ROOSEVELT, THE GREAT DEPRESSION,
AND THE ECONOMICS OF RECOVERY

ROOSEVELT,

THE GREAT DEPRESSION,

AND THE ECONOMICS

OF RECOVERY

ELLIOT A. ROSEN

University of Virginia Press
Charlottesville and London

University of Virginia Press

© 2005 by the Rector and Visitors of the University of Virginia

All rights reserved

Printed in the United States of America on acid-free paper

First published 2005

9 8 7 6 5 4 3 2 1

LIBRARY OF CONGRESS CATALOGING-IN-PUBLICATION DATA

Rosen, Elliot A., 1928–

   Roosevelt, the Great Depression, and the economics of recovery / Elliot A. Rosen.

      p.   cm.

   Includes bibliographical references and index.

   ISBN 0-8139-2368-9 (cloth : alk. paper)

   1. United States—Economic conditions—1918–1945. 2. United States—Economic policy—To 1933. 3. United States—Economic policy—1933–1945. 4. New Deal, 1933–1939. 5. Depressions—1929–United States. 6. Roosevelt, Franklin D. (Franklin Delano), 1882–1945. I. Title.

   HC106.3.R597 2005

330.973′0917–dc22   2005003930

TITLE PAGE IMAGE: President Franklin Delano Roosevelt, October 13, 1936. (AP/World Wide Photos)

CONTENTS

ACKNOWLEDGMENTS

D URING THE 1930S my mother took in sewing to keep the family in food and shelter. When I was old enough to become delivery boy for a growing dressmaking establishment, Frances Moley, one of her first clients, often suggested that I venture to the *Newsweek* building and have luncheon with Ray: "He likes history too." Likely, I was a college student before I summoned the courage to take up the offer; it soon became a regular affair. In February 1957 Raymond Moley proposed that I join him in framing an account of his service in the early stages of the Roosevelt administration. When I explained that I had scant background in the New Deal era, Ray reassured me: "You are a bright young fellow; I'm sure you can figure out the depression as well as FDR and I could." The effort required nearly half a century as I attempted to bridge the gap between historians and economists.

Encouragement over the years came from my colleague Henry Blumenthal and from Frank Freidel, both noted for their kindness to fledgling scholars. I met Henry when I joined the Rutgers-Newark faculty in 1957 and Frank soon thereafter in Ray's office. When I became a denizen of the FDR Library, I befriended its longtime director, Bill Emerson. I learned much about FDR from our exchanges in the reading room and at the Hyde Park diner and appreciated his support. On more than one occasion, when research funds ran dry, he came to my rescue while insisting that I put my thoughts on paper before my interment. Unhappily, all are deceased. I dedicate this book to these friends.

Throughout my career the Rutgers Research Council and the Graduate School-Newark afforded generous financial support including two fellowships. The American Philosophical Society awarded several grants for travel and photocopies. The Eleutherian Mills–Hagley Foundation supported my research at the Hagley Library in Wilmington, Delaware, and the Dirksen Center for the Study of Congress and Congressional

Leadership funded my exploration of the papers of Robert A. Taft. I am grateful also to the Carl Albert Center for Congressional Research and Studies for facilitating my study of the political economy of the Southwest and to the Harry S. Truman Library Institute for funding research in the papers of Will Clayton. The National Endowment for the Humanities awarded a Fellowship for College Teachers and Independent Scholars as well as two travel grants. Appointment as a Hoover Library Fellow and provision of several stipends as a Hoover Scholar by the Hoover Presidential Library Association facilitated a better grasp of the Hoover policies as well as the opportunity to experience Iowans' incomparable hospitality and to forge warm friendships. Finally, several FDR Freedom Foundation Research Awards and an Eleanor Roosevelt Institute grant enabled me to scour considerable portions of the material at Hyde Park and to befriend a series of archivists over the years.

Along the way I incurred profound personal obligations. My good friend and former colleague Herbert P. Meritt devoted a year to a detailed critique of the original manuscript. We engaged in frank give-and-take regarding length, exposition of economic ideas, and structure. I am grateful for his good humor and tenacity. Robert H. Ferrell offered pointed suggestions and challenges. Alexander Field kindly reviewed the economic interpretation found in the final chapter. I am also indebted to an anonymous reader who was as much a collaborator as a critic and to a thoughtful editor, Dick Holway, who guided the manuscript toward broader compass and greater coherence. My former student Leonard De Graaf helped to organize my research materials. Lastly, I tender my gratitude to the many archivists who shepherded me through their holdings over the years.

Part of my discussion of John Nance Garner's opposition to FDR's post-1936 legislative program is reprinted from *At the President's Side: The Vice Presidency in the Twentieth Century* edited by Timothy Walch, by permission of the University of Missouri Press. Copyright © 1997 by the Curators of the University of Missouri.

ABBREVIATIONS

AAA	Agricultural Adjustment Administration
AACO	Anderson, Clayton and Company
AFL	American Federation of Labor
C&S	Commonwealth & Southern
CCC	Civilian Conservation Corps
CES	Committee on Economic Security
CTI	Cotton-Textile Institute
CWA	Civil Works Administration
EPC	Economic Policy Committee
FCA	Farm Credit Administration
FERA	Federal Emergency Relief Administration
FHA	Federal Housing Administration
FPC	Federal Power Commission
FRUS	*Foreign Relations of the United States*
FSA	Farm Security Administration
FY	Fiscal Year
GDP	Gross Domestic Product
GNP	Gross National Product
HOLC	Home Owners Loan Corporation
NAM	National Association of Manufacturers
NIRA	National Industrial Recovery Act
NPB	National Planning Board
NRA	National Recovery Administration
NRB	National Resources Board
NRC	National Resources Committee
NRPB	National Resources Planning Board
PWA	Public Works Administration
REA	Rural Electrification Administration
RFC	Reconstruction Finance Corporation

SEC	Securities Exchange Commission
TNEC	Temporary National Economic Committee
TVA	Tennessee Valley Authority
UMW	United Mine Workers
WIB	War Industries Board
WPA	Works Progress Administration

ROOSEVELT, THE GREAT DEPRESSION, AND THE ECONOMICS OF RECOVERY

INTRODUCTION

HISTORY'S MIGHT-HAVE-BEENS can be as intriguing as the re-
cital of what happened. The threads that led to great decisions
in the past are intertwined with other strands, which, if they
had prevailed, might have brought about an entirely different aftermath.
What would have been the consequence for this nation if Roosevelt had
been felled by one of Giuseppe Zangara's bullets in Miami, on February
15, 1933? Would there have been a New Deal under an administration led
by Herbert Hoover had he been reelected in 1932? Would he have initiated
the interventionist state?

Historians have speculated on these questions with varying results,
and the degree to which Roosevelt's own ideas and inclinations (as opposed to those of his contemporaries) were essential to the formulations
of New Deal policies will be debated for years to come, as will the extent
to which these policies were consistent with those of his predecessor in
office. That said, it is the opinion of this writer that whatever ideas Roosevelt accepted from others, it was he who untangled the threads and he
alone who made the great decisions of the day. Herbert Hoover was no
Franklin D. Roosevelt but was unique in his own way in his contributions
to the American political system and the modern economy.

There is much to admire in the Great Engineer, the label that aptly
describes Hoover's contribution to the managerial and technological
change of the 1920s with its promise of a more abundant economy. Yet no
sharp line demarcated Hoover's economic ideology shaped during his service as secretary of commerce and his response to the Great Depression.
Businessmen, operating on the principles of voluntarism, would fashion
an efficient and abundant industrial base for an enduring prosperity. Government regulation and control of business, he believed, were clumsy,
incapable of adjustment to changed economic needs, and produced results
more detrimental than the ills intended to be remedied. The vast and

harmful tide of such legislation could be met by "organization of business itself," by business leadership that operated through voluntary associations which would preserve initiative and progress. Cooperation would eliminate waste in the form of destructive competition, business-labor strife, extremes of the business cycle, unemployment, and lack of synchronized standards. Such a system required organization, enforcement, and adoption of voluntary codes of behavior. Industry, in sum, was in the process of passing from extremely individualistic action into a period of associational activity managed by trade associations, chambers of commerce, craft unions, professional groups, and farmers' cooperatives. Collective action through self-governing industrial groups would stabilize output and employment and move society toward industrial democracy. Government, through the Commerce Department, would service business needs with statistical information and forecasts of demand and prices and would afford guidance in the direction of appropriate associational activities. Antisocial business behavior would be remedied by resort to antitrust.[1]

Associationalism, the core of Hooverian doctrine, collapsed like a house of cards in response to the economic downturn of the early 1930s. Yet Hoover did not deviate from principles developed in the New Economic Era. A devolutionist, Hoover announced that the federal government should not be the principal player in the economic crisis. "The American people have not forgotten how to take care of themselves," he admonished, and "should not delegate their welfare to distant bureaucracies." Thus was conceived Republican theology of the 1930s, or the "Ark of the Covenant," in Hoover's words, as he enunciated the theory of limited government at Madison Square Garden in the 1932 presidential campaign and in his critique of early New Deal policy, *The Challenge to Liberty* (1934).

Connecting the dots is not so easily accomplished in the instance of Franklin D. Roosevelt. An item in the gift shop at Hyde Park, a sphinx, its head in the shape of FDR's visage, a cigarette holder stuck firmly, almost defiantly, in his mouth, is emblematic of his challenge to those who would discern his operative philosophy. Unlike Hoover, Roosevelt was an experimentalist who did not hesitate to embrace unorthodox views. Roosevelt expanded the functions of the Reconstruction Finance Corporation to embrace a host of off-budget projects and thereby expanded the role of government well beyond Hoover's original strictures. Whereas Hoover regarded "a dollar as good as gold," economically and morally contractual and essential to social stability, the squire opted to reverse the deflationary tide that destroyed debtors and creditors alike. In the face of opposition from the Federal Reserve and his Treasury Department, Roosevelt followed the advice of the Lehman Brothers economist Alexander Sachs; René Léon, a retired banker and silver speculator; and Yale's Irving Fisher, who regarded reflation to predepression price levels as fundamental to recovery. Departure from the lock hold of the gold standard and the Sterling Equalization Fund, which Roosevelt held responsible for an appreciated dollar, was supplemented by domestic programs aimed at increased industrial and farm price levels. In the process, following the model created by Britain's chancellor of the exchequer, Neville Chamberlain, for self-sufficiency within the empire, Roosevelt moved the United States toward economic self-sufficiency.

Planning for industry was one of the persistent themes and enduring failures of the Roosevelt era. While industrialists initially divided on the merits of the National Recovery Administration as a recovery measure, fear of federal intrusion into the business system quickly led to opposition. In the event, there was no corporate commonwealth in the 1930s, a nexus of business, investment banking, and government. To the contrary, FDR regarded Wall Street bankers as crooks and sponsored legislation that discouraged business advance. Such legislation included measures that supported inefficient industries such as agriculture, mining, and textiles because they were large employers as opposed to corporations that were in the process of developing new technologies; it also included taxation of industry at wartime levels and discouragement of business-government cooperation in development of electric power systems and the railroads.

Relief and public works programs were designed as temporary measures, not as permanent accoutrements of a democratic society. Roosevelt abhorred the dole as leading to a dependent class in society. As framed by the secretary of labor, Frances Perkins, and by Edwin E. Witte of the University of Wisconsin, unemployment insurance and social security reflected the social justice component of the Progressive movement and the work of institutional economists that emphasized the vulnerability of the individual to the creative destruction that characterized an industrial-technological society. Unemployment insurance was not intended to sustain those permanently outside the workforce, only those temporarily unemployed. Social Security legislation, which originated as an annuity scheme, soon evolved as a measure for income redistribution. These programs cushioned the individual and the economy against the possibility of a future depression and expanded further in the postwar era.

Until the 1937–38 recession most economists assumed that the depression resembled earlier downward economic movements. These were cyclical in nature, with recovery responsive to renewed business investment encouraged by lower interest rates and wages. The persistence of high unemployment and limited investment in the recession within a depression led to acceptance of the concept of net federal contribution to the economy, or full use of resources and available labor, the work of Laughlin Currie, a Federal Reserve economist. In time, business economists and liberals in the business community came to accept compensatory federal expenditure as the least intrusive proposal for economic stabilization. Withholding of taxes from wages, begun in wartime, acted as a countercyclical device for economic stability as tax deductions dropped when incomes fell and increased in prosperous times.

Following Alvin Hansen's stagnation theory, which focused on the absence of technological innovation and the inability of private investment to absorb the rate of savings, the National Resources Planning Board wanted direct government intervention by means of a developmental economy. A government fiscal agency, the beneficiary of higher rates of taxation on industry and the middle class, would invest dormant savings in regional economic development projects modeled on the Tennessee Valley Authority, in urban redevelopment and selected industries, and in an expanded social welfare scheme that resembled Britain's Beveridge Plan. Government ownership would be introduced where necessary in the "public interest." Federal investment expenditure would be scaled upward or downward by an agency situated in the executive branch, its objective a full-employment economy, its operations funded by the Congress on a long-term basis. These objectives, featured in the full employment bill of 1945, were challenged by centrist economists and were moderated by the Congress in 1946.

That Alexander Sachs was tapped by nuclear physicists to convey their concerns to the president with respect to Germany's plans to build an atom bomb reveals much about his entrée to the Roosevelt administration. Sachs, master of the breadth and import of technological innovation in the interwar era, challenged Hansen's formulation of stagnation theory that pointed to mature capitalism or a permanent lack of investment opportunities. To the contrary, Sachs argued on reading Hansen's testimony before the Temporary National Economic Committee, business investment had been stifled by New Deal legislation such as the Public Utilities Holding Company Act; by TVA, which competed unfairly with unsubsidized private companies; by counterproductive high long-term interest rates and high levels of taxation on business; and by the antibusiness climate of the late 1930s. Business under siege by Felix Frankfurter's protégés, the "hot dog school," would not invest in a climate of uncertainty. Also, contrary to Hansen's stress on consumption as crucial to recovery, Sachs emphasized the need for private-sector investment and regional economic development as the best route to recovery.

Typical of most institutional economists, Columbia University's John Maurice Clark understood the need for fiscal stimulus in a depression. But he questioned the efficacy of developmental economics as a permanent policy. Underutilization of resources was not inherent in the American economy; rather its causes were structural, the result of stagnation in trade, an unsatisfactory tax system, excess labor supply in certain industries, and other factors. Permanent government spending would increase the national debt and lead to the logical assumption that future taxation and higher interest rates would follow, serving as a discouragement to investment.

While Hansen and his followers situated in various government agencies and departments worked in tandem with the National Resources Planning Board, a planning agency, Congress needed to be persuaded that it should convey fiscal authority, or at least its management, to an independent agency in the executive branch. Such a proposition had no future. A coalition of states' rights Southern Democrats led by Harry F. Byrd and old-line Progressives who detested concentrated authority either in business or government found added support as a result of Republican resurgence in the legislative branch under the leadership of Robert A. Taft, beginning with the 1938 midterm election. The conservative coalition, committed to curbs on the growth of executive power and the reassertion of congressional authority, terminated aspirations for a permanent planning agency. Refusal to fund NRPB continuance in 1943 and rejection of the full employment bill of 1945 ended the possibilities for planning through compensatory spending and a federal agency assigned the task of investment in the private and public sectors.

Multilateralists viewed reopened world markets and monetary stability as essential to prevention of another depression. They needed to wait for a decade or more to realize their ambitions through international organizations created to facilitate currency stability and removal of trade restrictions after war's end. Trade flow in the years after the Second World War expanded exponentially to the benefit of Europe more than the United States.

The common conception of a Third New Deal, or wartime adoption of Keynesian-style massive public expenditure as a cure for unemployment, neither reflected Keynesian analysis nor proved responsible for post–World War II economic growth. Rather, multifactor productivity, or technological advance and its application, educational levels, and other factors in the 1930s set the stage for U.S. economic growth and advantage in the postwar era.

Certain omissions or brief mention of New Deal programs customarily treated in the historical literature need to be explained in the spirit put forward by Stanley Engerman in his introduction to the third volume of the *Cambridge Economic History of the United States.* Economists and historians, he explains, "must learn to live together" and bridge the gap between their disciplines. Emphasis on depression causation and remediation—successes and failures alike—accounts for brief mention of the bank crisis of the early 1930s since the loss of depositors and investors in failed banks amounted to $2.5 billion as opposed to a decline of $30 billion in real Gross National Product in the early depression years. Attention instead has been given to the money supply decline and the failure of the banking system to play its traditional role of financial intermediary between investors and business.[2] Securities and Exchange legislation intended to bring about transparency in the market accomplished little as an inducement to business investment in an environment that was less than promising for risk.

While income inequality is a vital social issue, recent economic research suggests that it does not hinder economic growth. Minimum wage and maximum hour provisions as well as stimulus to unionization under Section 7(a) of the National Industrial Recovery Act, formalized under the Wagner Act (1935) and Fair Labor Standards Act (1938) likely proved to be counterproductive from a macroeconomic point of view. While these enactments briefly improved income distribution, they slowed down efforts at reducing unemployment and stimulating business investment. Despite the impact of unionization promoted by the Wagner Act and wage gains made after the Second World War, when unionization peaked, Claudia Goldin concludes that "neither the rate of productivity growth nor the rate of decrease in hours was much affected by labor organization." The fundamentals of economic advance in the twentieth century are best explained by technological development, adaptability of business to new technologies, workforce educational levels, natural resources, and private and public support for scientific institutions such as the Massachusetts Institute of Technology.[3]

As for Franklin D. Roosevelt, W. W. Waymack, editor of the *Des Moines Register and Tribune,* proved correct when he observed that "the very violence of the hate [with] which the 'right people' regard FDR now practically guarantees that 'the right people' of the next generation will canonize him—as the Great Conservator of the American Way."[4]

1 | FINANCIAL CRISIS

ONFRONTED BY DEFLATIONARY pressures, a massive decline in corporate income and investment, evaporated farm incomes, and widespread unemployment, Herbert Hoover attributed the Great Depression principally to international events beyond his control. As he put it in his *Memoirs,* "The great center of the storm was Europe. That storm moved slowly until the spring of 1931, when it burst into a financial hurricane."[1]

While such an analysis provided Hoover with a rationale for limited intrusion into the domestic arena, the impact on the U.S. economy by external events was not inconsiderable. These included the demand for remission of the debts and reparations settlements reached after the First World War; Great Britain's abandonment of gold, a policy which Hoover unwisely sought to reverse; and creation of the sterling trading bloc to the disadvantage of U.S. farm exports, which exacerbated the domestic agricultural crisis. Insistence by Hoover on maintenance of the dollar on the gold standard, a deflationary policy supported by the Federal Reserve Bank of New York and urged on Franklin D. Roosevelt, precipitated the massive price decline that ensued.

British prime minister Ramsay MacDonald opened the debts-reparations issue with the U.S. chargé d'affaires, Ray Atherton, in June 1931. The exchange occurred under conditions of accelerated economic warfare occasioned by gold transfer problems and imminent collapse of the international credit system based in part on the willingness of New York banks to renew short-term loans to Germany's local and state governments.

In previous talks with MacDonald, Chancellor Heinrich Brüning, pressed at home by both Left and Right, warned of the possibility of a government headed by the Communists or the Hitlerites. To placate the right-wing nationalists, the Brüning government demanded a revision of the Versailles Treaty that would allow the creation of a customs union with Austria, military parity with France, and a substantial abatement of reparations. Potentially most troublesome for Anglo-American relations was MacDonald's attempt to tie reparations relief to debts rescission. Great Britain, he insisted, served simply as a conduit for German payments made to it as reparations, then transmitted to the United States as war debts repayment, a position long since rejected by the Congress.[2]

MacDonald's message arrived in Washington at a critical juncture. With millions of farmers in distress, unemployment on the increase, country banks shuttered by the thousands, and federal revenues in decline, Hoover required the appearance of action as his earlier hortatory approach to these problems proved unsuccessful. Promises by business to maintain investment and employment, conferences in Washington that outlined voluntary action along these lines, establishment of a Federal Farm Loan Board to encourage farm cooperative marketing, would no longer suffice.

It is quite evident that by 1931 Hoover required a rationale for the internal collapse. There were two options: substantial federal intervention into the domestic economy, a course he would not take, or ascribing the depression to external causes beyond his control. The reparations–debts–international banking crisis of 1931 provided an opportunity for action in the international arena. Even with the MacDonald approach to Washington at hand, however, Hoover proved cautious: the so-called Hoover Moratorium on intergovernmental debts resulted from pressures that emanated from J. P. Morgan & Co.

At a June 5 luncheon meeting of the Morgan partners, Russell C. Leffingwell won unanimous endorsement of a memorandum on "Debts Suspension" initiated by General Electric's Owen D. Young, author of the 1929 Young Plan for reparations revision and a member of the board of directors of the Federal Reserve Bank of New York. In international banking circles it was feared that reparations repudiation under the guise of Germany's incapacity to pay, which was questioned, could well lead to repudiation of private debts as well. American investment in Germany had shored up both the private and public sectors for a decade in the form of short-term loans estimated at some $2 billion, half residing in commercial banks. A German default could well bring down some of the major New York financial institutions, the Chase and Guaranty Trust among them. While he sniffed at a "bankers' panic"—it should be noted that the Morgan firm was not directly involved in this system—Hoover went along. The resulting moratorium on intergovernmental obligations of June 1931 and arrangement of standstill agreements for the short-term private debts afforded a year's reprise for negotiating solutions to the mushrooming international economic crisis.[3]

With France facing a German reparations default, Hoover and Premier Pierre Laval met in Washington. The conversations of October 22–25, 1931, illustrate the disharmonious efforts at international cooperation opened up by MacDonald; too, they proved a prologue to the unsuccessful Lausanne Conference of 1932 and the disastrous World Monetary and Economic Conference of 1933. Despite a ranging agenda that included discussion of the gold standard, central bank cooperation in the stabilization of currencies, possible monetization of silver (a sop to U.S. mining and agricultural interests), disarmament, tariff reduction, revision of the Versailles Treaty, and France's requirement for political guarantees vis-à-vis Germany, not one of these issues could be resolved in the next few years. Whereas Hoover and Laval agreed on the desirability of an international monetary conference, which would secure maintenance of the gold standard and stabilization of the exchanges, MacDonald, who was in process of organizing a National government that went off gold and depreciated the pound, indicated a lack of interest in a monetary conference "at the moment." When the National government proved ready to stabilize a depreciated pound in 1933, Roosevelt, beneficiary of a rapidly depreciating dollar, proved unready. Such was the course of international economic affairs in these years.[4]

Efforts at debts-reparations rapprochement proved impossible and increasingly an obstacle to any sort of agreement on more important issues. The U.S. economic position was hammered out at an all-day meeting held at the offices of the Federal Reserve Bank of New York on October 19, 1931. In attendance were the Fed's principals, Eugene Meyer, governor of the Federal Reserve Board, and George Harrison, governor of the Federal Reserve Bank of New York; Assistant Secretary William Rogers and economic adviser Herbert Feis, representing the State Department; Acting Secretary of the Treasury Ogden Mills; and Walter Stewart of Case Pomeroy & Co. and S. Parker Gilbert of J. P. Morgan, spokesmen for the Wall Street banking community. The Wall Street conference arrived at a procedure which led to the Lausanne Agreement of 1932 and to the request for parallel concessions on the debts that descended upon the State Department as Hoover's term in office drew to a close. Germany should take the initiative and request its creditors to reconsider the reparations settlement. Germany's creditors meantime would be reassured by a Franco-American statement suggesting U.S. reconsideration of the postwar debt settlements through a reconstituted Debt Funding Commission.[5]

In his exchanges with Pierre Laval, Hoover refused to join in a general conference on debts, reparations, and monetary policy, a position accepted by MacDonald, or to call for a new Debt Funding Commission. He suggested to Laval, instead, willingness to review the debts with individual debtors by direct negotiation. Did this mean a quid pro quo conditioned on formal separation of debts from other financial issues? Had there been a wink of the eye, a nod that promised substantial debt relief to be afforded by the United States following a lowering of reparations?[6]

Hoover left for future scholars a memorandum, addressed to Secretary of State Henry L. Stimson (dated "October, 1931?") purporting to show that no commitments had been made beyond American willingness to consider capacity to pay. Contemporaneous evidence suggests otherwise. The memorandum, to begin with, was written in late 1932, not 1931, apparently to deflect charges made on the floor of the U.S. Senate that he had offered a debts-reparations quid pro quo. It is doubtful that Laval, in light of French feelings on the subject, would have suggested to German ambassador Herr Friedrich W. von Prittwitz und Gaffron that his government request a commission of inquiry on reparations without some understanding of equivalent concessions on debts. Such an interpretation is supported by the diary of Stimson, who was present at the Hoover-Laval exchanges: "The president. . . . brought forward the Mills suggestion the other day of invoking a conference under the Young Plan to determine Germany's ability to pay reparations during the time of the depression; to be followed by a reexamination of the debts. Laval didn't dispute this. I think he was a little surprised at the president making it."

The following day, as discussants considered a communiqué for public consumption, Stimson noted in his diary that the president conceded "if Germany was helped in their reparations, we would have to help our debtors on debts." This evidently was Laval's understanding. En route home, via London, he explained to Sir Frederick Leith-Ross at Treasury that "he had been led to understand that after the reparations question had been settled among the European powers, the American government would be willing to cooperate in a revision of other intergovernmental obligations."[7]

For a moment it seemed that the machinery had been set in motion for substantial relief from the debts-reparations albatross. The terse joint communiqué, issued in Washington on October 25, promised an effort toward an agreement on intergovernmental obligations "covering the period of business depression, as to the terms and conditions of which the two governments make all reservations." This last clause proved critical, for Laval needed to persuade the Chamber of Deputies and Hoover the Congress. Yet it soon became evident that the president refused to press for a permanent settlement of the wartime debts incurred by the Allies to the United States.[8]

In a cautious message to Congress in December, Hoover proposed repayment of debts due the United States during the moratorium year over a period of ten years beginning July 1, 1933. He suggested the need to make further temporary adjustments and to this end "re-creation of the World War Foreign Debt Funding Commission with authority to examine such problems that may arise in connection with these debts during the present economic emergency." In the congressional debate that ensued, leading to the joint House-Senate resolution of December 22, 1931, notice was served that debts would neither be canceled nor reduced in any circumstance. Suggestive of the isolationist attitudes of the decade, "Let any nation default that desires to do so," Senator Hiram Johnson of California challenged, almost hopefully, as a lesson to the interventionists of 1917. Fingers to the wind, Republican stalwarts joined in the display of nationalism. Even Hoover intimate David A. Reed of Pennsylvania wondered if debts reduction had been confected by Wall Street banks and bond houses that had made huge private loans to Europe in the 1920s. "We have cancelled all we are going to cancel."[9]

With Congress having "rapped my knuckles," in Hoover's words, leadership on the issue passed to France and Britain. During the course of the debate on the House-Senate resolution, Prime Minister MacDonald, an internationalist and a believer in Anglo-American amity, sent Secretary Stimson a blunt warning of events to come. "Reports have been made that Congress, in ratifying the one year moratorium, may attempt to impose conditions precluding further remission on the debts." The result, he predicted, would be an impasse. As conditions worsened in Europe, there seemed no prospect of reparations payments to England, leaving it unable to meet debts payments to the United States. "We hope," and MacDonald now mentioned the unmentionable, "that some means may be

devised which will enable us to avoid anything which might be represented as repudiation."[10]

Two distinct conferences met in Lausanne in June 1932. One dealt with
intergovernmental obligations, the other with the broad economic and
financial issues triggered by Britain's abandonment of gold in September
1931, the discard of its historic policy of free trade, and the devaluation of
the pound. The latter agenda, more difficult, involved the United States
and would be taken up at the World Economic Conference, held at London. As for the debts, France and Great Britain moved toward compromise in the belief that the United States would not press its wartime allies
into default for fear of its impact on international finance. The two European powers concluded that Germany could not or, in any event, would
not resume reparations payments. Hopeful of U.S. reciprocity and convinced of linkage between debts and reparations, Edouard Herriot, Laval's
successor, and MacDonald acceded to German demands. German commitments to its former opponents were scaled down some 90 percent contingent upon a commensurate forgiveness of war debts owed the United
States.[11]

The Hoover administration found itself divided, with the president
resentful of the agreement he had encouraged. In a series of exchanges in
mid-July, he and Stimson argued bitterly, the nationalistic Mills siding
with Hoover. At a tense luncheon Stimson counseled that the Lausanne
arrangements would prove helpful; Hoover countered that he and Stimson "really had no common ground; that he thought that the debts to us
could be paid and ought to be paid; and that the European nations were
all in an iniquitous combine against us." Stimson suggested that he ought
not to be Hoover's adviser, arguing that the New York Federal Reserve's
George Harrison, among others, perceived the Lausanne meeting as a
precursor of a genuine recovery. Most telling and correct in this series of
engagements was Stimson's claim that Ramsay MacDonald had made a
"gallant fight to do what he thought we wanted done." While the imbroglio cooled, Stimson remained unhappy, convinced that Hoover and
Mills, ardent nationalists, acted "from the standpoint of our domestic
politics [the 1932 political campaign]."[12]

While the war debts issue confirmed U.S. wariness of involvement in
Europe, considerably more destabilizing was Britain's abandonment of
gold in September 1931 followed by an equalization fund managed for the

purpose of a pound devaluated at the expense of the gold standard currencies. Creation of a sterling trading zone protected by tariffs on agricultural and other imports and an imperial preference system in 1932 severely limited U.S. agricultural exports to its principal outlet. From the perspective of London, the island nation could no longer afford the luxury of maintaining international liquidity and free trade, a critical component of economic growth in the century preceding the Great War. From that of the Hoover administration, abandonment of gold represented a departure from contractual and social norms and added to domestic political and economic pressures for an inflationary policy based on relinquishment of the dollar's tie to gold. War debts, it was hoped, could be traded for London's return to the gold standard.

Before the Great War the City of London functioned as the world's banker and as a force for stability in international money markets, with the Bank of England ready to exchange pounds for gold or for other currencies in relation to gold. With the bulk of world trade denominated in sterling, this system also has been described as an "international exchange-stabilizing sterling standard," sustained by Britain's investment of capital surplus abroad and willingness to take commodities instead of gold from its debtors. Britain profited not only from investment returns but also from the tendency for banking, shipping, and allied services to flow through London as the center of an international nexus of credit, trade, and insurance. The system worked well as long as there was minimal pressure on London's gold reserves, also as long as all major central banks took requisite, deflationary measures to defend gold reserves when necessary, even at the cost of local employment.[13]

The World War shattered the gold-sterling system. Its monumental cost enervated Great Britain as a financial power, compelled as it was to liquidate much of its foreign investments and borrow on a massive scale in the New York market. Subsequently, overseas earnings declined, and exports never recovered their prewar levels—much of that trade decline occurring in the dollar area—impairing the United Kingdom's financial capacity. Loss of dollar assets and earnings was compounded by the war debts owed the United States and a shift of financial services from London to New York.

The United Kingdom returned to gold at a prewar parity of $4.86 on April 28, 1925, leaving the pound overvalued by 10 percent. Gold advocates believed that a return to prewar parity would stimulate British trade and employment and forestall, in the words of Montagu Norman, head of the Bank of England, "nostrums and expedients other than the gold standard," meaning government experiments with paper money.

While a low interest rate strategy of the New York Federal Reserve Bank protected England's gold reserve for several years, in mid-1931 sterling came under pressure when the Macmillan Report revealed the extent of sterling balances convertible to gold and the May Report claimed that government deficits were a product of Labour's budgetary extravagance. Britain's international position had been further weakened by failure to attain a substantial postwar recovery as well as by sterling bloc trade deficits. More immediately, international loan funds, usually available from New York, Paris, and Berlin, dried up.[14]

On September 21, 1931, Great Britain abandoned gold, and the pound plummeted. Great Britain made no effort to cushion the impact on other nations, with MacDonald making it clear that stabilization of the pound was purely a British problem to be determined by business conditions. The effect proved catastrophic for exchange stability, for without gold and sterling as the common denominators of monetary values worldwide, the central banks of the principal nations would need to cooperate in maintaining agreed-upon currency parities in order to stabilize the marketplace, an impossibility in the depression environment.[15]

As national treasuries and central banks hoarded gold to protect their solvency, international economic warfare set in, ruthless and brutal. Twenty-one nations either abandoned the gold standard or prohibited gold exports, with the United Kingdom leading the way. Twenty-eight countries, including Germany and Italy, instituted foreign exchange controls, and eleven, principally smaller nations, imposed moratoriums on external governmental and commercial credit. Forty-four, among them the United States, France, Great Britain, Canada, Germany, and Italy, utilized general tariff increases or special tariff impositions as a further measure of self-preservation. Twenty-six made use of import quotas and embargoed certain exports to protect currency and gold reserves as well as the local market for domestic producers.[16]

The Hoover administration faced more difficulties. While Ramsay MacDonald, a Labourite, was anxious for joint effort with the United States, the National government formed in the wake of the October 1931 election was dominated by empire-oriented Tories, led by Chancellor of the Exchequer Neville Chamberlain, who framed its economic policies.

(Though the National government was theoretically a coalition of Conservatives, Labourites, and Liberals, the bulk of the Labour Party went into opposition.) In 1932 Chamberlain and the Treasury put forward a program designed to brake the United Kingdom's unemployment problem and its declining export trade, also to stabilize the pound at a level capable of maintaining London as the leading international center of trade and finance. At the same time Chamberlain proposed to protect key industries, often in decline, by safeguarding, or special tariffs and quotas; also by instituting general tariffs as a revenue-enhancing device. And he envisaged an Imperial Preference system designed to stimulate domestic manufactures and agricultural employment.

Sterling stability, local recovery through a low interest rate regime, and maintenance of British overseas markets took priority in establishing a new figure for the pound, $3.40. Especially grating from the standpoint of the United States was the establishment of the Exchange Equalization Account, announced by Chamberlain on April 19, 1932. British officials claimed that the equalization fund, managed at Treasury, served the purpose exclusively of smoothing out short-term fluctuations in sterling exchange rates. U.S. suspicion of sterling management to the dollar's disadvantage seemed more on the mark and plagued Anglo-American relations through the thirties.[17]

At the same time, to remediate the balance of payments problem and provide revenue enhancement to finance social programs, Chamberlain rammed a protectionist system through the cabinet and Commons. Chamberlain's "Trade Notes," in fact, reveal a broadly conceived neomercantilist program of managed trade, internal rationalization, and the use of tariffs to protect critical and declining industries, conserve employment, and shelter the nation's farmers from more efficient overseas producers. The result proved disastrous for U.S. wheat exports. British imports of American-grown wheat fell from a peak of nearly 4 billion pounds valued at $106 million in 1927 to virtually nil.

Imperial preference, the final component of Chamberlain's program, was taken up by the Ottawa Conference in the summer of 1932. Unlike its Continental competitors, which exported finished goods primarily to other manufacturing countries, 75 percent of United Kingdom exports remained within sterling area markets, which depended in turn on the export of raw materials. Self-sufficiency within the empire would assure reversal of the trade imbalance with foreign nations, conserve sterling, and assure, in turn, favorable access by the dominions and colonies to the world's leading importer of foodstuffs, raw materials, and forestry products.[18]

Canada's Richard B. Bennett, who presided over the Ottawa Conference, gave every appearance of becoming Chamberlain's ally in these proceedings. A proponent of attachment to the monarchy and the home country as bulwarks of freedom and independence and leader of the Conservative Party, he replaced the Liberal William Lyon Mackenzie King as prime minister in 1930 when Canadians already exhibited a desire to curb growing U.S. cultural and economic penetration. Whereas King favored a low-tariff system and detachment from Great Britain, Bennett campaigned on a high-tariff platform in 1930 in order to forge closer relations with the mother country behind a wall of tariffs and quotas. When Hoover signed the Smoot-Hawley Tariff, the Canadian leader pushed through, in response, the highest tariff in that nation's history.

As matters developed, the Ottawa Conference was reduced to an enterprise in haggling over preferences. The dominions wanted Great Britain to retain the preference granted in the 1932 Import Duties Act and negotiated further for a series of bilateral treaties which offered a system of quotas and licenses that would increase empire imports at the expense of foreigners in exchange for still higher tariffs on foreign goods. Satisfied with the result, Chamberlain believed the conference gave a positive turn to imperial relations.[19]

Chamberlain could now focus on war debts and reparations, which he regarded as deflationary and responsible for unsettled international relations. This hinged on U.S. forgiveness of the debts. Whereas Chamberlain wanted a final lump-sum debts settlement as a quid pro quo for the end of reparations, Hoover's rejection of the Lausanne Agreement, a turnabout in his view, left the chancellor of the exchequer troubled in the face of the December 15 deadline for renewed postmoratorium payments. His long-term objectives were clear: a prolonged moratorium of at least three years, sufficient to allow the issue to vanish in the U.S. Congress, and a small lump-sum final settlement, enough to allow the president to tell the Congress that he had made a valiant effort at collection. Short-term, however, Chamberlain faced a dilemma as the December 15 payment approached: "To pay or not to pay, that is the question." Angered at the obstinacy of the Americans ("they have no leaders"), he feared that outright refusal to pay would create a precedent that the De Valera government in

Ireland and other small European debtor nations would cheerfully follow. With the matter turned over to Stanley Baldwin, MacDonald, and the foreign secretary, Sir John Simon, a decision was made to pay as an advance against a final settlement. This was the situation presented by Mills and Hoover in their messages to Roosevelt during the interregnum.[20]

By the eve of the Roosevelt presidency, Chamberlain had put his program for British economic recovery into place. Chamberlain's policies rested on critical domestic problems whose resolution impinged on U.S. economic interests. Home agriculture, which he intended to preserve, could not even approach world market cost of production. Important sectors of British industry, iron and steel, cotton textiles, and coal especially, and certain sections of England and Scotland encountered long-term structural problems, a condition worsened by the depression though long in the making. As a consequence, he decided, Great Britain required advantages in international trade as its output no longer proved adequately competitive. To preserve social harmony and reduce unemployment, it seemed necessary, therefore, to pursue trade and monetary advantage. The abandonment of gold allowed the opportunity to wed a depreciated but stable pound with a tariff system keyed to the benefits of a captive market created at the Ottawa Conference. This program could be rationalized as beneficial in the long run to economic recovery, for general prosperity within the empire could be interpreted as a precondition to international expansion. He did not oppose lower tariffs worldwide, it should be stressed, but intended through bilateral arrangements and preferences, retained even with reduced tariffs, to maintain local and worldwide trade advantage.

Britain's abandonment of the gold standard placed the deflationary burden on American policymakers. With the New York Federal Reserve Bank determined to protect its gold reserves against capital flight, the result was a massive contraction leading to the ruinous deflation of the winter of 1932–33, capped by the bank crisis of late February–early March. In the process Hoover felt compelled to stave off domestic pressures for a depreciated dollar and to prevent the squire of Hyde Park from acceding to a reflationary program featured by relinquishment of gold.

Fearful of what Roosevelt might do, Hoover and Mills looked upon a devalued dollar with an attitude best summarized in memoranda formulated for them by the Federal Reserve Bank of New York. Fed economists held that a policy of a depreciated dollar or moderate inflation would lead inevitably to government's inability to control the process once it was under way. Political management of currency was a contradiction in terms. A devalued dollar would work only to the temporary advantage of the United States as it would drive prices further down in world markets and destabilize trade and exchanges. Available gold supplies were more than adequate to support the credit structure, and the price decline that began in 1929 could not be attributed to a gold shortage. The problem was neither one of inadequate reserves for an expansion of bank credit nor a shortage of money, but rather a reluctance to use the available supply due to a lack of confidence. Recovery would come about through normal business channels once confidence was restored.[21]

The Federal Reserve Bank of New York conceded that dollar devaluation would release part of the nation's gold reserve and make it available for additional credit and currency with the potential for a rise in commodity prices. But such a policy would undermine the financial system. A gold basis for currency was more a matter of psychology than of mathematics, as gold was rarely used in transactions. Business was done by credit or promises to pay, with only one dollar of gold required to sustain ten dollars of credit. Take away this confidence, and the "modern financial system goes to pieces." The obstacle to recovery, in the Fed's view, "is not shortage of money but fear and uncertainty" as abandonment of gold portended budget unbalance and unsound money. A decisive declaration by the new administration for sound money would remove these uncertainties.

Indeed, Federal Reserve policy in this period was contractionary. Remarkably, it sterilized (demonetized) gold inflows in light of its fear of inflation and abandoned open-market purchases of government securities in the closing months of 1932. At the same time real interest rates were abnormally high. Monetarists have concluded that deflationary Fed policies turned the downturn into a massive depression between the summer of 1929 and March 1993. Monetary currency and demand deposits fell by 28 percent, while industrial output declined by some 50 percent.[22]

Treasury Secretary Mills endorsed the deflationary position adopted by the Federal Reserve System. With the budget in balance, credit of the United States unimpaired, and Hoover's financial diplomacy brought to fruition in the form of currency stabilization and a return to the gold standard by Britain, Mills believed, the nation would endure "the foolish experiments" contemplated by Roosevelt. Defeated at the polls, the Republican president and his treasury secretary determined to press Roosevelt to sustain their priorities: budget balance, adherence to the deflationary gold standard, and renegotiated war debts.[23]

Differences in personality and style and inevitably bitter rivalry and calculation of future political advantage—Hoover and Mills ambitious for their party's 1936 presidential nomination, Roosevelt determined to hold the farm vote for the Democratic Party—played no small part in the Hoover-Roosevelt dissonance during the four-month 1932–33 interregnum. Hoover urged continuity between the two administrations on his own terms. This included a new Debts Funding Commission to reexamine capacity to pay, its membership overlapping with the ongoing experts committee preparing for the forthcoming World Monetary and Economic Conference, an outgrowth of Lausanne. Downward revision of debts presumably would lead to a second critical component of recovery, return of Great Britain to the gold standard.[24]

Such an agenda had no future. To begin with, war debts forgiveness required congressional approval, and the mood had not changed since Congress served notice in the joint House-Senate resolution of December 22, 1931, that Allied war debts would neither be reduced nor canceled in any circumstance, a position confirmed by congressional leaders.[25] Roosevelt was not about to expend political capital on the subject. Nor was he inclined to assume responsibility in matters that currently rested with "those now vested with executive and legislative authority."[26]

Hoover took a new tack, operating on squire theory, the notion that Roosevelt was no more than a mirror of his advisers. Evidently persuaded that he had a better chance if he bypassed Raymond Moley, Roosevelt's principal adviser in these negotiations, the president suggested the designation of Owen D. Young, Colonel Edward M. House, "or any other man of your party possessed of your views and your confidence and at the same time familiar with these problems," to sit down with members of his administration in order to "avoid delays of precious time" on these issues. Roosevelt offered to cooperate but refused joint responsibility. He would not be bound to a particular course of action. An angry Hoover released their correspondence to the press.[27]

Presumably the matter was closed, at least until Felix Frankfurter suggested Secretary Stimson as a bridge between the principals. Upon overcoming Hoover's objections, Roosevelt and Stimson conferred at Hyde Park. With Stimson convinced that he had persuaded Roosevelt to follow the Hoover administration's international economic priorities, a trade-off of debts for sterling's return to gold, a White House summit was scheduled for January 20, 1933. Stimson and Mills invoked cables from Ambassador to Germany Frederick M. Sackett that Britain planned to abrogate its debt commitment to the United States "without any compensation in regard to their attitude on the gold standard." (The British, in fact, had not the slightest intention of resuming the debts repayment or returning to gold.) After a long, hard discussion, it seemed to Stimson that Roosevelt had finally agreed to cooperate along the lines suggested by the Hoover administration. But Roosevelt cannily left Moley and Rexford Tugwell to negotiate with Stimson the contents of a message to the British ambassador, Sir Ronald Lindsay. The result proved a compromise that invited the British government to send a representative or representatives to discuss the debts and representatives "to discuss other related matters of mutual interest."[28]

The president made a final appeal to his successor on the eve of the transition to a new administration. Brazenly, likely for the record, Hoover implied that confidence had been restored until the rekindling of public fears in the fall and winter of 1932, the time frame of Roosevelt's campaign and election. Determined that there was ample provision for liquidity in the financial system, the lame-duck president called for renewal of confidence in the future by prompt assurance from Roosevelt "that there will be no tampering or inflation of the currency; that the budget will be unquestionably balanced, even if further taxation is necessary." Hoover also feared an expensive public works program which would encumber the power of the government to borrow. As he conceded to Senator David Reed, "I realize that if these declarations are made by the president-elect, he will have ratified the whole major program of the Republican administration; that is, it means abandonment of 90 percent of the so-called new deal. But unless this is done, they run a grave danger of precipitating a complete financial debacle."

As the nation's banking systems collapsed, Hoover held that the president-elect could have saved the situation had he pledged "the sanctity of 'the covenant' of the government to pay in gold," which would have resulted in a massive liquidation of values. In any event, as the most astute observer of this scene, J. P. Morgan's Russell Leffingwell, noted a year later, "The automatic gold standard, if it ever existed, came to an end in 1914. We have managed and mismanaged currency for 25 years, and I have no

notion that we can go back to an automatic gold standard in our time. . . .
The marvel to me . . . is that the correction was so long deferred."[29]

Roosevelt refused to assure maintenance of the dollar on the gold standard. Indeed, as early as the summer of 1932, he indicated to Henry A. Wallace his interest in currency-credit expansion and a devalued dollar.[30] While he promised budget balance at Pittsburgh during the campaign, he never made good. More open than his predecessor to experimentation, flexible in ideological and programmatic outlook, Roosevelt proved willing to unbalance the budget by provision for relief and public works. If budget unbalance evolved initially from social priorities and declining tax revenues, monetary policy represented a conscious endeavor to separate the dollar from both gold and management of sterling to the disadvantage of American price levels.

2 | NATIONALIZING THE ECONOMY

T
HE GREAT DEPRESSION sundered the special relationship between Great Britain and the United States, each now fending for itself. An industrial sector in decline, Britain depended on the processing of cheap raw materials from the empire into finished products, a protected home market, and a depreciated pound as a trading advantage vis-à-vis its competitors. With a mixed economy and with raw materials producers in the South and West dependent for recovery on appreciated prices for recovery, the United States, Roosevelt decided, more nearly resembled the British Empire than the British Isles.[1]

The decision to build an internal economy helps to explain the split in the new administration between advisers who stressed self-containment and the Atlanticist free traders, their outlook voiced by Secretary of State Cordell Hull. At odds with Roosevelt's domestic priorities, Hull was responsible for the Democratic Party's Wilsonian antistatist 1932 Chicago platform, the bible of conservative Atlanticists who opposed Roosevelt's domestic program for the balance of the 1930s. The platform urged a competitive tariff for revenue only, endorsed the agenda for the imminent international economic conference, with emphasis on the end of trade and currency warfare, condemned excessive interference in domestic affairs, and insisted on federal budget retrenchment.[2]

However much Ramsay MacDonald found encouragement in his early exchanges with Roosevelt, and however much he admired the experimentalism of the New Deal, his hopes for a grand all-around meeting of the minds to end international discord terminated abruptly when the London Conference turned into a shambles. That Roosevelt's policies proved exclusively responsible for this turn of events and the beggar-thy-neighbor monetary and bloc-trading atmosphere of the 1930s is questionable.[3] It was rather the economic agenda of Neville Chamberlain, MacDonald's Tory chancellor of the exchequer, which pushed the United

States toward self-containment. In the wake of the final and most devastating phase of a massive price collapse under way in the winter of 1932–33, Roosevelt moved toward a devalued dollar, convinced that the depression could not lift without an increase in the domestic price level. It became apparent, however, that the British equalization fund had maneuvered the dollar to a point where it appreciated to an unacceptable level.

As Roosevelt moved toward domestic priorities, he turned to unorthodox sources for an analysis of the depression's rudiments. Intranationalist economic theory was worked out by Raymond Moley and Rexford Guy Tugwell during the interregnum with the guidance of four economists: William W. Cumberland, a partner in the Wall Street firm of Wellington & Co.; Ralph West Robey, financial editor of the New York *Evening Post;* and Alexander Sachs and Paul Mazur of Lehman Brothers. This group called for a middle ground between self-containment and "philanthropic internationalism." Intranationalism afforded priority to domestic concerns since it interpreted the nation's problems as the consequence of skewed relationships among various sections, classes, and economic groups, agriculture and industry as an example. While it conceded the importance of restored trade with other industrialized nations, trade was secondary in the economic crisis. A return to international priorities could be achieved only after each nation attained internal recovery, a position reinforced by John Maynard Keynes. "International agreements," Robey concluded, "can be acceptable to us only if they assist us in strengthening our own economy." Mazur observed that during the previous one hundred years, internationalism had been "a British economy and the British philosophy of economics controlled."[4]

In communications to Moley and Roosevelt beginning in October 1932, then in a preinauguration discussion, René Léon, a knowledgeable retired banker and silver trader, explained depressed world price levels in intranationalist terms. Because the British sphere of influence embraced half the world's population, price levels as expressed in dollars or gold could not rise until London took the initiative. As the pound sterling and silver were both artificially depreciated, low price levels prevailed in the British Empire, Scandinavia, part of the sterling bloc, India, and, through India's depreciated silver currency, China's exchange. The result was depressed price levels worldwide, including the United States. According to Léon, deliberate depreciation of sterling to the disadvantage of the gold standard countries "must be broken up at all costs," since their obligations, fixed in gold, became more onerous as price levels fell. In the absence of international action, "local methods of protection must at once be adopted." The Hoover administration had mistakenly promoted a strong-dollar policy based on gold while U.S. trade evaporated, local production backed up into home markets, and price levels plummeted. Instead, the United States should "insist on . . . complete reversal of the [British] policy of price destruction."

Léon proposed resort to the wartime Trading with the Enemy Act of 1917, which authorized the embargo of gold shipments abroad, to drive the dollar down and the pound upward in international money markets. Foreigners, he contended, should not be permitted to use the dollar as a "lever against our prices," since free exchange of other currencies for the dollar had been used as a mechanism for depreciation of foreign currencies. In the instance of the sterling equalization fund, used to lower cost of production in the United Kingdom: "The dollar is the reciprocal equivalent of all other free gold standard countries. . . . When the Equalization Fund swaps pounds sterling for French francs or Dutch guilders, the resulting disparity between sterling on the one hand, and francs on the other, applies to the dollar in equal ratio."[5]

Roosevelt moved gradually toward divorce of the dollar from the sterling and gold standards. On March 6, as part of the bank holiday, the government prohibited private ownership of gold. Events soon demonstrated, as Léon predicted, that this measure secured no dollar decline. Gold during these weeks could be obtained under Treasury license for international transactions, and when speculators drained gold to Europe in exchange for dollars, Roosevelt embargoed gold exports altogether, a step taken on April 20. In the process he gained critical support from unexpected quarters, J. P. Morgan & Co.'s Thomas Lamont and Russell Leffingwell.[6]

The shift in Lamont's and Leffingwell's thought away from a gold dollar came about as a consequence of the farm crisis and the deflationary impact of bank closings. It required two to make a bargain, Lamont informed Roosevelt, and a return to the yellow metal seemed pointless so long as Great Britain used its depreciated paper pound to purchase American gold for its reserves, a course deflationary in its impact on the American economy. A return to gold at new parities required a tripartite agreement between the United States, Great Britain, and France. Currency ratios would be determined after a period of float and would be accompanied by reciprocal trade agreements and a debt settlement. In the interim a depreciated dollar would give farmers relief and promote a better equilibrium between an overvalued dollar and the undervalued pound. Worthy of note, also, was Lamont's proposed abrogation by the president and the secretary of the treasury of the gold clause in U.S. obligations. Payment should be made in dollars, as any other procedure would give creditors a "dishonest preference" over others, aggravating the current burden of indebtedness. According to Lamont, the United States was under no constitutional inhibition against violation of contract and possessed full constitutional authority over its money, a position long held by Oklahoma's Senator Elmer Thomas.[7]

When B. S. Carter of Morgan, Paris, questioned the reversal of long-held views on deliberate repudiation, Leffingwell parried, "Of course I believed in the gold standard, and want to get back on it." Then again, Leffingwell went on, he also believed in the *Mauritania*, but if she struck an iceberg and began to list, he would take to the lifeboats. The responsibility of defense of the old gold standard by the United States alone had been ruinous. Indeed, no nation had proved able to protect both the gold parity of its currency and its internal price level.[8]

With MacDonald en route to Washington for talks in late April, Roosevelt found himself torn between two approaches on currency and related economic issues. The internalist approach of Léon and the intranationalists required a lowering of the dollar's gold content in order to drive up local price levels for the output of farmers and industry. The Atlanticists, led by an unofficial adviser, the Manhattan banker James P. Warburg, seconded by the governor of the Federal Reserve Bank of New York, George L. Harrison, as well as by William Woodin and Dean Acheson at the Treasury Department, advocated joint Anglo-U.S.-French efforts toward a return to a gold exchange standard. The dollar, pound, and franc would be stabilized after a period of float in which the dollar would be allowed to depreciate.

The most knowledgeable of the Atlanticists in the Roosevelt entourage, Warburg was in a better position than those holding official posts to oppose monetary experiments. Recruited by Moley in late January to the small group advising the president-elect on issues scheduled for negotiation at the World Monetary and Economic Conference, Warburg quickly made his mark as the author of memoranda aimed at reestablishing Anglo-American economic entente and avoiding inflationary pressures in the United States. Like Hull, Warburg regarded trade agreements as the lubricant required to attain worldwide economic recovery. The United States, he believed, was capable of sacrifices toward that end. Unlike Hull, however, Warburg, a master of the weaponry of currency warfare, knew that trade reciprocity hinged on currency stability. For currency warfare would make trade agreements impossible to negotiate and, if negotiated, effectively null and void. Accordingly, the bulk of Warburg's efforts were directed through Treasury and the Federal Reserve in pursuit of multilateral agreement on currency parities.[9]

Given the quest for dollar-pound parity, complicated by French insistence on a quick return to gold to everyone else's disadvantage (France had long since satisfactorily depreciated its currency), the issue took shape as follows: What concessions would the MacDonald-Chamberlain government make toward Roosevelt's requirement for a depreciated dollar widely regarded as a stimulus to recovery? At what point would the United States completely abandon gold under Roosevelt, a nationalist course that would postpone Wilsonian internationalism to some distant time when the domestic depression was mitigated? And once the United States cut loose from the discipline of the yellow metal and the international bankers who managed it, would the dollar be stabilized at a point satisfactory to the needs of domestic raw materials producers or, conversely, to the requirements of the international bankers and the Chamberlain government? Given the economic primacy of the United States, Roosevelt commanded a pivotal position in these matters, a fact that he understood.

As the debts issue verged on paralysis—London agreed to a $10 million installment in silver, calculated at an inflated price, due on June 15 to keep the economic conference afloat—considerable energy was expended on dollar-pound stabilization during the preparatory discussions for the MacDonald-Roosevelt meeting. The issue was complicated by Roosevelt's April 20 ban on gold exports as MacDonald and his economic adviser, Sir Frederick Leith-Ross, made their way by ship to New York and Washington, as well as by the president's uncertainty regarding an appropriate figure for the dollar in relation to the pound. In the event, Roosevelt's abandonment of gold moved currency stability to center stage, at least from the British point of view, for it threatened a race toward devaluation and possibly a destabilized sterling, seriously impacting Britain's vital export trade.[10]

With a dear dollar stuck at $3.41–$3.42 to the pound, Roosevelt feared added deflationary pressures occasioned by the bank crisis. Some 10,500 banks had closed with deposits of nearly $5 billion in the decade 1921–32, severely damaging commodities producers in the South and the West. As "the great contraction" intensified in the early 1930s, capital losses and losses to investors and depositors spurred a massive decline in the stock of money, which fell by one-third. Commercial bank deposits fell by $18 billion, or 42 percent, and total deposits in suspended banks alone reached another $7 billion.[11]

The April 20 gold embargo reversed the bargaining position of Washington and London. Roosevelt acquired the dominant hand in the monetary poker game, the pound rising to $3.86 by April 24. In exchanges with British and French representatives, Warburg, anxious to pin Roosevelt down to a firm dollar-pound-franc parity, without which the London Conference could reach no trade agreements, broached a possible arrangement based on a reduced, uniform gold reserve of 25 to 30 percent (the optional 5 percent in silver a concession to western advocates of bimetallism). The proposed compromise, he anticipated, would also constrain pressures for monetary expansion.[12]

Customary assignment exclusively to Roosevelt of responsibility for failure of the World Monetary and Economic Conference to settle monetary and trade matters needs to be questioned as the very basis for the conference no longer existed after the preparatory Washington discussions of April 1933. Upon approval by Roosevelt and MacDonald of Warburg's proposed cutback of traditional bullion reserves from 40 to 30 percent, the agreement was submitted to London. In the belief that London would prove willing to return to a modified gold standard, Warburg proceeded to negotiate dollar-pound parity with Leith-Ross, who represented the British Treasury in the technical aspects of these negotiations. While the two settled on a dollar discounted in a range of 15 to 25 percent, considerably less than Roosevelt wanted, London's response sealed the matter and helps to account for the decision taken by the president to abandon negotiations for monetary parity.

Upon conferring with the Treasury in London, Leith-Ross put Britain's "Exchange Position" to Warburg in a formal reply. "The United States is the strongest creditor country in the world, with a favorable balance of trade and vast gold resources," the British memorandum began ominously. "The dollar was certainly not over-valued in relation to other currencies. . . . If the exchanges operated in response to economic forces, the dollar could not help remaining at or about the old parity," that of the winter of 1932–33. There was no give in the British stance, only the claim that a cheaper dollar would create havoc in world markets, "defy the law of gravitation," and render the conference "quite hopeless." Instead of a counteroffer, the Leith-Ross statement lectured "that the United States authorities should undertake pending the conference not deliberately to depreciate the dollar, and to support it at its present level of not more than 10% depreciation." The next day Roosevelt rejected the British proposal. French insistence on a dollar stabilized at current levels and Roosevelt's refusal to agree added fuel to the explosive end of the London Conference and its trade agenda.[13]

Warburg soon learned that he would serve at London in the unofficial capacity of intermediary between the European treasury–central bank negotiators and the U.S. delegates on the stabilization issue. As Warburg lacked legal authority, Roosevelt's formal representatives in currency matters were George L. Harrison, governor of the New York Federal Reserve Bank, and Oliver M. W. Sprague, adviser to the Treasury Department. The three agreed that de facto stabilization was necessary to prevent those nations still on gold from going off gold, a priority of the Fed-Treasury orthodoxy and the British cabinet, not the president. With the dollar in the process of decline on world exchanges (from $3.85 to $4.00 between April 29 and May 31), accompanied by a rise in domestic prices and industrial output, Roosevelt, on the eve of the London Conference, opted for reflation by means of a cheaper dollar.

Another problem emerged. Failed efforts at monetary stability meant that tariff reductions, even if negotiated by Hull at London, would prove meaningless. Roosevelt's secretary of state was not easily disregarded. A power in the Democratic Party since the Wilson era, he had helped secure Roosevelt's 1932 nomination and commanded considerable support in the South, as its economy was geared to exports. While Warburg's diary testifies to the secretary's inability to grasp the complex economic issues under discussion, Hull held to one belief: revival of global trade represented the surest way out of depression, whereas inordinately high trade barriers represented a sure road to international conflict. Also, an economy based on exchange of goods in a competitive environment worldwide assured minimal federal interference with the democratic process. Hull's model was the pre-Wilsonian world of open trade in open markets, with the United States taking the lead recently abandoned by Chamberlain. Yet tariff reciprocity proved elusive in the autarkic climate of the thirties. "I find frequently in conferences at the White House," Budget Director Lewis W. Douglas lamented toward the end of May, "the following statement made. We only export five percent of our production: Why, then, should we be worried about foreign markets."[14]

An open clash between Hull and Moley, his nominal subordinate, seemed inevitable. Once in office, Hull "prepared to work for legislation authorizing the State Department to negotiate reciprocal trade agreements based on the unconditional most-favored-nation clause and permitting substantial tariff reductions." While excluded from the Washington preliminaries because of the conference's stress on Treasury issues, the secretary of state looked forward to the meeting as a great stage on which he could put into play "the ideas I had entertained for nearly thirty years." Under Hull's tutelage his staff put together draft legislation that authorized the president to negotiate reciprocal trade agreements. And as he boarded the liner *President Roosevelt* for London, the hapless diplomat carried in his jacket pocket a copy of the trade agreement document, anticipating that the president would introduce it to the Congress as the ultimate achievement of the Hundred Days' session. Hull planned to present this proposal to the other delegations at London.[15]

When the World Monetary and Economic Conference organizing committee met in May, it agreed to a tariff truce for the duration of the London conference. Hull, elated, anticipated a permanent agreement with a rate reduction of some 10 percent. But the exceptions made by eight participating nations were vitiating. Worse still, from Hull's vantage point, news from Washington revealed that the pending agricultural-industrial program promised higher, not lower, tariffs as well as import quotas. Hull communicated his disappointment to the president. Roosevelt replied that attaining lower tariffs at the current session of Congress appeared "highly inadvisable and impossible of achievement."

The triad of issues that spawned the World Economic and Monetary Conference, a legacy of the previous administration, had been resolved. Roosevelt foreclosed discussion of debts and tariffs at an international conference. Gratified by a decline in the value of the dollar, he proved disinclined to stabilize even at current levels. A similar movement had taken place in London. The British government was inclined toward an empire rather than a world solution and fully intended to rid itself of the war debts.

Convinced that the conference could not fulfill the expectations of the internationalists, Moley determined to "clear the atmosphere by saying publicly what could be accomplished in London and what could not." Moley's views surfaced in a radio broadcast, then with his debut as a syndicated journalist. He cautioned against the optimism generated by the preliminary meetings held in Washington and explained that the major participants in the World Monetary and Economic Conference scheduled to open in London on June 12, the United States included, were en route to self-sufficiency. As for Hull's fixation on tariff barriers, "world trade is, after all, only a small percentage of the trade of the United States. This means that our domestic policy is of paramount importance."[16]

Hull viewed the statement as perfidious. The secretary of state gauged agricultural and industrial controls as "cutting the United States off from the rest of the economic world. . . . They [economic nationalists] wanted to concentrate on lifting prices and restoring business in this country by purely domestic measures." At his final meeting with the American delegation before their departure for Europe, Hull recalled, "I stood firmly for the purposes I had in mind for the London Conference, principally tariff reductions." Roosevelt could no longer waffle. Would he stabilize and take Hull's route to recovery through trade agreements? Or would he stay with the internalist agenda fashioned in the interregnum based on increased domestic price levels for industrial and farm output? Compelled to choose, the president opted for a nationalist program but retained the services of a compliant, internationalist-minded secretary of state who served in these years as a lightning rod intended to retain the loyalty of the old Wilsonians.

A depressed and hostile Hull would have his say in London. He attacked the "bootstrap methods" of the New Deal recovery program as Roosevelt accepted authority under the National Industrial Recovery Act to raise tariffs and impose import quotas. In the process Roosevelt notified Hull that he had put off until 1934 the issue of tariff reciprocity. "I left for London with the highest of hopes, but arrived with empty hands," observed an angry Hull. Moley would soon pay the price.[17]

There were two conferences at London in June 1933, one composed of statesmen and diplomats, the other of treasury and central bank representatives. The latter proved to be pivotal as France's demand for a temporary stabilization agreement to check speculative attacks on the gold currencies stood as a roadblock to discussion of trade and other issues. Between May 31 and June 12, when the conference opened, the dollar continued to depreciate, from $4.00 to $4.15 to the pound. When news leaked to the press that the treasury–central bank negotiators, including War-burg, Harrison, and Sprague, had reached a tentative agreement, the dollar rose, and securities in the United States plunged.[18]

On inquiry to U.S. negotiators at London, Roosevelt learned that the negotiators has agreed that in return for a pledge by Great Britain that it would refrain from use of its equalization fund to affect the price of sterling, Roosevelt would refrain from utilizing the provision of the Thomas Amendment to the Agricultural Adjustment Act that authorized the president to reduce the weight of the gold dollar up to 50 percent.[19] The Bank of England and the Federal Reserve Bank of New York would maintain a dollar-pound spread of 3 percent in relation to the gold franc, the dollar to be stabilized at a middle rate of $4.00 to the pound. The 3 percent spread translated as a range of $3.88 to $4.12. The Bank of England and the New York Fed would, if required, spend up to $60 million gold dollars to support their currencies at these levels.

Such an arrangement had no future. Recalling these events that summer, the president explained that "he told the delegation and the Treasury people before they left for the conference that he could consider no stabilization scheme which required the shipment of gold or a Treasury guarantee against loss to the Federal Reserve Bank." Convinced that his instructions were disregarded by Warburg, unhappy with the proposed arrangement, and about to embark on a seagoing vacation, Roosevelt summoned Treasury Secretary Woodin, Undersecretary Dean Acheson, and Moley to the White House. The president's instructions to the negotiating team, worked out by the group, rejected any agreement aimed at a close tie between the pound and the dollar. Instead, should the dollar fall to $4.25 to the pound, he would consider "unilateral action of some kind." Then again, in the event of a rise in the value of the dollar, "we must retain full freedom of unilateral action under the Thomas Amendment in order to hold up the price level at home."[20]

While the rejection sent the dismayed New York Fed's Harrison packing, Warburg stayed on, determined to force Roosevelt's hand on the issue of international economic comity. To keep the conference alive, would Roosevelt agree to a spread of $3.80 to $4.20? Roosevelt reiterated willingness to keep the pound from rising above $4.25, no more. The president insisted in a cable to Hull that "far too much importance is attached to exchange stability by banker-influenced cabinets. In our case it means only a very small (perhaps 3) percent of our total trade measured by production." Evidently, with the dollar now at $4.18, he would not stabilize.[21]

According to Moley, Roosevelt, in a discussion on the schooner *Amberjack*, remained open to a bargain. He might consider stabilizing at a middle point of $4.15, with a high of $4.25 and a low of $4.05. "I'm not crazy about it," Moley recalled Roosevelt's statement, "but I think I'd go that far." As one of the principal architects of intranationalism, he should have known better. Indeed, as Moley prepared to debark for London, a member of Lazard Frères, Frank Altschul, who had helped to fashion the policy of intranationalism, warned against currency stabilization on the ground that it would disturb the spring economic recovery, interpreted rightly or wrongly as due to Roosevelt's severance of the link that tied the dollar to gold. Recovery could only be attained as each nation first resolved its own domestic problems. International equilibrium would follow as a logical consequence of elevated price levels, whereas a currency agreement in London would perpetuate the current world disequilibrium.[22]

After Moley left for London, the Wilson intimate Colonel Edward M. House carried a monetarist argument against a premature parity arrangement to Roosevelt when the two met on the *Amberjack*. The Roosevelt-House relationship was affectionate, perhaps explained by mutual service in wartime, equally likely by Franklin's loss of his elderly father at a tender age. Their correspondence is marked by warmth and for the squire uncharacteristically revealing. "Mama," Sara Delano Roosevelt, was a guest at House's Beverly Farms estate at the very time that House and the president conferred. Confronted by pressures for monetary stabilization from Europe as well as his Treasury and Federal Reserve advisers, the president was "not yet firm in his own thinking," hence the importance of letters written by Benjamin Henry Inness-Brown that carried House's imprimatur.

A graduate of Harvard Law School, brilliant and articulate, Inness-Brown probably met Roosevelt in Cambridge or during his lengthy tenure as a partner in the downtown Manhattan firm of Kellogg, Emery, Inness-Brown & Cuthell. (Both Inness-Brown and Roosevelt maintained their business addresses in the Equitable Building at 120 Broadway from 1921 to 1928.)[23] According to Inness-Brown, detachment of the dollar from gold and the sterling equalization account would not suffice to raise price levels within the United States given the shrinkage of post-1929 purchasing power, which Inness-Brown attributed to a decline in velocity of turnover

TABLE 1. Demand Deposits and Velocity of Turnover (in billions of dollars), 6/30/29–3/31/33

	Currency	Demand Deposits (Check Money)	Total	Velocity of Demand Deposits
6/30/29	3.9	24.3	28.2	65.4
6/30/30	3.6	24.1	27.7	56.0
6/30/31	3.9	21.3	25.2	39.7
6/30/32	4.9	16.4	21.3	29.0
3/31/33	6.3	13 (est.)	19.3	25.2 (January)

Demand Deposits times Velocity		
6/30/29	24.3 x 65.4	$158.9 billion
3/31/33	13 x 25.2	32.7 billion

Shrinkage of Effective Money	$126.2 billion

Source: B. H. Inness-Brown to Colonel Edward M. House, April 25, 1933, box 63b, Edward Mandell House Papers, Manuscripts and Archives, Yale University Library.

in demand deposits amounting to $126.2 billion (table 1). This was the immediate cause of the depression, as velocity of turnover determined the price level of goods and services.

Shrinkage of effective money in circulation, if continued, would cause price levels to fall even further. It was imperative to provide more purchasing power as expressed in dollars, not gold, as all gold was owned by the Treasury and Federal Reserve. Individuals owned paper dollars and bank deposits, and only a doubling of dollars and demand deposits would impact price levels. The advantage of a higher gold price would be a broader base for issuance of currency and creation of credit. Any attempt to return to 1926 price levels depended on the writing up of demand deposits on the books of the nation's banks through the device of open-market purchases by the Federal Reserve of government securities. Despite assurances by the Fed, this had not been done, and there occurred no real inflation.

Inness-Brown's discomfort extended to the advisers around Harrison at the New York Fed, Woodin, Sprague and Acheson at the Treasury, and Lewis W. Douglas, Roosevelt's budget director, all deflationists. "People trained by the enemy" dominated the lower echelons at Treasury and the Fed. "It seems to me," Inness-Brown continued, we are in the midst of a struggle between the party of "Prices" (namely the people . . . who manufacture, produce, and sell), and the party of "Money" (namely the banking cult, who manufacture and sell money). The banking cult, who always treated the intricacies of monetary science as a mystical knowledge, is a priesthood to whom the sovereigns have been accustomed to surrender their initiative in this province of knowledge. . . . The money cult . . . which wished to keep its money stable in terms of a single commodity (gold) for its own convenience in transactions, has allowed such a terrific disaster to ensue upon the world that it is clear to me now that the party of Prices will win a victory in the United States, which will force a like victory in all countries.[24]

Inness-Brown regarded the president as a potential Kerensky, timid, too good-natured, too ready to harness inconsistent policies, too ready to carry out radical policies through conservatives who did not believe in them, paving the way for America's "Lenin, . . . already known and named and waiting in the Congress," that is, Huey Long. Central bankers, he added, were occupied with their own conference at London, holding their stabilization discussions independent of the nations represented there and unrepresentative of the needs of manufacturers, exporters, and workers. As Inness-Brown, a monetarist, preferred open-market operations in the range of $12 to $14 billion as opposed to near inaction by the Federal Reserve, Roosevelt's rejection of the stabilization agreement reached at London in June 1933, in his view, constituted only the first step in his separation of U.S. monetary policies from those of Harrison and the New York Fed.[25]

Keynes added public works to the mix in a series of articles published in the New York *Herald Tribune,* beginning June 27. "The assembled delegates in London compete with one another in their enthusiasm to raise prices by talk. But not one of them does anything definite or even makes a concrete proposal how to accomplish the desired object by joint action." Roosevelt, while justifiably nervous as he watched "the gang of verbalists" gathered at the Geological Museum, was himself subject to criticism on the ground that he had let talk outrun action, too dependent on psychological factors and a boom limited to consumption goods. "If he fails," Keynes warned, "it will not be because his measures are too drastic, but because he has been too tardy and too timid in his program of public works and in his efforts, by open-market operations and otherwise, to reduce the long-term rate of interest."

In Keynes's view the key to the situation could be found in the Thomas Amendment powers granted to Roosevelt. The conference should agree to devaluation in the range of 20 to 33 percent in the gold value of currencies, with the sterling and dollar blocs leading the way. (Stabilization required a transition period.) The resultant windfall profit should be appropriated by the treasuries of each nation and put into circulation by reduced taxes or by public works. The net result would be a more satisfactory basis for a worldwide rise in the price level than competitive depreciation. Keynes hoped that the British delegation would take the lead. If not, "why should not President Roosevelt, who does not lack boldness, bring the conference to the test by offering it to them? If they refuse . . . there lies hidden a deep and irreconcilable divergence of policy which justifies him in isolated action along his own lines."[26]

Moley's ill-fated venture to London needs to be considered in the context of a policy he had helped to initiate. A depreciated dollar and a rise in domestic price levels were essential as a stimulus to consumers and producers in a deflationary environment. His unsatisfactory personal relationship with Cordell Hull is a side issue. When MacDonald, Chamberlain, Guido Jung of Italy, and Charles Rist of France sought to reach a stabilization agreement, Moley fell into the error of direct negotiation. This gave Roosevelt the impression that his closest adviser had been taken in. Confronted by a rapid decline in the dollar-pound rate, with the gold currencies under pressure, French finance minister Georges Bonnet demanded on June 28 a declaration that the nongold countries would support the gold currencies at their current parities.[27]

It was in these circumstances, which included a divided American delegation uninformed of Roosevelt's variable monetary views, that Chamberlain and Leith-Ross approached Moley on June 29, the day after his arrival in London. To their surprise Moley "took over the responsibility for the conversations . . . and was prepared to go considerably further than had been expected." As Moley interpreted the compromise proposal drafted by the British and the French, "the representatives of the gold countries had apparently given up their insistence that the United States agree to some form of temporary stabilization as a condition to further participation in the conference." Rather, they would accept a "vague multilateral statement of ultimate principle." Whereas only days before, Roosevelt had said he would agree, if pressed, to a dollar valued at $4.05–$4.25, Moley believed he had gotten a better offer. Either Moley misunderstood the situation, lacking the requisite technical knowledge, or the gold bloc proposal urging ultimate stabilization of currencies had a different and accurate ring in Roosevelt's ears. For as Chamberlain's journal indicates, the June 29 statement hammered out at the American Embassy, which Moley felt assured Roosevelt would sanction, required "undertaking (inter alia) to stop speculation in exchanges," effectively a veto of the president's powers to secure domestic reflation.

The agreement proposed by the French and British read: "Each of the signatory governments whose currencies are not on the gold standard undertakes to adopt the measures which it may deem most appropriate to limit exchange speculation." According to Roosevelt, the Moley proposal depended on the willingness of the United States to check speculation and to stabilize the dollar. Roosevelt rejected the "compromise" agreement, in reality a concession to the deflationary philosophy of France, evoking his message of July 1. Given the dollar's continued decline, now at $4.33 to the pound, Roosevelt stated that "we must be free if gold or gold and silver are reestablished as international measures of exchange to adopt our own method of stabilizing our own domestic price level in terms of the dollar regardless of foreign exchange rates." He would not allow "any fixed formula of stabilization by agreement" at least until the United States demonstrated "the value of price lifting efforts." The president was correct in judging dollar depreciation at the time as a domestic issue, not subject to diplomatic negotiation.[28]

The old international gold standard was dead. While it provided stability of external exchanges, it had sacrificed stability of internal prices leading to an irreversible worldwide deflationary spiral. England, Roosevelt claimed, had left the gold standard two years earlier and only now sought stabilization. France, too, had followed its national interest. The conference, Roosevelt protested, had not been called to discuss the policy of one nation. For all practical purposes Roosevelt's angry message to the conference on July 3, the so-called "bombshell," terminated practicable negotiations at London. It categorized adherence of gold as a fetish of international bankers and made clear his intention to raise internal price levels. The conference, he recommended, should turn to more fundamental challenges such as coordinated expenditure for public works, a position opposed by Chamberlain.[29]

Once again, Roosevelt found support from the ranks of J. P. Morgan & Co. Leffingwell categorized the willingness of Harrison, Sprague, and Warburg to submit the question of United States monetary policy to international discussion as "one of the most amazing blunders in history." No major nation remained on the old prewar gold standard and no major nation had submitted its monetary policy to international mediation. In any event, it would be disastrous for the United States to stabilize the dollar at the time. Recovery was predicated on policies that remained to be implemented, particularly in the areas of inflation and public works. Great Britain, he observed, once the exemplar of the gold standard, had been doing relatively well since its abandonment of gold in 1931. It was unfortunate for Roosevelt, Leffingwell observed scathingly, that the Treasury's technical advisers, Sprague and Walter Stewart, a Wall Street economist, among the few in the United States who understood money and exchanges, had learned their subject in England. "The British knew enough to go off gold themselves. No doubt it would suit their book to have America back on gold . . . leaving the world to the British oyster."[30]

The gold bloc, Keynes observed, devalued their currencies following the war by a percentage considerably higher than that contemplated by Roosevelt, virtually eliminating their internal debt. As for the United States, "Their debt structure is a problem which would remain as a social disease even with employment restored to normal, if prices and wages remain at their recent level." Keynes advocated for both Great Britain and the United States a policy of devaluation combined with public works and lower long-term interest rates. "We have to determine . . . whether or not to join the Administration of the United States, in the company of the British Dominions and of India, South America, and Scandinavia, in a concerted policy of increased loan expenditure, public and private, at home and abroad, in pursuit of the twin purposes of raising prices and of restoring employment." That decision rested on the outcome of a contest between Chamberlain and the dominions.[31]

Chamberlain entered the conference, like the gold bloc, determined to yield nothing to Roosevelt's requirement for price reflation. Additionally, the British government insisted that the imperial preference system could not be breached by discussion of the most-favored-nation clause in commercial treaties. Finding Roosevelt's stance offensive and unacceptable, pressured by the *Times* of London and Keynes to adopt an expansionary budgetary policy, which he opposed, Chamberlain prepared a statement for submission to the British delegates at the conference. The chancellor of the exchequer claimed that "stabilization had always been recognized as an essential factor in the situation," a view countered by the dominions. Jan Christian Smuts of South Africa drafted a memorandum, supported by Stanley M. Bruce of Australia, Bennett of Canada, and Sir Henry Strakosch, a member of the Council of India, that endorsed the president's "outrageous statement" (Chamberlain's words), since they urged empire support for public works, credit expansion, depreciated sterling, and reduced taxes. Chamberlain backed off for the moment.[32] On this, Chamberlain's biographer observed, "As primary producers, as borrowers, as seed-beds of experiment, their [the dominions'] sympathies were much inclined to Roosevelt: this he [Chamberlain] would resist, hoping to carve out of the international ruins some actual agreement for the broad space of the Empire." The chancellor of the exchequer won the intraempire contest when he secured a restatement of the Ottawa principles, or protected trade within the empire. In Chamberlain's view he had diverted the dominions "from the dangerous path of currency depreciation and public works," which might well induce inflationary public expenditure.[33]

In his correspondence with his sisters, Chamberlain explained: "There are always a number of people who will have more faith in a quack than a qualified practitioner. That sometimes enables the quack to be successful where the qualified man has failed and we must hope that the Roosevelt experiment will succeed. But it hasn't succeeded yet and in the meantime he has certainly torpedoed the conference." The chancellor of the exchequer preferred his own "slower and less sensational methods," since they would prove more satisfactory in the long run. A discussion with Thomas Lamont, the Morgan partner, soon reinforced these views. Ever the politician, playing to both sides of the ocean, Lamont expressed a lack of "faith or confidence in Roosevelt (whom he has known all his life) and he considers that he is making a series of experiments so disastrous that his only hope lies in his belief in the probability of their not being proceeded with."[34]

The burden now rested with Roosevelt, surrounded by orthodox monetarists. He was "magnificently right," Inness-Brown echoed Keynes, provided he had a program and deputies willing and able to carry it out.[35] Indeed, a speculative increase in inventories in the hopes of higher price levels was dashed by a sharp decline that began in the summer of 1933. Consumer purchasing power proved insufficient to absorb output. This compelled consideration of another controversial step, reduction of the dollar's gold content.

While a depreciated dollar was necessary to U.S. recovery, manipulation of the dollar's gold content would not result in the controlled inflation Roosevelt contemplated. Recovery also depended on expanded Federal Reserve open-market operations, adequate credit expansion, lower real interest rates, and increased public works expenditure as well as growth in private-sector investment and employment. U.S. leadership along these lines was requisite for worldwide prosperity. Yet the Fed never undertook a serious expansionary policy in the 1930s, and no tolerable level of public works funding could meet the deficit in private-sector investment.

3 | DOLLAR DEVALUATION
AND THE MONETARY GROUP

OOSEVELT'S REJECTION OF the stabilization agreement negotiated by Chamberlain and Moley at the London Economic Conference opened the way to unilateral pursuit of price-raising measures. That development led to the first substantial internal debate of Roosevelt's administration—a debate that helps to clarify two matters: the belief that the president proved subject to capture by his advisers and his choice of a domestic as opposed to international priorities in approaching the Great Depression.

The argument that Herbert Hoover framed the New Deal's programmatic approach to the economic debacle, originated by Walter Lippmann, can be tested in the context of the dollar's divorce from the gold and sterling standards. Whereas Hoover championed the gold standard as basic to recovery, the yellow metal as a mechanism both for settling international accounts and for assurance of price stability had become a fiction. Gold fluctuated as readily as any other commodity and possessed only symbolic import. Yet Hoover continued to insist on its retention after the 1931 collapse despite its deflationary impact, a disastrous course pressed on Roosevelt that he refused to follow.[1]

As to Roosevelt, he was scarcely imprisoned by the "gold-dust twins," Cornell University's agrarian economists, George F. Warren and Frank A. Pearson. He believed, correctly, that commodity prices needed to be raised, and that adherence to the gold standard proved a hindrance to this end. After a brief experiment in the autumn of 1933, the president quickly abandoned the Warren-Pearson thesis which claimed that domestic prices were ineluctably tied to the price of gold. Instead FDR fixed its price and opted for increasing price levels by the device of production controls on commodities, a policy which Warren vehemently opposed on the grounds of undue interference in the economy. Nor would the president heed the advice of James P. Warburg, the New York Fed, and his Treasury advisers who worked to retain the dollar's tie to a modified gold standard managed by the City of London and the Wall Street banking establishment, a device intended to tie his hands.

Recovery for the United States, Roosevelt held, required higher price levels for raw materials output and manufactures in hopes that reflation would provide solvency for producers and their creditors. Here Roosevelt met considerable internal resistance institutionalized at Treasury and the New York Federal Reserve Bank. Given the Federal Reserve's unwillingness to pursue an expansionary monetary policy on the ground that ample credit existed in the banking system to meet the demands of creditworthy borrowers, the policy of "expanding the money" by means of open-market operations was left to the executive branch. Roosevelt, under considerable pressure exerted both by inflationists and orthodox monetarists, chose a course that satisfied neither point of view.[2]

Opposition to monetary expansion crystallized initially under the informal leadership of James P. Warburg, who emerged as the prime mover of the "monetary group" formed by Roosevelt in the late summer of 1933. In the end Roosevelt followed his own muse. No adviser or cluster of advisers dominated the final decision to devalue the dollar.

With the World Monetary and Economic Conference a shambles, a troubled Cordell Hull summoned the U.S. delegation's financial adviser, James P. Warburg, to his quarters. While the secretary of state surely knew by then that the president operated outside normative administrative channels, evidently he had not grasped the full import of Roosevelt's bombshell messages beyond the certainty that his subordinate, Raymond Moley, was through. In Hull's view "the whole monetary question [was] now still open to discussion and deliberation" at London. Warburg believed to the contrary that there remained little if anything to be discussed other than resignation from the American delegation. He would "finish . . . [his] association with the administration," Warburg noted in his diary. Gradually, Warburg's mood changed. The scrappy young banker determined to make a fight of it with "the new school in Washington," namely Yale's James Harvey Rogers and Cornell's George F. Warren.[3]

En route home, Warburg organized his thoughts for presentation to Roosevelt. Warburg placed the blame for the conference's failure on "the changed attitude of America between the [April] Washington conversations and your messages of late June and early July," a situation, he allowed, dictated by events. Presumably this afforded the president the opportunity to recant in a new message to the conference, one that assured the gathering of his commitment to international cooperation. While Warburg claimed that he did not understand sufficiently what informed the president, he had talks with John Maynard Keynes and Sir Josiah Stamp, a highly regarded businessman-economist, hopefully sufficiently radical in their monetary views, and had developed ideas for "stabilizing the purchasing power of a currency which may fit in with the thoughts that have been recently developed in Washington."[4]

Warburg also drafted a mea culpa for Roosevelt's signature, intended for a dispirited MacDonald. The president should have informed the prime minister in the course of his Washington visit that monetary stability was temporarily out of the question and should not therefore have encouraged the convening of a conference that summer. The letter would also concede that the United States, meaning Roosevelt, had been the "stormy petrel of the conference," hence responsible for its failure. And it pledged that America would not embark on a course of isolationism or nationalism. Once the United States had put its house in order, it would devote itself to neighborliness in its international relations.

On his return to New York, Warburg conferred with Walter W. Stewart, Budget Director Lewis W. Douglas, and Moley. Douglas proposed that they rally conservatives against the inflationists in a last-ditch fight for dollar-pound parity in the context of a revised international gold standard. He also assured Warburg that they could rely on Moley, who professed that he was "on the side of conservatism."[5]

For Moley it was the onset of a trek that culminated in a warm friendship with Herbert Hoover and an alliance with anti–New Deal Republicans. He was skeptical of inflationist theory on the ground that the price of gold "doesn't affect prices when the dollar isn't tied to gold." In an effort to protect the Brains Trust's domestic priorities, he gravitated to monetary and fiscal conservatives: Walter Stewart, a deflationist Wall Street banker; William Cumberland of Cumberland & Co.; Ralph West Robey, a budget hawk and financial writer for the New York *Evening Post*; Swagar Sherley, former chairman of the House Appropriations Committee; and Warburg. These and other members of the Democratic Party orthodoxy, Bernard Baruch and W. Averell Harriman, had become intimates and advisers on economic policy, foreign and domestic.[6] Indeed, when Moley's

State Department office was manned by Baruch during his absence in London, the president inferred that Moley had placed the financier in a position to become a major figure in the shaping of economic policy.[7]

Lewis Douglas's assurances to Warburg of Moley's support were soon confirmed by W. Averell Harriman. "He [Moley] feels as I do about the whole situation." Harriman, the principal force in the investment banking firm of Brown Brothers Harriman, urged the young banker not to break with Roosevelt. The "swing to the left" required Warburg's return to Washington. Harriman, a supporter of FDR in the 1932 campaign and the New York State chairman of the Emergency Reemployment Campaign, reassured Warburg that Moley was "scared to death of what was going to happen and that he felt sure he would be a powerful ally in restoring sense." In any event, the two agreed on the need to organize in order to counter the influence of the Committee for the Nation, a group of inflation-minded businessmen who subscribed to the Warren thesis in the belief it would forestall federal intervention in the economy.[8]

Warburg locked horns with Roosevelt at the White House on July 24. After he categorized Roosevelt's bombshell message as unfortunate in substance and tone, Warburg read the apologia intended for MacDonald and requested the president's signature. Roosevelt, angered, denied that he had changed his monetary policies in midstream. When Warburg countered that the president had indicated in May that he was prepared to enter a tripartite monetary agreement, the president "said he had never done any such thing." In the heat of the moment, neither recalled that it was Leith-Ross, spokesman for a British cabinet opposed to concessions on the stabilization issue, who ended that earlier discussion. The Tugwell diary indicates that when the U.S. negotiators proposed a three-party stabilization fund which would act to keep the dollar, franc, and pound in an understood relationship to each other, "They [the British and French] were not prepared to accept this."[9]

A brief interruption by Secretary of the Interior Harold Ickes provided a cooling-off period. Warburg then presented a memorandum on currency matters, and Roosevelt apparently agreed to it, an unfortunate habit, for Roosevelt tended to agree with his last caller, then would proceed in another direction. The memorandum intended to tie the president to the orthodoxies of Atlanticist internationalism. According to Warburg, recovery was best achieved by international means and by offering the business community monetary stability. The threat of inflation promised a flight of capital and constituted a menace. As a consequence, Warburg empha-sized U.S.-British comity. In the process Britain would serve as senior part-ner in order to protect the American Congress and presidency from the pressures of a powerful and insistent agrarian–small town constituency. Once these two major powers stabilized their currencies, subsequent negotiations would determine the ratio of their paper to gold, in effect a return to a modified gold standard. Other nations, Warburg predicted, ini-tially the sterling-oriented Scandinavian countries and the dominions, eventually the gold bloc, would follow suit. While periodic but infrequent changes in the price of gold would be permitted to counter a rise or fall in commodity prices, the revised gold standard would be managed by cen-tral banks, a check on the influence of the inflationists on monetary pol-icy. In order to enter into prompt negotiation with other nations on these issues, a commission of experts would be created to determine the amount of dollar devaluation and the gold content of the dollar. Monetary policy would be removed from the political process.[10]

Roosevelt refused to adopt the internationalist agenda. Rather, as War-burg soon learned from Dean Acheson, the president, by no means con-vinced of the merits of their position, planned a debate at Hyde Park that pitted Warburg against James Harvey Rogers and George F. Warren, newly appointed as monetary advisers to the president. Significantly, the econ-omists were domiciled at Commerce, not at Treasury, as Roosevelt had decided to put measures for restored price levels beyond the reach of the orthodox monetarists. At the same time, there emerged an effort, typical of Roosevelt, to fuse disparate views, especially those of Warren, a nation-alist, and Rogers, who like Warburg, preferred the international route to depreciation but considered public works expenditure as the sure route out of the morass.[11]

The Yale University economist Rogers gained entry to the Roosevelt circle through the offices of Secretary of Agriculture Henry A. Wallace, Adolf A. Berle Jr., and Colonel Edward M. House. Rogers was rooted in South Carolina, cotton, and the need for export markets, hence the attrac-tiveness of his views for Wallace. Like Warren, Rogers favored an increase in the price of gold; but unlike Warren and his mentor at Yale, Irving Fisher, Rogers regarded a depreciated dollar as inadequate in meeting the economic crisis.[12]

With the depression's onset, Rogers emerged as a proponent of "con-trolled inflation." His book *America Weighs Her Gold* (1931), widely reviewed and summarized for public consumption in a series of syndicated articles, treated the depression in a framework of failed international relations and a massive maldistribution of gold toward the United States from Europe since 1914. The United States, the world's principal creditor nation, held 42.7 percent of the world's gold monetary stock yet engaged in a "shameless" high tariff system, leading to economic disaster. A modern standard of living, marked by a worldwide division of labor and internationalized industry, required expanded trade, which in turn depended on the ability of debtors to repay their obligations by the sale of their products to the United States. Smoot-Hawley and its predecessor tariffs instead forced debt repayment by the export of gold to the United States. With much of this gold inflow sterilized by the Federal Reserve, there had been no substantial price rise; rather, a vicious cycle of deflation ensued, compounded by a rigid wage-price system. This left the brunt of the disaster to fall on the shoulders of the commodities producer.[13]

Rogers did not advocate abandonment of the gold standard, only of its rigidities. Initial remedy required reliance on a smaller gold base and expanded open-market operations to arrest price declines and facilitate long-term borrowing. But this no longer sufficed, for credit expansion simply turned into excess bank reserves once the crisis deepened. Reconstruction Finance Corporation loans to banks, railroads, and insurance companies helped to fill a gap left by paucity of private-sector securities issues but did not put adequate purchasing power in the hands of consumers. In any event, the RFC was limited by principles of prudent investment. The gap should be made up by federal expenditure for public works based on wartime spending and on private-sector investment in the 1925–26 years of prosperity, or $700 million per month. At the same time, Rogers proposed increased Federal Reserve member bank reserves, trade-off of war debts for reduced tariffs, and international agreement on stimulus to purchasing power by governmental capital expenditure.[14]

Like the monetarists, Rogers eschewed agricultural and industrial planning as representative of a drift to state socialism at worst and, once proven as failed, responsible for uncontrolled inflation. Rogers also opposed independent revalorization of the dollar, the Warren–Pearson–Committee for the Nation scheme, as ineffective and potentially harmful. Unilateral devaluation would afford only temporary stimulus to foreign purchases in the United States, that is, until other countries followed suit. Simultaneous international devaluation, on the other hand, would avoid a competitive race, increase monetary gold stocks, and redistribute the world's gold supply, and it could serve as a basis for the funding of public works that would put purchasing power in the hands of spenders.

Warren, Rogers, and Warburg offered their views on monetary policy to Roosevelt at Hyde Park. All agreed that the president should remove the uncertainty that surrounded the dollar. How to accomplish this and at what precise point proved another matter. Roosevelt observed that he wanted to see first what the NRA could accomplish for domestic price levels. Moreover, he could see no harm in the current situation. Warburg contended otherwise, then claimed that fear of currency inflation and monetary experiments prevented a recovery, since current price levels outstripped business activity. In the international arena an undefined U.S. monetary policy would lead to chaos, with the gold countries forced off gold and a vicious cycle of competitive devaluation the result.

To forestall the crisis he anticipated, Warburg suggested that all monetary projects be concentrated in the Treasury Department, where, he hoped, Lewis Douglas would succeed the ailing William Woodin, and in the antiexpansionary Federal Reserve. These agencies would be advised by experts—the subsequent monetary group—who would formulate recommendations to the Treasury. The United States should fix the amount of dollar devaluation by October 1, subject only to a 10 percent variation to bring about price level adjustments. The United States and Great Britain would fix the ratio of their currencies to gold at the same time and within the context of a debt settlement.

Once the amount of dollar devaluation had been determined by the monetary group, accepted by the Treasury, and authorized by the president, and once conversations had been initiated with Great Britain— Warburg proposed a 70-cent dollar—central banks would publish weekly the official buying and selling price of gold, with the right to raise or lower gold prices by 0.5 percent weekly. This would continue until de jure stabilization was achieved. Monetary gold would be confined to central banks, which would use it for the settlement of the international balance of payments and as cover for note issues. Gold cover for note issues would be reduced to 25 percent, 80 percent in gold and 20 percent optionally in gold or silver. Once de jure stabilization was achieved, central banks would adjust gold prices periodically to offset exaggerated fluctuations in the world price level, a tall order in the autarkic climate of the 1930s. For all practical purposes this was the same proposal made by Warburg to

Roosevelt and Leith-Ross in April, a general return to gold as a confidence builder in the business community, with an added fillip: the revised gold standard would be managed by orthodox advisers beyond Roosevelt's immediate reach, i.e., the Treasury Departments and central bankers in New York, London, and Washington.

With Warburg done, Warren produced several charts which seemingly demonstrated that the price of gold directly impacted all other commodity prices, which would render the NRA irrelevant. "The president," Warburg noted, "seemed quite impressed." Warren then stated his belief that Roosevelt should keep the dollar under his control and "cut it enough and keep it declining."[15]

Warren opposed the acreage controls feature of the Agricultural Adjustment Act on the ground that commodity prices could be raised and the depression ended only by forcing the gold value of the dollar downward until the desired price level was reached. As for the optimum amount of devaluation, Warren held the greater the reduction, likely in a range of $32 to $35 per ounce, the sooner the recovery; this would make any discussion with the British on the subject pointless. Once the value of the dollar had been depreciated adequately to sustain a price recovery, the value of future money would be based on a commodity dollar. Legislation would prescribe that the weight of gold (or gold and silver) in the dollar would vary weekly based on an index of wholesale commodity prices.[16]

The four-hour debate nearly ended when Roosevelt expressed support for Warren's proposal for domestic gold purchases, but at $29 an ounce. (In fact, he had already indicated that he would so instruct the Federal Reserve in a private discussion with Warren.) Warburg questioned the legality and efficacy of this approach, based on an opinion, offered by Acheson, that under the act of March 14, 1900, Treasury could buy gold only at $20.67 an ounce. He did not mention that Acheson had qualified his comment when he noted that under the Thomas Amendment the president could reduce the gold content of the dollar and fix a new price which then would apply to the act of 1900. Why not instead, Warburg projected, authorize the Federal Reserve and Treasury to fix the price of gold both in terms of domestic purchases and overseas shipments? Warren and Rogers concurred. Once again, Roosevelt insisted that he would not permit gold exports; he wanted to establish a market for newly mined gold without reference to exports or imports.[17]

At this juncture both Warren and Warburg gave priority to monetary measures as these left basic economic decisions on prices, wages, and investment to the private sector. Warburg seemed ready to concede the issue of periodic, or weekly, adjustment of the gold content of the dollar, at least as a matter of practical political necessity. But Warren's scheme, clearly nationalist, placed responsibility for dollar depreciation on the presidency and was predicated on an absolute correlation between commodity prices and the gold price of the dollar. Warburg insisted on Anglo-U.S. comity and early stabilization of the dollar, with monetary authority situated in a group of experts at Treasury and the Federal Reserve in order to fend off popular pressure and nostrums. Warren offered a theory of recovery dependent on appreciated prices, Warburg on business confidence subject to currency stability. Neither regarded the balance of the New Deal program as credible.

The Warburg position that Anglo-U.S. currency stabilization would reassure credit and investment markets and move industry in the direction of greater borrowing and production was not convincing. Basic obstacles to recovery existed beyond business confidence: the weak position of most potential users of capital; the uncertain impact of the NRA codes on cost of production, and the question, still unanswered, whether the NRA could deliver on its promise of recovery. The immediate prospect for recovery and price increases depended on increased demand for materials and labor spurred by public works.

At the same time, no evidence existed to prove Warren's theory, which held that price levels and business activity would correlate with shifts in the price of gold. Historically changes in the gold content of the monetary unit followed currency depreciation accompanied by a higher price level, not the reverse. There was, however, one advantage to a change in the price of gold, as it would result in a paper gain in the value of the metal held by the Federal Reserve Banks. If taken by the government, a certain amount of money could be added to circulating medium through public expenditures without adding to the tax burden or to borrowing. As matters developed, however, the Fed, fearful of inflation, sterilized its gold holdings.[18]

From the perspective of the president then, Warburg and his Treasury Department stood firmly against domestic gold purchases at increased dollar prices ostensibly on legal grounds, more likely on policy grounds. From that of Wall Street and the bulk of the business community, willingness to resume investment depended on the monetary and fiscal policies advocated by the anti-inflationists in the informal monetary group. Surely, if he was to contravene the orthodoxy in pursuit of a cheaper dollar and the goal of an internalized economy, Roosevelt would need to end traditional Wall Street–City of London control of monetary policy, a point hammered consistently by Inness-Brown.

Proposals by Warburg and Dean Acheson for membership in the monetary group were rejected by the president. Included in the Warburg list were Keynes, Stamp, Sir Arthur Salter, and Leith-Ross, evidently a product of his belief that monetary stability could be achieved only as a joint enterprise under British leadership. Roosevelt selected no British advisers. The informal monetary group consisted instead of Treasury Secretary Woodin; Lewis Douglas; Sprague, a Treasury adviser; Rogers; Eugene Black, governor of the Federal Reserve Board (a cipher in the deliberations that followed); Harrison; Stewart; and Warburg. Herbert Feis, State's economic adviser, was included later on the advice of Felix Frankfurter.[19]

Nor was there a meeting of the minds between Roosevelt and Warburg on the monetary group's agenda. Just how, Warburg inquired, could a new gold standard achieve flexibility without the risk of political mismanagement, implicit in a managed currency? If the United States was to reduce the gold content of the dollar, Warburg wanted to know "by how much?" In whom should such authority be vested? And at what point should other nations be consulted? No commission, Roosevelt observed, could determine "what kind of dollar we are going to have" and "how big a dollar we are going to have in the future." Why not, Warburg parried? "Because I myself can't answer that," the president retorted, obviously disinclined to delegate such authority, given high unemployment. How could he determine what kind of dollar he wanted under current conditions? Warburg countered that the president could not, in any event, buy gold in the domestic market at $29 an ounce, a return to their Hyde Park debate over the legality, if not the efficacy, of such a move. Roosevelt declared that he could force the Fed to do so under his Thomas Amendment powers.[20]

Secretary of the Treasury Woodin tendered the group's Interim Monetary Report to the president at the end of August. Essentially Warburg's work, the report cleverly offered lip service to a dollar with constant purchasing power and debt-paying power, the Warren thesis, an economic impossibility, but required in reality a revised or modified gold standard agreed upon by Great Britain and the United States. Monetary flexibility would be provided through the use of discount rates and open-market operations by cooperation of the world's major central banks, equally impossible. For long-run control the monetary group recommended "periodic but infrequent changes in the price of gold" managed by "a highly intelligent authority" and whenever possible by international agreement in order to preclude a race for depreciation.[21]

Before Roosevelt responded—in fact the day after the report was dispatched to the president—one of its own members undercut Warburg's argument. Sprague, former adviser to the British Treasury, knew the British position better than Warburg. Skeptical about the results of a conference with Great Britain on currency matters, Sprague predicted correctly that the United Kingdom would muddle through to a trade recovery with easy money. A moderate further depreciation by the United States would likely raise prices all around, including gold, sterling, and the dollar, a not unacceptable result.

When Warburg challenged this view, Sprague insisted on getting to the essence of the matter. "Do you . . . believe that successful negotiation with the British sets up a bulwark against the advocates of depreciation?" he inquired. "Or do you hold that an agreement with the British will tend to establish economic conditions that will render depreciation . . . less desirable?" Warburg's reply was candid: An agreement with Great Britain "is the very best thing that we can erect against various forms of lunacy, including greenbacks. . . . The alternative is, as I see it, having no commitment to anyone; we shall be free to run amuck."[22]

While in agreement with Warburg's objectives, the principals of the Federal Reserve System preferred a more discrete approach to counter pressures on the president for "monetary panaceas," the work of the Harvard economist John H. Williams, an adviser to the New York Fed. Williams questioned Warburg's strategy on the ground that it would stir up the inflationists. Rather, the Fed should refrain from engaging in open-market operations beyond the legal minimum on the ground that recovery was on the way.

Also fearful of inflationary pressures, Governor Harrison, satisfied with the current $700 million in excess bank reserves, saw no need for additional purchases of government securities. According to Harrison, the nation's banking system was fully able to meet legitimate demand "on the basis of good credit risk," this last point signaling rejection of an expansionary monetary policy. Further open-market purchases by the

Fed could be justified only on a political basis, to fend off inflationary pressures from the president and the Senate. Since to quit such purchases completely, however, would precipitate pressure for inflation, Harrison decided on modest, concessionary open-market purchases made in the early fall of 1933, which were abandoned during the balance of the 1930s; hence, Roosevelt's decision to move independently of the Fed under his Thomas Amendment powers.[23]

Convinced that politics rather than economic reasoning governed Roosevelt's decision-making process—in fact, both political and economic conditions often proved operative in his process of arriving at a policy—Warburg decided to take on Roosevelt again, encouraged by Robert A. Lovett, a partner in Brown Brothers Harriman and by executives of life insurance companies. Lovett prepared a letter to be sent to policyholders by their insurers "setting forth the damage they had already suffered by reason of depreciation of the dollar and urging them . . . to get in touch with their congressmen and senators."[24]

In the course of a discussion with Roosevelt in late September, Warburg protested the decline of the dollar, which now approached $5.00 to the pound, for the president had authorized domestic gold purchases at increased prices. Warburg argued that further dollar decline would impair savings and depress the value of insurance policies and bonds and would impose hardships on wage earners. He pressed for a public pledge by the president that recovery would be built on "orderly processes" and a sound credit structure. And he insisted that the dollar be fixed at its present value through joint endeavor with Great Britain. Once that was accomplished, the president should return his Thomas Amendment powers to the Congress.[25]

As Warburg unveiled these proposals, Roosevelt interrupted; he wanted a weaker dollar still. "I asked him," Warburg recalled, "whether that meant that he wanted a $5.00 sterling rate or that he wanted a further depreciation of the dollar in terms of gold. He said that he wanted both. I told him that in March, when the pound was $3.40, he would have been satisfied with $3.75; that in April, when it was $3.75, he would have been satisfied with $3.90; that in May, when it was $3.85, he would have been satisfied with $4.00; that on the 17th of June, when we suggested stabilizing at $4.00, he would have been satisfied with $4.25; . . . in August, when it was $4.50, he would have been satisfied with $4.86; now that it was $4.85, he would be satisfied with $5.00 . . . and so on ad infinitum." Roosevelt countered that Warburg simply did not appreciate the importance of an upward move in cotton and wheat prices, and if this were not done, "we would have 'marching farmers.'" Warburg persisted: perhaps the president was under pressure by the inflationists, Warburg suggested. It was not a matter of pressure at all, but one of conviction, Roosevelt replied, and if further depreciation impacted property owners, it was the lesser of two evils.

Beset by reporters as he left the White House, Warburg endorsed an anti-inflation editorial that had appeared in Frank Knox's *Chicago Daily News.* An angry Roosevelt noted in his own hand, "Warburg no longer advised me after Sept 20 1933." It was, for Warburg, the first open step toward a formal alliance with Knox and other anti–New Deal Republicans.[26]

On the heels of his exchange with Roosevelt, Warburg confided to Lewis Douglas his intention to break with the administration. At this point he hoped for leadership by a conservative Democrat, David F. Houston, Woodrow Wilson's agriculture secretary and currently president of the Mutual Insurance Company of New York, or James Cox of Ohio, the party's 1920 standard-bearer, a newspaper publisher who had headed the U.S. delegation to the London Conference. The potential alliance soon broadened. Walter Stewart agreed to recruit the American Federation of Labor economist Leo Wolman. George L. Harrison protested to Warburg that as head of the Open Market Committee, he could no longer see his way clear to continued open-market purchases of government securities designed to inflate currency and credit. He, too, planned a showdown with the president. At the same time Treasury Secretary Woodin stated his intention to get out but feared that it might put him in a position where he could do nothing to avert a catastrophe. Warburg riposted that he "also would not prevent it by staying in."[27]

Warburg put a motion to the monetary group intended to pressure Roosevelt, who had never made a formal reply to the Interim Monetary Report. The resultant analysis, transmitted by Woodin to the president, advised immediate preparation by the Treasury for discussion with Great Britain aimed at fixed dollar-sterling parity and a return of both currencies to a modified gold standard. Steps to be taken included the export of gold to prevent the dollar's fall below the historic $4.86 and suspension of open-market operations by the Federal Reserve, which Roosevelt had ordered to inflate currency and credit.[28]

Warburg also urged on the monetary group public notice, timed for the arrival in Washington of Sir Frederick Leith-Ross on a debt accommodation mission, that in no circumstances would the United States further depreciate the dollar, a stance the group refused to adopt. As the breach widened, Warburg prepared a letter that detailed his abhorrence of New Deal policies. His points included the rapidity with which the banks were reopened on the grounds that it would lead to another crash or a socialized banking system; abandonment of gold; discard of the theory that prices could be raised by monetary means, the price- and wage-fixing features of the NRA, and the Thomas Amendment; opposition to the 1933 Securities Act "on the grounds that it would make a free flow of capital into investment impossible"; and rejection of "the various forms of 'trick currencies,'" particularly a dollar of constant purchasing and debt-paying power.[29]

Scarcely the captive of his advisers, an angry president rejected the monetary group's proposals. These had judged events from the perspective of the New York banking community as opposed to the nation's broader requirements. Britain was not prepared to negotiate a dollar-pound cross rate. Indeed, Roosevelt stood prepared to see the dollar go to $5.00 or more in relation to sterling. And open-market operations should continue in order to meet banking and exchange requirements. "Tell the committee," he admonished Woodin, "that commodity prices must go up, especially agricultural prices." And the advice he required should meet these guidelines. "I wish our banking and economic friends would realize the seriousness of the situation from the point of view of the debtor classes—i.e., 80 percent of the human beings in this country—and think less of the 10 percent who constitute the creditor classes." Roosevelt instructed Woodin to continue open-market purchases, a position opposed by the monetary group. According to FDR, "There is no doubt in my mind that you and I are being subjected to all sorts of silent pressure by some members of the banking fraternity who do not want to make loans to industry. They are in a sullen frame of mind, hoping . . . to compel foreign exchange stabilization and force our hands."[30]

An equally determined Warburg pushed the monetary group toward a head-on confrontation with the president. "How to Raise Prices," the monetary group's final effort in the art of persuasion, was explicit in its critique of early New Deal legislation and its monetary policy. When the president inquired instead how he could purchase gold "at any price he liked," in Warburg's words, which, in the event, he proceeded to do, Roosevelt was informed that no legal authority existed for such a program.

Soon, news leaked of off-the-record remarks made by Roosevelt at a press conference. He placed responsibility for the recent price collapse on the bankers, and he charged the existence of a conspiracy by the banks against the administration program. These views Warburg categorized as "communistic." In essence, the monetary group rejected the New Deal recovery program.[31]

Convinced that the monetary group's proposals had failed to persuade Roosevelt to abandon gold purchases, a despondent Warburg unburdened himself to Leith-Ross at the British Embassy in Washington. This exchange and others between Leith-Ross and members of the monetary orthodoxy, including Acheson and Douglas, reveal a basic unwillingness on the part of the British Treasury to negotiate a compromise satisfactory to Roosevelt on the issues of debts and monetary policy or to open the British-dominated sterling market to freer trade. They also demonstrate that the United Kingdom's leadership at Treasury believed the island nation was well on its way out of the depression based on a policy of low long-term interest rates and empire preference. In fact, the sterling bloc was now joined by Scandinavia and Argentina. Refusal to coordinate sterling with dollar depreciation was based on the premise that Great Britain could muddle through satisfactorily on its own terms, which it did.

During his meeting with Warburg, when Leith-Ross expressed the view that Roosevelt had moved "leftward," Warburg followed with an emotional outburst: Roosevelt could not be trusted to follow any consistent policy. "He [Warburg] feared that all the president's confidence was based on his physical condition and that if things turned wrong he might suddenly become a helpless cripple." Warburg urged that Great Britain divorce itself from the Roosevelt policies, which might well result in an abrupt crash, and should stand firm on the debts issue. Leith-Ross offered assurances. "We have no apprehensions that we were going to move far on this question." Nor would London budge on devaluation. "London regarded devaluation as the worst of alternatives and would prefer . . . to let things drift." Leith-Ross's exchanges with Walter Stewart and Lewis Douglas proceeded along similar lines. Stewart feared an uncontrolled inflation based on an excess of open-market operations. Douglas offered that the United States was en route to a collapse and "a vast program of socialism."[32]

Each nation went its own way in the 1930s with devastating consequences for the world economy and for peace. British Treasury officials dismissed Keynes's proposals for a public works program as costly and ineffective as opposed to the dole and a policy of low interest rates. Whereas American policymakers relied on reflation and a devalued dollar, British officials lacked interest in the subject; Britain had already abandoned gold and devalued the pound to its satisfaction. The Tories were satisfied with the status quo based on imperial preference and protected export markets based on the Ottawa arrangements and on bilateral treaties negotiated by the Board of Trade. Inefficient industries were protected for the moment, but not to long-term competitive advantage in the world marketplace.[33]

As for Roosevelt, bent on autarky, despite fierce resistance by Acheson at Treasury, Harrison at the New York Fed, and the monetary group, he instituted purchase of newly mined gold on the domestic market at increasing prices as of September 8, 1933, in the light of a decline in price levels for agricultural and industrial output. This, of course, was based on the Warren theory, which correlated higher prices for commodities precisely with higher prices for gold. When this policy failed to produce the desired result, Roosevelt, scarcely given to tables of organization, charged Henry Morgenthau Jr. at the Farm Credit Administration—a devout believer in Warren's theories—with gold purchases in the world market. Since both the Fed and Treasury questioned its legality, the procedure was financed by a subsidiary of the RFC. In these circumstances Warburg would need to look elsewhere for support in his campaign to check Roosevelt's inflationary program.[34]

4 | MONETARY POLICY AND
THE HOOVER-STRAWN GROUP

THE 1930S DEFLATION proved more crippling in its impact on the nation's economy, indeed more insurmountable, than wartime inflationary cycles. Collapsed price levels discouraged business investment that would prove to be unprofitable, and a decline in incomes stymied consumers' propensity to buy the output of industry. Debtors defaulted and brought down thousands of banks with them. Those banks that survived proved reluctant to lend given their own parlous circumstances. Adherence to the gold-sterling standard under the Hoover administration fed the deflationary tide. Any potential price recovery was regarded as inflationary and under the so-called rules of the game required higher interest rates and investment curbs, resulting in increased unemployment. This scenario served as the basis for the Federal Reserve's defense of its gold holdings as dictated by precedent and statute and as a consequence was responsible for the final financial collapse in the winter of 1932–1933.[1]

Abandonment of the gold standard protected Roosevelt's initial program for recovery, which was based on the principles of autarky, reflation, and planning. Elimination of abuses in the American system might well be accomplished without reference to external affairs. But establishment of a structured economy based on an artificially induced rise in price levels for the output of industry and agriculture required a drop in the purchasing power of the dollar and insulation of the American economy from the vicissitudes of sterling, gold, and the world market. According to Rexford Tugwell, "We wanted recovery, we wanted a balanced economy, we wanted to institutionalize the balance and prevent future depressions. We had to shut off interference."[2]

While the Thomas Amendment to the Agricultural Adjustment Act authorized the president to reduce the dollar's gold content, Roosevelt faced the problems of timing and degree of depreciation. In the process

Roosevelt encountered the opposition of two groups determined to check the dollar's nationalization: internationalists at the Treasury and the Federal Reserve Bank of New York, the latter a mirror of Wall Street orthodoxy that predicated recovery on stable currencies as basic to restored world markets, and the antistatist Warburg–Hoover–Silas Strawn group that regarded dollar devaluation as the first step in the direction of overhead management of the nation's economy.

Hoover's insistence on a dollar as good as gold is consistent with his broader objections to the New Deal, the belief that limited federal authority and reliance on local and individual initiative should not be sacrificed on the altar of economic policies that centralized decisions in the nation's capital. Hoover's missionary zeal for a return of both the dollar and the pound to the gold standard at their pre-1931 ratio was intended to erect a barrier to financing the social and economic experiments contemplated by the New Deal. This goal required also, as he saw it, a party realignment. Maverick Republicans who accommodated the New Deal's domestic policies, especially cheaper money, would join the Democratic Party; antistatist Southern Democrats would ally with like-minded members of the GOP. To view Hoover otherwise, as responsible for the first leg in a relay race toward the interventionist state, plays havoc with his legacy.

Above all, Hoover desired adherence to basic constitutional principles, especially a delimited presidency and separation of powers; and he resisted Roosevelt's encroachment on these fundamentals. Seen in this light, when the Congress by the Thomas Amendment delegated the powers to issue unbacked currency and to reduce the dollar's gold content up to 50 percent to the president for the duration of the emergency, it abrogated its constitutional responsibility to determine the value of the dollar and to fund public expenditure.

In the effort to check Roosevelt's monetary experiments and secure a return to gold at the "legal" price of $20.67, both Hoover and Warburg repaired to the city of Chicago as the epicenter for the GOP's reemergence as a potent conservative antistatist force in American society. Then the nation's second city, Chicago and its business community offered the opportunity to tap into a well-positioned and experienced commercial-banking-manufacturing elite, the core of the Republican Party's reactionary wing. The Chicago group, the political base for Herbert Hoover's continued presidential aspirations, believed that Roosevelt's monetary policy constituted a threat to social and economic stability and a step toward creation of an excessively powerful presidency. This philosophical bias served also as a cover for the hostility of commodities processors of the upper Middle West who opposed higher raw material costs induced by an inflationary monetary policy and the price-raising features of the Agricultural Adjustment Act.

Upon his arrival in Chicago on October 20, after he had severed his ties to Roosevelt, Warburg conferred with an old friend, James Henderson Douglas Jr. Douglas, an attorney associated with the investment bank Field, Glore & Co., served as assistant secretary of the treasury in the final year of the Hoover presidency. At Warburg's request Douglas gathered some of Chicago's leading Republicans, among them presidential aspirant Frank Knox, publisher of the *Chicago Daily News;* John Stuart, who headed Quaker Oats; the iron and steel manufacturer Edward L. Ryerson, who had been a member of President Hoover's National Advisory Committee on Unemployment; and George Ranney, vice president of International Harvester, whose president, Alexander Legge, had chaired Hoover's Federal Farm Board. The meeting's upshot was a draft program along the lines that Warburg had argued in Washington, designed to secure the endorsement of leading conservative economists.[3]

The nascent movement against dollar devaluation took on added impetus with Roosevelt's October 22 radio announcement of his intention to pursue a reflationary policy designed to "make possible the payment of public and private debts more nearly at the price level at which they were incurred." He did not know what the permanent value of the dollar would be, Roosevelt explained, but was determined nevertheless "to control the value of the dollar at home" and detach its valuation from the accidents of international trade and the internal policies of other nations by establishing a domestic gold market. "I am authorizing the Reconstruction Finance Corporation to buy gold newly mined in the United States at prices determined from time to time after consultation with the secretary of the treasury and the president. Whenever necessary to the end in view, we shall also buy or sell gold in the world market. . . . We are thus continuing to move toward a managed currency."[4]

Upon appraisal of the text of Roosevelt's message, the Chicago group concluded that he had burned his bridges on the issue of increased price levels through monetary means, and that gold purchases managed by the RFC were illegal. Warburg, Knox, and James Douglas expanded their organizational base, while Warburg drafted the "Chicago platform," which

condensed his earlier arguments: a higher price level resulted from business recovery, not the reverse, as the Warren theory claimed, and increased
business activity required a reasonable likelihood of profitability and
monetary certainty.[5]

Hoover anticipated that the Chicago group, conservative economists,
and the Crusaders, a group of antistatist businessmen, would reinvigorate
a reconstituted GOP merged with conservative Democrats such as Virginia's Senator Carter Glass, Bainbridge Colby, Bernard Baruch, and Lewis
Douglas. At the same time, it would shed its Progressive component,
George Norris, Robert La Follette Jr., Hiram Johnson, New Mexico's Bron-
son Cutting, and others of similar bent. To this end, Hoover drafted a statement of principles for the Republican National Committee and the GOP's
congressional remnant. It offered the view that the Democratic administration had violated fundamental constitutional principles and retarded
recovery by its departure from sound economics. Recovery, Hoover held,
required "re-establishment of a sound monetary, financial, and fiscal system" and the repeal of New Deal emergency legislation.[6]

According to Hoover, economic recovery based on budget balance and
a stable currency had begun under his auspices, only to be aborted by
Roosevelt's penchant for monetary nostrums. The Thomas Amendment,
which empowered the president to reduce the dollar's gold content by 50
percent, he wrote to Senator Simeon D. Fess of Ohio, who had led the
floor fight against the amendment, "is the greatest and most unnecessary
gamble with the future of the American people ever proposed in our history." It portended a dictatorship; threatened socialism or communism;
and empowered a single individual, the president, to alter values and implement economic transfers from insurance policyholders and savers to
speculators, large corporations, and those who held equities. Foreigners
would benefit at the expense of their American creditors, private and
public, through a 50 percent savings in their dollar obligations. Much of
this argument lacked credibility at a time when a deflated dollar increased
the purchasing power of these very groups, domestic and foreign, at the
expense of commodities producers and those who possessed little or no
savings or equity.[7]

Following a late September conference in Chicago with some forty to
fifty businessmen, Hoover put into motion a behind-the-scenes strategy
coordinated with Frank Knox and Ogden Mills calculated to compel reluctant congressional Republicans to openly oppose the New Deal agenda

on general constitutional principles and to challenge Charles McNary's minority leadership in the Senate, which generally accommodated the Roosevelt program; to checkmate any conceivable move toward fiat money; and, if possible, to float a program for a return to the traditional gold standard. Warburg's conferences with the Chicago group comported with this strategy, as did a Hoover-Baruch exchange at Palo Alto in which the two men apparently agreed on monetary issues. In addition, Hoover planned the formation of committees by conservative academics and groups such as the Crusaders, the American Federation of Labor, and the American Legion.[8]

Hoover circulated a memorandum to conservative economists contending that both Great Britain and the United States should commit to a restored gold market, with each nation committed to purchase gold at its former price, $20.70 and £4 2s. Other nations presumably would follow suit. The result would be, instead of devaluing the dollar, devaluation of gold in ratio to other commodity prices by allowing it to decline to the "standard price."

When Hoover forwarded his views on a return to former gold parities to Princeton University's Edwin W. Kemmerer, research professor in international finance and adviser to numerous governments on currency management, Kemmerer replied that a return to the pre-1931 gold standard was unlikely. While initially opposed to Roosevelt's abandonment of the gold standard, Kemmerer held that it was nevertheless an accomplished fact. The Hoover proposal for a return to gold, however desirable in theory, would induce another deflationary spiral, too painful a prospect and politically impossible. Instead of a return to the old gold parity, Kemmerer preferred stabilization at current levels.

Hoover backed off momentarily. Taking his cue from Kemmerer, he conceded the need for devaluation at current levels as "the least damaging disaster." Monetarist opponents of the Roosevelt-Warren program now pressed for the end of political management of the currency, abandonment of commodity dollar theory, and abnegation by Roosevelt of the power to issue fiat money and further reduce the dollar's gold content.[9]

With his access to members of the Eastern Establishment, Warburg on his return to New York successfully recruited business and banking leaders and conservative economists to the sound money movement. These included Marshall Field, who headed the Chicago investment banking firm of Field, Glore; George Davison of the Central Hanover Bank of New

York; James Brown of Brown Brothers Harriman; Walter E. Spahr, New York University economist who with Edwin Kemmerer founded the Economists' National Committee on Monetary Policy; Elihu Root, former secretary of state; Grenville Clark, head of the National Economy League; and Arthur Ballantine, the last three partners in Root, Clark, Buckner & Ballantine; and a score of others. In Philadelphia, Warburg enlisted George Lorimer, publisher of the anti–New Deal *Saturday Evening Post*, the *Country Gentleman*, and the *Ladies' Home Journal*, as well as officers of Penn-Mutual, Insurance Company of North America, Drexel & Co., and Gerard Trust.[10]

Statements in opposition to Roosevelt's monetary policy, largely Warburg's work, shared certain common claims, attacking money management as "greenbackism," accusing the policy of favoritism of one group (commodities producers) over the larger (business) community, as well as suggesting that the economic unsettlement had been occasioned by Roosevelt's monetary experiments. Absent at this date was the usual demand that the dollar return to its former gold parity lest such a policy lead to a disastrous deflation. Instead, emphasis was placed on stabilization, with or without Britain, at current parities. Sophisticated economists had long since departed classical thinking on the ground that even the gold standard was a managed one, especially in the years after the Great War, and that automaticity, known as "the rules of the game," in its operation had become a fiction and if followed produced unemployment. Actually at issue in this contest between Roosevelt and the orthodoxy of business, bankers, and economists led by Hoover and Warburg was the locus of economic management and its end, or in Warburg's estimate the question of "a non-political note-issuing bank or a political government." Hoover and Warburg viewed Roosevelt as the captive of wild-eyed neopopulist inflationists; Roosevelt viewed monetary policy under the New York Fed as controlled by the New York banking interests, with their focus on a return to a system of fixed currency parities. Roosevelt was more nearly correct.

The sound money movement was formally launched in November by the Chicago Committee on Monetary Policy, a permanent organization of Midwestern business leaders including Sewell Avery (Montgomery Ward); James H. Douglas Jr.; Albert Lasker and Ralph M. Shaw (Winston, Strawn & Shaw); Albert A. Sprague (wholesale grocer); and John Stuart (Quaker Oats). A statement drafted by Warburg and Douglas and endorsed by a dozen Chicago area economists claimed that recovery rested on an increased volume of business, which in turn depended on confidence in the dollar and in the national credit.[11]

Hoover and Warburg broadened their agenda to include fiscal policy based on budget balance, constitutional limits on presidential power, and distrust of centralized authority, the fundamental tenets of antistatists. The prominent Chicago attorney and Hoover intimate Silas Strawn, a former president of the U.S. Chamber of Commerce—a group currently headed by the pro–New Deal Henry I. Harriman—carried the fight into the Chamber's precincts. Strawn, like Hoover, was determined to undermine Chamber support under Harriman's leadership of agricultural and industrial controls and to shift the Chamber toward a new role, opposition to Roosevelt's statist policies.

In this effort Warburg collaborated with the national Chamber's currency and finance committee on the basis of a resolution he pushed through the New York State Chamber of Commerce which demanded a return to the "old gold standard," or the dollar's former value. Repeating his earlier claim that "we made a mistake to treat Roosevelt as a sane man," Warburg urged in a meeting with Leith-Ross that Great Britain should "show our teeth on every occasion" and take "definite offensive action against the American experiments."[12]

But Strawn and others of the anti–New Deal group in the U.S. Chamber wanted a broader protest. This surfaced in a series of resolutions issued on November 18, the very day that Roosevelt castigated his opponents as Tories opposed to experimentation before a large crowd at Savannah, Georgia. In the area of monetary policy, the Chamber insisted on an early return to a gold basis and avoidance of fiat money. Another resolution devoted itself to a critique of Public Works Administration expenditures that duplicated or competed with private-sector activity. The TVA–Muscle Shoals experiment and federal housing programs also were condemned as unwarranted federal intrusion into private-sector activity. And the Chamber insisted on greater industrial self-government under the NRA, translated as greater code authority for business as opposed to government in the face of increased union activity. As Strawn put the NRA issue to Hoover, "Fatal mistake number 1 was inserting in the NRA Act Section 7(a), which has encouraged labor to attempt to unionize everything."[13]

In tandem with Hoover and Walter Lichtenstein of the First National Bank of Chicago, a member of the Chamber's department of finance,

Warburg also secured endorsement of their monetary views by the Federal Advisory Council. Created under the Federal Reserve Act to advise the Fed on business conditions, open-market activity, and other statutory functions, this group of orthodox bankers reiterated the Warburg formula for recovery: higher price levels would come about as a result of greater volume of business activity and employment, not as a result of monetary stimulus. Restored business activity depended on long-term investment in durable goods industries by the private sector, and that necessitated a stable money policy based on gold.[14]

As Dean Acheson and O. M. W. Sprague resigned from the administration, thirty-eight members of the Columbia University faculty advocated the end of the ongoing gold purchase policy. The group, which included Leo Wolman, James W. Angell, Howard Lee McBain, John Maurice Clark, Wesley C. Mitchell, Ralph West Robey, Edwin R. A. Seligman, and H. Parker Willis, called for a return to gold and an international stabilization agreement with Britain, but "not necessarily," it needs to be noted, "a return to a gold dollar of the former weight and fineness." Also worth noting was the refusal of Arthur Burns and Arthur Gayer to sign the Columbia University round-robin. In the current circumstances, they asserted, it seemed wise to allow the president and the Congress maximum leeway. The petition failed to recognize that a middle ground existed between extreme inflation and stabilization at current price levels, as well as that current price levels were unsatisfactory and needed to be raised, though not necessarily to the 1926 level, in order that "the present debts can be more easily borne." A similar call from seven Cornell University economists, George Warren's colleagues, denied the agricultural scientist's thesis that the economic depression could be explained by a gold shortage and rejected the claim that monetary policy should be determined by the movement of commodity prices.[15]

At the New York Fed, Harrison concluded that the imminent fall of the French government and its abandonment of the gold standard would be attributed to the American gold-buying program. Harrison convinced the president to halt gold purchases for a week and received permission to inquire of Montague Norman, governor of the Bank of England, whether "the British government would be willing to join the United States government in *de jure* stabilization of their currencies."

When Harrison and Norman discussed the overture by telephone, Norman agreed to de facto stabilization for two weeks only, because the pound had now been driven to a 10 percent premium. Roosevelt noted in a private memorandum that he had been pressured by "New York bankers and by political forces led by Ogden Mills and . . . [by] British sources to create definite sentiment in this country to have the gold content of the dollar fixed by the United States. As part of all this, assurance was given by the same sources that if the United States would go back on gold that Great Britain would follow." A skeptical Roosevelt jotted down for the record: "My advices were (a) that England would not go back on gold simultaneously with us; (b) that England would like to have us go back on gold but would not follow . . . thereby keeping her favorable trading position liquid. In order to place England on record, and solely for that purpose, and not because we intended or expected to go back on the gold standard, George Harrison made this unofficial interrogation of Montagu Norman. As we expected, it was turned down by the Bank of England and the British Treasury."

The British were not prepared to tie their hands in the current environment. To begin with, Norman was anxious to keep the price of gold down in order to help the French, while Roosevelt, pleased with the gold experiment, remained determined to push the gold price upward. Then again, according to Norman, "With gold prices where they are and a general conspiracy everywhere in the United States, South America and the British colonies to raise [commodity] prices, the situation is so uncertain that England cannot afford to stabilize *de jure* now." Only the United States had the wherewithal (sufficient gold) to support such a move. Norman did support a temporary biweekly arrangement "provided the United States would hold the price of gold where it is now," though he acknowledged that the dollar would rise as a consequence in world exchanges.

Norman soon reversed himself. He could not stabilize at current rates as "a great many people in England feel that the sterling rate as against the dollar should be much lower than it is now." Harrison proposed a return to the old dollar-sterling rate of $4.86 but again found Norman unreceptive. Whereas the British believed the dollar was undervalued, FDR was convinced that "for the U.S. to stabilize first would enable Great Britain to get an advantage by reducing the value of the pound further before it was in turn stabilized."[16]

In this situation of stalemate, the British Treasury determined that the time had come to go it alone. A devalued dollar, it developed, had no measurable impact on internal sterling prices. Weekly index numbers of wholesale prices in the United Kingdom barely fluctuated from July 1 to December 2, 1933, varying no more than 1 percent.[17] Treasury seemed content with the price of gold established by Roosevelt in January 1934, as it left the equalization fund with a profit of £15 million and pulled the price of sterling down 38 percent without equalization fund intervention. "The result is satisfactory enough for us," Sir Warren Fisher at Treasury advised Chamberlain, "apart from the new threat to the gold countries." In the event, Britain took the position that it could rely on its trade agreements to cushion a race toward depreciation, and its foreign policy soon focused on possible hostilities at opposite ends of the globe and its inability to engage simultaneously in both spheres.[18]

"As motley a group as ever assembled in a common cause," Albert U. Romasco categorized the loose alliance that endorsed Roosevelt's monetary policies. Romasco cited the Committee for the Nation, a group of businessmen-inflationists committed to the views of George F. Warren, Irving Fisher, James Harvey Rogers, Idaho's Senator William E. Borah, Father Charles E. Coughlin, and the publisher William Randolph Hearst.[19] But there are difficulties with this catalog of those who desired reflation through the device of a devalued dollar. Rogers, who emphasized reliance on fiscal policy and public works, regarded the Warren theories as fallacious. Fisher, an early exponent of an increased money supply and reflation, now urged the end of gold purchases as unsettling to the economy. And the list should have included as well the Harvard economist Frank Taussig, Walter Lippmann, Benjamin Henry Inness-Brown, and Russell C. Leffingwell, supporters of dollar devaluation who offered cogent advice to Roosevelt and whose explanations of early New Deal monetary policy are closer to the mark. Subsequent limited monetization of silver simply expanded the monetary base and did not lie at the heart of New Deal economic policy.

Roosevelt's decision to fix the price of the dollar at $35 to the ounce of gold, or 59.6 percent of its former gold value, elicits two basic questions. What impelled him to close out the experiment with the Warren theory that held that commodity prices were inextricably linked to the price of gold? In the long run, what was the economic impact of dollar devaluation on the pace of recovery? Roosevelt's motives are best explained by the correspondence and memoranda lodged in the President's Secretaries and Official Files at Hyde Park. Unlike the often frank cabinet minutes found in the British archives at Kew, Roosevelt's notations on paper, as well as his face-to-face exchanges, in which he often filibustered, rarely reveal his motives. Whether a reaction to a domineering mother, as psychologists might explain, or simply the desire to force historians to guess at his calculations, which amused him, his reticence compels one to reason out the basis for his decisions.

The failure of recovery to take hold in the summer and autumn of 1933, after the spring upsurge, resulted when a speculative rise in the prices of primary products did not generate sufficient additional demand because farmers made use of enhanced incomes to repay debt—hence Roosevelt's gold purchase policy. Currency depreciation offered the potential of increased price levels in substantial parts of the economic system as well as export goods, especially agricultural products. A depreciated dollar also promised increased incomes and stimulus to demand for all other goods. While speculative activity in the spring of 1933 drove prices to unsustainable levels, a devalued dollar, once it attained a point of equilibrium, realized by the mid-1930s, produced price levels lower than their 1926–29 peaks but higher than before reflation commenced.

The views of J. P. Morgan's Russell Leffingwell likely had considerably more influence on Roosevelt's policy of dollar devaluation than those of the monetary cranks. In private correspondence with the president, Leffingwell credited his gold policy with avoidance of a more severe collapse and endorsed his refusal to join efforts made during the London Economic Conference to peg the dollar to sterling and the gold currencies. Although Leffingwell believed in monetary stability, this needed to wait on a satisfactory level of wages and prices as well as the stability of foreign exchanges. Pressures for a return to the old gold standard were "simpleminded."

While in the past the gold standard and stable currencies served as vehicles that facilitated commerce, in the current autarkic climate, according to Leffingwell, they were a force for instability. It would take time to find new parities. These would be conditioned on experience with domestic price levels, the level of foreign exchanges, achievement of domestic equilibrium and budget balance, and the willingness of other nations to make complementary decisions. Closed economies required monetary management attentive to restored internal price levels. International currency agreement based on revised parities would follow, not precede, the achievement of domestic objectives. In the current deflationary climate, gold served as a drag, and the only recourse was its abandonment. Nor did it appear appropriate in these circumstances for government to honor the gold clause in contracts. "The controlling principle . . . is that the sovereign, the State, had and must have control of its currency and therefore of obligations payable in its currency. . . . This power it cannot obligate or contract away."[20]

For all practical purposes Roosevelt was determined to transfer the shaping of monetary policy from the New York Federal Reserve and the City of London to Washington. The Gold Reserve Act provided a flexible dollar in order to increase internal price levels. Sound money was a means to an end and not an end in itself. In the current depression it had become evident that one could not, except for short intervals of time, have stable internal prices, business, and prosperity and stable foreign exchanges, as these were incompatible in the depression.[21]

With respect to the immediate decision to stabilize, it quickly became apparent in light of the decline in economic activity toward the end of 1933 that neither domestic gold purchases nor purchases made in the London market served to push farm prices upward. Rather, commodities sagged as the gap widened between New York and London prices for the yellow metal. In the process it became evident from sources that could not be dismissed that the gold standard had long since become a hindrance to reflation.[22]

Yet halving the dollar's gold content would not double commodity prices, contrary to the Warren theory. In practical terms this meant a unilateral return to the former sterling-dollar rate of approximately $4.86 since the dollar had declined by 37 percent, the level of depreciation of other currencies used in four-fifths of international trade. Irving Fisher, hardly a monetary crank, advised that the time had arrived to stabilize. The nation, he cautioned, "is again trembling in the balance as it was several times before, before plunging back into depression." Roosevelt's opponents had waged a potent campaign of fear which threatened the same result. At the same time, it was necessary to take the wind out of the sails of the radical inflationists. The public had become perplexed by divided counsels. "Announce that you will devalue the dollar 50 percent and proceed to do so," Fisher admonished.[23]

The Gold Reserve Act, which revalued the dollar to 60 cents, or $35 to the gold ounce, won a mixed reception. It offered a wide base for currency management yet afforded a degree of assurance to the psychological needs of gold-minded bankers and economists. At the same time, the decision to stabilize represented a defeat for the theories of George F. Warren. The Committee for the Nation, committed to a return to 1926 price levels, echoed Warren's disenchantment with the New Deal's tendency towards enlargement of government's role in the economy and advocated a dollar inflated to $6.08 in relation to the English pound. Indeed, Warren's inflationary policy represented an alternative to Roosevelt's interventionist domestic programs, not a return to $4.86. Herbert Hoover also remained unreconstructed. His policies, he claimed through the balance of his years, had turned the depression. The time had come "to fix the value of the dollar today, make it convertible in gold payable in coin over the counter." The result, he believed, would be a quick recovery, a doubtful proposition.[24]

On December 29 Roosevelt asked for a transfer of the gold held by the Fed to the Treasury "without resort to a formal executive order." A presidential proclamation then fixed the weight of the gold dollar under the Thomas Amendment to the Farm Relief Act of May 12, 1933, and authorized the Treasury to purchase gold at the rate of $35 to the ounce through the Federal Reserve Bank of New York, acting as fiscal agent for the account of the United States. With the Treasury an issuer of currency and credit based on upwardly valued and monetized gold reserves captured from the Fed under the new law, Roosevelt could now meet the requirements of a moderately expansionary fiscal policy.[25]

In response to direct pressure by Roosevelt and congressional inflationists, the Fed grudgingly purchased $385 million of government securities between May and October 1933 and then closed out open-market activity, a decision taken despite a shrinkage of some $9 billion in currency and checking money between 1929 and 1933 and a decline in velocity of demand deposits by more than half, resulting in a shrinkage of $126.2 billion of effective money. In the face of Fed passivity based on its fear of inflation, Treasury, which became a coproducer of money and credit with the passage of the Gold Reserve Act, took up the slack, resulting in average annual growth rate of monetary base of 13 percent in these years. The locus of power in monetary management shifted still more from New York to Washington with the Banking Act of 1935. Emphasis subsequently was placed on Treasury financing of public works through instrumentalities such as the Reconstruction Finance Corporation and reliance on deficit expenditure.[26]

Yet Roosevelt had never been convinced of the efficacy of monetary policy as sufficient to secure reflation and turn the depression. "My chief difficulty," he explained to Duncan U. Fletcher, chairman of the Senate Banking Committee, "is in the acceptance of the theory that the price level will of necessity follow the supply of dollars. As you know, most banks have an abundant supply of dollars and credits, yet they do not seem to be using them—at least in any way to put up prices," a problem which persisted through the decade, since banking institutions concentrated on their liquidity. Roosevelt instead concentrated his energies on federal investment in regional infrastructure: the Tennessee Valley experiment, economic development of the Columbia River valley in the Pacific Northwest and Santee-Cooper in South Carolina, the Rural Electrification Administration, and public works. These would stimulate domestic purchasing power and meet the longer-term structural problem of regional underdevelopment outside the northeastern quadrant.[27]

The early New Deal years also witnessed elaboration of the agenda developed by Roosevelt and the Brains Trust: stimulus to agricultural and industrial price levels, implementation of an expanded public works policy designed to cushion the unemployed against the impact of unemployment, and provision of social insurance to fend off future depressions. These, in tandem with the objective of regional economic balance through infrastructure investment by the federal government, served as the essentials of early New Deal planning. Radical New Deal planners, Rexford Tugwell in the lead, wanted more: the abandonment of a market economy and the introduction of genuine overhead management by experts of prices, output, and investment, with production and investment geared toward socially useful purposes.

5 | FISCAL POLICY AND REGIONAL DIVERSITY

R ELEASE FROM THE requirements imposed by the gold standard was the first step in Roosevelt's strategy for achieving economic recovery. It liberated domestic policy from the lock hold of needlessly high, deflationary interest rates, credit restriction, and budget balance.

As it has been argued that Hoover's thought on demand management was more advanced than Roosevelt's, it may be appropriate to examine Hoover's legacy to Roosevelt's fiscal policies. This leads to the question, at what level could the Roosevelt administration unbalance its budgets and add to the national deficit? One might also ask, on what rationale did Roosevelt seek recovery, since Keynes's views on countercyclical spending, which evolved in the early 1930s, were not published in *The General Theory* until 1936 and were not widely accepted by American economists until the decade's end. In any event, would the multiplier, which promised a ripple effect on the economy beyond public expenditure, have had any significant impact on private-sector spending for investment in the depression?[1]

The Hoover rationale for a bank of public works, shaped in the aftermath of the post–World War depression and the 1920s environment of budget surpluses and reduced deficits, was a theoretical exercise in macroeconomic demand management. In practice, as public revenues evaporated and deficits grew in late 1931 and in 1932, Hoover and Treasury Secretary Mills sought cuts in expenditures and revenue enhancement. Budgetary discipline was the theme of Hoover's annual message to Congress on December 8, 1931, in which he cited enlarged deficits and the need for balance, with the exception only of debt retirement. The next day, he requested huge cuts in the funding of the Agriculture Department, the United States Shipping Board, the armed forces, and the Federal Farm Loan Board. The burden of employment, Hoover held, was the responsi-

bility of private enterprise, not the federal government. "We cannot squan-
der ourselves into prosperity," he decreed, as "rigid economy [was] a real
road to relief." Expenditure for public improvements needed to wait for a
return to prosperity. By July 1932, in the belief that the depression had
turned, Hoover would have—if Congress approved—cut the budget by
$700 million.[2]

In order to enhance federal income, Hoover signed a new revenue bill
that provided for increased tax rates approaching wartime levels on corporate profits, estates, and personal incomes, setting the tax structure for
the 1930s. Treasury Secretary Mills also secured from Congress a wide
range of excise taxes on items that ran the gamut from soda pop, toilet-
ries, and radios to automobiles.

In an effort to mask increased budget deficits, which could not be
avoided in view of revenue shortfalls, Hoover turned to the device of the
Reconstruction Finance Corporation in January 1932. The RFC was instituted to fund capital spending in the private sector (refused by Congress
until June 1934), self-liquidating public works, and loans to banks, railroads (which were large employers), and those states no longer able to
finance relief payments. This stands as his major contribution to New
Deal fiscal policy, for Roosevelt immediately recognized the possibilities
of a dual budget, one for normal expenditures and one for off-budget
finance of self-liquidating projects.[3]

Actually, under Hoover, whereas Congress authorized over $3 billion
in RFC borrowing and lending authority—these funds borrowed from
the Treasury—a tight-fisted RFC kept lending at $2 billion. Loans to
banks were made on fully secured or quality paper, resulting in a drain on
sound capital. Most such banks failed in the winter 1932–33 financial collapse. As for capital loans on offer by the RFC to public bodies, these were
limited principally to self-supporting projects and made at above-market
interest rates. Equally restrictive was Hoover's insistence that unproductive or non-revenue-producing public works be held at $575 million; the
same is true of the requirement that loans to states should be conditioned
on their certification of inability to raise funds for relief purposes in the
market, which implied the state's insolvency. Few such loans were made.
Up to October 1932, when RFC activity nearly halted, relief loans to the
states totaled only $35 million.[4]

At the root of these constraints and Hoover's contest with the Congress
on the issue of public works and relief spending was his belief that the

states should remain free from federal interference and the conviction that individuals in distress should rely on the community and private charities for sustenance in depression. Emphasis was placed on local responsibility for the relief-unemployment problem by the device of community chest drives, also on well-publicized meetings with business executives who pledged maintenance of employment and expanded investment. While initially helpful, voluntarism proved unproductive as localities could no longer fund relief or infrastructure projects.

Roosevelt viewed the RFC as more than a fig leaf designed to cloak budget unbalance. He enhanced its lending capacity and converted a policy of loans conditioned on inability to borrow funds to grants for the states. Most importantly, Roosevelt used RFC expenditure for relief, public works, subsidy of rural electrification, and a host of programs (WPA, CWA, TVA, FCA, FHA, CCC, and more) as a vehicle for remediation of regional economic imbalance, which he regarded as basic to recovery and avoidance of future depressions. By 1935, banks aside, the RFC had loaned $10.6 billion to the business sector and government agencies. During World War II it funded $40 billion for business expansion.[5]

Like Hoover, Roosevelt proved responsive at first to the widespread certainty in the financial community, the Congress, the press, among most academicians, and the public that recovery was conditioned on budget balance. The Hoover-Roosevelt logic is readily explained by the conviction in the business and investment communities, joined by economists, that substantial budget deficits damaged the broader economy through increased interest rates, which put a lid on credit availability. Unlike Hoover, however, Roosevelt clearly intended to expand federal functions and proved unconstrained by the principle of balanced budgets in practice. As the economist Herbert Stein observed in his classic study of fiscal policy, "The belief [in budget balance] was probably real enough, but it was not so high in Roosevelt's scale of values that he was prepared to sacrifice much for it." Still, the preponderance of economic thinking in England and the United States in the 1930s stressed budget balance and a responsible monetary program as crucial to recovery. A revision in fiscal policy required "a change in basic facts. There had to be a coordinated or progressive monetary policy, so that government deficits would not force up interest rates to an undesired degree."[6]

It was widely argued, further, that a public works program was not particularly effective as a remedy for large-scale unemployment as public projects were slow to get under way, their cost was high relative to the number employed, and useful projects were limited. As Sir Frederick Phillips at the British Treasury noted in a memorandum, expenditure of £191.9 million on public works approved between June 1929 and August 1931 resulted in an average of 62,906 employed on public works in the period June 1929–March 1933, at a time when total unemployment amounted to 2.6 million. According to Phillips, "To anyone who has ever studied the question it is a commonplace that fluctuations in the fortunes of some great industry such as coal, cotton, or shipbuilding may affect the live register as much in a month as a determined expansionist policy of public works affects it in two years." Indeed, Keynesian theory to the contrary, British policy relied on the dole as more efficacious in meeting the problem of unemployment, a plan followed through the 1930s.[7]

Assuming Roosevelt's ability to quickly implement a public works (federal investment) program of $3.3 billion under Title II of the National Industrial Recovery Act, a questionable assumption, such an enterprise would scarcely make more than a dent at a time when gross U.S. private domestic investment plummeted from $16 billion (1929 dollars) to $344 million in 1933. If one accepts the Keynes-Kahn multiplier of 1.5 to 2, which was generous, as it is likely in the 1930s economic environment that a goodly percentage of public expenditure would be used to reduce indebtedness or would go into savings (the Keynes liquidity trap), new federal spending would need to reach some $7.5 to $10 billion to close the gap at a time when total federal expenditure for goods and services amounted to $2.6 billion. At the same time, state and local spending would need to be doubled, which proved impossible. At best, a policy of low interest rates and deficit spending could meliorate the worst of the depression; it could not remediate deep structural problems.[8]

Behind the demand for shrinkage in federal expenditure stood the Grand Pooh Bah of American finance, Bernard M. Baruch. After he had amassed a considerable personal fortune as investor and speculator, Baruch managed the nation's wartime effort on the domestic front as head of the War Industries Board. Following the war, he financed several powerful Southern Democratic senators as well as the presidential campaigns of party hopefuls, including that of Roosevelt. In view of estimates for fiscal 1934 (July 1, 1933–June 30, 1934), with revenue at $2.5 billion as against projected spending of $3.8 billion, Baruch wanted an immediate plan for closing the gap; specifically, budget cuts of $800 million and a beer tax of $150 million, which presumably would stimulate business activity sufficiently to bring about virtual budget balance. Relief expenditure should be separated from the normal budget and financed by bond issues supported by new revenue specifically allocated for the purpose and adequate to pay interest and amortization over fifteen years. Agricultural relief would be financed by the processing tax in order to preclude an impact on the budget.[9]

Baruch's views were echoed by the National Economy League, headed by Admiral Richard E. Byrd, brother of Virginia's Senator Harry F. Byrd, both insistent on budgetary stringency. At its core were members of the Eastern Establishment, including John J. McCloy and Grenville Clark, reinforced by a bipartisan group of prominent political, legal, and business luminaries, among them Calvin Coolidge; John W. Davis, the Democratic Party's 1924 presidential nominee; Archibald B. Roosevelt, son of Theodore; Elihu Root; and Newton D. Baker. Antistatists regarded budget tightening as an opportunity to eliminate current entitlements, especially benefits paid to veterans who suffered no wartime disability, lest new constituencies emerge for the beneficence of government.[10]

With Roosevelt pledged to arrive at a balanced budget in his Pittsburgh speech in the course of the 1932 campaign, he tapped Lewis W. Douglas, scion of a wealthy copper-mining family, Arizona congressman, and a budget hawk, to serve as his budget director. Wartime service in France in the American Expeditionary Force left Douglas with firm impressions of Germany's responsibility for the conflagration, of American failure to prepare adequately and then after the war its failure to ensure the peace with membership in the League of Nations. Like his father, a personal friend of Clemenceau, he advocated alliance with France against a resurgent Reich. These attitudes carried him, some two decades later, as another war broke out in Europe, into active work for military preparedness through the interventionist Century Group and William Allen White's Committee to Defend America by Aiding the Allies.

In the intervening years, upon election to the House of Representatives in 1926 at age thirty-two, Douglas identified himself as a Jeffersonian Democrat and proponent of states' rights. He also urged war debts forgiveness and became an admirer of fellow congressman Cordell Hull of Tennessee, "my father confessor and guide," and his free-trade philosophy. Douglas cemented lasting friendships with men of similar viewpoint, members of the Eastern Establishment: F. Trubee Davison, son of a

J. P. Morgan partner, Hoover's assistant secretary of war; John J. McCloy, an Amherst classmate who married Peggy Douglas, Lewis's sister; the economist Walter Stewart, a deflationist; and Dean G. Acheson, a member of the Washington, D.C., law firm of Covington, Burling & Rublee. In 1932 Acheson assisted the Arizona congressman as they shaped proposals for reduced veterans' benefits.

The selection of Douglas for a post critical to financial management and its impact on the broad economic policy represented an attempt to maintain a wide spectrum of ideological opinion in the Democracy, in this instance conservative antistatist internationalists who had drafted the party's 1932 platform. A balanced budget promised to keep federal intrusion at a minimum, fed business confidence theory, and offered the Wilsonians the hope that once the bottom had been turned, there would be a reversion to open-market doctrine.[11]

During the Seventy-second Congress, Douglas served as protagonist in the efforts of the bipartisan House Economy Committee to reduce the current budget deficit by $263 million. He opposed the so-called Garner-Wagner pork-barrel (so labeled by Hoover) or relief bill approved by the House and the Senate in July 1932, with its provision for massive loans by the RFC for public works, a measure vetoed by the president. And he joined Hoover in support of a national sales tax, disguised as an excise tax on manufacturers, a proposal quashed in the House by a Progressive coalition led by Fiorello La Guardia, described by Douglas as "the Socialist from New York." Draconian federal retrenchment, which Douglas favored, or a 25 percent budget cut, required halving expenditures for veterans of $1.12 billion and the curbing of government services. The alternative, he warned the House, was impairment of the credit of the United States.[12]

In the contest for the presidential nomination, the young congressman favored the conservative, Newton D. Baker, Woodrow Wilson's secretary of war and widely regarded as Wilson's heir apparent. While unhappy with the Roosevelt-Garner ticket (the latter was a "cheap, yellow political trixter" who had sold out Hoover to the Progressives in Congress on relief expenditures and the sales tax), he viewed the states' rights–internationalist Chicago platform, with its pledge of budget balance, trade reciprocity, and international currency stabilization as "the greatest human document ever framed by a political party." His support of FDR in the campaign rested on the platform and the Pittsburgh pledge of a 25 percent cut in federal expenditures.

Invited by Roosevelt to formulate proposals for recovery in late November, Douglas urged on the president-elect a national sales tax, forgiveness of international debts, and currency stabilization with Britain and France. With the international economy stabilized and tariff reciprocity implemented, he offered, recovery would surely follow. When Roosevelt refused to pursue the sales tax route, to disavow large-scale spending for public works, favored by congressional Progressives, or domestic allotment for agriculture, or in early December to join with Hoover in formal debts negotiations, Douglas was miffed. But with Roosevelt seemingly pledged to close the budgetary gap and to participate in the forthcoming World Monetary and Economic Conference, Douglas agreed to serve as his budget director.[13]

Immediately prior to taking office, Douglas offered several areas for budget reduction: interest payments on and amortization of the national debt, military spending, federal construction projects and agencies, especially the Commerce Department, which had grown considerably under the New Era's managerial philosophy, and federal salaries and payrolls. Veterans' benefits, at $1.1 billion, or 25 percent of the federal budget, perceived by the economizers as an undesirable precedent for entitlements, seemed most vulnerable to the economy drive, though politically risky, given the strength of the American Legion in virtually every congressional district.[14]

Working quickly in view of the likelihood of congressional hostility to specific budgetary cuts, especially of veterans' benefits, Roosevelt and Douglas framed "An Act to Maintain the Credit of the United States Government" (the economy bill), dispatched to the Congress on March 10, 1933. Noting that "too often in recent history liberal governments have been wrecked on rocks of loose fiscal policy," Roosevelt requested discretionary authority to reduce veterans' benefits by $470 million and federal salaries by $150 million, or a total cut of 13 percent in expenditures contemplated for the fiscal year commencing July 1, 1933. Douglas projected budgetary savings of $900 million, almost half from a reduced federal payroll. Despite congressional opposition, the bill quickly made its way through both houses and was signed by the president. Roosevelt also asked the Congress to legalize 3.2 beer as a constitutional amendment for repeal of the Prohibition Amendment made its way through the states. Taxes on low-alcohol beer, it was estimated, would add some $100 to $150 million per annum to federal revenues, further implying budget balance.[15]

Yet the magnitude of federal budget deficits and lending suggests a different scenario. Federal expenditure for what was then regarded as a base peacetime period, the years 1926–29, exclusive of debt retirement, averaged just over $3 billion, reached $4.6 billion under Hoover in the fiscal years 1932 and 1933. By FY 1934 (July 1, 1933–June 30, 1934), the first under Roosevelt's management, federal expenditure rose to $6.7 billion, remained at $6.5 billion for FY 1935, then escalated in 1936, an election year, with congressional insistence on veterans' bonus legislation, to nearly $8.5 billion. Budget receipts in fiscal years 1933–36 were less than half of federal expenditure, excepting only FY 1935 when receipts equaled 57 percent of outgo. As a result of record peacetime deficits, total gross national debt rose from $22.5 billion to $33.7 billion in the fiscal years 1933–36.[16]

E. Cary Brown's measure of net contributions of government fiscal policy to effective demand arrived at the widely cited conclusion that a program of fiscal stimulus was untried. "The direct effects on aggregate full-employment demand of the fiscal policy undertaken by all three levels of government was clearly relatively stronger in the thirties than in 1929 in only two years—1931 and 1936," those marked by veterans' bonus legislation. But Brown lumps federal with state and local expenditure and tax policy, thus mitigating the effect of increased federal spending for relief and public works. And he excludes as well RFC lending of $10.6 billion by the end of 1935. There are other problems with Brown's conclusion: the concept of "net federal contribution" to effective demand was not developed until the mid-1930s by Laughlin Currie at the Federal Reserve, nor was it openly endorsed by administration economists until the 1937–38 downturn. Indeed, prior to 1931, the context for Hoover and Roosevelt, the largest peacetime budget deficit reached $89 million in 1909.[17]

While the concept of countercyclical spending in depression was at least a decade old, extending back to the President's Conference on Unemployment held in 1921 in the wake of the postwar depression, limitations were imposed. Hoover insisted that public works be financed by a reserve fund which never materialized, and that these must be on an "economical" as opposed to a relief basis, which precluded expenditures beyond the decisively limiting category of self-liquidating projects customarily undertaken by the state and local governments. With most states under constitutional mandate to follow the principle of budget balance and their ability to borrow limited by revenue decline and market conditions, major construction programs fell considerably, as did construction by the bankrupted railroads and the troubled public utilities. The burden was now shifted to the federal government.[18]

In the course of the New Era, William Trufant Foster and Waddill Catchings added considerably to the rationale for increased public expenditure in depression. Catchings, a Harvard Law graduate who made a career as a steel manufacturer and investment banker with Goldman, Sachs & Co., developed an interest in business cycles with the postwar depression and funded the Pollak Foundation to this end. Catchings recruited Foster, a Harvard classmate, to head the enterprise. In *Profits* and *The Road to Plenty*, they claimed that sustained production required sustained consumer demand, a counter to Say's law of markets, or classical theory, which held that consumer demand followed automatically from capital consumption. Foster and Catchings explained underconsumption partly in terms of consumer reluctance to spend when prices fell and also in terms of price distortions, maldistribution of income, and the tendency of business to finance capital requirements from earnings, thus sterilizing savings. The result was industrial overcapacity as consumer purchasing power declined. Public works would be required periodically to stimulate purchasing power. Unlike Hoover's proposed bank of public reserves, however, they advocated deficit spending as a more satisfactory way to achieve sustained demand. Despite a lack of professional credentials and the conservative bent of professional economists, Foster and Catchings broached the possibilities of monetary and fiscal expansionary policy.[19]

While Roosevelt had noted in his copy of *The Road to Plenty* that its prescription for an economic downturn was "too good to be true," the President's Secretaries File at the Roosevelt Library contains a typescript and marked-up copies of articles published by Foster after the depression's onset. Their location in those files the president regarded as most pertinent to his administration makes it likely that Foster's arguments for a public works program gained FDR's attention. Foster preferred the Lloyd George public works program of England's Liberal Party to the dole, favored by the Tories. Public funds, Foster held, could be wisely utilized for bridges, highways, slum clearance, and the development of electric power.

In 1932 Foster proposed a $3 billion public works program: "This is no time to balance the budget, not, in any event, the budget of new capital expenditures." While Hoover and Foster had jointly proposed such a program to the 1928 Governors Conference at New Orleans in the form of increased capital expenditure by the states during a downturn, this proved an economic and constitutional impossibility. Hoover subsequently opted for the gold standard and a strong dollar. Since this decision required that every effort be made to balance the budget, Foster distanced himself from Hoover. He preferred currency management, currency-credit expansion, and if need be a modified gold standard, claiming that the alternative would be massive repudiation of debt. If repudiation was required, "that means Federal control; that means national planning; that means collective action on a scale hitherto untried in the United States."[20]

Advice on the subject of demand management also came to FDR from abroad. Viscount Astor dispatched to the White House advance copies of two articles published by Keynes in the *Times* and the *New Statesman* (March 13–16, 1933), packaged in the United States as *The Means to Prosperity*. Keynes challenged as worse than useless Chamberlain's objective, announced at Ottawa, of raising commodity prices by imposing limits on output. Reduced demand would follow, in Keynes's view, and with it shrinkage of retrenched producers' income. Higher price levels required increased investment expenditure and increased aggregate spending power. In normal circumstances cheap and abundant bank credit would restore industry's working capital, traditionally a step toward recovery. But in the current climate business expectations were so devastated that monetary policy, while helpful, would not stimulate capital outlay.

Restored aggregate spending power required increased loan expenditure for public works, undertaken simultaneously worldwide, to alleviate the principal cause of the depression, namely, the drying up of U.S. lending at home and abroad. This meant abandonment of counterproductive balanced budgets that diminished spending power and hence national income. Economic stimulus be afforded the division of budgets into two parts, one for short-term expenditure and the other for capital purposes. Increased income from public employment would spread throughout the system and in the end stimulate both employment and national income, thus compensating for lowered business expectations. Only at this point in the recovery process, he argued, would cheap money impact business investment.[21]

Initially, Roosevelt's fiscal proposals encompassed multiple options:

enlistment of Douglas and introduction of the economy bill to satisfy the budget balance group; use of the Reconstruction Finance Corporation to finesse the Democratic platform and the Pittsburgh pledge when necessary for public works and relief; and the remediation of structural distortions, which historically favored the industrial financial Northeast as opposed to the commodities producers of the West and the South. This last effort would direct public expenditure for recovery to underdeveloped and exploited areas of the United States.[22]

The first signal that the Pittsburgh pledge might not be redeemed in view of the inherent contradictions of fiscal policy jolted Douglas even as he and Roosevelt conferred on the message that accompanied the economy bill, which presumably marked the initial step toward a draconian $3 billion budget for fiscal 1934. (Actual budget expenditures totaled more than double that figure, or $6.7 billion.) When the president suggested that they incorporate $300 million for the Civilian Conservation Corps, a pet project, Douglas objected: "It was difficult if not impossible, for him to go in two different directions at the same time, in the same legislation and the same message to the Congress. It was either important to maintain the credit of the United States and to establish a firm control over public expenditures, or it was not." (In a letter to his father, Douglas speculated "that eventually I might be compelled to resign.") Within the week Senators Robert F. Wagner, Robert M. La Follette Jr., and Edward P. Costigan presented to Roosevelt a bill for $500 million in direct federal relief grants as opposed to loans to the states; Roosevelt's approval was anticipated since it included creation of the CCC and would be financed by the RFC.[23]

In a message to Congress, Roosevelt called for provision of unemployment relief through three mechanisms: the CCC; grants to the states for relief work; and creation of a broad public works program, which was legislated under Title II of NIRA. Congress soon agreed to the CCC (established by executive order on April 5), and on May 12 FDR signed into law the Emergency Relief Act. It appropriated $500 million on a grant-in-aid basis to be distributed through the states and created the Federal Emergency Relief Administration; Harry Hopkins was in charge.[24]

"More and more congressmen and senators," Douglas noted, "are protesting against stopping the construction of post offices, proposed cuts in the army, navy and other departments," a situation reversed to Douglas's chagrin by the $3.3 billion spending proposal incorporated in Title II of NIRA. In order to keep the budget balance fig leaf intact, Roosevelt appointed Douglas to head a special advisory committee which projected a 1⅛ to 1½ percent levy on all manufactures, an indirect sales tax, a proposal that necessitated the president's active support in the face of congressional hostility. With Roosevelt backing and filling, the House passed an assortment of nuisance taxes instead, with amortization of public works left to repeal of the Eighteenth Amendment and passage of alcohol and beer levies. An unhappy Douglas noted that he proved powerless to bring about the president's endorsement of a sales tax.[25]

By early September the dual budget, adopted informally, came under challenge. The conservative journalist David Lawrence, writing for the anti–New Deal *Saturday Evening Post*, forecast an accumulating federal deficit in the face of revenue shortfalls. With fiscal year 1934 as his theme, Lawrence projected an ordinary budget of $2.773 billion for the regular operations of government; an emergency budget for public works of $3.3 billion; and an RFC budget of $1 billion, which embraced the farm land banks, disbursements to farmers, relief for the states and cities, $200 million to the Home Owners Loan Corporation, and $50 million for irrigation and smaller projects. The list totaled $7 billion of possible disbursements in the current fiscal year. Excluded from the total was an additional $4 billion authorized for mortgage refinancing, in effect a contingent liability, resulting in potential federal expenditure and liabilities of $11 billion.

Lawrence conceded the likelihood that many of the RFC loans would eventually be repaid and also the possibility of some salvage from self-liquidating public works and various loan programs. But there remained a substantial shortfall in the absence of an adequate revenue base. Despite rising rates, income tax receipts had shrunk to $750 million in the last fiscal year. Liquor taxes would not prove the panacea that many predicted. Lawrence projected instead some $150 million annually in beer taxes and $350 million in hard liquor taxes with repeal. Cigarette and tobacco taxes would yield $400-plus million more. In the end business would pay the bulk of the taxes. For when all was said and done, Lawrence predicted, with governments notoriously inept and corrupt, plagued by inefficient fiscal managers to boot, the Roosevelt program would burden the profit system with its "new social theories" and a dubious economic reconstruction.[26]

During the summer and fall of 1933, an increasingly frustrated budget director challenged the Roosevelt policies, at least in private, as dominated by labor, as a portent of a ruinous inflation due to the departure from gold, and as a step taken toward state capitalism through the vehicle of the Reconstruction Finance Corporation. An internationalist, he was also distressed by the wreckage of the London Economic Conference. When Roosevelt asked for his opinion of the bombshell message, Douglas condemned its nationalism. "I think," he recalled saying, "You have cast the die for war." Asked to explain, the irate budget chief invoked the three pillars of nineteenth-century peace and stability: free trade, gold-based currencies, and the British fleet. "You have boshed it," Douglas protested.[27]

The fracas continued. Roosevelt perceived a bankers' plot to destroy his faltering recovery program through the device of loan limitation. He expected to counter this maneuver, Douglas complained, by substitution of public for private capital. Calculations of $1.4 billion in emergency expenditure for the fiscal year commencing July 1, 1934, seemed to escalate as rumors circulated that Roosevelt contemplated public works expenditures in excess of the $3.3 billion authorized in NIRA's Title II. Douglas tired of the subterfuge that distinguished ordinary from emergency expenditure, since both increased the deficit and the national debt. Equally alarming, items stricken from the normal budget under authority granted to the executive by the interregnum Congress and in the Economy Act found their way into the public works program. As an example, while naval expenditure had been cut to $50 million under general expenditures, $238 million for naval construction could be found under emergency measures.[28]

Douglas lost this round when Roosevelt created by executive order the Civil Works Administration under Harry Hopkins in order to accelerate public works spending. A response to the economic downturn of the closing months of 1933 and the snail's pace associated with Harold Ickes's PWA, the CWA provided four million jobs in the winter of 1933–34 and then was phased out in the spring at a cost of $950 million.[29]

The dispute heated up in the closing days of 1933. Roosevelt evidently was determined to shape fiscal policy as readily as he controlled monetary policy. Douglas seemed stung, also, by the appointment of Henry Morgenthau Jr. as William Woodin's successor at Treasury: "The administration . . . has acquired stupidity and Hebraic arrogance and conceit in Morgenthau." Preparation of the budget message for fiscal 1935 focused the debate. At two meetings with FDR, Douglas protested the size of public works expenditure. Roosevelt countered that it should be considered in a five-year time frame. Nor could the two agree on the policy of reliance on the Reconstruction Finance Corporation. Douglas viewed the RFC as an instrument for circumvention of deficit spending and desired a quick burial effective June 30, 1934. Roosevelt refused to scuttle the RFC: "Lew, you don't understand. Heretofore banking has been undertaken by private individuals for profit. Hereafter, it will be a governmental function." Douglas asserted that the net result would be governmental control of all credit and economic activity. When Douglas pressed that government could not replace business as an employer, Roosevelt rebutted that "he did not know what the future held."[30]

The exchange concluded, Douglas presented Roosevelt with a memorandum on fiscal 1935 projections. It estimated $6.6 billion in Treasury financing for the next six months, over $4 billion in refunding operations and $2.5 billion in new issues, a pace that exceeded wartime requirements. The outcome, he claimed, would be social upheaval. The budget director did not question the need for direct relief but continued his opposition to continuance of the RFC: "I do not believe you want the government to be the complete and absolute dictator of credit and of all the human activities that flow from credit." The result, he predicted, would be state capitalism and the end of private enterprise as an employer of people. Brazenly, Douglas proposed that Roosevelt reread his Pittsburgh address and his March budget message.[31]

All to no avail. While Roosevelt's fiscal 1935 budget message of January 3, 1934, promised eventual budget balance, Douglas projected a near-record peacetime budget of just over $6 billion, based, however, on no new authorization for public works as there remained $2.45 billion in unexpended funds. Instead, the president requested an additional authorization of $2 billion based on continued need for relief and recovery. For all practical purposes, as Dean Acheson observed, Douglas's voice had been stilled. Acheson, who was convinced that the Roosevelt budgets would lead necessarily to inflation and permanent subsidy of "great sections of the country," gauged Douglas as nominally in control of expenditures but actually maneuvered by Roosevelt merely to "fuss with details" and certain to be "saddled with the responsibility for all the trouble."[32]

When at a cabinet meeting Roosevelt "asked me where the bill was appropriating the two billions," Douglas replied that it would be unwise since veterans' benefits were again under debate in the Congress. Roosevelt claimed that no relationship existed between the two; Douglas countered that if that was true, he would exceed his budget. "Why, yes, of course," said the president. "What," FDR pressed, "are you going to do about unemployment and relief?" Whereas Douglas found relief acceptable, he pointed out that public works expenditure of $2.5 billion would provide direct and indirect employment for only 800,000 people. Roosevelt put off his decision.[33]

When Congress effectively repealed the previous year's Economy Act, restoring $228 million in veterans' benefits and $125 million in salaries paid federal employees, Roosevelt wielded the veto, and Congress overrode it. "It did not have the ring of conviction," Douglas complained, and in any event the president seemed indifferent to the outcome.[34] In the circumstance, Douglas insisted on a commitment to hold the 1935 budget deficit below $1.5 billion and to seek actual budget balance in fiscal 1936. This could be done by phasing out RFC expenditure and public works, while allowing $750 million for relief.[35]

The budget director now targeted the balance of the Roosevelt program: artificial maintenance of wages and prices, restricted production, higher tariffs, an attack on business profits, public works, and the Securities Act, which "if not amended means that the government becomes the exclusive capitalist and therefore permit [sic] the Tugwellians to plan our economy," leading inevitably to a communistic or collective system. "Torrence," a code name for FDR in Douglas's correspondence, had become, further, increasingly vindictive toward businessmen and bankers. They were crooks, and increased strikes by labor had been caused by the "arrogance of employers."

At a conference with Roosevelt and Morgenthau on April 23, Douglas opposed an additional $500 million for public works—the CWA was succeeded by the Emergency Work Relief Program, administered by a division of Hopkins's FERA—as it would make impossible their projected balance of the 1936 budget. Roosevelt declared, "That is too far in the future." Douglas repeated his belief that the spending program crippled private investment. Roosevelt replied, "Lew, you are crazy—you have an obsession on the subject of a balanced budget and the investment of capital for private purposes—there is no such need." Douglas persisted, "I had hoped you would now want . . . to . . . taper off the spending program." Roosevelt vowed, "No, I do not want to taper off until the emergency is passed."[36]

The denouement came with a proposal for $525 million in drought relief for rural areas, or more specifically whether it should be funded by a $3 billion relief bill, passed by the Congress on June 4, 1934, or whether new funding should be requested. Douglas held that Roosevelt had ample funds available for the purpose. Roosevelt countered that he wanted "a kitty and would take a kitty for five billions if Congress would give it to me." Douglas then

> asked if he [Roosevelt] proposed to spend at the rate of three to four hundred millions a month [Keynes's recent proposal]. At this he became angry, banged his fist on the desk and said, "I am getting God damned sick and tired of having imputed to me things I have never said." Shaking his finger at me he continued, "You have been reading Arthur Krock and Maynard Keynes."
>
> I said, "Yes, I have, and if you aren't going to spend at that rate I don't see what you need the money for."
>
> Still angry, he said, "I never said I was going to spend at that rate and I don't like to have you or anybody else infer I am going to." Then, more quietly, "I am just as Scotch as you. I have some Dutch in me also, and I want to save just as much as you want to save."[37]

The Senate Appropriations Committee reported a deficiency bill limiting the president's power to divert $400 million in RFC funds for the Public Works Administration and relief. Angered, Roosevelt "wanted that limitation out," he instructed Douglas, and asserted "that if it weren't taken out he would have to call Congress back into session and that then we would probably get the La Follette proposal for $10,000,000,000." Conceding the issue a few days later, Douglas went along with HR 9830 and its emergency provision for $2.5 billion, "far beyond the real necessities of the situation."[38]

Distressed by the continued, even expanded, public works program, by FDR's evident unwillingness to close the federal deficit, and by the "undermining of the American system," Douglas eased the way toward his resignation with a leave of absence during the summer of 1934. Roosevelt, suspicious of Douglas's motives and activities, claimed at a cabinet meeting that his budget director had set out to "make a written record. He makes a written record of everything. If things go wrong he wants to be in a position so he can show that on such and such a date he advised the president not to do thus and so. Of course, he makes a good watch dog of Treasury, but I don't like it."[39]

An exchange with Russell Leffingwell in New York City provided no succor for Douglas, as it revealed the Morgan partner's continued support of Roosevelt's monetary and fiscal policies. "Says would have gone through a deflation so intense . . . only way out is inflation. Of course I do not agree." Opposed to the administration's entire legislative and social agenda, to Roosevelt's tendency to substitute New Deal supporters for traditionalists in the Democratic Party, which foreshadowed a subsequent attempt at political realignment, and to the likely appointment of the "nutty" Marriner S. Eccles, an advocate of countercyclical spending, to head the Federal Reserve Board, Douglas wrote FDR that "it would be better to replace me with someone who is in more complete accord with your budgetary policies."[40]

When the two met at Hyde Park on August 30, Roosevelt, reluctant to part company even with ideological dissidents in view of his desire to maintain a broad base for the Democratic Party, swore allegiance to budget balance—several years off. He could not abandon relief and public works "and let people starve." No longer persuaded by the argument, if he ever was, Douglas countered that vested interests dependent on federal spending had mushroomed under the New Deal's largesse. Asked where he would cut federal expenses, Douglas cited the CCC, PWA, RFC, now even relief; he countenanced only a dole based on an allowance less than could be had in private employment. Roosevelt granted that the Civil Works Administration proved costly and promised to replace it with a similar but more economical program. When Douglas insisted on a broadened tax base by means of a decrease in the income tax exemption to $500 and an increase in the normal rate to 10 percent in order to induce public resistance to federal spending, Roosevelt protested that those who lived on low incomes would be hurt.

Unsuccessful with this line of argument, the president claimed inability to prepare a new budget for fiscal 1936 without Douglas's input. Again he encountered a stone wall. Douglas argued for a normal budget of $2.5 billion, with a modest sum added for relief; all other expenses would be eliminated. A totally frustrated Douglas insisted on commitment to "the competitive system" and adherence to the party platform. The outburst concluded, Douglas handed over his letter of resignation. Roosevelt predicted that it would mean the loss of Congress to the Republican Party in the coming congressional campaign, invoked the usual marching farmers, and charged cowardice in the face of the enemy, unable even now to concede that he was the enemy.[41]

With Lewis W. Douglas exited from the Roosevelt circle, Warburg and Douglas could openly join forces. In a debate before the Economic Club of New York with the popular economic writer Stuart Chase, who favored countercyclical federal investment in depression, Douglas aired his views publicly after the congressional election. Acquisition of consumer goods had scarcely been affected by the depression, according to Douglas, whereas capital goods expenditure had declined by 65 percent. Further, employment had declined 16 percent in consumption goods and 50 percent in producers' goods industries. Past depressions had been liquidated by capital expenditure for plant and equipment replacement, new buildings, and semipermanent goods once costs fell and profit possibilities resumed. No federal public works program could meet this void, as capital expenditure normally ran from $25 to $35 billion. Unbalanced budgets and manipulated currencies destroyed confidence and private-sector investment.

Budget balance, Douglas maintained, required the end of the public works program, the CCC, and government credit facilities such as the RFC. These would be replaced by block grants to the states for emergency relief, some $1.25 billion, under conditions similar to Great Britain's means test. States and localities would be left free to supplement such grants to carry out relief programs of their own choice, including direct relief. In effect, it was a program of devolution, a return of the relief–public works function to the states, a reiteration of his 1920s Jeffersonian states' rights ideology of minimal central government.[42]

With the approach of the 1936 presidential election, Warburg also condemned Roosevelt's discard of the Democratic Party's 1932 platform and his Pittsburgh pledge of budget balance and a sound currency in *Hell Bent for Election*. Pierre S. du Pont, a mainstay of the bitterly anti–New Deal American Liberty League, underwrote its dissemination (27,000 copies). Lists were furnished by the National Association of Manufacturers, John Kirby's Southern Committee to Uphold the Constitution, and Du Pont. The New Deal represented, the disenchanted Warburg wrote, with its $5 billion per annum budget deficits for relief and public works, compulsory unemployment insurance program, and the Social Security Act, a "fulfillment of . . . promises . . . made by the Socialist candidate, Mr. Norman Thomas." The Democratic Party platform had indeed pledged such programs, but under state auspices with federal financial assistance. The platform had not provided for agricultural output restricted to the domestic market or antitrust suspended to foster "business controlled by dictatorship," Warburg's view of the National Recovery Administration. Roosevelt, in sum, had flouted the Constitution, assumed dictatorial powers, and taken on an air of indispensability as he centralized authority in the federal bureaucracy. Domestic issues, as Warburg saw them, were home rule, states' rights, and constitutional democracy, which "would suit me pretty well as an alternative to the New Deal."[43] Internationalist economic priorities, economy, and devolution of governmental authority were the themes preached by Warburg and Douglas as they met with Governor Alf M. Landon of Kansas in April 1936.[44]

Writing in the context of the fiscal revolution that marked the post–Second World War era, Herbert Stein termed Roosevelt's first-term fiscal policy inadequate, since it ignored the possibility, through public works and relief expenditure, of large, indirect multiplier effects upon employment. "The limitations of the spending program did not result from failure to conceive of it as a 'recovery' program rather than a 'relief' program, but from the decision to confine relief to the neediest cases and to provide it on a minimum scale." Overall, Stein observed, the Roosevelt administration "never produced any general theory of the fiscal policy under which [it was] working"—at least, it needs to be added, until the 1937–38 recession.[45]

Yet the question can be put, just how fully was Keynesian (and multiplier) theory developed in the 1930s? No Western nation offered a workable Keynesian model in these years. In fact, Roosevelt's fiscal policy and public works program proved more expansionary than Neville Chamberlain's. In the period 1929–35, the United Kingdom budget remained in surplus, excepting only the year 1933, with total receipts quite stable. In the United States tax revenues fell steeply and recovered to the 1929 level ($4 billion) only in 1935, while total expenditure more than doubled, from $3.2 billion to just under $7 billion.[46]

Which leads to the related question of the multiplier effect of public works programs in depression. That it came under discussion is clear. But monetary and fiscal policy alone or in combination could be not be demonstrated as proven factors in assuring a recovery in light of a preference for liquidity by individuals and banking institutions and the existence of profound structural problems. Such limitation was illustrated again at the century's close, when Japan proved unable to fend off a long-term steep recession with the limited weapons of near-zero interest rates and massive expenditure for useless public works. There were severe lim-

TABLE 2. Federal Interregional Transfers, 1933–38 (in millions)

	Internal Revenue Collections 1934–1938	Federal Benefits 3/4/33–6/30/38
NORTHEAST REGION		
New England Division		
Maine	$48.5	$ 188.1
New Hampshire	30.9	71.8
Vermont	13.9	94.1
Massachusetts	667.0	784.7
Rhode Island	108.4	111.3
Connecticut	285.0	243.9
Total	$1,153.7	$1,493.9
Middle Atlantic Division		
New York	$4,246.1	$3,075.2
New Jersey	761.5	944.7
Pennsylvania	1,613.8	1,773.6
Total	$6,621.4	$5,793.5
NORTH CENTRAL REGION		
East North Central Division		
Ohio	$1,082.1	$1,717.6
Indiana	372.8	736.2
Illinois	1,719.2	1,875.1
Michigan	1,016.4	1,218.2
Wisconsin	351.0	817.0
Total	$4,541.5	$6,364.1
West North Central Division		
Minnesota	$ 272.3	$ 773.7
Iowa	105.2	778.1
Missouri	481.3	748.1
North Dakota	7.4	386.3
South Dakota	7.7	385.8
Nebraska	67.2	559.9
Kansas	101.8	605.8
Total	$1,042.2	$4,238.3
SOUTH REGION		
South Atlantic Division		
Delaware	$ 228.4	$ 40.9
Maryland	334.3	380.7
District of Columbia	100.2	375.8
Virginia	705.0	426.7
West Virginia	75.0	302.7
North Carolina	1,464.9	495.0
South Carolina	67.3	350.3
Georgia	136.9	314.5
Florida	135.2	340.9
Total	$3,247.2	$3,027.5

East South Central Division		
Kentucky	$486.4	$ 395.0
Tennessee	111.6	469.0
Alabama	58.5	486.7
Mississippi	18.6	441.7
Total	$675.1	$1,792.4
West South Central Division		
Arkansas	$ 23.7	$ 455.2
Louisiana	148.7	460.8
Oklahoma	246.6	564.4
Texas	451.1	1457.3
Total	$870.1	$2,937.7
WEST REGION		
Mountain Division		
Montana	$ 25.7	$ 369.3
Idaho	12.7	263.3
Wyoming	10.1	133.0
Colorado	112.6	347.0
New Mexico	7.8	186.2
Arizona	12.7	237.1
Utah	26.8	301.5
Nevada	14.9	102.3
Total	$223.3	$1,939.7
Pacific Division		
Washington	$ 115.2	$ 523.0
Oregon	48.9	344.3
California	1,081.7	2032.7
Total	$1,245.8	$2,900.0

Source: G [Grace Tully]: "Memo for Mary, for President's locked drawer," PSF 178; for similar studies see memorandum, E. E. Lincoln, "Federal Non-recoverable Relief Expenditures by States, Compared with Internal Revenue Collections, July 1, 1933, to June 30, 1937 . . ." and accompanying table, f. 771, box 1, Pierre S. du Pont Papers; "Summary Operations Report of Federal Funds Loaned and Expended from New and Emergency Appropriations, March 4, 1933, through December 31, 1937," *Cong. Record*, 75th Cong., 3rd sess., vol. 83, Senate, April 14, 1938, 5386–87.

itations on federal spending. In an era of modest national budgets, accelerated public expenditure could have a measurable economic impact, but not sufficient to induce a full-employment economy. Public expenditure of a magnitude sufficient to turn the tide of unemployment on a major scale, actually at wartime levels, required a state apparatus unknown in peacetime and of doubtful acceptance. And the concept of the multiplier that provided this justification—suggesting that public works had effects in the economy greater than the expenditure itself—lacked a rationale pending economic analysis in the 1937–38 recession. Roosevelt opted for remediation of structural imbalances as basic to recovery.

The raison d'être behind Roosevelt's structural approach to recovery stemmed largely from his perception of the resemblance of the U.S. economy to that of the British Empire, with London the financial center and exploited raw-materials producers Canada, Australia, and South Africa at the periphery. In this instance, Wall Street was at the center, while underdeveloped and exploited and dependent extractive economies, the South and the West, were at the periphery. The Roosevelt program proposed instead, as had the original Brains Trust, redirection of "surplus income" away from New York toward the hinterland.

To remediate regional economic imbalance, the New Deal recovery program provided for interregional transfers calibrated to achieve not simply better distribution of purchasing power but over the long run economic diversification in the nation's commodities-producing areas. A study formulated for Roosevelt based on internal revenue collections and federal benefits for 1933–38 points to the provision of economic transfers toward the poorer states (table 2). As an example, the South Atlantic division (Delaware, Maryland, the District of Columbia, Virginia, West Virginia, North Carolina, South Carolina, Georgia, and Florida) shows collections of $3,247 million and benefits of $3,027.5 million. If Delaware, with its economy based on the profitable E. I. Dupont de Nemours, the state's principal employer, and Virginia and North Carolina, both favored by tobacco and mixed economies, are excluded, the poorer South Atlantic states paid in $848.9 million and received $2,064.9 million. Collections in the Middle Atlantic states (New York, New Jersey, and Pennsylvania) yielded $6,621.4 million, with benefits paid out totaling $5,793.5 million. In the Mountain West, dependent on extraction of minerals at depressed prices, collections amounted to $233.3 million as opposed to benefits of $1,939.7 million, a pattern repeated in the Pacific region, the Gulf states, and the Upper Plains area.

Overall federal nonrecoverable relief or "pump-priming" expenditure for the period March 4, 1933, through December 31, 1937, in the United States and its territories amounted to $17.153 billion, distributed through the following programs: Agricultural Adjustment Administration; Farm Security Administration; Civil Works Administration; Federal Emergency Relief Administration; Civilian Conservation Corps; Bureau of Public Roads; Social Security; Public Works Administration; Works Progress Administration; Emergency Relief Appropriation Acts of 1935, 1936, and 1937; Reclamation Service; and Public Buildings (Treasury). These outlays do not include either the ordinary expenditures of government, approximately $17.246 billion, or an additional $14 billion in loans made by the Reconstruction Finance Corporation, Farm Credit Administration, Commodity Credit Corporation, Farm Security Administration, Home Owners Loan Corporation, Public Works Administration, Rural Electrification Administration, and other federal lending agencies. Such loans, while recoverable, were nevertheless largely a "contingent liability," or debt, of the U.S. government with guaranteed debt on June 30, 1937, at $4.7 billion.

Federal expenditures (FY 1933 through FY 1937) of over $34 billion, half pump-priming and redistributive in nature, half ordinary, were made against income, corporate, and inheritance taxes of $17.682 billion and an additional $2.6 billion derived principally from alcohol, tobacco, and social security taxes; motor fuels; and customs receipts. Gross national debt increased from $22.5 to $36.4 billion.[47] Traditionalists shuddered at the magnitude of these numbers, at the thought of a citizenry dependent on federal largesse and the growth of the federal government's role in economic and social management at the expense of the states.

6 | THE MYTH OF A CORPORATE STATE

P LANNERS BELIEVED THAT the economic implosion of the early 1930s could not be remedied in the absence of structural reform. Plans for control of investment and production, fair pricing, limits on entry, and increased employment and wage levels emanated from diverse sources. Protagonists included business leaders, members of the Roosevelt Brains Trust, the U.S. Chamber of Commerce, raw materials producers, economists, and popular writers. With profits evaporated and 25 percent unemployment, most such proposals reflected the belief that a market economy had become an anachronism and needed overhead management either by trade associations or by a federal economic council. These developments led to an attempt to stabilize production and employment, to provide for minimum wages and maximum hours, and to assure unions' right to organize plant and business's need to return to profitability.

To many observers the War Industries Board served as a model for cooperation between business and government. Yet industrialists prevailed; they hoarded materials, catered to the civilian market, and were tempted to profiteer. Bernard M. Baruch's loosely administered agency, based on voluntarism—he took charge on March 4, 1918—scarcely resolved the tension between industrialists' fear of central control and wartime need for bureaucratic organization.

The trade association movement of the 1920s also represented a flawed model. Voluntarist principles proved illusory. Organized labor lost ground, and wages and purchasing power lagged profits. Success depended on the presence of a dominant firm. Older industries and a preponderance of raw materials producers, on the other hand, could not achieve market or price stability in the face of high fixed costs and excess capacity. As Colin Gordon notes, "Visions of organized markets and industrial democracy may have danced in the heads of a few enlightened capitalists, but few corporate solutions transpired beyond Herbert Hoover's subject files."[1]

With the coming of the depression, business clamored for antitrust suspension, price stability, and market division. The Swope Plan, introduced by the General Electric president Gerard Swope at a dinner of the National Electric Manufacturers Association in September 1931, depended on trade associations. These business groups would coordinate output with consumption, afford employment guarantees, and provide for unemployment, old-age, and widows' insurance, with costs to be shared by employees and management. The plan also featured cost and earnings statements to end below-cost sales used by marginal, low-wage competitors to the detriment of ethical producers, translated as General Electric. Necessarily, the Sherman and Clayton Acts would be modified to permit cooperative trade association practices, their agreements to be filed with the Federal Trade Commission and the Justice Department.[2]

Statists distrusted such an approach and promoted collective planning controlled by a government agency. Representatives of labor, consumers, and small business would be included, with investment and social policy guided by a council of experts. They urged control of industries marked either by excess profits or by ruthless pricing and wage practices, especially raw materials producers; suggested mechanisms for ensuring stability of workers' earnings and minimum social guarantees; and they explored the role of public works as a form of relief and as a stimulus to purchasing power, private-sector investment, and employment.

Stuart Chase's *A New Deal* serves as an example. A popular writer on economic subjects and a proponent of Taylorism, or scientific management, he championed a "third road," neither Black nor Red, as he put it. Such a middle way would transform the denotation of profit. Profiteering, defined as business retention of the margin between corporate income and outgo, would give way to release of that margin to the community at large. This required control from the top, including currency management; long-term government budgeting, which would allow for temporary budget unbalance as a means of accommodating public works and works reserves; minimum wage laws; stiffened inheritance and income tax levies; scaled-down tariffs; regulated foreign investment; and "an industrial budget of national requirements and industrial capacity to meet them," as well as "national and regional planning boards to coordinate the whole."[3]

In the last analysis, all such plans depended on centralized investment decisions rather than reliance on the market. In "The Principle of Planning and the Institution of Laissez Faire," Rexford Tugwell urged a refuge from insecurity, "a kind of economic Geneva," with government in a managerial role. A national plan, he proposed to Roosevelt during the 1932 campaign, would include surveys of potential demand, investment and price controls, rearrangement of industry to meet the plan, and protection of the disadvantaged, defined as farmers, wage earners, and consumers. Management would be put in the hands of an Economic Council, and antitrust would be suspended. Initially the council would rely on persuasion, though in time, however, "it might be necessary to implement its power by constitutional change and enabling legislation."

Tugwell urged economic balance in a framework he described as disproportionality theory. Imbalances in the economy included the disparity between profits and wages, accumulation of corporate surpluses at the expense of investment in new technologies, and disparities between sections, especially between urban-industrial and farm income. Absolutely essential, Tugwell believed, were "fundamental changes of attitude, new disciplines, revised legal structures, unaccustomed limitations on activity . . . if we are to plan. . . . This amounts, practically, to the abolition of 'business.' This is what planning calls for." He rejected an outmoded faith in the profit motive. Labor, he felt, had no stake in corporate earnings, and the separation of ownership and control established by Gardiner C. Means's work convinced him that even management had a minimal profit incentive. Surplus corporate reserves, in the event, led to overcapacity.

Other factors also pointed to the substitution of planning for laissez-faire. The new technology of work elimination required coordination and control. Otherwise another economic disaster would follow. Planning also required social control of economic activity. Tugwell viewed as inadequate the creation of a central group of economic experts charged with planning, existing as an advisory body, proposed by GE's Swope. It could not stem speculation in the form of profit making. Planned production and planned consumption required the social control of profits. By social control Tugwell meant federal planning for every industry and every facet of the economy. "Planning implies guidance of capital uses; this would limit entrance into or expansion of operations. Planning also implies adjustment of production to consumption; and there is no way of accomplishing this except through control of prices and profit margins."[4]

Planning of any type, business-dominated or statist, faced critical impediments, a point expressed by GE's chairman of the board Owen D. Young and the Lehman Brothers economist Alexander Sachs. Since there was little experience with the planning mechanism in peacetime and "a limit to the capacity of man to act wisely in diversified activities spread over wide areas," planning, according to Young, needed to be fashioned organically, over a period of time, and should prove its efficacy to the public at large. Planning should be designed to secure greater volume to stimulate employment, ensure higher wages, and increase purchasing power; also to promote a flow of production to larger, more economical units. Inefficient producers would be amortized over time. In order to clothe enterprise with a public interest, government representatives would sit with the developing industrial councils, and the administration would exercise control by taxation of excess profits.[5]

The concept of a cooperative commonwealth proved to be an elusive goal. Planning schemes, regardless of source or objective, relied on superimposing a parallel economic government on the nation's political and constitutional fabric, requiring a curb on legislative authority. Such schemes scarcely comported with the nation's decentralist ideology despite the rationalization that planning had long since existed in the nation's cities, its business structure, in wartime, and in government agencies. The worst of the depression having lifted by 1934–35 and the cooperation movement now a memory, planners faced a market mentality that rejected centralized controls, however administered.

The basic study of the origins of the National Industrial Recovery Act, which details multiple origins, treats the outcome as largely the work of cartelists who aspired to suspension of antitrust. This would charge business self-government with maintenance of price and production controls. But such a victory by any single constituency never occurred in the making of NIRA, and the ambitions of those who wrote the law were more complex and even contradictory.[6]

Prior to Roosevelt's inauguration, Raymond Moley, impressed with Henry I. Harriman's memorandum, "An Economic Program," noted, "Keep in immediate file and show to the governor." The utility magnate's credentials in the Roosevelt circle had been established in the campaign when he furnished the agricultural economist Milburn Lincoln Wilson and Tugwell with mechanisms critical to the working of acreage allotment, particularly an excise tax on processors for redistribution of income from urban consumers to agriculture at no cost to the federal budget. Like Tugwell, Harriman proposed a National Economic Council, but one that was voluntary and based on industry, agriculture, and labor. Its purpose would be the transfer of national income into wages and agriculture by means of business limitation of profits, or through "a system of taxation that will put them [businessmen] out of business." Harriman also proposed a minimum wage program as a stimulus to consumption as well as amendment of the Clayton Act permitting trade conferences to abolish unfair practices within an industry. On the vote of 60 to 70 percent of a trade group, unfair methods of competition would be prohibited, provision made for maximum hours and minimum wages, and production tailored to demand. Once approved by a government agency—government's role was limited to a veto—trade agreements would bind. Harriman's program also included credit extension to industry through the Reconstruction Finance Corporation or the Federal Reserve System, to stimulate production, employment, and purchasing power.[7]

The most widely circulated of the packages for private-sector stimulus through government subsidy was the Moulton-Jacobstein Plan, a product of Harold G. Moulton, president of the Brookings Institution, and Meyer Jacobstein, a former member of Congress from Rochester, New York, currently president of that city's First National Bank and Trust Company. Moulton-Jacobstein proposed a National Board for Industrial Recovery that would select industries best able to stimulate economic activity, determine what percentage of production increase would be desirable, allocate increases by industry and region, form wage and employment policies (including labor representation), stabilize prices in select industries, and provide for a minimum government guarantee against losses. All such proposals, whether they called for a cooperative business commonwealth and/or stimulus packages, mandated suspension of antitrust enforcement in order to keep government's role at a minimum.[8]

Given the variety of plans for industrial recovery, their potential cost, and ideological tensions, Moley, burdened by preparations for the MacDonald visit and the Economic Conference, turned the matter over to James P. Warburg, who evaluated proposals for industrial recovery principally in terms of budgetary impact and their portent for a welfare state. When these were summarized in a document that testified to dissonance on the subject, Roosevelt and Moley concluded that business thinking had not clarified sufficiently to justify consideration of industrial planning in the current emergency session of the Congress.[9]

While Warburg favored the subsidy approach to industrial recovery, evidence was absent to support the argument that government loans to industry would stimulate employment or increase purchasing power, since gains in one area might lead to losses in another. Expense might be considerable as there was no assurance that the government could recoup loans made through the RFC. In the absence of a stimulus to demand in the shape of a public works program, price rises would choke newly expanded production. As Moley put the issue to Warburg, he would also need to convince Senators Costigan, La Follette, and Wagner that public works were less effective than subsidy plans designed to stimulate increased output.

Anxious to relieve himself of the assignment—like Moley, he was focused on the London Conference—Warburg met the senators, convinced on his departure that he had sold them on government loans to industry as superior to public works. He proposed as capable of framing a recovery plan Malcolm Rorty, author of the Rorty Plan, which resembled that of Moulton and Jacobstein; the New York banker Fred I. Kent; James H. Rand of Remington Rand; Moulton; Virgil Jordan of the National Industrial Conference Board; David L. Podell, an attorney specializing in antitrust; Representative Clyde Kelly; and the United Mine Workers economist W. Jett Lauck. Lauck and Moulton collaborated on the initial draft of the National Industrial Recovery Act based on Lauck's experience with the bituminous coal industry and Moulton's advocacy of business-government cooperation based on the WIB model.[10]

Lauck established his credentials as a Progressive economist while serving as secretary of the National War Labor Board. An exponent of the "democratization of industry"—government mandate of collective bargaining as well as a role for organized labor in managerial decision making—he was employed as an economic aide to John L. Lewis and the United Mine Workers. By the mid-1920s, with bituminous coal burdened by too many mines and miners, the industry floundered. Typical of the failure of the postwar cooperation movement was the demise of the Jacksonville agreement, negotiated in 1924 by Hoover, Lewis, and a major operator, George G. Moore. It provided for high wage scales ($7.50 per day) in the Central Competitive Field, in order to eliminate inefficient, low-wage, small-scale producers by promotion of mechanized mining. When the agreement collapsed, union members migrated to the southern nonunion fields in search of employment. Competition from anthracite and petroleum producers exacerbated the situation. With profits in decline, the National Coal Association abandoned the cooperation theme, reduced wages, and laid off workers. Lewis turned to Lauck in an effort to revitalize the UMW and fend off radical dissidents.[11]

Lauck focused on the Copeland-Jacobstein bill (1928), which became the Davis-Kelly bill of 1932. In exchange for exemption from the Sherman Act, producer combinations in coal would recognize "the right of workers through chosen representatives" to bargain collectively. Management would forgo the right to discharge workers for union membership or activity. Unskilled workers would be assured the right to earn a living wage. Equal pay would be provided for women in industrial occupations. Child labor would be prohibited in mines, and the workday limited to eight hours and workweek to six days. Regulatory authority would be vested in a bituminous coal commission, forerunner of the NRA code authorities.[12]

Politically astute, Lauck suggested a marriage of bituminous coal with other stricken industries such as agriculture, lumber, textiles, natural gas, copper, and petroleum. Emergency boards would be charged with governance of price and production agreements. As opposed to the Swope–Chamber of Commerce Plan for industrial self-government, Lauck insisted on "government interference and regulation," a theme taken up by Lewis in testimony (1931) before Senator Robert La Follette's Committee on National Planning and Stabilization. Lewis's national coal commission would fix maximum prices, license and regulate producers and shippers in interstate commerce, and control shipments into glutted markets. Industry would accept the collective bargaining guarantees that became Section 5 of Davis-Kelly. In subsequent testimony before the Senate Finance Committee, the UMW head called for a Board of Emergency Control directed by the president, empowered to control output and prices in basic commodities including agriculture. The board would tailor output to the needs of the domestic market and would be empowered to stimulate purchasing power and limit hours of labor and the length of the workweek.[13]

Unable to persuade the Hoover administration to take a stand on Davis-Kelly, the UMW turned to Roosevelt in the course of the 1932 campaign. Philip Murray, UMW vice president, and others of the union leadership met twice with the governor and secured a pledge, privately and then in an address at Terre Haute, Indiana, that if elected, he would call a conference of miners and operators and "force action on the stabilization of the industry." These developments served as a basis for Lauck's quest for industrial democracy based on a living wage through collective bargaining as essential to the nation's recovery.[14]

At a meeting with Moley, who had previously conferred with UMW officials, Lauck presented his plan for stability in soft-coal mining. Moley conferred with Warburg, who expressed preference for government agency loans to business. Undeterred, Lauck dispatched memoranda to Warburg and Moley outlining the Davis-Kelly bill, which would require all corporations engaged in mining and shipping bituminous coal in interstate commerce to secure a license from a U.S. coal commission. Operators would be permitted to form marketing pools if price schedules and trade practices were not held to be restraints of trade. Section 5 of Davis-Kelly accorded mine workers the right to deal collectively through representatives of their own choosing in making wage agreements and provided that no coal firm in the pool could require mine workers to refrain from union membership as a condition of employment. These principles soon made up the essence of NIRA's Section 7(a) and other components of the bill.

When Lauck learned of the decision to incorporate Davis-Kelly into a broad measure for industrial recovery, leaked in an Arthur Krock column in the New York Times, he insisted on inclusion of the right to bargain collectively. John Gall, assistant general counsel of the NAM, confirmed that Moley, Baruch, Moulton, and John Dickinson at Commerce had moved in the direction of a modified version of the War Industries Board, authorized to set price and production schedules and stimulate output. That evening, at a meeting sponsored by the Brookings Institution, the Black bill, which would limit workers to thirty hours per week, came under discussion. Present likely were Moulton and other Brookings economists, also Gall, Dickinson, and representatives of the Federal Reserve Board. The group concluded that the Black bill, or work spreading, would prove unworkable unless attached to a broader program.[15]

Passage by the Senate of the Black thirty-hour-week bill on April 6, 1933, endorsed by the AFL's William Green, reopened discussion of work spreading, a nostrum that had won a wide spectrum of adherents in the business community. Black reasoned that work spreading would create six million jobs. Indeed, the Accord de Matignon, which forced French employers to adopt a similar plan in 1936, led to decreased output and greater unemployment. Roosevelt, desirous of revision, dispatched Frances Perkins to the House Labor Committee. The secretary of labor proposed shortened hours of labor, minimum wages in industries where reduced hours threatened substandard income, also relaxed antitrust enforcement in order to allow industries to cooperate in eliminating unfair trade practices. Whereas Chamber of Commerce proposals entrusted production controls, minimum wages, and social insurance to the private sector subject to scrutiny by an agency of the federal government, Perkins specified Labor Department oversight. Such a scheme had no future. The AFL's Green opposed minimum wages as tantamount to maximum wages, a proposition that would undercut the rationale for unions; and businessmen feared government control of industry. Support for the Black bill dissipated.[16]

As Roosevelt backed away from the Black-Perkins formula, businessmen seized the chance for antitrust revision with John Dickinson's assumption of the role of deus ex machina, at least from the perspective of the NRA as a corporatist triumph. Dickinson "declared war from within the administration on the Perkins substitute" on behalf of the Chamber of Commerce and the NAM, with wages and hours serving as an entering wedge for industrial self-government.[17] The picture was more complicated. It is doubtful that the Perkins substitute enjoyed backing. Roosevelt told Moley that he would not delay the close of the emergency session of Congress on behalf of the thirty-hour bill; and Dickinson's argument, made to Moley, did not deprive the labor secretary of final authority in event of passage.[18]

The Dickinson memorandum challenged the rationale for a shortened workweek. Recent technological advances made possible a reduced workforce that could produce commodities in fewer hours than required in the past. In normal circumstances, according to Dickenson, the Black bill would correct the evils of technological unemployment. In the current environment, wages were too low to support a thirty-hour workweek. Given an environment of falling prices and a decline in economic activity, businessmen, unable to pass on increased costs to the consumer, would resist wage increases. The result would be increased friction between labor and capital. Or, if business could pass on increased costs to consumers, the result would be decreased purchasing power.

In place of the Black-Perkins proposal, Dickinson suggested that products of night work by women or children or of sweated labor (defined as more than fifty-four hours per week) would be prohibited from interstate commerce. As a universal code would cripple the economy even further, members of individual industries should agree upon a code of labor standards based on maximum hours and minimum wages. Such codes would require approval by the secretary of labor. The labor secretary could summon a conference to this end on her own motion and, if agreement was not reached, could impose a code on the industry for the duration of the emergency.[19]

Moley, Warburg, and Wagner arrived at a consensus. The Davis-Kelly bill framed by Lauck for stability in the bituminous coalfields would be replaced by "a general measure for stabilization of industry." Wagner was charged with the effort. The decision was made on April 25 to suspend the antitrust laws, to institute price and production controls, and to introduce labor safeguards. A Moulton-Lauck subcommittee was designated to draft a bill which included a public works proposal. Preliminary drafts authorized an Industrial Recovery Board and later added a federal emergency administrator of public works who would make grants and loans for both public works projects and private-sector industrial expansion to the tune of $5 billion. The notion of subsidies for selected businesses was discarded in subsequent drafts as these were considered too slow in generating purchasing power, promised open-ended government subvention without results, and averted the industrial controls envisaged by the planners and incorporated in the Wagner industry control bill.[20]

The Lauck-Moulton draft was integral to the National Industrial Recovery Act. This included its declaration of policy, expanded in the final version, and, more basic, provision for a National Board for Industrial Recovery, the subsequent National Recovery Administration. The board would organize cooperative trade groups where none existed and work with existing trade associations to establish minimum reasonable prices, correlate production plans, and license business engaged in interstate commerce. It would consist of seven members, including the secretaries of commerce and labor, with the balance, appointed by the president with the Senate's consent, to represent industry, finance, labor, agriculture, and consumers. No corporation would be entitled to ship goods in interstate commerce without a license issued by the Industrial Board; the licensing process would include negotiation between the board and employers of hours of work. Section 4(2) provided that "employees shall be guaranteed the right to organize and bargain collectively through representatives of their own choosing," and Section 4(3), that "no licensee shall make it a condition of employment that its employees shall not become members of a labor organization." Designated industries were to organize a committee to prescribe operating rules and recommend to the board price and allocation schedules. Marketing pools or joint selling associations approved by the board could operate in interstate commerce, provided that such a pool was not an unreasonable restraint of trade.[21]

Lauck and Moulton turned over their effort to the second Wagner conference, held May 2, then to an enlarged drafting committee headed by Dickinson. The final version of the law represented a fusion of the Lauck-Moulton effort and subsequent input by Dickinson and General Hugh Johnson, who had served under Baruch as administrator of the WIB. The draft, completed on May 14, extended on the principles of the original Lauck-Moulton proposal based largely on Johnson's belief that Congress should cede control of the codes to the presidency in order that all of industry should be codified under the centralized direction of government. Then, too, comporting with the Brains Trust's drift toward self-containment, he insisted that import controls were required to protect domestic price levels. Moulton, opposed to cartelization, departed when the group agreed to allow base cost pricing tied to production costs. He soon opposed other features of the NRA including its coverage of hundreds of industries, import controls, excessive delegation by Congress to the presidency, and its tendency to undermine the free market.[22]

Title I of the National Industrial Recovery Act provided for "the general welfare by promoting the organization of industry for the purpose of cooperation among trade groups." Section 3(1) of the Lauck-Moulton draft had authorized the board "to promote in industries the development and organization of cooperative trade associations, institutions, or groups."

The NIRA strengthened federal controls by empowering the president to establish agencies to implement Title I, likely reflecting Johnson's views of a centralized system of economic controls. Lauck and Moulton had entrusted the board to set up machinery for this purpose. The Swope–Chamber of Commerce–Harriman proposal reposed authority in the private sector, leaving industrial stabilization (as well as provision for social insurance) in the hands of trade associations, controlled only by a veto power residing in the hands of a federal agency.

The Lauck-Moulton draft provided for the law's end with a president's declaration that the emergency was over; the act allowed two years, though the experiment could be terminated earlier by a congressional joint resolution—leaving greater discretion on this score in the hands of Congress.

Trade association agreements under the Lauck-Moulton draft, which provided for reasonable prices and production plans correlated to consumption, were to be approved by the Industrial Recovery Board. Under NIRA, codes of fair competition required presidential approval. These could be submitted to him by a trade association; or, in a grant of power (likely Johnson's addition) that exceeded the Lauck-Moulton provisions and was scarcely contemplated by business proposals, he could impose such a code on an industry.

The NIRA made no mention of the marketing pools or joint selling associations provided for by Lauck based on his coal industry experience.

Section 3(e) of NIRA reinforced the Lauck argument, sustained by Johnson, for an economy managed on a domestic basis. It empowered the president to limit imports that competed with domestic output through the device of Treasury licensing.

Both the May 1 draft and NIRA called for licensing of corporations engaged in interstate commerce. This proved to be a sticking point in early deliberations, when the trade association attorney, David Podell, insisted on discard of the proviso on the ground that it would prove a restraint on business. Lauck countered, successfully, that licensing would serve to restrain a business community relieved of antitrust enforcement. Whereas the Lauck-Moulton proposal mandated licensing as a means of enforcing compliance with provisions for hours and collective bargaining, NIRA gave the president the option to invoke licensing when he deemed it necessary for the purposes of the act.

Also, the president was empowered to prohibit the transportation in interstate or foreign commerce of petroleum in excess of the amount permitted to be produced under state law. While this was not a feature of the Moulton-Lauck draft, Lauck had long since advocated proration for petroleum in tandem with control of coal output.[23]

The main struggle, Lauck later recalled for John T. Flynn, who wrote a series of articles on NIRA, was not the issue of suspension of antitrust urged by the Chamber of Commerce and the National Association of Manufacturers before congressional committees for the purpose of price and production controls. This had already been decided: "Only one hearing was held on these various purposes before the House Committee on Judiciary." Thus, "when Senator Wagner called his meeting and Dr. Moulton and Mr. Jacobstein were appointed a committee to draft a bill, we were all in agreement . . . as to the suspension of the Anti-Trust laws provided there were fundamental guarantees to labor, and . . . also that it contained provisions for adequate economic planning and control."

From the perspective of organized labor, the major issue in the interval between the original drafts and June passage of the law was an attempt to water down the import of Section 7(a) waged before the House and Senate committees charged with review of the legislation by the Chicago labor attorney Donald Richberg, who had grown conservative. Richberg, commended by Moley to Johnson as a labor expert, proposed an amendment to Section 7(a) stating, "No employee or no one seeking employment shall be required as a condition of employment to join any organization or refrain from joining a labor organization of his own choosing." This was also the position of the National Association of Manufacturers in a resolution adopted on June 3. The NAM insisted that Section 7(a) be modified "so as to make it clear that there is neither the intention nor the power to reorganize present mutually satisfactory employment relations, nor to establish any rule which will deny the right of employers and employees to bargain either individually or collectively in such form as is mutually agreeable to them." When an attempt was made to amend Section 7(a) along these lines on the floor of the Senate, Lauck, Lewis, and Henry Warrum, the UMW counsel, buttonholed Nebraska's George W. Norris. They claimed that the revised wording not only would jeopardize the labor guarantee of organization and collective bargaining but would validate company unions. Norris, Wagner, Wheeler, La Follette, and Costigan opposed the Richberg amendment on the floor of the Senate, and it failed of passage.[24]

Over the long term the National Recovery Administration's labor policies promoted unionization and paved the way for social gains such as wages and hours legislation and limitations on child labor. During its two-year existence until the *Schechter* decision of May 1935, further, employed labor's wage gains were substantial and surpassed price increases; income redistribution also benefited those who were employed. Yet these immediate gains in nominal wages were nullified at the macroeconomic level by wage-price inflation, which absorbed the increase in money supply that resulted from monetized gold imports. According to a quantitative analysis, these developments diminished the real money supply and real wealth while increasing interest rates, hence reducing the potential for reemployment and investment. The net result was an economic contraction.[25]

There were other problems. Conveyance of code authority by the president to Hugh Johnson who, in turn, created hundreds of code authorities controlled by large, dominant corporations or by trade associations offered the potential of a cartelist regime imposed on a market economy. The NRA lacked a coherent rationale in the absence of congressional guidelines, and there existed no real enforcement authority beyond moral suasion. Prices were raised ahead of stimulus to purchasing power, which depended on government expenditure for public works. The codes tended to favor older, larger inefficient industries to the discouragement of investment in newer, innovative technologies. Yet older industries, as in the case of agriculture and textiles, were large employers of unskilled labor. The Federal Reserve should have pushed interest rates downward, nearly to zero, and flooded the banking system with liquidity. The alternative was regulation in the form of overhead economic management by government, impossible in a market economy.

In the absence of a huge state enforcement apparatus, the hundreds of codes formulated by trade associations and the National Recovery Administration had not the slightest chance for acceptance beyond Administrator Johnson's late summer–autumn 1933 campaign for mass adoption, termed the President's Reemployment Agreement. This, in fact, proved to be the NRA's zenith. By late autumn, when the economy suffered a relapse, Johnson and the code apparatus came under broad attack. Alexander Sachs, the NRA's research chief, who had exchanged views on industrial policy with Johnson since the 1932 campaign, headed for the door.[26]

According to Sachs, valorizing inflated postwar values would not reverse the decline, and a normal, cyclical recovery was improbable. Corporate income showed a net deficit of $6 billion, and corporate debt proved to be excessive as a result of heavy borrowing at high interest rates in the optimistic environment of the 1920s. In prior depressions it sufficed to rely on a rising level of demand. But the nation's capital structure, inflated in the New Era, required a reduced burden of debt, the ratio of debt to wealth standing at 75 percent in 1932. In the event, Sachs never accepted planning in the form of Tugwell's or Swope's overhead, or top-down, economic management. He preferred a piecemeal intervention where needed, with emphasis on severely distressed sectors. "I found General Johnson in agreement with the thesis," Sachs recalled, "that we had to avoid the cartelization of industry and that any process of price inflation would soon lead to a serious reaction because there would not be the accumulated gain of purchasing power which absorbs goods at higher prices. . . . The focus of the memoranda and plans submitted to and accepted by General Johnson was the reactivation of capital goods industries."[27]

Unemployment statistics supported the Sachs thesis. Rough estimates for 1932, already available, indicated that more than half of industrial sector employment could be attributed to the capital goods sector. Of the 10,385,000 unemployed in the nation's industries, 5,525,000 were attributable to the capital goods decline. Unemployment in consumption goods was a fraction of this number, or 1,550,000.[28]

Vitally important, Sachs wanted the components of the proposed law separated out by discrete laws and agencies for administration of public works, social ends, private works, and industrial recovery. He preferred, in place of the NRA's code machinery, altering the function for the Federal Trade Commission by abandonment of emphasis on antitrust in favor of rationalization of competitive practices. This meant that hearings would be held on the requirements of sick industries (coal, oil, and textiles), and the results would be thoroughly researched and submitted as the basis for legislation by Congress.

Selected by Roosevelt to head the National Recovery Administration, the impetuous, dynamic, confrontational, temperamental, and hard-drinking Johnson, onetime cavalry officer, scarcely fitted Sachs's prescription for careful study of the needs of the extractive raw materials industries and other sick industries. Sachs, a statistician, an econometrician, and an analyst of economic cycles and the vagaries of fluctuations in consumer purchases, scarcely comported with Johnson's sense of immediacy in a drive to orchestrate the economy along the lines of the War Industries Board. Planning could be tested only by limiting its scope to the depressed natural resources industries, particularly coal and petroleum, and by limited regulatory power. Planning might have worked, as Sachs and Owen Young proposed, if carefully evaluated for results. Otherwise, it had no future. In a diverse and market-oriented economy, the business community quickly returned to the tenets of capitalism.[29]

B USINESS LEADERS AND peak organizations such as the U.S. Chamber of Commerce quickly backed away from planning, wary lest the National Recovery Administration, subject to presidential authority, bring about federal control of the economy. U.S. Chamber of Commerce endorsement of an industrial recovery plan rested on two assumptions: trade association primacy, with the federal government possessed of no more than a veto power over industry management of pricing, marketing, wages and hours, and child-labor controls; and the belief that Section 7(a) of the National Industrial Recovery Act tolerated company unions and bargaining with separate groups of employees within the same plant. When these assumptions proved baseless, a disenchanted Henry I. Harriman aired his views at the board of directors meeting in September 1934. The Chamber president deplored strikes occasioned by organizational disputes among labor unions supported, in turn, by the "forces of anarchy and communism."[1]

Corporate liberals, Harriman included, accepted Section 7(a)—if separated from the codes and if strikes were permitted only when called by ballot, since workers presumably were more pliant in such matters than union leaders. Fact-finding boards would head off strikes with the right to work protected from violence and intimidation. A new version of Section 7(a) would define collective bargaining as inclusive of representatives of all employee groups, would protect minority rights in the bargaining process, and would ensure that no employee was required to join a union as a condition of employment.

Nor was Harriman satisfied with the NRA's administrative arrangement, which was not intended, he claimed, to apply to intrastate business or to small firms, to engage in price fixing and codification of minutia, to condone impossible wage pressures, or to facilitate the principles of revolution. In a revised Recovery Act, government authority would be rescinded and bureaucratic interference eliminated, with each industry responsible for its own code, subject simply to government revision and approval. Business, moreover, could accept or reject such "requests" by the bureaucracy and would have the final say in acceptance of a code. Price-fixing would be limited to natural resource industries and all codes confined to interstate business.[2]

As Herbert Hoover predicted, there occurred no sharp chronological or ideological divide in the emergence of business antagonism to the Roosevelt program. "The industrial code program will work in the early stages of enthusiasm for unity and recovery. . . . It will be ultimately bogged down by conflict in details and released human nature when the scare is over." Conflict in sentiment is reflected in Willard M. Kiplinger's digest of business opinion in the early summer of 1934 based on 2,000 replies to a questionnaire sent to his newsletter clients. Manufacturers represented a majority of respondents, with a minority engaged in finance and distribution. Asked to what extent their business had been helped or hurt by Washington policies during the previous half year, a bare majority felt aided by the NRA. Slightly less than half reported no improvement, with inability to secure working capital from banking institutions wary of lending, and uncertainty as to future government policy the principal deterrents.

The question "What do you need most from Washington?" induced Kiplinger's respondents to urge an end to government harassment and experiments, especially monetary schemes, inflation, budget deficits, the NRA, price control policies, and debilitating taxation. A substantial majority evidenced contradictory sentiments. Thus codes that ended destructive trade practices were lauded, but the NRA's principles were deplored; most business representatives favored higher wages for labor while they condemned Section 7(a)'s labor provisions; businessmen opposed price-fixing but favored price controls, and so forth. Ambivalence, the contradictory nature of these responses, and division on basic issues, Kiplinger pointed out, could not be sorted out by the size of firms. But most firms proved unequivocal on the issue of the AFL efforts to unionize industry, which they condemned. Overall, some 70 percent of those canvassed were "sour on Washington." Southerners proved more favorable toward New Deal economic policies, while New York, New England, and Midwest businessmen were more critical.[3]

An attempt to sort out acceptance of or hostility to the NRA on the

basis of large versus small business does not work; nor does capture theory, which assumes ipso facto business needs as the basis for regulatory
policy. The clearly defined positions of spokesmen for peak organizations
such as the Chamber of Commerce and the National Association of Manufacturers scarcely reflected the complex, disorganized, and contradictory quality of business reaction to New Deal policies. This varied from
section to section, industry to industry, and even within firms presumably supportive of planning. Reaction often depended on degree of technological innovation, profitability, even personal ideology.[4]

Differences between General Electric's Gerard Swope and Owen D.
Young illustrate the lack of unanimity in major firms, as GE's principals
divided on industrial policy. A revised Swope Plan was presented to the
Business and Advisory and Planning Council of the Commerce Department on November 1, 1933. Commerce and industry would organize into
self-governing units. Each trade association would elect an executive authority to carry out code provisions. Enforcement would be the responsibility of the Federal Trade Commission and/or the Department of Justice.
A peak association, a National Chamber of Commerce and Industry, an
enlarged Chamber of Commerce of the United States, would gather statistics and standardize products. A Board of Governors, made up of the
commerce secretary and "the highest type of businessmen," would act as
an arbiter in the enforcement process. In response to criticism, Swope
modified the structure by adding representatives of labor, transportation,
farm groups, the Federal Reserve, and the secretaries of labor, agriculture,
and treasury.[5]

Whereas Swope was an enthusiast of planning by trade groups, GE's
board chairman Owen D. Young viewed his colleague's plan as the forerunner of a corporate state. An advocate of bottom-up planning, or a
gradualist approach based on experience, Young challenged the revised
plan for trade association management of the economy as the basis for "a
separately organized economic government with power to coerce the political government." He could support an economic council set up by government and empowered to induce trade associations toward cooperative
activity, gather data and experience for a year, then suggest appropriate
legislation to Congress. But a National Chamber of Commerce and Industry, aimed at quick results, would threaten freedom of individual
action and foment a reaction against the idea of economic organization.
"However willingly the American people may accept an organized effort

like the NRA in time of disaster . . . they do it only as a matter of expediency, half heartedly as to principle, fearful lest it run into an overpowerful bureaucracy."

The NRA, as viewed by Young, originated as a relief measure to spread work and avoid the dole. Subsequently, it was enlarged to become a device for increased purchasing power through higher wages and to meliorate disastrous competition by suspension of antitrust. In the end, it threatened to become a permanent bureaucratically controlled program which would undercut the Constitution and the law.[6]

Increased business criticism of the Roosevelt program also found expression through the *Baltimore Sun*'s John W. Owens in June 1935, in a piece based on a weeklong series of off-the-record interviews in New York City with industrialists and financiers. A majority proved sympathetic to the NRA to the extent that it had tempered competitive excess in a deflationary cycle and steadied wages and hours of employment. A minority viewed the NRA as a mistake, and a majority was critical of its management under Hugh Johnson; most were convinced that it was doomed to fail as it proved incompatible with political democracy and capitalism. "Their judgment is that the NRA, with its scheme for control of production and for control of prices by the businessmen, and . . . for massing of . . . labor behind equally rigid wages-and-hours regulations, raised a wall directly in the path of free competition."[7]

Whereas General Electric's executives represented a capital-intensive sector of the economy under pressure from competitors, Sears, Roebuck's Robert E. Wood, spoke for a new breed of mass-market, low-cost retailers. When *Forbes Magazine* polled "men of affairs"—defined as industrialists, bankers, and mercantile, utility, and advertising executives—to discover those best qualified to offer the president guidance, Wood appeared on the list of twenty chosen for the encomium. Wood's attitudes also reflected a large segment of midwestern sentiment in the interwar years. His views on money and credit were decidedly expansionary. A xenophobe who advocated strict immigration control and who later on claimed that U.S. diplomacy was dominated by eastern bankers and Jewish financial interests, Wood nevertheless endorsed Cordell Hull's reciprocal trade efforts and supported barter arrangements to get rid of the agricultural surplus. His return to the Republican fold as the worst of the depression crisis lifted mirrored the shift in midwestern political opinion in the 1930s.[8]

Wood's support of the early Roosevelt program, symbolized by service on the Commerce Department's Business Advisory Council, can be explained in the context of his economic and business philosophy. Provision for monetary and credit expansion, social security, unemployment insurance, minimum wages, public works, housing, and enhancement of rural income comported with his views on the importance of expanded purchasing power. Further, he lauded the chief executive's exceptional tendency to "work for the benefit of the South and West, and not alone of the industrial East. He has established a balance of power."[9]

Yet early on, Wood signaled an independence of mind that eventually modified his initially favorable appraisal of the New Deal program. In concert with many business leaders, he deplored the price-fixing tendencies of the NRA codes as beneficial only to huge combinations such as U.S. Steel. His experience with the NRA Industrial Board convinced him that consumers would fare better under mass distribution and price-cutting policies instituted by Sears. Nor was he content with Section 7(a) or more generally with New Deal labor policy. In typically candid fashion, a memorandum dispatched to Roosevelt questioned "universal trade unionism" as a mechanism for the attainment of better wages and working conditions. Employees should be free to join or not to join a labor organization, and employers should not be coerced to sign shop agreements if they were not so inclined. He feared labor tyranny as much as that of capitalists and urged publicity for union expenditure and disclosure of the salaries of union officials. Wood also deplored the failure of the president and the business community to find common ground on budget balance, reduced taxes, and curtailment of Harry Hopkins's social philosophy. Our society, he argued, did not owe relief to loafers, incompetents, or aliens. But Wood's most bitter censure was reserved for Rexford Tugwell's address delivered at the Olympic Auditorium in Los Angeles on October 28, 1935.

Ever the lightning rod in the Roosevelt entourage, Tugwell recently had attended one of the so-called Moley dinners with "a lot of first-rank businessmen, putting to them the challenge which the depression presents, the necessity for the assurance of work . . . for reaching such an arrangement as will produce and distribute goods and get them into consumers' hands." Fifteen participants, among them Wendell L. Willkie, Tugwell observed, responded with "querulous complaints . . . about the lack of confidence which businessmen have in the present administration," specifically government disorganization, fiscal policy, and its antibusiness stance. "The discussion at the end degenerated into so many complaints about the attitude of the mob, as they called it, and the administration's responsiveness to it . . . that I took the occasion to wind up the discussion by saying . . . that what they were really afraid of was . . . the American people and the trend of their thinking."

Tugwell's October address assumed the form of a call to arms to statist liberals. It condemned "the well-stocked Tory citadels" that tended to prevail by the "very cohesiveness of inaction," and it invoked ideas suggested in his *Industrial Discipline and the Governmental Arts,* which judged that freedom of enterprise had been abridged only in traditional ways. Tugwell contemplated yardstick acquisitions by government, or federal entry into areas of enterprise dominated by monopoly pricing. Finally, equally ominous to some was his call for an alliance of "the great masses of our people who have been helped most by our policies and from whom we draw our strength—the farmers and workers."[10]

Under attack from within the Senate and by businessmen, Tugwell lost the contest for statist regulation of the business community through the device of a redesigned NRA, the battle being fought in the White House as he and Roosevelt handicapped the outcome of the *Schechter* case in May 1935. Upon agreement that the Supreme Court would soon decree the NRA unconstitutional based on a recent decision[11] on the ground of excessive transfer of legislative authority to the chief executive, Tugwell argued that the 1936 campaign should focus on a constitutional amendment designed to broaden national power over interstate commerce. This would sever conservative Democrats from the party and compel an ideological realignment. Southern reactionaries would join with GOP conservatives and the Chamber of Commerce, while Roosevelt would cement a new Democracy based on a farmer-labor coalition. The time had come, Tugwell argued, to sort out the sheep from the goats, as he put it, and shed from "our side" the likes of Senator Josiah W. Bailey of North Carolina, Virginia's Harry F. Byrd, Thomas P. Gore of Oklahoma, and Alfred E. Smith. Reactionaries of this ilk were "more dangerous inside than they would be outside." A New Deal Democratic Party would seek expanded federal authority to embrace "anything which affects the stream of commerce."

Tugwell and Harry Hopkins found the president in his study on May 31. With the *Schechter* decision, Roosevelt wanted a new law that limited hours and provide minimum wages for labor; perhaps, too, it would authorize trade groups to make voluntary rules that regulated standards of competition. Tugwell noted the growth of irreconcilable differences with Roosevelt, for he desired more decisive action in the shape of Mordecai Ezekiel's Industrial Adjustment Act, modeled on the Agricultural Adjustment Administration.

Ezekiel, an economic adviser to Henry A. Wallace, had come up with a scheme later published as *$2,500 a Year: From Scarcity to Abundance*. This proposed that the federal government underwrite expanded output and when necessary purchase and warehouse the inevitable surpluses, an industrial version of the ever-normal granary, normally applied to farm output. Government-owned enterprises would be introduced, if needed, to compel price competition in the private sector. Benefit payments to cooperators, actually tax rebates along the lines of Agricultural Adjustment Administration payments to farmer-participants, would retain voluntarist principles and would be financed by taxes on the entire industry, leaving outsiders to the mercies of the market. Government-business contracts would incorporate reduced prices, increased payroll levels, and an annual minimum income for workers of $2,500 achieved in the span of a few years as a stimulus to demand. Like most such proposals, Ezekiel's was based on the belief that the market economy no longer functioned in a regime of fixed prices, oligopoly, and trade association dominance.[12]

Roosevelt refused to commit to a scheme which might well eventuate in direct government intrusion into the decision-making process of business and lead to huge costs incurred for the purchase of surplus output. Entering the fray, Harry Hopkins agreed with the president that legislation could be set up to regulate basic industries on a piecemeal basis. When Felix Frankfurter joined the group, he endorsed the Roosevelt-Hopkins approach. Tugwell lamented "we have lost many of our gains and . . . nobody is in a position to get any of them back." At a cabinet meeting on June 5, 1935, with Tugwell in attendance for Henry A. Wallace, Roosevelt announced the NRA's continuance—as a record-keeping shell. For all practical purposes the NRA had ended. The Roosevelt program had reverted, as Tugwell put it, to the unsatisfactory "one-thing-at-a-time" method.

Tugwell attributed the loss of his theory of overhead economic management to the zealotry of the "old man" on the Supreme Court, "Isaiah," as Roosevelt referred to Louis D. Brandeis, the antediluvian apostle of the cult of littleness, or, conversely "the horrors of bigness." (Tugwell also resented the transmission of these views into the White House by Felix Frankfurter and his acolytes.) Overhead economic management, Brandeis related to Milo Perkins, assistant secretary of agriculture, immediately after the unanimous *Schechter* decision, required superhuman abilities and made tyrants of little men in minor posts, stifled creativity, and undermined economic democracy best promoted at the community level. While Brandeisianism served as the basis for Tugwell's and Moley's subsequent explanation of abandonment of the planning concept, they had also lost out to the growing belief that the NRA hindered economic recovery.

Roosevelt's frequent expression of his wish for a revised NRA does not mitigate the fact that it lacked a business constituency. Nor was the publication of the Brookings Institution's study promising for NRA renewal, with its conclusion that "in trying to raise the real purchasing power of the nation by boosting costs and prices the NRA put the cart before the horse." In the event, at the close of 1935 Treasury reported a general improvement in consumption and producer goods such as autos, food, textiles, iron and steel, and textiles, also that payrolls reached satisfactory levels. And it predicted continued improvement in 1936.[13]

The NRA was not a point of entry to a cartelist regime or to national planning; in reality the so-called corporate commonwealth was stillborn. Only the petroleum industry was rationalized, as a result of a unique set of circumstances. These included confinement of crude output to a handful of states, principally Texas; international controls on crude withdrawal by informal arrangements commencing with the "As-Is" agreement of 1928, reached by Standard of New Jersey, Shell, and Anglo-Persian; Gulf Coast pricing, an arrangement based on Gulf Coast prices, which prevented price-cutting worldwide; expanded consumption, especially in the United States, a result of increased automobile registrations and usage; technological improvements that kept prices low; an emergent conservation movement based on the knowledge that petroleum is a limited resource; and the possibility of shortages in the event of war. Such circumstances were not replicated elsewhere.[14]

A glut in crude output that began with the opening of Oklahoma's Seminole Field in 1927, followed in late 1930 by the discovery of vast new fields in east Texas, resulted in a disastrous drop in crude prices from 90 cents to 10 cents a barrel. Passage of the National Industrial Recovery Act exposed a basic tension between the majors, represented by the American Petroleum Institute, and the independents, most represented through the Independent Producers Association of America, which favored federal price-fixing under the NRA. Whereas the independents, reliant on crude output and more vulnerable to short-term market fluctuation, sought a price umbrella, the better-financed and integrated majors feared federal price-fixing as a first step toward public utility status. This was not an unrealistic assumption in light of increased awareness of the limited supply over the long term in the face of navy reliance on petroleum. Fear of federal control heightened with appointment of Interior Secretary Harold Ickes as petroleum administrator on August 29, 1933.

A compromise based on state control of output satisfied both the majors and the independents. Excess output of crude based on the rule of capture or unlimited withdrawal was replaced by state agency proration or output control through limits placed on oil shipments, a procedure dominated by the Texas Railroad Commission subsequent to the East Texas discovery. This device was made viable by the concentration of the major fields in a handful of states, which enabled state controls to be federalized upon passage of the Connally Act (1935). State proration was enforced by federal boards through certificates of clearance for interstate oil shipments since these proscribed shipments of "hot oil" in excess of state-mandated quotas. In the process the Texas Railroad Commission, guided in setting output quotas by forecasts of demand by the Bureau of Mines, met independents' needs through a mechanism that protected their high-cost output from market pricing. This system, put into place by the Interstate Oil Compact of 1935 and based on quotas, price maintenance, and shelter of high-cost producers, further aided by import controls, ordered the domestic market and remained in place until 1972.[15]

Elsewhere the NRA had no measurable impact on business rationalization. Firms at the forefront of technological advance were hampered by the codes, industries in decline were stabilized only temporarily, and bitterly competitive industries remained competitive. Several illustrations suffice to support this generalization. In the case of automobile tires, bitter competition among the industry's dominant firms, between the industry leaders and medium to small firms, and at the retail level precluded practical code agreements. With the NRA ineffective, and Goodyear, Goodrich, and U.S. Rubber opposed to price controls in the tire-manufacturing code, patterns that emerged in the 1920s remained unaltered: domination by large manufacturers, code violations, and price warfare at the retail or replacement level led by Sears, Roebuck and other mass retailers.[16]

There is scant evidence, if any, that automobile producers, the nation's principal industry, sought government intervention. Here the market was permitted to operate unimpeded and unaided. Three producers dominated the market—Ford, General Motors, and Chrysler—responsible for 75 percent of production. After a steep decline through early 1933, the industry recovered, and by 1937 employment and total wages approximated 1929 levels, with production slightly lower at 4,809,000 units.

Under pressure from NRA administrator Hugh Johnson and Roosevelt, the industry leaders (Henry Ford excepted) went through the motions and submitted a code that effectively exempted automobile manufacturers from Section 7(a). Beyond fear of industrial unionism, the heads of the nation's leading industry exhibited either hostility (Ford) or indifference to the Recovery Act, convinced that demand followed from a general recovery and not the price of automobiles.[17] GM's Alfred P. Sloan Jr. noted after *Schechter:* "I do not think the NRA principle is practical or desirable. . . . Now that things are getting better, it would be nothing short of a crime to go back and agitate the NRA scheme of things, which was a complete failure. . . . The sooner we get government out of business . . . the better off the community will be."[18]

Whereas newer, profitable industries such as chemicals and aircraft also opposed federal intervention,[19] bituminous coal proved another matter. Fragmented and demoralized bituminous producers turned to government and John L. Lewis's United Mine Workers for a modicum of price stability. In the year 1929 the industry suffered a net loss of over $11 million; in 1930, $42 million. From a peak of 704,000 wage earners in 1924, employment declined to 293,000 in June 1933; and those still employed were working short hours and an average of less than half a year. With wages at 60 to 65 percent of production cost, unionized, high-cost northern, Central Field operators, along with Lewis, sought government regulation and regional price-fixing under the NRA. Together, Roosevelt, Lewis, and the Central Field group fashioned a coal code (October 2, 1933) administered by five regional authorities delegated the task of maintaining a "fair market price" and reducing North-South wage differentials, essential to price maintenance. Mines in operation soon increased by 85,000, wages by 70 percent, and annual wages from $677 to nearly $1,100.

Coal prices stabilized briefly, and wages and working conditions improved. But by the winter of 1934–35, cooperation evaporated under challenge by the NRA's Consumers' Advisory Board, which opposed price-fixing and by southern producers and small operators who undercut pricing arrangements.

The two Guffey Acts, Guffey-Snyder (1935) and Guffey-Vinson (1937), symbolized a return to the original purpose of national planning for so-called sick industries, yet they proved unable to stabilize bituminous coal. The work again of Lewis and the Central Field operators, the Guffey Acts quickly broke down under litigation and the resistance of southern non-union, low-cost operators. Also involved were technical problems such as code loopholes, inability to gauge relative market value of differing grades and sizes of coal, and freight differentials; continued overcapacity driven by a price umbrella; and the incapacity of agencies created to enforce the Guffey Acts. Over the long run, neither industrial self-government nor government intervention could overcome deep structural problems and the availability of energy alternatives such as petroleum, waterpower, and natural gas.[20]

As in the instance of bituminous coal, the cotton textile industry, severely depressed and marked by excess capacity, foreign competition, and the emergence of alternatives, particularly rayon, initially supported government stabilization under the NRA. This typified unprofitable industries in decline, as did the subsequent split within the textile industry between more mechanized, nonunion, low-cost southern mills and high-cost, unionized northern firms.[21] But unlike bituminous coal, the mid-1920s collapse in textile profitability led to the creation of an effective industrywide trade group, the Cotton-Textile Institute. Unable to stabilize prices in the face of excess output or to maintain profitability under Herbert Hoover's vague associationalist doctrine, the CTI with the coming of the depression moved toward acceptance of a substantial degree of government authority.

Under the NRA, the Cotton-Textile Institute served as the industry's Code Authority. It enforced production limits under the 40–40 arrangement (two forty-hour shifts as opposed to twenty-four-hour operation), child-labor restrictions (no one to be employed under sixteen years of age), and a minimum wage of $12 per week in the South and $13 per week in the New England mills in order to narrow the traditional regional wage differential. Unlike bituminous coal, the textile industry enjoyed some cohesion under an umbrella organization controlled by producers, with the code enforced by the CTI. This arrangement, which offered the potential of a cartel regime, disintegrated under an assortment of pressures. The Consumers' Advisory Board and Leon Henderson and Victor von Szeliski at the NRA's Research and Planning Division challenged price-fixing on the ground that price and production controls hampered recovery. There emerged also intraindustry objections to stifling controls and management's loss of autonomy, inability to resolve the issue of the cotton-processing tax under AAA that furthered the competitive advantage of rayon, continued overproduction, the belief of southern mill owners that the Cotton Textile Code tilted toward the northern operators in the shape of equalized labor costs, large-scale failure to achieve profitability, and management's unwillingness to countenance the purport of Section 7(a).[22]

The NRA scarcely impacted long-term industrial trends. Whereas the New Deal program cushioned the declining natural resource industries, it could not generate a level of investment needed to employ new entries into the job market or to generate a large-scale increment to purchasing power. Where large, integrated companies dominated—automobiles, petroleum, chemicals, and food processing—profitable operations resumed by mid-decade as a result of efficiencies in operation, product development and differentiation, and in some areas renewed and expanded consumer demand. Indeed, overall, if finance, transport, and public utilities, especially hard-hit areas, are excluded, manufactures realized annual average corporate profits for 1936–37 at only 9 percent less than the average for 1923–29, or $3.837 billion (1936–37) against $4.213 billion (1923–29). For all manufacturing corporations, rate of return from operations of 8.39 percent in 1936 equaled that of 1929, and return on total equity in 1936–37 exceeded that of 1926–28. Other statistics support the argument for a recovery in manufactures to 1929 or predepression levels. Employment of nonproduction employees (1,290,037 in 1929 and 1,217,171 in 1937) and production and related workers (8,369,705 in 1929 and 8,569,231 in 1937) had returned to predepression levels; yet unemployment remained high as industry failed to absorb new entries into the workplace, resulting in downward wage pressures of 10 percent.[23]

Structural unemployment is explained by industry's productivity growth and a secular shift from older, heavy manufacturing industries—agriculture, mining, textiles, iron, and steel—that traditionally employed unskilled labor en masse to newer technologies that required less labor for their output. By the 1920s an emergent and affluent middle class enjoyed higher incomes and, spurred by advertising and consumerism, responded to newer products such as automobiles, chemicals, housing, and processed foods. In normal circumstances these newer industries would displace traditional employers in response to a shift in consumer appetites. But the financial collapse interrupted the process at an early stage. Absent massive public investment, full recovery in the 1930s depended on private-sector finance of new technologies in the process of displacing the old industrial order. Here business uncertainty with respect to future profitability curtailed investment, demand, and employment.

There were other related problems. Capital requirements in the newer industries were lower than those of the basic industries associated with late nineteenth-century capitalism. Industries that took up the employment slack in the post–World War II era—government, services, and communications—did not yet make a major impact. Finally, industry proved unable to absorb surplus agricultural labor as the farm sector moved into the era of mechanized and scientific agriculture. Small farms, while perhaps socially desirable, had become uneconomic, a situation which lessened the need for farm labor. The net result was secular stagnation, a problem compounded by the financial collapse, expressed in human terms as chronic unemployment.[24]

As early as July 1933, while still associated with the NRA, Alexander Sachs warned Roosevelt of a low-level recovery based on productivity growth. With 100 units produced by 2.3 billion man-hours per month in 1920 as a base, by early 1933 it required only 1.33 billion man-hours per month to turn out the same volume of output. This growth in productivity resulted in lower employment, failed purchasing power, and excess plant capitalized long-term at a high level of fixed cost, with the burden of corporate retrenchment falling on wages and employment. At the same time, in view of fixed interest charges and a decline in purchasing power, corporations found no respite. Recovery hinged on reinvigorated capital markets and abandonment of punitive antibusiness policies embodied in the Public Utilities Holding Company Act of 1935, the excess-profits tax, the current munitions makers inquiry, and uneconomic government expenditure that undermined capital markets.[25]

Sachs offered Roosevelt indicative planning based on business-government partnership through the device of nonpartisan regulatory boards that would integrate public- and private-sector investment while bringing private utilities under social control.[26] Potentially one of the most imaginative proposals made for stimulus to private investment and coordinated public- and private-sector management of industries clothed with a public interest, essentially utilities, housing, and railroads—large employers and potential consumers of idle capital—it was doomed by increased hostility to the business sector within the Roosevelt administration.[27]

Sachs desired railroad rehabilitation through salvage of the nation's Class I carriers and abandonment of insolvent carriers, all currently supported by RFC lending aimed at liquefying bank and insurance portfolios, a practice which simply maintained bankrupts. Government financial assistance to Class I railroads would induce their modernization, serving in turn as a stimulus to the steel industry. A leasing authority would finance the program. When Roosevelt turned the Sachs proposal over to Joseph Eastman, federal coordinator of railroad transportation under the Emergency Transportation Act of 1933, Eastman balked. Railroads remained a sick industry. Roosevelt never consented to forced consolidation.[28]

Analysis of Sachs's proposed southeastern power pool, designed to resolve the Commonwealth & Southern–Tennessee Valley Authority controversy, illuminates his growing critique of the New Deal's shortcomings as well the private-sector attack on New Deal economic policies beyond the usual portrayal of capitalists' hatred for the squire of Hyde Park. Sachs interceded with Roosevelt in the David E. Lilienthal–Wendell L. Willkie imbroglio on the basis of what he considered uneconomic public-sector spending. Public expenditure that duplicated electric power in areas where adequate power existed, in this instance the projected TVA service area, resulted in investors discounting C&S bonds. The outcome nationwide was curtailed expenditure by private-sector utilities for new construction, averaging a current $100 plus million annually as opposed to some $800 million in the 1920s. If the multiplier were to prove effective, according to Sachs, public expenditure must not inhibit private-sector investment lest it become limited in its impact.

It is misguided to categorize Sachs's role in the TVA-C&S controversy, as did Lilienthal, as simply "a scheme to limit TVA and municipal power expansion." Sachs did not offer a direct challenge to the Norris-Lilienthal-Roosevelt vision of a Tennessee–lower Mississippi Valley experiment

intended to bring a mixed economy to one of the nation's most impoverished regions and to serve as a model for economic development in the
Pacific Northwest. Rather, he proposed a mixed public- and private-
sector approach to management and development of regional electric
power modeled on the British grid system as a stimulus to utilities investment. Duplication of existing private-sector facilities by a federally subsidized TVA, Sachs held, would deter the investment potential of private
utility companies. This meant at worst a net loss to the economy of an
annual $800 million in private utility expenditure as opposed to a frac-
tion of that amount in proposed government expenditure for public
power, or at best a trade-off in total capital investment.[29]

The Tennessee Valley controversy, like the great river, originated with a
number of tributaries. These included Roosevelt's belief that Wall Street
dominance of the private utilities industry, which he associated with
watered stock issued by an unneeded layer of holding companies in the
1920s, created an environment of excess profits funneled upward to bankers
and investors at the top of the securities pyramid at the expense of consumers. Also at stake was Roosevelt's conviction that a durable recovery
depended on a mixed economy in impoverished regions. Likely, too, given
his New York experience, he suspected that state regulatory agencies were
frequently subject to capture by those interests they regulated and in any
event could not effectively control utilities that crossed state lines when
packaged into large units by interstate holding companies.

Equally central to the shape of TVA was Senator George W. Norris's gas
and waterworks socialism, the belief that municipally owned systems, fed
by federally operated multipurpose dams, would generate power at lower
cost than profit-making utilities for the benefit of impoverished ruralites
and small towns in a number of the country's regions. Also basic to the
public-power approach was Roosevelt's and Lilienthal's embrace of a
multitude of social and economic functions that would bring additional
benefits to the rural South, namely, cheap water transport, education in
better farming practices, school and health services, and other programs
designed to eliminate poverty.[30]

The Tennessee Valley Authority, legislated on May 18, 1933, served as the
basis for a broad design that fitted well Roosevelt's concept of economic
balance based on regional planning. The act provided that electric power
generated at Muscle Shoals and elsewhere in the region under agency management and distribution would effect flood control, reforestation, indus-

trial development and employment, and improved navigation. Essential to these ends was federal capital investment for generation and distribution of electricity at low cost, the most controversial feature of TVA's early history.[31]

Under the terms of the statute, power produced by the authority would serve as a yardstick for measurement of the relative costs of public and private generation of electrical energy. Public-power advocates were convinced that TVA, like Canada's Ontario Power, would demonstrate the excessive charges levied by the private utilities. State-chartered public agencies in the TVA service area would receive preference in the purchase and sale of power under contracts that called for self-liquidation of construction cost of distribution systems and surpluses to be applied to reduced rates. While power could be sold to private utilities for resale, the authority also could build transmission lines to farms and smaller communities not serviced by the private sector.[32]

The three-member TVA board declared its intent to provide electricity for the entire drainage area of the valley, including its larger municipalities, and beyond the region if required, a program assigned to Lilienthal, one of its directors. Lilienthal pursued with a near-religious and unbureaucratic passion the Section 11 mandate that public power "shall be considered primarily for the benefit of the people of the section as a whole and particularly its domestic and rural consumers . . . [so] as to encourage increased domestic and rural uses of electricity." A Wisconsin public-power Progressive, Lilienthal, like Roosevelt, regarded private-sector utilities as parasitical and possessed of no essential role in this great undertaking. Holding companies were "tapeworms sucking the nourishment out of the operating companies," and he announced a flat rate of $1.50 per month for small users (50 kilowatts) as opposed to $2.58 charged by the Commonwealth & Southern companies in Alabama and Georgia.[33]

Public-power Progressives considered private-sector control and operation of huge regional power networks as dominated by investment bankers who mulcted operating companies and consumers through various devices: watered stock, profits funneled upward to management, and the levy of excessive charges on the operating companies by so-called service companies. With this situation brought to light by congressional investigations, Lilienthal, Norris, and other champions of public power, Roosevelt included, felt justified in their crusade for publicly owned regional networks operated by quasi-governmental boards in the public interest. The latter would give preference in sales at the bus bars, where power was converted for resale, to municipally owned operating companies as well as rural electric cooperatives subsidized by the Public Works Administration or the Rural Electrification Administration, a program intended to bring power to underserved ruralites.

Unfortunately, at least from Lilienthal's perspective, with TVA unprepared to distribute power on its own at this stage, he was compelled to negotiate with the equally tough-minded Wendell L. Willkie, president of Commonwealth & Southern, which dominated the area. There was another difficulty. Willkie could well argue that C&S, like several other holding companies formed in the 1920s, served a perfectly legitimate purpose by meeting capital needs of operating utilities that could no longer afford the technology developed for integrated networks. It was also true that many were formed by engineers and managerial types, not investment bankers. Indeed, relatively pristine as holding companies went, C&S did not neatly fit Lilienthal's characterization once it was reorganized in 1929 and geared to production rather than the financial artifices associated with holding companies.

With Wilson Dam at Muscle Shoals alone capable of power output at the time, the adversaries managed a truce on January 4, 1934, when a contract was signed for the sale of certain C&S properties. C&S also agreed to purchase surplus TVA power, and TVA agreed to refrain from direct competition in the C&S service area. Since the contract ran either for five years or until the Norris Dam was capable of power output, expected completion of that dam in 1936 brought the conflict to a head. Willkie wanted a long-term contract extension, and Lilienthal opposed it.

In the interim the picture was complicated when a group of Alabama Power preferred stockholders sought to enjoin the sale of properties to TVA and challenged PWA grants and loans to municipalities for the construction of competing systems, the basis for the *Ashwander* case. On February 17, 1936, the Supreme Court affirmed the right of the authority to sell Wilson Dam power and to purchase the properties it had contracted for, yet it avoided the issue of TVA's constitutionality. There ensued the *Nineteen Power Companies* suit, which challenged TVA's constitutionality, with C&S subsidiaries in the lead.

As these suits wended their way through the judicial system, Willkie emerged as a combative spokesman for private property. The public authority, he claimed, capable of writing off costs of dams for power output to flood control and navigation, enjoyed unfair advantage. According to Willkie, TVA paid lower taxes to localities and could secure substantially lower interest rates for its bonds thanks to government backing. (From Lilienthal's perspective, such a claim sustained the argument for lower-cost public power.) Privately, Willkie complained of a plan on the part of Washington intellectuals to "Sovietize" the United States by the device of public ownership. In a more restrained address before the U.S. Chamber of Commerce, Willkie attributed the lag in economic recovery to government hostility toward business. And with passage of the Public Utilities Holding Company Act of 1935, which empowered the Securities Exchange Commission to dissolve holding companies which owned operating utilities that were not interconnected, the so-called death sentence, he refused to register C&S with the SEC. He pursued instead a constitutional challenge in the courts.[34]

At this juncture Sachs proposed a compromise in the shape of a Southeastern Power Pool. In light of the failure of planning under an overreaching National Recovery Administration and the *Schechter* decision's claim of excessive delegation of power and a lack of standards, Sachs suggested indicative planning in the form of a blend of public and private power managed by a broadly representative quasi-public board endowed with clearly specified authority. While he conceded to Roosevelt the need for lower power rates and the predepression practice of overvalued property as the basis for reproduction cost theory, it made no sense to use limited federal resources to duplicate facilities that were on hand.[35]

Following a meeting with the president at the White House in late February 1936, Sachs presented the case for responsible public utility holding companies as opposed to an environment of "political attack and struggle." With FDR's consent Sachs consulted with executives associated with private utilities, Willkie included, as well as James Landis, chairman of the Securities and Exchange Commission. The holding company chiefs proposed power pools that blended public and private facilities. Landis and Sachs agreed that strict enforcement of the Holding Company Act's Section 11, the death sentence clause which limited tiers devised by holding companies, would inevitably be followed by a reconsolidation as the criteria would prove too negative for a rational restructuring of the industry.[36]

For all practical purposes, Sachs put on the table a concrete business-government program of stimulus to investment in the nation's infrastructure. Perpetually in the background and deeply involved in these events, the framing of the Holding Company Act included, Felix Frankfurter soon countered by massaging Roosevelt's anti–Wall Street bias. "A friend of mine who sits on the board of a financial concern with very large utility holdings reports, in deepest confidence [Roosevelt delighted in confidential reports emanating from the Street], the following comments made by their counsel, John Foster Dulles," to the effect that SEC litigation against Electric Bond and Share would likely be very prolonged and "might never reach the Supreme Court on the basis of the present [Holding Company] Act." In a decisive thrust Frankfurter reminded Roosevelt of the SEC's reputation under Landis for lenience in its relationship with large economic units.

The issues clearly drawn, Roosevelt refused to junk the public-power school of thought, partially from deep-seated hostility toward holding companies, also because of his desire to retain the political support of the anti–big business, anti–Wall Street midwestern Republican Progressives in the upcoming 1936 presidential contest. In reality, most of the holding companies that survived the crash no longer represented the model Roosevelt had fought as governor of New York.[37]

As Willkie and Lilienthal disputed the terms of renewal of their contract—Willkie asked that "a mutually agreeable period of territorial integrity and protection be given to the balance of the territory in which the company operates"; Lilienthal riposted that such proviso exceeded the terms of the original agreement—Sachs telegraphed Roosevelt that he had completed a plan for a power pool and model grid in pursuance of his instructions. The plan, Sachs anticipated, would promote reemployment "in industries awaiting . . . constructive stimulus." When Roosevelt and Willkie conferred on May 20, Roosevelt promised "a possible solution of the relationship between the private utilities and the Government." In a letter to the president the next day, Willkie maintained that as long as unfair public competition continued, the private utilities, "fighting for their lives," found themselves compelled to litigate, a hedge vital to the economic interests of his firm.[38]

In the summer of 1936, the presidential election at hand, Roosevelt authorized Sachs; Basil Manly, vice chairman of the Federal Power Commission; and Louis B. Wehle, a private attorney, to formulate a satisfactory plan. Manly, inclined toward public power, fearful of capture by the utilities, suggested that Sachs and Wehle prepare a draft proposal for a public utility trust controlled by the federal government, capable of leasing transmission lines from the present owners. It would control wholesale transmission and power sales to the public under a uniform rate schedule. This structure, or regional power pool, would allow TVA and private utilities to own and operate generating plants and avoid the difficult valuation issue. At the same time, this model could be applied to the proposed Bonneville bill, with the provision that public facilities provide the bulk of power generated in the Pacific Northwest. At a meeting with Sachs in July, J. P. Morgan's Russell C. Leffingwell, Thomas Lamont, George Whitney, and Henry P. Davison, concurred.[39]

Sachs offered the president a preliminary plan for a Southeastern Power Pool, based on interconnection, coordination, and allocation of credits and debits modeled on the British grid which provided for pooling between public and private utilities. Established by the Electricity Supply Act, a Central Electricity Board served as a public entity organized and administered by engineers and managers independent of the civil service. Capable of raising its own funds by sale of nonvoting securities, the power pool could engage in planning and construction, maintain the public-private status quo, and integrate business and public management freed of political interference.[40]

The power pool plan would encompass a region with a 250-mile radius, part or all of twelve states, with the eleven TVA dams expected to be completed by 1943 a component of the pool. It promised economies of scale, avoidance of duplication, savings to consumers, rural electrification, and security to investors, as well as the ability of C&S to refund high-interest bonds. The pool, administered by a public entity under the oversight of the Federal Power Commission, would be initiated by a long-term contract between C&S and TVA. Generating facilities, transmission lines, and substations would deliver energy to wholesale load centers for resale to pool members; and charges to retail customers would be regulated by state and federal agencies. The formula would apply as well to the Bonneville area and other valley development programs.

Long-term leases would provide stability for the private sector. Alternatively, compensation for acquisition of private facilities would be determined on the basis of investment value administered as a going concern or market value, a principle to be followed by municipalities seeking to acquire existing private distribution systems. Before a member of the pool would be afforded another's market, the applicant would be required to demonstrate public benefit by such acquisition, in which case compensation would be determined by the regulatory body or arbitration. Sachs also challenged PWA loans at below-market interest that subsidized municipal plants as well as TVA's threat of forced sales of private entities.[41]

The Sachs proposal prompted Roosevelt's call for a September 30 White House meeting of utility executives, federal agencies, engineers, and economists. The president cited a remarkable degree of agreement on the cooperative pooling proposal that had the potential for lowered costs and utility rates.[42] The gathering included representatives of government administrative bodies: Frank McNinch, the FPC chairman; Basil Manly, vice chairman; Frederic Delano, the National Resources Committee; Morris L. Cooke, charged with the Rural Electrification Administration; and representing TVA, Arthur E. Morgan, chairman, and Lilienthal; representatives of private utilities, including Willkie; and of industry and banking, GE's Owen D. Young and J. P. Morgan's Thomas W. Lamont. Sachs and Wehle also attended.

Roosevelt suggested a piecemeal approach to the problem at hand, one that secured "the benefits of pooling through cooperative arrangements between governmental agencies concerned with power and the private utility industry." This assignment would be given to the Federal Power Commission. Lilienthal countered that the TVA had already amassed the requisite staff and data. Sachs and Wehle supported the president's proposal on the ground that the Holding Company Act vested jurisdiction over interconnection in the FPC. Roosevelt turned to McNinch and Manly: "You have the facilities and the space for carrying out these duties." More immediately, given the imminent expiry of the TVA-C&S contract, FDR designated Wehle as contract arbitrator for institution of the power pool, the concept to serve as a model for joint government–private-sector power development.[43]

The proposed Southeastern Power Pool for a blend of public and private financing of utilities under a government board foundered on the issue of public control. While the proposed agreement called for mutual confidence between the parties, Cooke, long engaged in conflict with the holding companies, claimed that fair value and compensation, essential to the Sachs plan, promised lengthy and acrimonious litigation, which played into the hands of the utilities. Further, the utility board was easily subject to capture. Also compelling, the aging apostle of public power, Nebraska's Norris, dispatched a passionate appeal to the president in which he observed that "these negotiations are going on with our enemies. They are trying to reach an agreement with the Commonwealth and Southern, an outfit you know would destroy you in a moment, if they had the power." There followed an indictment of C&S and the cost of litigation inflicted on TVA, the claim that Willkie violated the terms of the 1934 contract, also that Wehle, appointed by Roosevelt to mediate, was under the influence of C&S. "I agree with you. Don't worry," the president promised.[44]

Conscious of the denouement, Willkie dispatched a letter to Roosevelt, which contained a statement written on September 30, 1936, but withdrawn because of the presidential contest. While supportive of the Sachs plan, the C&S head insisted that unfair TVA competition was the nub of the problem. "We can survive under either regulation or competition, but we cannot survive regulated as we are against a subsidized unregulated competitor." Willkie insisted on government purchase at a fair price or freedom to operate in an environment free of invasion by government agencies.[45]

The matter closed on January 25, 1937, with Roosevelt's dispatch of a letter drafted by Lilienthal which advised the participants that a sweeping preliminary injunction by Judge John J. Gore in the *Nineteen Power Companies* suit precluded further negotiation of the power pool proposal. Sachs countered that the court proceedings were well known to all participants from the beginning and pointed to Willkie's expressed willingness to defer the suit in return for TVA discontinuance of its policy of duplication of C&S facilities, a proposal refused by Lilienthal.

Sachs denied involvement in any effort to compromise the essential elements of Roosevelt's power program. Rather, he explained to the president, he had participated in the previous year's negotiations as "an exponent of economic planning under the aegis of federal authority." His proposals were exploratory and modeled on British and Swedish experience. This included the principles of equality of treatment on property account in the taking of privately owned utilities by municipalities, fixing of fair investment value in such takings, uniformity in accounting, and removal of uncertainty for the private sector. Roosevelt suggested, dismissively, that he take the issue to a new committee headed by Frederick Delano and Interior Secretary Ickes, assigned responsibility for a national power policy.[46]

Effectively, Lilienthal, who disapproved of holding companies in light of their past record, was determined to sell TVA power to municipalities and to bar C&S, as he saw it, from the exercise of monopoly power in the region. Willkie felt obligated to protect C&S from unfair competition and expropriation in its traditional territory by resort to litigation.[47]

Sachs's effort at indicative planning through coordinated public-private investment went by the boards. Whether or not a power board was subject to capture or offered a viable route out of the depression as opposed to the Frankfurter-Corcoran anti–big business philosophy, is open to speculation—though it needs to be observed that Thomas Corcoran's agenda proved unproductive. Roosevelt, never enamored of the private utilities, was now committed to the view of public-power advocates that regional resource development should be undertaken exclusively by the federal government.

The stage was set for two conflicting methods of achieving reemployment and a recovery. Business confidence theory held that anti-business attitudes fostered by a new group of advisers, the protégés of Felix Frankfurter, manifested in the original Securities Act, the Public Utilities Holding Company Act, and excessively high taxes on industry, retarded investment and recovery. The National Resources Committee, on the other hand, was already in the process of offering the president an alternative based on multipurpose regional planning under the management of public authorities. Following the 1937–38 downturn, the National Resources Planning Board, successor to the NRC, presented Roosevelt with a plan for a developmental economy and a welfare state based considerably on European practice.

8 | TRADE RECIPROCITY OR THE
LAND USED AS CONCEALED DOLE

ROM A MACROECONOMIC POINT of view, "the effect of the agricultural depression on the level of aggregate activity in the United States . . . appears to have been small" compared with the deflationary impact of the international currency crisis of 1931.[1] Then again, in terms of rural poverty and national income, the agricultural depression loomed large. The structure of national income in the interwar years showed a marked level of disparity between those employed in manufacturing, or 20.7 percent of the national total and less than half, 9.5 percent, for agriculture. Median income of families for 1935–36 was $1,230 for New England, $1,260 in the north central area, $960 in the South, $1,040 in the mountain and plains states, and $1,335 in the Pacific states. Family income disparities appeared within a region when urban-industrial centers were compared with rural areas.

Intermediate and short-term trends exacerbated the situation that confronted commodities producers. Europe's need to conserve hard currencies, the Ottawa agreements aimed at empire self-sufficiency, then the capture of Eastern Europe, Scandinavia, and Latin America for the sterling bloc, cut off traditional outlets for U.S. exports, principally wheat and cotton, exacerbating commodities price declines. Wheat exports fell from a peak of 280 million bushels in 1920, when Europe had not yet recovered from the recent conflict, to a range of 80 to 96 million in the years 1927–31 and a low of 2 to 17 million bushels in the mid-1930s. Wheat prices declined from $1.30 per bushel (July 1929) to 48 cents (July 1932). Cotton exports fell less precipitously in these years, yet producers faced newly emergent foreign competition in the world market, and prices fell by half between 1929 and 1932.

Modern technology and the use of hybridized seeds and fertilizers compounded the problem of evaporated overseas outlets. Millions of small farmers, tenants, and laborers were made redundant by increased output per acre and reduced demand for labor. At the same time, small-scale entrepreneurs could not afford the required investment in land and machinery.[2]

Manufacturing employment, a traditional outlet, could not absorb marginalized farmers and unneeded farm labor. Factory employment stagnated in the interwar decades: 10.5 million were employed in 1920; the number declined in the postwar depression, stabilized at 9.5 to 10.5 million in the years 1923–29, then contracted to a low of 6.8 million in 1932. Industrial employment gradually returned to the 1920 figure only in the late 1930s. These developments served as background to a debate on the best route to agricultural recovery, with internationalists pitted against corporatists bent on autarky.[3]

Several alternatives for remediation of the farm depression emerged: maintenance of inefficient and heavily subsidized small operators "as a kind of concealed dole," a policy adopted in industrialized countries, especially Europe; or in the case of the United States, the purchase of marginal land by the federal government accompanied by a shift of impoverished ruralites to self-sustaining and unproductive homesteads, a potentially expensive scheme favored by Department of Agriculture planners and undertaken by the Resettlement Administration, later by the Farm Security Administration. Wilsonian antistatists favored negotiation of reciprocal trade agreements intended to reopen overseas outlets. Then again, economic nationalists, led by George N. Peek, accepted autarkic behavior as the norm and favored resort to barter and dumping of the surplus in the world market.

Domestic allotment, the most controversial feature of the Agricultural Adjustment Act of May 12, 1933, originated with the premise that in the absence of urban employment opportunities or adequate overseas outlets for their surplus output, agrarians needed to be sustained by acreage controls tailored to domestic demand. Owners would be compensated by payments for curtailed production. Yet over the long term, rationalized land use meant elimination of marginal producers—some 50 percent of farmers—from the land,[4] as the other half produced 89 percent of farm products that entered the market and could easily produce the balance and thereby attain a satisfactory level of farm income. This process, cushioned by subsidies, culminated with industrialization of farm life. In the interim a land-purchase program inaugurated on a small scale in December 1933, transferred to Tugwell's Resettlement Administration, then to the Farm Security Administration, provided minimal relief but met fierce resistance by conservative legislators and commercial farmers.[5]

Antistatists maintained that reliance on acreage limitation under the Agricultural Adjustment Administration portended a permanent bureaucracy that would undermine economic and political independence in rural America. According to this group, wheat and cotton producers, the nation's principal exporters, could not regain their former income and be freed from management of farming by Washington until foreign outlets for their surplus reopened. Beyond this point antistatists divided. The contingent led by George N. Peek, the initial head of the AAA, sought for agrarians the tariff equivalent enjoyed by manufacturers under the post–World War protectionist system. In effect Peek's was a nationalistic scheme based on government-controlled barter and dumping of surplus farm output into the world market. Cordell Hull–Wilsonian internationalists viewed autarky as a threat to domestic freedom and as fomenting eventual warfare. In due course the debate over trade policy became enmeshed with the issue of potential U.S. involvement in what many sensed was an inevitable replay of the Great War. Hull's defeat of Peek's ambitions for autarky marked the first victory of the internationalists toward global interdependence.

The Hull-Peek controversy centered initially on the secretary of state's pursuit of unconditional most-favored-nation agreements based on traditional multilateral movement of goods. Peek insisted instead on barter for selected, noncompetitive imports. Peek's views had become increasingly isolationist and xenophobic since his experience with the War Industries Board. There, associated with Hugh Johnson and Bernard Baruch, he became infatuated with corporatist notions of business-government cooperation for market and price stability. The postwar agricultural depression inspired a similar approach for farmers, who operated through cooperatives and processor-managed marketing agreements. Peek observed, further, that eastern business and financial interests had exploited the farmer, selling to agrarians on a protected market while farmers were selling into an unprotected and competitive world market at distress prices.

The solution, "equality for agriculture," took legislative form in the various McNary-Haugen farm bills based on Peek's computation of prewar parity for farm and industrial prices. In theory, by segregation of the farm surplus from anticipated domestic demand and sale of that surplus, when necessary at a loss through an export corporation at world market prices, farmers would enjoy parity. Since the bulk of output would be sold at a profit on the domestic market, with the establishment of orderly internal marketing farmers would enhance their net income.

Stubborn and uncompromising, a superb proselytizer and a Jeffersonian antigovernment corporatist, Peek, following the failure of the Moline Plow Company, which he attributed to a decline in farm income, devoted his energy to promotion of his two-price high-tariff regime in the wheat-growing areas of the Midwest and Northwest. But serious questions were raised with regard to the workability of McNary-Haugenism from the outset. The plan would stimulate output and lead to insurmountable costs to be borne by the proposed export corporation. Also, farm cooperatives, upon which Peek relied as market stabilizers, could not serve that function if members bore the cost of the equalization fee while nonparticipants reaped the benefits. There were other difficulties. McNary-Haugenism's simplistic formulas and assumptions could not be carried over to cotton, unlike wheat principally an export crop. In the event, Europeans not only needed to protect gold and currency reserves but viewed maintenance of population on the farm as an unemployment cure. Yet, while an impediment to trade, high tariffs enjoyed wide appeal among Progressive Republicans on whom Roosevelt depended for agricultural and other legislation and attracted nonexporters such as small business, dairy and truck farmers, and sugar beet growers, as well as industries such as steel faced by worldwide overcapacity.[6]

Recruited on the basis of his following among wheat farmers and grain processors, Peek helped frame the Agricultural Adjustment Act. His appointment as its administrator proved anomalous as he opposed production controls and anticipated in their stead a corporative arrangement that would consist of processors and producers who operated through marketing agreements. It would be chaired by a proponent of industrial self-government, possibly Bernard Baruch. While Title I of the law authorized voluntary agreements for acreage reduction, advances on basic crops stored on the farm, and marketing agreements with processors, Peek also secured Section 12(b) authorizing use of the processing taxes for export subsidies in the belief that dumping and bilateral trade treaties would suffice to achieve parity. Unable to manage processors opposed to higher commodity prices and antagonistic to crop controls, Peek resigned his post in December 1933. Roosevelt, torn between the Hull and Peek views on trade, appointed Peek to the post of special assistant on trade policy to the president.[7]

For Hull, Peek's assumption of the newly created trade post was another cross to bear. He had bested the high-tariff Democrats, the Du Pont–Smith–Raskob group, in 1931–32, when he helped to wrest control of the party from their embrace. He then wrote his low-tariff views into the party's 1932 platform. Whereas Hull favored extension of unconditional most-favored-nation treatment to all, the benefits of lowered tariffs negotiated with one country accorded to those nations that reciprocated, Peek favored conditional treatment or barter as the basis for expanded exports. Peek also promoted a centralized agency modeled on the British Board of Trade to control foreign commerce through complicated devices such as quotas, import licenses, subsidies, and capital and currency controls, all anathema to Hull and not a simple matter as U.S. trade was largely multilateral in nature. No sooner had Peek been appointed special adviser on foreign trade by an executive order than he publicly endorsed bilateral barter agreements as the best route to killing off "the regimentation movement."[8]

Passage of the Trade Agreements Act, June 12, 1934, which permitted the president to negotiate tariff agreements downward by as much as 50 percent, failed to resolve the Peek-Hull controversy. Each interpreted the statute as an endorsement of his approach. Whereas Hull believed his views reflected those of the president, Peek seemed closer to Roosevelt's frequent references to Yankee horse trading and more aligned with the brief and the vague terminology of the act, which was intended to avoid congressional aversion to large-scale imports.[9]

There were contradictions on both sides. Hull described the Trade Agreements Act at congressional hearings and in public addresses in terms of enhanced exports for American commodities, not in a framework of export-import balance. This approach dominated U.S. negotiation of reciprocity agreements, the Canadian-U.S. treaty of 1935 serving as a prominent example. Peek's attack on the AAA as regimentation proved equally disingenuous, since the controls he envisaged required a greater degree of planning, both internal and external, than the Roosevelt administration contemplated. Indeed, Peek's proposed trade board more nearly resembled Germany's managed economy than that of the British Board of Trade. Then again, the antistatist internationalists proved amenable to congressional delegation of authority to the presidency in the cause of reciprocity, not for domestic purposes. In the event, reciprocity under Hull and State soon became entangled with the movement against U.S. involvement in Europe's affairs.[10]

An undecided Roosevelt turned over to State administration of the Trade Agreements Act, while Peek was authorized to negotiate barter agreements subject to presidential approval. On the hustings and in a letter to Roosevelt, Peek denounced Hull's program as un-American and as "unilateral economic disarmament." The trade adviser's arrangement of a barter deal with Germany—cotton would be exchanged for dollars (25 percent) and German currency to be used for U.S. imports of German goods—marked the beginning of the end for Peek. When Hull opposed the deal on grounds of trade inequality and the nature of the German regime, Roosevelt withdrew his approval.[11]

Peek, joined by Raymond Moley, continued the debate into 1935. Their objective, neomercantilist planning meshed with the movement for separation of the United States from Europe's affairs. Still a member of Roosevelt's circle of advisers, Moley, while supportive of passage of the Trade Agreements Act, quickly assembled arguments against State's management of the law. Hull, "a doctrinaire free trader," would be inclined to sacrifice domestic employment on the tariff adjustments altar. An embargo of those nations determined to have violated the disarmament pact under negotiation at Geneva would bring the United States into the next war. He was concerned, Moley later confided to Father Charles E. Coughlin, with a foreign service sympathetic to British diplomacy. Impressed further with Walter Millis's *Road to War,* which critiqued U.S. willingness to supply the Entente during the Great War, Moley, adamant, favored an embargo on all arms shipments and loans to belligerents.[12]

With the neutrality debate in the Congress and Mussolini's invasion of Ethiopia as background and with the western Progressives split on the question of congressional delegation of power to the presidency, Moley vented his concerns to the president. Roosevelt opened the exchange when he declared untrue editorials published in *Today* that categorized negotiation of the Canadian-U.S. trade agreement as furtive, outside the purview of public hearings. FDR also protested the charge that most-favored-nation treatment obviated the use of bilateral treaties. "In actual practice we are making bilateral treaties insofar as 99% of the articles affected are concerned." Moley's detailed response took the argument well beyond bilateralism.

State and the Foreign Service, Moley retorted, were imbued with a foreign spirit, which Roosevelt had rejected in the 1932 campaign. The internationalists, he reminded the president—Newton D. Baker, Columbia University president Nicholas Murray Butler, the *Baltimore Sun*, and the *New York Times*—had opposed his nomination and much of his domestic program. While favorable toward the Canadian treaty, he questioned the most-favored-nation principle. Why not, he wanted to know, achieve the same end through bilateral arrangements? Moley also suggested that those vested with the conduct of U.S. diplomacy, the same group that guided Wilson into war, "one foot at Broad and Wall and the other at Geneva," believed in the transcendence of international questions, hence U.S. involvement in "international coercive movements." Echoing the views of former World Court justice John Bassett Moore—he studied with Moore in his graduate student days at Columbia when both opposed U.S. entry into the World War—Moley rejected discriminatory embargoes as a denial of neutrality, since discretionary power was the prerogative of the Congress, not the executive branch.[13]

As head of the Export-Import Bank in October 1935, Peek broadened the effort to separate commercial policy from State Department control in an address before the National Industrial Conference Board. Foreign trade policy would be shaped in a framework responsive to domestic requirements by an independent board modeled on Great Britain's Board of Trade or Germany's Economic Ministry. Such a body, detached from State, would also secure a policy of neutrality for the United States. Before a War Industries Board reunion on Armistice Day, 1935, Peek expanded his agenda to include tight immigration controls; strict federal oversight of imports and exports, including capital exports; stabilization of the dollar at an "American price level"; tariff reduction on a country-by-country basis; strict neutrality and cash-and-carry in the event of war in Europe. To Roosevelt, the address sounded like a Hearst editorial; to Peek the time had come to go into opposition.[14]

A frustrated Peek charged in *Why Quit Our Own?* that Hull and Henry A. Wallace, "with the implied approval of the president, are using the Trade Agreements Act to break down the American protective system and to involve the country in the affairs of the world." While the United States might well in the future abandon the American System and "join the low-wage family of nations," such a scheme should be subjected to the polls and approved by the Congress.[15]

During these years Peek's high-tariff views proved vulnerable in the Midwest as it became evident that Smoot-Hawley's tariff schedules could not prevent a price collapse. Corn commanded 10 to 20 cents a bushel in 1932 despite a tariff of 25 cents, wheat 30 cents a bushel under a 42-cent tariff. Midwestern opinion divided between high-tariff states such as Illinois as opposed to Iowa farmers more open to reciprocity; between wheat producers who faced Canadian competitors and cattle producers who desired cheap feed. In this environment the American Farm Bureau Federation's Edward A. O'Neal gradually maneuvered farm entrepreneurs toward endorsement of reciprocity. At the same time the Cowles-owned *Des Moines Register and Tribune,* edited by William Wesley Waymack, also chipped away at Peek's appeal in the nation's midsection. The influential editor mustered support from a younger generation of farmer-entrepreneurs and Des Moines insurance and business interests.[16]

Like the eastern internationalists, with whom he allied, Waymack's concerns were catholic in their dimension; but unlike that group his views more closely identified with an agrarian constituency. He regarded the Agricultural Adjustment Act as a mixed blessing. Farmers, he well knew, had diverse economic interests; one shoe did not fit all. Thus southern farmers, disposed toward cotton production controls, turned acreage set-asides under the AAA to feedstuffs for greater cattle, sheep, and pork production and readily underpriced midwestern farmers and drove down their income. Waymack believed that the Hull open-markets program could accommodate both sections.

A Wilsonian and a liberal Republican, Waymack feared both external and internal threats to constitutional and economic norms. Conscious of the imminence of renewed worldwide war, Waymack promoted educational campaigns at the state, regional, and national levels aimed at a redefined liberalism in an autarkic and nationalistic climate. Waymack believed that democratic institutions were menaced from the outside by communism and fascism, from within by power aggregated into the hands of a chief executive and Congress overly responsive to interest groups and engaged in a process of self-contained decision making. He acknowledged the need to accommodate the centrifugal tendencies of the twentieth century; but he wanted the opinion-shaping process to include the citizenry, which he defined as enlightened and intelligent liberals.[17]

Engaged in a war of ideas scarcely limited to producer prices, Waymack encouraged the work of the Commission of Inquiry on National Policy in

International Economic Relations, organized in January 1934 to study and report on capital movements, monetary policy, and trade barriers. The group, financed by the Rockefeller Foundation, sponsored by the Social Science Research Council, and headed by the University of Minnesota economist Alvin H. Hansen, endorsed Hull-internationalist doctrine: cooperation with the League of Nations short of involvement in European conflicts; U.S. adherence to the World Court; repeal of the Johnson Act, which prohibited loans to nations in default on their debt payments; immediate settlement of the war debts; downward tariff revision and increased noncompetitive imports to achieve a better trade balance in goods; and prompt negotiation of reciprocal trade agreements. Hansen's work evidently led to his appointment as chief economist (1934–35) for an interdepartmental committee created to administer the Trade Agreements Act.[18]

Waymack soon joined with Nicholas Murray Butler, president of Columbia University and an ardent Wilsonian; Brooks Emeny, Foreign Affairs Council; Ralph Flanders, a Springfield, Vermont, industrialist, later U.S. senator; Brooks Hays, a liberal Arkansas attorney; Charles P. Taft II, the liberal-internationalist member of the Taft family; the journalist William Allen White; Lewis W. Douglas; and Alvin Hansen to form the Economic Policy Committee. This group was funded in time by the Carnegie Endowment for International Peace. The EPC's founders, ambitious for a wide membership, promised study of the international economic relations of the United States and their connection to preservation of peace.[19] This group was soon joined by Alexander Sachs, Thomas W. Lamont, Winthrop W. Aldrich, Will Clayton, and Dean G. Acheson. With the outbreak of war in Europe, the EPC members proselytized the public toward greater U.S. support for the Allied and British causes and influenced as well, through the likes of Clayton and Acheson, postwar economic diplomacy, which moved toward a global economy in the second half of the twentieth century.[20]

Douglas's membership in the Economic Policy Committee reflected his continued commitment to an internationalist agenda as well as a return to budget balance. A vice president of American Cyanamid, Douglas continued to proselytize for currency stabilization—achieved by the Tripartite Agreement of 1936—on the ground that it assured recovery and would lead to an Anglo-U.S. agreement on trade policy. Continued protectionism, he held, distorted capital investment, sheltered inefficient producers, and resulted in a static living standard (fewer goods at higher prices). He preferred a competitive world geared to increased consumption in a deregulated domestic economic environment. To achieve these ends, Douglas joined with Newton Baker and the AFL economist Leo Wolman in a letter to the *New York Times*, June 2, 1936. Some background is helpful.[21]

Atlanticists offered a coherent alternative program to the New Deal's insular program: Anglo-American comity in diplomacy and economic affairs, U.S. cooperation with international bodies as a step toward greater involvement in Europe's affairs, and the reopening of world markets to obtain recovery and avoid another Great War. These policies would render unnecessary the internal economic controls that led ineluctably to the loss of free enterprise and democratic institutions elsewhere. Baker, typical of other antistatist internationalists, found in Cordell Hull's trade agreements program the administration's redeeming potential. Further, neutrality legislation served as a surreal exercise in legalisms, for should warfare erupt in Europe, the United States would be drawn in. With Adolf Hitler's rise to power and Germany's subsequent withdrawal from the League of Nations and the League-sponsored disarmament negotiations, Wilsonians determined that they needed to reach a wider audience. Like Henry A. Wallace, Baker was convinced that "America Must Choose" between international economic comity through exchange of goods and a low-level recovery followed by certain destruction.[22]

In this environment Baker and Norman Davis, U.S. ambassador-at-large and delegate to the disarmament talks at Geneva, proposed a coordinated effort by the Woodrow Wilson Foundation and the Carnegie Endowment for International Peace for joint activity in the direction of international cooperation. The timing of the Baker-Davis proposal (May 1933) coincided with the failure of the McReynolds resolution to get through the Senate Foreign Relations Committee. Favored by Davis, Hull, and behind the scenes by Henry L. Stimson, it would have authorized the president to cooperate in a potential international arms embargo against an aggressor nation, though it hedged by retaining freedom for the Americans in determining the aggressor. The Johnson Amendment, offered by Senator Hiram Johnson (California), required instead that an embargo announced by the president would apply equally to all belligerents, a mechanism designed to keep the nation out of another European war. Baker and the others of the Wilsonian persuasion regarded the concept as an illusion, as another world war could only be avoided by U.S. participation in international deliberations in the framework of Kellogg and Briand and the Pact of Paris. At a joint meeting of the Academy of Political Science and the Carnegie Endowment, Baker, seconding an address by Owen D. Young, asserted, "Economics and the perfection of science will one day force us into world affairs." Such a proposition had no future in a climate permeated by munitions maker theory, the belief that the United States had fought to preserve investment of Morgan & Co. in the Allied cause, and the sense in some quarters that Germany had been dealt a draconian peace.

With German rearmament and the beginning of the Italo-Ethiopian conflict bringing on renewed tensions in Europe and Senate defeat of U.S. membership in the Permanent Court of International Justice in the background, Nicholas Murray Butler chaired an international conference at Chatham House in London in March 1935 and on his return to New York sponsored a series of roundtables that lasted nearly a decade. These focused on Anglo-U.S. comity, trade liberalization, exchange stabilization, and restored lending.[23]

While in London for the Chatham House talks, Thomas Lamont pressed for war debts settlement with Montagu Norman and Neville Chamberlain in order to resuscitate Anglo-U.S. relations. Neither proved receptive. Dollar-pound parity, Norman held, could not work while Roosevelt retained the power to further devalue the dollar given distrust of his motives since the failed London Conference. When meeting Prime Minister Stanley Baldwin, Lamont proposed British relinquishment of the 10 percent principle taken from the Lausanne settlement, since the debts impasse was critical to resolution of other matters. Baldwin confirmed mistrust of Roosevelt and claimed that economic issues were in the hands of Chamberlain and George Harrison of the New York Fed. Evasive responses in London reflected competition for market share, rearmament pressures, the potential of war in both Europe and Asia, and the need to protect a farflung empire for which Britain was unprepared. America was viewed as isolationist, its president unreliable, and Congress the captive of sectional interests.[24]

The Baker-Wolman-Douglas epistle, drafted by Lippmann, which reflected the views of influential Atlanticists opposed to Roosevelt's domestic as well as his foreign policies, anxious for Anglo-U.S. entente on economic issues, had as its immediate aim prevention of a landslide victory in the 1936 national contest. Lippmann condemned cost-price increases under the NRA as counterproductive and suggested instead dollar-franc-pound stabilization and lowered tariffs as the preferable route to higher price levels and recovery. This, he believed, would undercut support for the Johnson Act and hopefully open the American market to supplies for France and U.S. capital for Britain in the event of war.

Troubled by congressional delegation of power to the presidency and fearful of "planned collectivism," as he saw it, Lippmann inquired of Baker if he anticipated that he would support Roosevelt in the national election. Both expressed distaste for the Republican Party's leadership yet abhorred Roosevelt's sponsorship of class warfare and self-interested minorities. At the same time they questioned the efficacy of a third-party movement based on a coalition of antistatists. Douglas, at first tempted toward coalition politics, soon concurred on the ground that liberal Democrats could scarcely join with the hopelessly reactionary GOP in stemming the New Deal's collectivist tide. "The real fight," Lippmann agreed, "would have to be made within the Democratic party." With the group anticipating Alf M. Landon's nomination, Lippmann framed the Douglas-Wolman-Baker declaration of principles to appeal to Hull; Wallace, fundamentally an internationalist and never comfortable with acreage controls; and the senatorial opponents of the New Deal, particularly Virginia's Carter Glass and Harry F. Byrd.[25]

In the end, Lippmann endorsed Landon in the 1936 contest. He abhorred one-man rule under Roosevelt, as he viewed the president, and accepted private assurances offered by Landon's running mate, Chicago newspaper publisher Frank Knox, that a Landon-Knox administration would not adopt a policy of economic nationalism based on Smoot-Hawley.[26]

Douglas proved amenable to Landon's private blandishments at a six-hour session in Topeka intended to resolve the Republican Party's contradictory tariff position. On the one hand, the Cleveland platform promised adjustments to promote international trade and currency stabilization; on the other, repeal of the Trade Agreements Act so as to shelter the farmer against "importation of all live stock, dairy, and agricultural products . . . which will depress American farm prices," in reference to cattle imported from Mexico into the Southwest and the impact of the recent Canadian-U.S. reciprocity agreement. Douglas emerged certain that Landon was low-tariff but uncertain that he would take a strong position on the subject if elected. While Landon praised the Hull leadership as courageous, he raised the issue of stiff congressional resistance. Reciprocity would be achieved by a body similar to the Board of Trade in Great Britain, Peek's position; the Board of Trade, in fact, favored high tariffs. When Peek's advocacy of bilateral barter agreements came under discussion, Landon described them as "the handmaiden of a governmentally regulated economy," then endorsed them. Motivated largely by abhorrence of Roosevelt's budget policies, Douglas endorsed Landon, while he commended Hull's efforts as exemplary.[27]

While Douglas and Lippmann found their way into the Landon camp, others of the internationalists either remained with FDR or fell silent. Thus Grenville Clark (Root, Clark, Buckner, and Ballantine), an economizer in the manner of Virginia's Harry F. Byrd, supported Roosevelt on the contingency of another war, which he regarded as imminent. Clark preferred the experienced leadership of Roosevelt and Hull. While Baker went fishing, James P. Warburg returned to the Democratic fold based on the Hull trade policies.[28]

Also compelled to choose between the Hull program and his constitutional views, Dean G. Acheson, a participant in these exchanges, opted for reciprocity. According to Acheson, the tendency to hand over to government the myriad problems that confronted society had not brought any greater wisdom or ability to their resolution. "By turning to the government to say what shall be produced . . . and how much of it, or to fix prices or wages, or the practices of business, or to finance or direct the financing of industry, farming or private building, we can not escape from the limitations of individual ability. . . . All these decisions must still be made by men and women." By centralizing the decision-making process, society had created omnipotent, not omniscient, government. Government could neither create nor execute a plan for 120 million people, and Americans would not submit to such a plan. At the same time, Acheson condemned business's centralizing tendencies, its search for order, control, stability, and government interference as a replacement for competition. Such a predisposition exaggerated errors, stifled initiative, and weakened character. Neither corporate nor government control had proven capable of producing more goods at lower prices. Controlled output cost too much and led in the end to authoritarianism.

To Alexander Sachs, Acheson suggested that the Supreme Court decision which voided the AAA was inevitable given the New Deal's propensity to enact legislation so sweeping as to violate the basics of the federal system. With Baker, Acheson represented the Duke Power Company in its suit to declare the PWA grants for municipal power plants unconstitutional. Tempted to support Landon on fiscal and sound money grounds, Acheson declared for Roosevelt. Landon's attack on the Hull program represented a challenge to the secretary's effort to revive international trade: "I must be on his [Hull's] side."[29]

Landon endorsed the Peek-inspired platform planks that promised economic nationalism in campaign addresses designed to secure the electoral vote of the farm states. At Des Moines, with the Canadian-U.S. reciprocity treaty creating apprehension, Landon pledged an American price, the tariff equivalent, for farm products; at Minneapolis he supported reciprocity and criticized the treaty with Canada on the ground of increased imports of cheese, commodities, and livestock. In the words of his biographer, Landon failed to explain "how trade barriers could be lowered while giving farmers additional tariff protection."[30]

Peek claimed that the Canadian-U.S. reciprocity treaty would induce greater importation of commodities from Canada into the United States. He rejected the assertion of Hull and Wallace that the exchange would stimulate the wages and purchasing power of industrial workers, thereby benefiting farmers. Actually, implementation of the Canadian treaty hardly altered trade patterns, which tended to follow earlier economic trends. U.S. exports benefited more in these years than Canada's exports into the United States. The United States, in fact, maintained its predepression favorable trade balances wherever trade treaties—few in number or importance—were negotiated. Nor is there evidence that American farmers suffered from the trade increase with Canada. Indeed, the Landon-Peek analysis found itself undercut on the heels of the Minneapolis speech by a significant rise in agricultural prices, hogs from $2.50 per hundredweight in 1932 to $9.10 in 1936; eggs from 8 to 17 cents a dozen; butterfat, 16 to 29 cents per pound.[31]

Like Waymack, William L. Clayton, a member of the internationalist-oriented Economic Policy Committee, dwelled on diminished exports and market share—in this instance for cotton, which impacted his firm's business volume. A hard-driving entrepreneur, Clayton believed that society benefited from efficiency and lowered costs, with resulting economic friction a necessary price to be paid. These bedrock assumptions served as the basis for his opposition to trade barriers as ruinous to the southern cotton producer, to those dependent on him for employment, to consumers, and to American living standards.

Born to an unsuccessful cotton farmer near Tupelo, Mississippi, Clayton attributed his emergence as the nation's leading cotton broker to the opportunities afforded by an open economy, one that rewarded initiative and business acumen. It was government's function to furnish a level playing field, free from bureaucratic interference and special privilege, whether in the shape of excessive controls, market rigging, or corporate-inspired barriers to free trade. Committed to comparative advantage, he lectured Senator Arthur Vandenberg (Michigan) at a 1940 Senate hearing on extension of the Reciprocal Trade Agreements Act—Republican protectionists were opposed—that "the next peace must be based upon the principle of the division of labor on a worldwide basis." "Only in that way," he argued elsewhere, "can the standard of living of the backward nations of the world be raised, and only in that way can our own standard of living be maintained and improved."[32]

These views came early in life. In the course of service as a court clerk in Memphis, where he moonlighted as a stenographer-typist, Clayton transcribed a speech for William Jennings Bryan on the deleterious impact of the tariff on the rural economy. He became a convert. While in Memphis, he also met Jerome Hill, a St. Louis cotton merchant, moved to New York with Hill's American Cotton Company, then to the Texas Cotton Products Company, also organized by Hill. In 1904 Clayton, his brother-in-law Frank Anderson, and Monroe Anderson formed Anderson, Clayton and Company, capitalized at $9,000 and based in Oklahoma City. Clayton emerged as the firm's leader. In time, ACCO moved its headquarters to Houston to secure access to a major port and warehouse facilities, then branched out into other southern trading centers as well as Los Angeles. During and after the World War, ACCO also moved into markets once dominated by European factors based on Clayton's business strategy, which included bypassing the middleman in cotton shipping, finance, and brokerage. In the 1920s ACCO emerged as the world's leading cotton factor.[33]

A major shift in the cotton trade in the interwar years reinforced Clayton's low-tariff view. Historically, raw cotton had been the nation's principal export as expressed in dollar value. While world consumption of

U.S. cotton exports grew in the 1920s, even before the depression other producers increased their market share. He attributed the American share decline to the postwar high-tariff regime and the inability of Europeans to amass dollars and gold for purchases here. With the onset of depression, Clayton maintained that congressional policies met a purely political agenda when Smoot-Hawley shut out imports. Further, Federal Farm Board purchases overhung the market and depressed prices. "Commerce left free," he insisted, "automatically purges itself of its own ills." Recovery could be achieved only with "retirement of government from all economic activity in competition with its citizens." Tariffs functioned as a tax on consumers for the benefit of inefficient producers and were totally worthless to commodities producers who had lost access to vital overseas outlets. The tariff as a defense of the nation's living standard was a myth, and Cordell Hull was "the soundest thinking man in public life today."[34]

Clayton condemned Roosevelt's agricultural program as readily as he had Hoover's. Under the AAA, producers could rent cotton lands to the secretary of agriculture for cash, received options on surplus cotton in storage, supplemental parity payments, and loans amounting to 10 cents a pound. Prices for basic crops were guaranteed by the Commodity Credit Corporation as of October 1933: farmers were offered crop loans at predetermined price levels and given the alternative of withdrawal from storage or abandonment if market prices fell below support levels. In testimony before Alvin Hansen's commission of inquiry, Clayton claimed that artificial stimulus to American cotton prices through acreage reduction (15 million acres for 1934, 10 million projected for 1935), crop loans, and other devices would allow foreign output to displace that of southern producers. Further, Wallace's proposed middle course—acreage controls an interim measure en route to a return to a low-tariff regime which was basic to peace and prosperity—published as America Must Choose by the Foreign Policy Association in 1934, would not work for cotton as long as the American price exceeded that at offer on the world market. Artificially high domestic prices would also encourage substitution by synthetics, the end result a loss of 1.5 million jobs for farmers, laborers, and those involved in shipping, ginning, and processing.[35]

Passage of the Bankhead Cotton Control Act of 1934 further diminished U.S. output when it instituted strict production controls and assured a minimum price to farmers. While the cotton loan–acreage control program provided an adequate standard of living for the farmer, government could not regulate the world price of cotton within the confines of the United States unless prepared to abandon its principal export.[36]

Clayton's forecast of declining market share for the United States and for cotton as opposed to rayon proved to be accurate: the U.S. share of world output steadily declined from 68 percent before the AAA (1930–32) to an average of 45 percent in the crop years 1935–39, or 8.7 million bales pre-AAA as opposed to 6 million under the AAA.[37] While curtailment of domestic cotton output and cotton loans raised domestic U.S. cotton prices from 6 cents to 12–14 cents, according to Clayton, Farm Board and AAA policies stimulated new production and added to the surplus. In effect, American high price–low volume policies served as a protective wall behind which new areas overseas could be opened. Yet support for the Reciprocal Trade Agreements program kept Clayton in the Roosevelt camp. "A vote for Roosevelt," he told the press in October 1936, "is a vote to keep Secretary Hull in office."[38]

In Clayton's weltanschauung more than cotton exports were at stake. The United States had led the world astray in the interwar period and proved substantially responsible for the pattern of strangled trade that led to a depression and spawned dictatorship in Europe. It was incumbent on this nation, consequently, to lead the way out of the morass toward a world order in which benefits would accrue on all sides. "For years we have sold much more to Europe than we have bought from her. When this war ends," he declared in 1940, "[we must] be prepared to trade our goods for theirs, scrapping the tariff in the process." The alternative, a self-contained economy, would so severely damage the American standard of living that democracy likely would not survive.[39]

When situated in the context of twentieth-century agrarian economic trends, the New Deal farm program was neither as radical nor as defective as claimed then or since. The farm crisis, long in the making, was not quickly resolved. In 1940, 23 percent of farm operators (1.5 million farms) owned less than 30 acres. Few of this group proved able to sustain themselves on a commercial basis. Of farmers who operated 30 to 100 acres, another 2 million farms, only the largest and most productive were potentially economically viable, provided they received government support. This left only half the nation's farmers capable of earning adequate income in the absence of government supports.[40]

New Deal programs hardly proved able to address deep and long-standing structural problems, especially in the Old South. In that region the New Deal agricultural program proved neither as helpful to owners nor as harmful to tenants and sharecroppers as is sometimes suggested. Legislation oriented to agriculture cushioned the downward movement of farm prices, which had reached its nadir in 1932. But recovery required the movement of unproductive farmers to alternative occupations for which too often they were unprepared or which proved unavailable in the 1930s, and it also required restored external markets. While cash receipts of farmers rose from a low of $4.7 billion in 1932 to $8.7 billion in 1936 and $9.2 billion in 1937, followed by the 1938 setback, the 1929 income level for agriculture was attained only in 1941. Benefit and rental payments were not as substantial as often implied. These started at $131 million in 1933, rose to $573 million in 1935, declined in the next three years, and increased to $807 million in 1939. More important was the indirect impact of general recovery and relief expenditure.

In the Midwest price stability and new sources of credit encouraged trends under way: farm mechanization, greater productivity stimulated by use of better land due to acreage controls, and improved horticultural practice. The net result was greater output per acre and reduced labor needs on the farm. Whereas, for example, 100 man-hours of labor were required for a yield of 100 bushels of wheat in 1900, 87 hours were needed in 1920 and 47 in 1940. In the case of cotton, output of 100 bales before and after harvest required 147 man-hours of labor in 1900, 113 in 1920, and 83 in 1940. Acreage controls impacted the traditional sharecropper system, though not as substantially as often claimed by anecdotal evidence. (Once crop yield passed a certain point, it became more economical for the landowner to shift to hired labor.) White croppers declined from 339,343 to 205,089 between 1930 and 1940 in the ten cotton-belt states, black croppers from 380,911 to 290,032. As a result, "sooner or later . . . the tenants and farm laborers of the Southeast would have had to leave the farms and seek their fortunes in cities and towns."[41]

The Roosevelt peacetime program cushioned the farm economy. It did not alter long-term trends in agriculture. A European-style, state-supported, small-scale agriculture hardly enjoyed a future in a society already committed to industrial capitalism, agriculture included. In the process, income inequality in the United States, which rose in the 1920s and early depression years, was reversed by productivity gains in agriculture which exceeded those of industry and by the resultant migration of a substantial segment of the rural labor force to urban areas in order to take up other employment.[42]

Although the antistatist, open-market globalists made scant headway in these years, they had overcome George Peek's approach to agricultural recovery based on autarky and a corporatist economy. Claimants on behalf of global markets and comparative advantage would have their day, as Newton D. Baker predicted—after another World War.

9 | RELIEF, PUBLIC WORKS, AND SOCIAL INSURANCE

ROM THE INCEPTION OF the New Deal, the Roosevelt Brains Trust conceived that relief and public works programs would tide people over until the industrial system recovered sufficiently to offer adequate employment. But even in normal times the business system proved subject to cyclical swings that brought on temporary unemployment and discarded those too old to work. The answer lay in provision for the unemployed and the superannuated through social insurance. Hopefully, social insurance would also help to inure the economy against another depression. The sources of these programs lay in the social justice component of progressivism; the success of workmen's compensation instituted at the state level, which served as a model for unemployment insurance based on state management; the claims of institutional economists that workers required protection from the vagaries of industrialization; the programs of radical social reformers such as Abraham Epstein and Isaac Rubinow who cited Europe's advances in the area of social protection; and the women's movement, supported by such women as Grace Abbott, Katherine Lenroot, and Frances Perkins, which aimed to protect dependent women and children.

The New Deal programs for relief, public works, and social insurance had important long-term consequences. Public works programs led to the building of a vast infrastructure: valley resource development and regional economic diversification; highways and air transport facilities; electric power generation and transmission, especially for rural, underdeveloped areas; water supply and sewers, as well as flood control; national park facilities; and urban housing.

Analysis of federal, state, and local contributions to the economy for these programs in a framework of "fiscal federalism" also reveals the growth of fiscal cooperation and interdependence between the central and state governments. In the span between the New Economic Era of the 1920s and the New Deal's peacetime years, total government expenditure at all levels, federal, state, and local, as a percentage of GNP grew from 12.8 percent in 1927 to 17.36 percent in 1934 and 17.86 percent in 1940. The federal share of total expenditure increased from 30.57 percent in 1927 to 38.6 percent in 1934 and 44.91 percent in 1940; total state share grew from 12.98 percent in 1927 to 16.83 percent in 1934 and rose to 17.51 percent in 1940; local share of fiscal expenditure in this period declined from 56.44 to 37.88 percent. This process was marked by centralization of programmatic and fiscal authority in the federal government, by increased fiscal transfers from the federal government in light of its broader tax base to the states and localities, and by decentralization of responsibility for implementation of social legislation and public construction to the states and localities. Overall, cooperative grants for programs administered jointly by federal and state governments, 1933–40, cost some $27 billion, with $16 billion allocated to relief programs. The magnitude of relief expenditure at a level of $2 billion per annum is best understood when expressed in 1996 dollars: $240 billion or 4 percent of GNP. Total new construction in 1940 alone was funded by the federal government at $2.13 billion and by the states and local government at $1.5 billion, or a total of $3.63 billion. The states met matching requirements by revenue enhancement through personal and corporate income taxes and sales taxes.[1]

Fiscal cooperation emanated from the very nature of the federal system and variations in state and regional living costs. Initially Roosevelt was determined that the states should shoulder a degree of responsibility for assistance to the indigent and until the 1939 amendments to widows and dependent children. Congressional pressures for state management of relief and old-age assistance programs stemmed from a desire to maintain the federal system and from differences in local social attitudes. Social security aside, there were no uniform standards for the level of payments in social programs administered by the states.

Relief, the most expeditious way to deliver assistance to those in need and to stimulate aggregate demand, was tackled first. In the course of hearings held by Wisconsin's Robert La Follette Jr., chairman of the Senate Subcommittee on Federal Aid for Unemployment Relief in the winter 1932–33 session of the Congress, Harry Hopkins, after discussion with the president-elect, outlined the basics of New Deal relief policy, namely, replacement of loans by grants to the states that would amount to $600 million to $1 billion and creation of a separate federal agency empowered to deal directly with the states as opposed to local units of government. Roosevelt affirmed these objectives in a message to Congress soon after taking office and asked for the appointment of a federal relief administrator (a task assigned to Hopkins) who would also implement a broad public works program.

On March 27, 1933, Senator Robert Wagner introduced an emergency relief bill for a Federal Emergency Relief Administration. Under this legislation the Reconstruction Finance Corporation was authorized to borrow $500 million for relief, with its role delimited to that of fiscal agent. Expenditure was the responsibility of FERA. Of this sum, the states were allotted $200 million based on relief expenditure in the previous three months and $300 million at the discretion of the relief administrator who was charged with maintenance of an adequate standard of relief.

When he signed the Federal Emergency Relief Act, Roosevelt indicated his reluctance to bring the federal government into the relief business on a permanent basis on the grounds of state and local responsibility. FERA expenditure of funds was limited to the unemployed, leaving local government to care for the destitute unemployable—widows, orphans, the handicapped, and aged. In practice, the dividing line between the unemployed and unemployables blurred and proved difficult to enforce, as local officials shifted unemployables onto federally funded relief programs. Overall federal grants to the states under FERA increased from $502 million in 1933 to $1.6 billion in 1934 and $1.7 billion in 1935 and then tapered off in the late 1930s to $700 to $900 million per annum. State and local funding for relief also increased steadily in the years 1933–35, from $558 million to $954 million, decreased in 1936–37, and after the 1937–38 collapse rose in 1939 to just under $1 billion.

While Roosevelt and Hopkins were uncomfortable with federal involvement in relief except as a temporary measure at a time when states and localities were financially strapped and viewed home relief as debilitating to the individual, public works lacked the stigma associated with relief. Some sort of work for the unemployed, if appropriate, it was assumed, would engender self-respect, maintain skills, and stimulate purchasing power. At issue was the level of expenditure for a works program which would necessarily add to budget imbalance.

At this juncture Wagner reintroduced a bill which originated as the Emergency Relief and Construction Act of 1932 and culminated in a $3.3 billion public works initiative incorporated into the National Industrial

Recovery Act. This resulted in a Public Works Administration headed by Interior Secretary Ickes.[2]

There were problems. Ickes, a careful and deliberate planner, tended to subcontract work to construction firms that hired from the ranks of skilled labor rather than the unemployed. Also, large-scale infrastructure projects proved slow to get under way and required substantial overhead costs for planning and materials. When the speculative burst of early 1933 faded by the late summer and early fall, Hopkins put a more radical plan to Roosevelt at a White House luncheon on November 2. A dynamic social work administrator, Hopkins had eased away from an approach based on subsistence relief and the casework method of social workers. He preferred work relief and cash wages entrusted to recipients to be spent at their discretion. While FERA established a national pattern for relief, pushing aside the old poor boards, and resulted in a 93 percent increase in family benefits (May 1933–May 1935), it was compelled nevertheless to rely on relief investigators who applied a means test and supervised family budgets. More immediately, Hopkins seemed prodded in part by a nationwide relief census undertaken in October that showed more than 12.5 million Americans dependent on public assistance.

Aubrey Williams, a southern liberal and a key aide, had suggested to Hopkins replacement of relief by an expanded FERA Work Division that would scrap the means test and social workers' supervisory role in favor of a daily wage tailored to skills and workplace experience. The new federal agency would become national employer of last resort and would federalize the process by serving as its own works projects contractor. The proposal, accepted by Roosevelt, resulted in an executive order for the Civil Works Administration. The CWA expended some $950 million in half a year on small works projects such as airports, playgrounds and parks, sewage and irrigation, highway and street repairs, an emergency education program that employed teachers in adult and vocational studies, a women's work program, and various initiatives for the arts and white-collar workers such as manuscript editing, murals, and musical productions. Driven by engineers and industrial managers committed to market wages and genuine employment, at its peak, in January 1934, the CWA was the nation's largest employer by far. It provided work for some 4 million "employees," expending 75 percent of its budget for wages. Though hours were limited to encourage CWA employees to seek employment in the private sector, CWA hires enjoyed medical benefits and disability coverage for workplace injuries under the Federal Employees Compensation Act of 1916.[3]

Yet the CWA was doomed virtually from its inception. When Hopkins informed the president in early January 1934 that funds for the program would soon run out—nearly $1 billion had been committed over three months—Roosevelt ordered an immediate cutback in employment and hours and the CWA's termination at winter's end. Roosevelt explained his reasoning at a meeting of the National Emergency Council, a group formed by the White House to coordinate New Deal recovery programs:

> If we continue CWA through the summer, it is going to cost seven or eight million [billion] dollars, and secondly, it will become a habit with the country. We want to get away from CWA as soon as we can. The CWA ends the end of April, and next winter, if there is still a great deal of relief needed, the matter can be taken up again. But they must know that it is going to end this year at the end of April. . . . We all agree there has got to be a limit to CWA and the people must look to the time when it will have ended. . . . We must not take the position that we are going to have permanent depression in this country, and it is very important that we have somebody to say that quite forcefully to these people.[4]

Clearly unwilling to be overtaken by a newly created, highly motivated bureaucracy, Roosevelt did not regard relief and public works as a permanent federal responsibility. Whereas Hopkins expounded a philosophy of "real jobs for real people," translated as a guarantee of employment in the depression, Roosevelt regarded temporary federal employment as within a relief framework. He intended no permanent dependent class. Rather, the private sector eventually would resume its employment function and release the national Treasury from onerous expenditure connected with relief and public works activity.

From a budgetary standpoint the CWA, however well-intentioned, proved unrealizable. While Roosevelt's claim of its total cost of $7 to $8 billion per annum seems exaggerated, Corrington Gill, at the CWA's Division of Finance, Research, and Statistics, estimated an annual outlay of $4.224 billion for wages alone. An additional 25 percent for cost of materials, administrative expense, and the potential of disability claims under the Federal Employees Compensation Act added up to some $5 to $6 billion annually as opposed to federal receipts (fiscal 1934), exclusive of processing taxes on commodities, of $2.745 billion. A chastened Hopkins, in a turnabout, evidently having gauged the consequence of Moley's departure from Roosevelt's priorities, conceded at a meeting of the National Emergency Council the political dangers involved in the centralizing tendencies of New Deal emergency programs.[5]

In his annual message to Congress on January 4, 1935, Roosevelt announced that the federal government should quit the business of relief, which he described as a narcotic, "a subtle destroyer of the human spirit ... fundamentally destructive of the national fibre." He declared: "I am not willing that the vitality of our people be further sapped by the giving of cash, of market baskets, of a few hours weekly work cutting grass, raking leaves or picking up papers in the public parks. We must preserve not only the bodies of the unemployed but also their self-respect, their self-reliance and courage and determination."

Observing that 5 million people were currently on relief rolls, Roosevelt suggested that work must be found for the 3.5 million employables, victims of "depression caused by conditions which were not local but national." Here the federal government alone possessed resources adequate to finance a works program. The balance, 1.5 million unable to work, or unemployables, defined by Hopkins as the aged, widowed, tubercular, mentally ill, and physically disabled, should be sustained by the local community or private charity. The distinction between employables and unemployables reflected Roosevelt's and Hopkins's belief that state and local governments had fobbed off onto the federal government their own responsibility for funding relief, a claim modified by the president's willingness to offer federal categorical assistance in the form of matching grants for aid to the aged, mothers with dependent children, and the blind.[6]

Roosevelt created the Works Projects Administration by executive order, May 6, 1935, as a replacement for FERA which would allow the federal government to "quit this business of relief" by year's end. A $4 billion appropriation, plus $880 million from unexpended previous authorizations, provided funding. Unlike Ickes's Public Works Administration, the WPA was obligated to take on employables from relief rolls, with payments limited to $800 per annum and restricted to one family member. Eighty-five percent of WPA expenditure was for wages, with states and localities required to furnish materials and other nonlabor costs. WPA's wage policy, labeled a security wage, was intended as a compromise between FERA's smaller relief wage and CWA's market or prevailing wage policy. Subsequently, in 1936, under union pressure, the WPA paid prevailing hourly wages but reduced hours worked and capped monthly income at security wage levels. Earlier arts, white-collar, historical, and similar projects were continued, and WPA activity was broadened to include the Resettlement Administration, rural electrification, the National Youth Administration, and projects of similar stripe. Overall, WPA employment averaged some 2 million workers over the next six years, and total expenditure amounted to $11.365 billion.[7]

The framing of unemployment insurance and social security legislation and their economic implications required a different tack. Unlike relief and public works, Roosevelt and his labor secretary, Frances Perkins, viewed old-age annuities and unemployment insurance as permanent fixtures of a modern industrial economy in light of its cyclical nature and the need to pension off older workers. While unemployment insurance, it was believed, needed to be federalized in order to assure conformity with the Supreme Court's interpretation of the commerce clause, old-age insurance was nationalized as a result of workers' mobility over a lifetime.[8]

In recent years comparative studies have placed social insurance in a framework of cultural and institutional differences, economic growth rates or level of industrialization (convergence theory), polity types, the relative strength of trade unions and labor parties, evolving bureaucracies, pursuit by monopoly capitalists of "the commoditization of labor," and in the United States the impact of regionalism, especially southern dominance of the legislative process (racism and control of black labor), and in terms enunciated as "politics matters" or "bringing the state back in." In this last context Theda Skocpol's analysis of the contextual origins of social policy in the United States proves most helpful. In Great Britain and Western Europe, social insurance plans were devised in highly centralized political systems and by powerful bureaucracies. In the United States bureaucrats lacked such independent authority in a fragmented, decentralized system. Labor unions were preoccupied with workplace issues and their own expansion or very survival. Nor were politicians necessarily the captives of welfare-state capitalists. The answer lies, instead, Skocpol offers, in the need for politicians to forge "compromises . . . of social interests in ways congruent with the operating needs of the political institutions within which they pursue their careers."[9]

Another school of thought views national social insurance policy as the outcome of pressures from the business community driven by the rising cost of industrial welfare schemes initiated by large northern firms. Industrial regulation, including the Wagner and Social Security Acts, it is argued, were supported by welfare capitalists—GE's Gerard Swope, Walter C. Teagle of Standard Oil, New Jersey, and Marion Folsom of Eastman Kodak—who desired the equalization of labor costs across the geographic spectrum and the elimination of disparities in state welfare legislation. Such an argument is open to question. Dominant northern manufacturers were scarcely subject to unacceptable wage pressures or the likelihood of serious southern competition comparable to that exerted by the South in textiles and coal. In the event, social insurance in the private sector did not represent a burden as it was discretionary and niggardly, given at the sufferance of management.

A survey of private-sector plans for unemployment insurance adopted to May 1931, the peak year for such coverage, revealed only fifteen company plans for guarantee of employment or payment of unemployment benefits, and several of these were inoperative. Such schemes covered only 116,000 employees, with 50,000 eligible for benefits, or less than 1 percent of the workforce. That of the Dennison Manufacturing Co. of Framingham, Massachusetts, founded in 1916 and funded by employer contributions for five years, then by accrued interest, was depleted by the depression. S. C. Johnson & Son of Racine, Wisconsin, adopted a plan in 1922. Also funded by employer contributions, benefits ranged from $1 to $4 per day for the initial 100 days of unemployment. During the plan's eight years' existence, it paid out $4,241. Proctor & Gamble offered a guarantee of full pay up to forty-eight weeks per year, provided after six months of service for those earning less than $2,000 per annum. Covered employees were required to join the firm's profit-sharing plan and to subscribe to a stated amount of company stock. By far the largest company plan was that of General Electric, funded equally by employer and employees. With the depression's impact on the plan, weekly benefits were gradually reduced, then limited to those in need.

The inadequacy of welfare capitalism is also demonstrated by established legal theory, which treated private pensions as a gratuity. When the firm faced financial embarrassment, or if employees left the job or were fired for cause, pensions were invalidated. The Rockefeller-owned Consolidation Coal Company discontinued its pension plan in August 1928 in light of the industry's distressed circumstances. As a gesture, the board of directors set aside a total of $500 per month for the relief of "worthy" indigent and disabled employees or their widows. These "donations" ended when the West Virginia firm went into receivership in May 1932. Employers usually required twenty-five to thirty years of continuous service for vesting, and once granted, a pension could be dropped for cause. All in all, there were 420 voluntary plans in firms employing 3.5 million, most of these large firms. Estimates of private-sector pensioners range from 140,000 to 165,000 in the years 1931 through 1935 in a total population of 7 million over age sixty-five.[10]

Once the recovery program was under way, Roosevelt and his labor secretary, Frances Perkins, looked to limitation of future downswings of the economic cycle through the device of social insurance. Appointment of a woman for service in his cabinet seems secondary to other factors: Perkins's involvement with passage and enforcement of progressive labor legislation, her pragmatism, her commitment to social insurance along lines that differed from that of Great Britain, and her capacities as an administrator. Perkins believed that social justice was workable, that the power of the state could be brought into play to correct social abuses, and that government could serve as an instrument for the control of the new industrial system's excrescences. Nurtured in a comfortable New England environment, she was influenced by social Christianity, as well as by the economist Simon Patten's belief that sufficient wealth had been generated by industry to fund social provision. Tough, yet capable of compromise, ambitious, an astute observer of industrial conditions, she quickly climbed up a ladder that opened up to talented middle-class women: schoolteacher, settlement house worker, labor and safety expert, and administrator, this last as state governments, particularly in the industrialized Northeast, began to focus on the workplace environment for women and children.

Perkins cut her teeth as legislative lobbyist in Albany, New York, for the Consumers' League when she pressed for passage of the so-called fifty-four-hour bill, which limited hours for workingwomen. She soon won the respect of Alfred E. Smith and Robert Wagner, then rising Tammany protégés, and in turn guided them toward factory safety reform in response to the Triangle Factory fire in New York City. She was appointed by Smith in his first term as governor to the new state Industrial Board in 1919, which she chaired as of 1924. Roosevelt elevated her to the post of industrial commissioner when he won the governorship.

Both wanted passage of social legislation at the state level, particularly unemployment insurance. Roosevelt hesitated on the ground that no state could burden business with such an expense lest its industries lose out to competitors. Perkins was more decided on the issue and, when offered the post of secretary of labor in Roosevelt's cabinet, conditioned her acceptance on a public works program and passage of social insurance. Her position was grounded on social principles and in the belief that such policies would stabilize purchasing power. Roosevelt's response reflected both past and future attitudes on the subject: "You know, Frances, I don't believe in the dole and I never will." The president-elect need not have been concerned.[11]

Dispatched by Roosevelt to London to study the British system, Perkins published on her return an "American Plan" for unemployment insurance. While supportive of relief expenditure, she deplored the blurred dividing line in England between compulsory insurance against unemployment and the dole. (The postwar depression in England led to "uncovenanted" or extended benefits, which resulted in the waiver of contributions by employees and employers and the abandonment of limits on the number of weeks such benefits could be received.) Employers, she argued, should pay for unemployment insurance, with recipients required to endure a waiting period of one month in order to rule out payments for brief spells between jobs. It would provide for "stable workers for whom payments can be made into the fund on an actuarial basis. . . . It does not touch the situation of the unstable or unskilled worker . . . the worker in a disorganized industry . . . nor the unemployable."[12]

Roosevelt dispatched a message to Congress on June 8, 1934, on the subject of a projected social insurance program intended to "prevent a recurrence of collapse" and to afford protection "against the hazards and vicissitudes of life . . . especially those which relate to unemployment and old age." Later that month, by executive order, Roosevelt assigned the task to a Committee on Economic Security. The CES consisted of four cabinet members, labor (Perkins, who chaired), treasury (Henry Morgenthau Jr.), agriculture (Henry A. Wallace), and the attorney general (Homer S. Cummings), and the federal relief administrator (Harry Hopkins).

Edwin E. Witte, chairman of the University of Wisconsin's economics department and an experienced legislative draftsman, served as executive director, charged with formulation of concrete proposals for social insurance. A student of the labor historian John R. Commons, Witte had been recruited by Perkins on the advice of her assistant secretary, Arthur J. Altmeyer, another Commons Ph.D. who had served as secretary of the Wisconsin Industrial Commission, which administered that state's labor laws. Witte, Altmeyer, and other Commons protégés represented the Wisconsin idea in the field of unemployment insurance, promoting federal-state cooperation and reliance on state-legislated programs. Witte's staff included Barbara Armstrong of the University of California-Berkeley law school, author of *Insuring the Essentials: Minimum Wage, Plus Social Insurance—A Living Wage Problem* (1932), and J. Douglas Brown, an economist affiliated with the Industrial Relations Section at Princeton University, who, with Murray W. Latimer, a former corporate pension planner responsible for the Railroad Retirement Act of 1934, helped to draft the Social Security Act's old-age insurance provisions.[13]

An Advisory Council, appointed by the president and the CES, was chaired by Frank P. Graham, president of the University of North Carolina. The choice of Graham, a southern progressive, as chairman was intended to blunt the animus toward the program expected from southern conservatives. The council consisted partly of corporate members—Eastman Kodak's Folsom, GE's Swope, and Standard of New Jersey's Teagle—who were welfare capitalists favoring a nationally standardized and administered unemployment insurance program.[14]

The presence on Witte's staff of Bryce M. Stewart and Murray W. Latimer, affiliated with Industrial Relations Counselors, Inc., and J. Douglas Brown of Princeton's Industrial Relations Section, both funded by John D. Rockefeller Jr., is explained by Rockefeller's interest in improved labor relations following the Ludlow Massacre, a fierce battle on April 20, 1914, between coal miners and state militia at the Colorado Fuel and Iron Company which left a number of men, women, and children dead. At issue were working conditions and union recognition. Determined to bind labor and capital as partners, Rockefeller-controlled firms adopted employee representation schemes, or company unions, and eventually added employee benefits.[15]

Aided by his counsel, Raymond B. Fosdick, Rockefeller formalized his interest in reducing labor strife with the employment of labor relations specialists in the Fosdick law firm, spun off as Industrial Relations Counselors, Inc., in 1926. The group, made up of exponents of labor welfare plans, published definitive studies of corporate pension and unemployment compensation schemes in the United States, Canada, and Europe, including Latimer's *Industrial Pension Systems in the United States and*

Canada (1932–33) and Stewart's *Planning and Administration of Unemployment Compensation in the United States* (1938).[16]

Roosevelt's house capitalists aside, most industrialists opposed social insurance on the basis of cost and state intrusion into the private sector. Whereas the U.S. Chamber of Commerce—for the moment—and the National Retail Dry Goods Association supported the Economic Security Act, the National Association of Manufacturers, Manufacturing Chemists Association (6,257 member firms), Connecticut Manufacturers Association, Ohio Chamber of Commerce (some 4,000 members), and Illinois Manufacturers Association (2,500 members), among others, opposed it. Thus the New York State Economic Council requested that the president and Congress defer compulsory social insurance pending business recovery, and the NAM platform of American Industry, adopted in December 1934, claimed that federal legislation designed either to establish a compulsory national system or to subsidize state systems constituted an unconstitutional invasion of state and local activity.

In May 1935 the U.S. Chamber of Commerce reversed field. "We question the propriety as well as the constitutionality of any effort by the Federal Government to take jurisdiction over the subject matter of this proposed legislation," read a Chamber resolution. The business group objected to the impact of the payroll taxes on recovery. With the momentum of the 1920s welfare capitalist movement faded in the depression, most business leaders and organizations strongly opposed national and state-level pensions and social insurance, as did the mass of smaller manufacturers, wary of its immediate cost and oblivious, perhaps correctly, to the theoretical argument that they could pass these costs through to the consumer.

Neither support from welfare capitalists nor opposition from others in the business community was basic to Roosevelt's decisions in the matter of social insurance or its coverage, at least until the 1939 amendments when welfare capitalists allied with the Hansen-NRPB planners and those who favored income redistribution. No social radical knew this scene better than Abraham Epstein, founder of the American Association for Old Age Security. Epstein, who favored a national plan for unemployment compensation, noted "the opposition of well organized American employers to social legislation," led by their research directors, state chambers of commerce, manufacturers associations, and trade groups. Roosevelt was left with the support of Marion Folsom, Gerard Swope, Winthrop Aldrich, and other liberal members of the Commerce Department's Business Advisory Council.[17]

Massive unemployment and the success of existing workmen's compensation legislation at the state level, which served as a model, led the Committee on Economic Security to focus on unemployment reserves. Two approaches emerged: state-administered programs funded by employer contributions based on experience rating—the tendency of a plant or industry to maintain a steady employment level—favored by the Commons-Witte-Wisconsin school and passed as the Groves Act (1932) or a national plan with national standards supported by an alliance of welfare capitalists and radical social reformers on the Advisory Council.

The Wisconsin state-based plan suffered a major handicap: if implemented by some states, unemployment reserves would put local industries at a competitive disadvantage with those states which failed to follow suit. In a quest for advice, Walter Raushenbush, the Wisconsin law's administrator, turned to his father-in-law, Justice Louis D. Brandeis, who directed Raushenbush to the 1927 case of *Florida v. Mellon,* 273 U.S. 12, as instructive. The Sunshine State had lured wealthy retirees by abjuring inheritance taxes. Congress, in the Revenue Act of 1924, provided for a federal inheritance levy that allowed an 80 percent offset against state estate taxes, upheld by the Supreme Court in the Florida case. Presumably, since the same principle could be utilized in the field of unemployment insurance, Brandeis proposed a federal payroll tax on employers, to be offset by payments to state unemployment reserve funds. But there were significant differences between the two proposals. The federal death tax credit made no attempt to induce the states to adopt policies that traditionally fell under their residual police powers, and the Constitution gave no explicit power to the central government to legislate on the subject of unemployment insurance. Federal action, Brandeis believed, was limited to grants-in-aid to the states on a matching basis or to exemption of private employers from the federal income tax for payments to unemployment insurance funds (tax-offset).

At a series of Washington dinners, Walter and Elizabeth Brandeis Raushenbush, the prime movers; Lincoln Filene, a Boston merchant, and Henry Dennison, a Massachusetts stationery and paper goods manufacturer (both progressive social and economic planners); Wagner; Thomas Corcoran; Isador Lubin, commissioner of labor statistics; Perkins; and members of her legal staff, Charles E. Wyzanski Jr. and Thomas Eliot, agreed on tax-offset. This served as the mechanism for the Wagner-Lewis bill, introduced in Congress in February 1934, which provided for a 5 percent federal payroll tax on employers of more than ten persons, to be offset by unemployment insurance levies under state law. The states were left free to choose a plan based on plant reserves, industry reserves, or pooled funds.[18]

Roosevelt hesitated to act. Industrialists questioned their ability to manage a sizable payroll tax when prices and profits were under pressure. Also, it was common knowledge that Robert L. Doughton, the North Carolinian who headed the House Ways and Means Committee, and Pat Harrison of Mississippi, chairman of the Senate Finance Committee, both of whom reflected the views of southern conservatives, were equivocal if not openly opposed to the bill.

The president also needed to reconcile the views of the federalists and the nationalists, the latter in favor of a uniform, nationalized system as opposed to the Wisconsin advocates of state-based plans that allowed for experimentation and local variations. William Leiserson and Isaac Rubinow, who wrote the Ohio Plan, rejected Abraham Epstein's insistence on emulating the British model, an insurance system based on employer, employee, and state contributions, with the size of its payout geared to the number of the insured's dependents. "Such a provision," according to Leiserson, "completely changes the character of the law so that it becomes a relief measure rather than an insurance scheme. . . . I do not want to mix relief measures with insurance legislation. . . . Insurance in my mind is limited to plans which pay benefits in accordance with premiums contributed and regardless of the means or resources possessed by the recipients."[19]

On the issue of a federalized versus a nationalized system of unemployment insurance, Witte gained Felix Frankfurter and Louis D. Brandeis as valuable allies. The United States was not a "tight little island like England," Frankfurter urged. Schemes of social legislation, while a necessity, needed to evolve over time, respect variation from state to state, and provide for the gradual development of relations between the central government and the states. Frankfurter preached an evolutionary process that would determine the balance between centralized and decentralized administration. A visit with Justice Brandeis at his Chatham, Massachusetts, summer home not only confirmed Brandeis's support for tax-offset but suggested to Witte that only social insurance managed by the states would pass muster with the Supreme Court. Witte noted that Brandeis "believes that we will never again have another depression like the present; in any event, we have to plan on that basis. Believes strongly that all forms of social insurance should be state administered." Witte required little persuasion in the matter of a federal-state system for unemployment reserves. As he saw it, the Constitution, as interpreted by the courts, limited federal authority to protection of the states when they used the police power in providing unemployment legislation; also the states served ideally as laboratories for experimentation with unemployment reserves. The Supreme Court soon substantiated the argument for limited federal authority; and, in any event, as Witte noted, a substantial majority in Congress opposed federally imposed uniformity.[20]

Immediately applicable to the question of nationalizing social insurance was the Supreme Court decision in the case of *Railroad Retirement Board v. Alton Railroad Co.,* decided May 6, 1935, which led the Congress to doubt that a national program could overcome legal doctrine. The Court declared that establishment by Congress of a compulsory retirement program for employees of interstate carriers violated the commerce clause. A fund had been created to be administered by the Retirement Board based on compulsory, uniform contributions by employers and employees of Class I railroads. The majority opinion that uniform contributions met social ends, not the federal government's authority or need to regulate interstate commerce, and hence were void undermined the likelihood of a nationalized plan for unemployment or old-age insurance. The Court also held that uniform contributions by all carriers represented a taking of property, violating the principle of due process of law.[21]

Bryce M. Stewart of Industrial Relations Counselors fell back on a compromise proposal favored also by the AFL and social welfarists led by Abraham Epstein. Stewart suggested a national system based on grants-in-aid to the states and uniformity of benefits which he held likely to pass muster with the Supreme Court. This plan failed to resolve the split with the Wisconsin progressives who favored state collection of payroll taxes, with benefit levels governed by loose federal standards.

When the CES convened, Perkins, Morgenthau, Wallace, and Hopkins endorsed the federal-state program. They reasoned that tax-offset was more likely to be held constitutional by the Supreme Court in the light of its decision in the case of *Florida v. Mellon.* In the event of an unfavorable court decision, under the federal-state tax-offset plan the states might well continue with their own unemployment insurance schemes as they would have passed laws that levied a payroll tax. Disagreement within the committee on the amount and longevity of benefits, coverage for seasonal and part-time employees, employee versus employer contributions, and employer experience rating could be resolved at the state level, which allowed for state and regional differences. Critical to the CES decision, it needs to be added, was Roosevelt's insistence from the outset—a view he repeated to Perkins, Altmeyer, Witte, and Eliot at the White House—that "we've got to leave all that we can to the states, all the power shouldn't be in the hands of the federal government."

Just before Christmas, Perkins convened a meeting at her home. Six hours of debate led to a federal-state system with loose national standards, approved by the president following a presentation at the White House by Perkins and Hopkins. It provided coverage for employers of eight or more persons, levied a federal tax ascending from 1 percent of payroll in 1936 to 2 percent in 1937 and 3 percent in 1938. The plan also provided for a 90 percent offset against approved state plans based on pooled funds. The question of constitutionality, as well as both presidential and congressional insistence on retention of considerable autonomy in the hands of the states, proved to be decisive.[22]

Provision of old-age insurance took a different trajectory from that of unemployment reserves since no state plan furnished a usable model. All imposed a lengthy residence requirement, and most relied on counties for funding through property taxes. Typically, Ohio's scheme required state residence for fifteen years, proof of poverty and good character, and a lien against one's home claimed on death by the state for the purpose of reimbursement. Old-age assistance reached only 231,000 persons by 1935, less than 3 percent of those over age sixty-five. Average monthly assistance ranged from $26 in Massachusetts to a more usual sum of less than $10 elsewhere. Workers' mobility over a lifetime also increased the need for a national plan.

Given the technical problems involved, Witte, persuaded by M. Albert Linton, president of Provident Mutual Life Insurance Company, Philadelphia, brought experienced actuaries into the picture. The actuaries determined on a partial reserve or pay-as-you-go system, the reserve amounting to $15.25 billion. Unlike a full reserve system, a partial reserve called for federal contributions sufficient to maintain this level at some future date when out payments exceeded income from contributions and interest. A full reserve system, it was believed, meant the accumulation of some $50 to $60 billion over time, a sum regarded as too large to be managed by the U.S. Treasury. It also was argued that a large reserve would tempt politicians to use it for other purposes and would require unacceptably high payroll taxes that would soak up spending power in the depression.

The original bill drafted by actuaries provided for a payroll tax on earnings up to $3,000, at a total rate of 1 percent, 0.5 percent each for employers and employees for the years 1937–41, with provision for gradual increases until the total reached 5 percent. The surplus projected in the plan's early years would be drawn down gradually by beneficiaries until 1965, when the federal government would be required to meet an anticipated deficit from general revenues, estimated at $124 million beginning in 1965, rising to $1.1 billion by 1980, figures that were unrealistically low.

Monthly annuities became payable beginning in 1942, lump-sum death benefits to survivors in 1937. Because early retirees, scheduled initially to collect monthly stipends beginning in 1942, would qualify for a 24 cents per month annuity calculated on an actuarial basis at a monthly wage of $50, 48 cents if they earned $100 monthly, the plan provided for a $10 monthly minimum, those with greater incomes and the young subsidizing those nearing age sixty-five. Yet this was not fundamentally a need-based system, since benefits in due course would be scaled to reflect prior income.

The Social Security Act also provided for federal grants to the states for the blind and handicapped, child welfare, maternal and child-related health assistance, and public health services (categorical assistance). Aid to dependent children (mothers' pensions), which made the federal government responsible for one-third of the cost of state services, came about at the insistence of Grace Abbott, Katherine Lenroot, and Secretary Perkins. While the original bill presented by the CES covered all employed persons, domestic workers and farm laborers were excluded by the House Ways and Means Committee, based on Treasury's claim that it would be overwhelmed by a broader plan. On the other hand, old-age assistance did not exclude farmers and farm labor if they were covered under state law. Health insurance failed to get off the ground given objections by the American Medical Association.

When Roosevelt learned from Henry Morgenthau Jr. that tax rates, scheduled to reach a total of 5 percent of payrolls in 1957, would not suffice over time to meet contractual obligations, requiring resort to general revenues, he balked. Opposed to "the same old dole," he ordered a recalculation which led to the Morgenthau amendment calling for escalated payroll taxes. This change, carried to Roosevelt and then the Congress by Morgenthau, emanated from Treasury's and Roosevelt's concern that a pending five-year public works program, intended to employ 3.5 million people and estimated to cost $17.5 billion, with nearly $5 billion to be expended in the year beginning July 1, 1935, alone, would severely impact the federal budget. (Also pending was congressional passage of early payment—some $2 billion—of the veterans' bonus.) As for the possibility that a broad-based income tax on the middle class would suffice to cover the cost of old-age insurance, the Twentieth Century Fund estimated revenues from this source at only $200 million per annum. It was anticipated, further, that funds collected under Title VIII of the Social Security Act would help finance unfunded, noncontributory old-age pensions provided under Title I of the law.[23]

As presented to the Congress by Morgenthau, payroll levies were projected to begin at a rate of 2 percent (1 percent each for employer and employee) in 1937, rising at intervals, reaching a total of 6 percent by 1949. If implemented, these higher rates would have generated a reserve fund estimated at close to $50 billion by 1980 instead of the $15.25 billion reserve proposed by the CES; the larger sum was regarded as adequate to meet future liabilities. Altmeyer, Perkins, and Eliot, the law's legislative draftsman, worked out a compromise: a small contribution in the first year, with rates rising rapidly in the ensuing years in light of the group's belief that escalating payroll taxes would be so large as to be confiscatory and would be scaled back by Congress, as they were in 1939. In fact, payroll taxes were frozen at a total of 2 percent under the 1939 amendments, and benefits were expanded to include widows, surviving parents, children of deceased workers, and the children and spouses of retirees.[24]

Congressional hearings centered on the old-age assistance feature of the bill. Byrd of Virginia, supported by southern members of both the House Ways and Means Committee and the Senate Finance Committee, claimed that the bill would vest authority over the states in a federal department, seen as a wedge for federal interference with the handling of "the Negro question." Watering down of the federal government's supervisory role in the form of a vague proviso for "a reasonable subsistence compatible with decency and health" resulted in a wide divergence in such support, ranging from $6.37 per month in Mississippi to $32.39 in California, with 50 percent of the cost paid by the federal government.

At one point, based on the claim of dubious constitutionality of old-age insurance, leading members of the House Ways and Means Committee told the president that support was so lacking as to necessitate its removal from the economic security package lest it endanger passage. The Senate Finance Committee, dominated by southern conservatives, appeared even less enamored of old-age insurance, particularly with the May 6 decision of the Supreme Court holding the 1934 Railroad Retirement Act unconstitutional in language that seemingly applied to the social security bill. With passage doubtful, Pat Harrison delayed a committee vote and gradually worked to win over opponents. (Byrd and North Carolina's Josiah Bailey absented themselves from the final committee vote.) But for Roosevelt's endorsement, according to Witte, "the old age insurance titles would be completely stricken from the bill." Roosevelt signed the law on August 14, 1935. The principles of insurance as the basis for social security and state management of the assistance program explain congressional support.[25]

From their inception the potentially huge reserves and high payroll taxes called for by the Morgenthau amendment, contrasted with the law's limited coverage, left the Social Security Act's old-age insurance provisions vulnerable to attack by divergent interests. These included insurance company executives and their actuaries allied with Michigan's Senator Arthur Vandenberg, who favored a pay-as-you-go system, or limited reserves; radical critics, led by Abraham Epstein, who viewed social insurance as a vehicle for income redistribution; advocates of purchasing-power theory who pointed to high payroll taxes as regressive and responsible for the 1937–38 downturn; the Twentieth Century Fund and spokesmen for welfare capitalism who favored lower taxes, hence a current-cost-basis system; and academic experts, notably Eveline M. Burns and Paul H. Douglas, as well as the principal Social Security administrators, Arthur J. Altmeyer and Wilbur J. Cohen, who pushed for benefits extended to widows and orphaned children.

The differences between Epstein and Edith Abbott on the one hand and Witte on the other proved to be fundamental. Witte held that social assistance, which expressed the community's obligation to its needy, as in the instance of mothers' pensions (aid to dependent children) or rehabilitation programs for the disabled, should be financed from general tax sources. Contributory insurance programs, on the other hand, should meet problems generated by industry: unemployment, accidental injury, health needs, and the superannuation of workers. Edith Abbott of the University of Chicago expressed "little faith in social insurance, believing that it is very costly and will not take care of a large part of the people who are dependent. . . . Miss Abbott is particularly opposed to contributions by employees, whether to unemployment insurance or old age pensions." Abbott stressed the development of a permanent system of relief for the unemployed and the dependent, with the federal government imposing standards and sustaining most of the cost.

Epstein, supported by J. Douglas Brown, viewed social insurance in terms of "social stability or social security of the existing society which can now be accomplished only through the assurance of a minimum of purchasing power" and in terms of a more equitable society. "Whereas private insurance is based on the principle of paying the greatest benefit to those who can afford to pay the highest premiums, social insurance aims rather at the establishment of a minimum level of economic sustenance. . . . Since its chief aim is to accomplish socially desirable ends, the premium rates are determined by social policy; not by the actuary." Insurance executives and actuaries, fearing the loss of highly profitable industrial, or burial, policies sold to the working class, sided with Epstein. Linton pushed forward increased early benefits sufficient to assure an adequate or minimal living standard and expanded coverage, or a blend of old-age assistance and old-age insurance, creating a system that would not compete with insurers' products.[26]

The resulting 1939 amendments, effective the next year, provided increased benefits overall, particularly for low-income workers, and new benefits for widows and survivors of insured workers and for their dependent children and parents. The suspension at the same time of pending increased payroll taxes led to a pay-as-you-go system.[27]

Witte, a member of the Social Security Advisory Council, challenged the actuarial basis of the 1939 revision, predicting that younger, longer-lived future beneficiaries either would receive lowered benefits or would be assessed inordinately high payroll taxes, a claim easily dismissed at a time when payroll tax collections far exceeded annuity outgo. In fact, actuarial estimates made in 1935 had proven flawed. The prediction of 35 million enrollees by 1980 had already been exceeded, thus understating future obligations and overstating future reserves. In Witte's view terminating the reserve system evaded the issue of accrued liabilities. The answer rested either in retaining payroll levies at current rates or adopting multiparty contributions at the outset, payable by government, employers, and employees. Modeled on the British system, a tack later taken by Alvin Hansen, the latter method made clear federal responsibility for the likely shortfall. Opponents argued that such liabilities were meaningless when applied to the federal government as opposed to private insurers, as the former possessed unlimited power to tax to meet its obligations.[28]

Lacking support, Witte lost the debate to the social justice advocates, the American Keynesians and the planners at the National Resources Planning Board who allied with Altmeyer and Cohen. Marriner S. Eccles, chairman of the Federal Reserve Board, addressed the concerns of the public-spending contingent: "The present plan is operating as a gigantic saving device," he complained, "at a time when there is a surfeit of saving; it is decreasing consumption when we have inadequate consumer buying power."[29]

Morgenthau reversed his earlier stand, caving, according to Witte, to Hopkins, Eccles, Hansen, and the Federal Reserve economist Laughlin Currie, who believed in social security as a mechanism for economic stabilization and who abjured reserves beyond a period of three to five years. Roosevelt, Witte also claimed, preoccupied with war preparedness, capitulated to congressional pressure for frozen rates and expanded benefits and to Republicans responsive to the Townsend movement. "The inevitable day of reckoning would come," Witte predicted, as the Advisory Council, the Congress, and the administration overrode his construct of social insurance.[30]

HE 1937–38 RECESSION WITHIN a depression was profoundly disappointing as it followed a gradual recovery achieved by the mid-1930s. The recession was attributable to a misguided Federal Reserve policy of increased interest rates and bank reserve requirements, a decline in federal expenditure, and a surfeit of manufacturers inventory that needed to be drawn down. The cure was contested initially within the National Resources Planning Board and subsequently in the Congress.

While institutional planners led by the NRPB economist Gardiner C. Means advocated federal micromanagement of industry, particularly output and wage maintenance, this approach to a permanent recovery came under challenge by Laughlin Currie, a Federal Reserve Board economist, who advocated a compensatory fiscal policy based on net federal contribution to the economy. Currie sought to rationalize public expenditure by determination of an amount sufficient to stimulate both consumption and use of idle savings for investment beyond public works. Harvard's Alvin Hansen took the argument into the realm of macroeconomic management through fiscal policy for agricultural programs such as land use planning, public investment in valley resource development, urban housing, an expanded social insurance program, and if need be investment in industrial expansion. Such expenditure would come under the aegis of an independent agency staffed by experts that reported to the Congress. This agency would accelerate or decelerate public expenditure in response to the business cycle. According to Hansen, such a policy required blueprints (advanced planning for public expenditure) that could be implemented as needed by experts, not after the fact by the Congress. "We do not have a choice between 'plan and no plan.'"

The initial rationale for public expenditure as a stimulus to the economy was provided by Currie, who won a wide and influential audience in the Roosevelt administration. Outlets for savings in the 1920s based on rapid population growth, the emergence of the automobile industry, foreign loans, and state and municipal capital expenditures had dried up. Only federal government borrowing and expenditure could compensate for excess saving and deficiency of private spending. Currie claimed that several problems needed to be addressed: abandonment of the concept of annual budget balance in favor of net federal contribution sufficient to induce full employment other than by make-work and development of a rationalized tax system designed to put more spending power in the hands of lower-income groups. An expanded social security program, extended to workers' dependents and other beneficiaries, Currie and Hansen also believed, would meet the need for social equity, stimulate purchasing power, and if financed by other than exclusive reliance on payroll taxes would further rationalize the theory of net federal contribution to the economy.[1]

While Currie and Means debated their respective proposals for an attack on the depression under the aegis of the National Resources Planning Board, an anti–New Deal coalition of Southern Democrats and Republicans took shape in the Congress. The "conservative coalition" was bent on defeating proposed public investment in infrastructure based on the economic cycle and administered by an independent agency domiciled in the executive branch, to these congressmen another example of Roosevelt's overreach. Unable to repeal the New Deal, congressional conservatives determined to staunch its progress.

The process of developing a theory of net federal contribution to the economy to end the depression began with the appearance of Marriner S. Eccles before the Senate Finance Committee in its quest for recovery measures during the grim days of February 1933. The Utah banker proposed federal stimulus to the economy by financing reemployment in order to reverse the economic cycle. He attributed the depression to excess saving in the twenties funneled into capital expenditure and to diminished purchasing power, which resulted in a $30 billion decline in national income. Credit expansion by the Reconstruction Finance Corporation would not do. Only increased volume and turnover of bank money would raise price levels and yield sufficient federal income to finance recovery.

Heir to a business-banking empire in the Mountain States, Eccles challenged the view held by Bernard Baruch and Herbert Hoover that massive scaling down of debt would induce recovery.[2] Rather, continued debt liquidation devalued assets held by fiduciary institutions and endangered the solvency of those still afloat. Eccles relied on countercyclical theory: resolution of the depression crisis required substantial expenditure for public works funded either by a bond issue or by issuance of currency by Treasury through the Federal Reserve banks. In addition, government must assume active management of the economic system by promoting more equitable distribution of wealth and income in order to restore a balance between output and purchasing power.[3]

From Salt Lake City a discouraged Eccles viewed with skepticism much of the early New Deal program. The economy bill would reduce purchasing power and increase unemployment. The Farm Credit Act and Home Owners Loan Act, like RFC loans, introduced greater liquidity into the economy but did not create new purchasing power. A devalued dollar would afford only a temporary lift to exports, since other nations would follow suit. The National Recovery Administration restricted output when it should have stimulated consumption. Eccles concluded that the current situation differed from earlier depressions that had been resolved by renewed capital expenditure when prices and wages fell substantially. Reliance on credit expansion would not work; financial institutions continued to contract loans in pursuit of liquidity and failed, in the event, to find creditworthy customers. The consequent decline in bank money amounted to $15 billion, a problem complicated by falling turnover of checking account money. An increase in the quantity of money would not suffice as only 10 percent of purchases were made with cash. "The need is not for more money but for more spending." Whereas bankers could not supply credit at a time when one-half of productive property lay idle, government could ignite a crippled economy because of its power to spend and tax. Also, because poor income distribution had caused the depression, remedy depended on adequate purchasing power in the hands of those who would spend, not save. This required government expenditure for public works financed by taxation of high incomes, estates, and corporate surpluses.[4]

These views were carried by Eccles to Tugwell, Ezekiel, Wallace, Hopkins, and Jerome Frank at a Washington dinner in November 1933, then to Henry Morgenthau Jr. one month later. Commodity prices, Eccles told the treasury secretary, could not be raised by pursuit of George Warren's theories, only by increased bank money through federal expenditure and by stimulus to turnover. Morgenthau offered him the post of special assistant charged with monetary and credit matters; while committed to budget balance, the head of the Treasury employed dissenters so long as they kept their opinions in house.[5]

When nominated by FDR to the post of governor of the Federal Reserve Board in the summer of 1934, Eccles conditioned acceptance on a restructured Federal Reserve System based on central control and management of the monetary mechanism as an instrument for acceleration or tempering of business activity. With money management diffused and under the control of the twelve regional governors of the system, the money supply tended to be procyclical: it expanded with increased rate of business spending and contracted when it declined. Eccles held that reversal of procyclical policies required a strengthened Federal Reserve Board given control over open-market purchases and sales of bills and securities. In the past, Eccles noted, the twelve autonomous governors, "profoundly influenced by a narrow banking rather than a broad social point of view," had dominated open-market policy. He wanted a reconstituted Open Market Committee, with policy control in the hands of the board, which represented national needs.[6]

The 1935 Banking Act met Eccles's criteria. It marked a shift from a system based on diffused power to a newly created Board of Governors of the Federal Reserve System. A reorganized Open Market Committee consisted of five representatives of the regional banks and the seven members of the board, the latter positioned to set open-market policy and interest rates. At the same time the board's power to set reserve requirements was expanded, since the new legislation made permanent a section of the Glass-Steagall Act (1933) which permitted Reserve Bank advances on any satisfactory security. The concept of eligible paper thus ended.[7]

Lack of formal training in economics led Eccles to recruit Laughlin Currie, a Treasury Department economist, for service on his staff as assistant director of the Division of Research and Statistics. Currie provided Eccles and a coterie of New Dealers with a rationale for recovery based on deficit spending. Born in Nova Scotia, he was educated at the London School of Economics and Harvard, where he took his Ph.D. Currie's dissertation, "Bank Assets in Banking Theory," published as *The Supply of Money in the United States* (1934), offered a critique of the Fed's monetary policy. It suggested a policy based on general business conditions as opposed to emphasis on liquidity and the quality or productiveness of commercial loans. To accomplish greater central bank control and a counter-cyclical monetary policy, Currie also urged better use of open-market techniques and discretionary management of reserves.[8]

Like Eccles, however, Currie came to regard deficit spending as indispensable to recovery, a position he took in a letter cowritten by six Harvard economics instructors and sent to the White House in late January 1934, then published in the New York Times. Since the letter departed from the orthodox (anti–New Deal) views of the senior members of the Harvard economics faculty, Currie, barely into his thirties, moved to Treasury on the assumption that he had no future at Cambridge. As assistant research director of the Fed, he provided an economic rationale for purchasing-power theory. This proved to be no small achievement. Before Keynes's General Theory—and even after its appearance—advocates of deficit spending faced formidable obstacles. Wartime aside, no precedent existed for budget unbalance. Fiscal policy in peacetime consisted of an accounting of federal income and expenditure; depression era deficits were involuntary, not an instrument of macroeconomic policy. Deficits were equated with reckless spending and required higher interest rates and taxes. The result was additional unemployment and reduced output.[9]

Currie challenged budget balance in depression as lacking logic: "Balancing the budget requires either a curtailment of expenditures or an increase in taxes, or both. . . . A contraction of expenditures means . . . a contraction of the demand for goods, which in turn involves further contraction of incomes. With each decline in incomes the ability to pay taxes and the yield of taxes at given rates decline." Like Eccles, Currie viewed relief expenditure as simply maintenance of current demand, or bare subsistence. Only increased government expenditure on durables would stimulate demand for output, as these industries, particularly construction, represented the bulk of unemployment. Currie charted the decline in the construction industry since the second half of the 1920s (table 3). Remediation required a massive federal public works program financed by deficits.

In his estimates of the pump-priming deficit required over time to bring about full employment, Currie differentiated among several categories of government deficit expenditure ranked in proximate order of their effectiveness: durable goods and housing, federal funding of rail improvements, rural electrification, utilities, and relief. He also questioned the notion of a uniform multiplier, since one could not apply the current

TABLE 3. Estimated Construction (millions of dollars), 1925–33

	Average, 1925–29	Average, 1930–33	1933
PRIVATE			
Residential	2,818.6	811	222
Commercial	1,007.8	388	89
Other	403.8	193.5	169
Total private	4,230.2	1,392.5	480
Railroads and Utilities	2,976	2,245	1,088
PUBLIC			
Cities	1,365.6	1,198	400
Counties	744.8	391.6	100
State	466.2	681	300
Federal	258	493.3	500
Total public	2,834.6	2,763.9	1,300

Grand total (approx.) in billions

1925–29	1930	1931	1932	1933
10 to 11	10.1	7.5	4.4	3.1

Source: Federal Employment Stabilization Board, appended to Laughlin Currie, "Memorandum on Confidence" [1934], box 72, Eccles Papers.

income velocity of all money to any given amount of new money as the latter might well differ from the former. He predicted only a tendency for income and expenditure to be increased beyond the amount expended, as the multiplier varied with the nature of federal spending.

Implicit in this was a definition of pump priming that differed from its normal usage, or government expenditure that served as a quick jolt to recovery—impossible in light of the massive decline in durable goods output. Rather, Currie proposed continuous pump-priming expenditure until a housing recovery was secured and excess industrial capacity was eliminated. As a counter to budget balance theorists, he contrasted net national debt of the United States, at $19 billion (deducting recoverable loans, gold, and cash balances from gross interest-bearing debt) with that of the United Kingdom, at $37 billion in 1934. With the United Kingdom's income at $19 billion, its debt stood at two times national income; with U.S. national income at $55 billion, current U.S. debt stood at a mere .35 times income. Service on U.S. debt amounted to 1.3 percent of current income; for the United Kingdom, 7.3 percent. Based on this analysis, Currie estimated that the United States could sustain a debt of $110 billion, several times the current level. Annual expenditure that proved insufficient to afford the required stimulus to private expenditure would build up a large debt and still not counter the depression.[10]

While the general notion of federal investment as a stimulus to economic activity was not a novelty, Currie buttressed the concept by a monthly series compiled with the assistance of a former student, Martin Krost. Designed to measure federal income-increasing expenditures required to bring about full recovery, the Currie-Krost series served as a pioneering step toward the emergence of macroeconomic fiscal policy and the goal of a full or maximum-employment economy. Currie and Krost rejected official Treasury figures that measured the deficit as an unsatisfactory indicator of government's contribution to private incomes. Instead, they distinguished among income-increasing, income-decreasing, and neutral Treasury activity. Income-increasing expenditure was defined as money that changed hands as a payment for current services, e.g., public works and relief. Most government receipts fell into the income-decreasing category. Loans to financial institutions designed to increase liquidity were treated as neutral in impact. Measuring the activity this way, Currie and Krost estimated federal income-increasing expenditures for the fiscal years ending June 1933, 1934, and 1935 at $1.9, $2.47, and $3.28 billion, respectively, as against the $4 billion they deemed necessary.[11]

Toward the end of Roosevelt's first term, Currie's observations on fiscal policy reached several influential economists and advisers, including Leon Henderson at the WPA and Isador Lubin at Labor. Through Henderson, who served as economic adviser to the Democratic National Committee in the 1936 campaign, Currie's contacts expanded to include Thomas Corcoran and Benjamin Cohen, Jerome Frank, William O. Douglas, Harry Hopkins, and Henry Wallace.

With the 1937–38 recession and the Eccles-Currie disinterest in monetary policy as the lever for recovery, fiscal policy overtook the monetary approach. In the interim, however, while the Currie-Krost studies offered the New Deal a sound statistical base for deficit spending as a recovery device, strong opposition remained. Economists and businessmen, by and large, were not yet amenable to deficit spending. Thus in early 1936 the U.S. Chamber of Commerce membership, convinced that a natural recovery was under way and antagonistic to the Roosevelt policies, overwhelmingly endorsed a referendum calling for budget balance to be achieved by reduced expenditure.[12]

Indeed, Eccles aside, Currie's analysis of the role of federal expenditure in the economic process received scant support at the Fed. Emanuel A. Goldenweiser, director of research and Currie's immediate superior, blocked publication of the Currie-Krost findings in the *Federal Reserve Bulletin*, and the study could be secured only on request. "I was in hostile territory at the Federal Reserve," Currie recalled, "and completely dependent on Eccles's support."[13]

Even as Currie broke new ground on federal income-increasing expenditure, the federal deficit narrowed with increased revenues while the Board of Governors tightened reserve requirements in order to check excessive credit expansion. This was achieved in three steps, in August 1936 and March and May 1937, with the concurrence of the New York Fed's George L. Harrison and the bank's economic adviser, Harvard's John H. Williams. As a result, reserve requirements were doubled, removing some $3 billion of reserves as a base for monetary expansion. Currie, unopposed to this tightening, concluded that the economy was midway to recovery, with national income at $64 billion as opposed to $40 billion in 1932. To tame price rises and speculative inventory accumulation, he supported the firming of interest rates, the wiping out of excess bank reserves, and budget balance. "It is better to aim at relatively full employment in, say, three years' time, and in the meantime to carry the unemployed, than it is to seek full recovery in a year or so," lest price pressures, a shortage of skilled labor, and inventory building lead to a boom and a bust.[14]

These conclusions reflected the widespread belief that a natural business recovery was under way, and with it the possibility of reduced deficits, possibly eventual budget balance through increased revenue by means of a tax on the undistributed profits of large corporations, a measure passed by Congress in June 1936. The stage was set for the 1937–38 recession, brought on by monetary tightening, in which Currie concurred, a decline in federal net contribution to the economy, disincentives toward private-sector investment as a result of unusually heavy taxation of corporations, and a rise in prices and business inventory.

The notion of heavy taxation of the corporate surplus was well received in the administration, as Roosevelt, Morgenthau, and Eccles converged on the issue of corporate power. Large corporations, they believed, especially those closely held, retained earnings as a means of assisting wealthy shareholders in tax avoidance, since corporate tax rates were lower than those on high incomes. A tax on retained corporate earnings would force idle funds into the economy, while drawing down excessive investment in plant (overcapacity).

Roosevelt's endorsement of an undistributed profits tax met severe resistance in the powerful Senate Finance Committee led by Harry F. Byrd (Virginia), William H. King (Utah), Walter George (Georgia), and Josiah Bailey (North Carolina), all Democrats and supporters of the business view that the bill was actually an anticorporate measure assuming the guise of tax legislation. The result was a compromise: an undistributed profits tax graduated at 7 to 27 percent (the president asked for 33 percent) and a normal graduated tax on corporations of 8 percent of the first $2,000 of net income to 15 percent of income in excess of $40,000. While the act released some $1.1 billion in cash and other assets, it placed smaller businesses at a disadvantage, since larger corporations proved more readily able to meet capital requirements in the open market.[15]

By early autumn 1937, with a deflationary trend clearly under way, sensitive to a replay of the failed budgetary policies of the early 1930s, Currie questioned the decline in net government contribution to national income, now virtually nil. The president had not grasped the seriousness of the situation, he complained to Eccles. Currie urged increased WPA expenditure, speeding up of other federal spending activity, tackling the slack in building activity, which he attributed to price and wage rigidities, and resort to substantial open-market operations.[16]

Roosevelt conferred with Currie, Henderson, Lubin, and Hopkins in November. Hopkins undoubtedly arranged the four-hour discussion at Henderson's prompting. The Commerce Department economist had been provided a table by Currie that documented the recent decline in net federal contribution to community expenditure. Was this a temporary decline or the start of another depression, Henderson queried? Wall Street attributed the recession to the tax on undistributed earnings, capital gains taxes, and the administration's failure to balance the federal budget. Henderson suggested instead that it had been induced by price increases and reduced government spending. In language inspired by Currie, he claimed: "The net contribution to community expenditure is determined by visualizing the governmental income (taxes) and its actual disbursements as a flow. If the government takes away from workers or corporations and uses these in bookkeeping items, such as Old Age Reserve Accounts, gold purchases, debt retirement, etc., and the amount exceeds what is paid for men and materials, then there is a deficit." Henderson's fears that the recession might well deepen failed to persuade Roosevelt, who was convinced by Henry Morgenthau that budget balance was a prerequisite to business confidence and a recovery.[17]

As the recession persisted, antimonopolists, influenced by the work of Gardiner C. Means and Mordecai Ezekiel, administration economists, argued the theory of stuck or administered prices in a noncompetitive environment (at least in certain key industries), a theory that inspired the antimonopoly investigations by the Temporary National Economic Committee. While Currie allied with this group, probably for practical purposes, his own work concentrated on compensatory fiscal policy rather than industrial structure and monopoly pricing. Currie explained the recession in terms of an excess of business collections from consumers over disbursement for the making of goods (an inventory buildup); dividend payments retained rather than returned to monetary circulation; cost-price pressures that followed from unionization (or fear of unions) responsible for substantial wage increases in large industries, concessions too readily passed off through higher prices; and, most importantly, shrinkage in net federal contribution to community expenditures from $335 million per month in 1936 to $60 million per month in March–September 1937. National income, he noted, reached an annual rate of $72 billion in the first nine months of 1937 as opposed to $40 billion in 1932 at a lower price level and $81 billion at a higher price level. With "normal unemployment" at 3 million, by the summer of 1937 it had fallen to 4 million, a figure that promised a return to general stability. Currie held that if housing expenditures and government contributions combined had been greater by some $4 billion on an annual basis, inventories could have been stabilized at the higher price level.

Currie rejected explanations based on misguided monetary policy. Absorption by the Federal Reserve of excess bank reserves, Currie held, represented a legitimate effort to contain inflationary pressures that showed up as a result of inventory building and a shortage of skilled labor. Tightened credit, he claimed, was balanced by desterilization of gold and open-market operations—though these measures were taken by Treasury and the Fed once the recession had turned. Rather, he pointed to major problems in the management of fiscal policy, especially a lack of month-to-month flexibility in expenditure and tax collections, the inadequacy of prior-year estimates, and the unpredictability of the political process.[18]

These observations were later disputed by monetary economists, especially Milton Friedman and Anna Jacobson Schwartz's account, more recently by Allan H. Meltzer. Based on an absurdly high interest rate policy and unwillingness to utilize open-market purchases, Fed policy failed in the depression. Indeed, the Fed was totally inactive except to help induce the 1937–38 downturn as Currie and Eccles fastened instead on the uses of fiscal policy.[19]

A full-employment economy, Currie maintained, required $80 to $90 billion in national income and some $17 to $18 billion of capital expenditures, the latter figure based on consumer savings of $12 billion and business savings of $6 billion. This compared with expenditures for producers' durables and residential building of $13.6 billion in 1929 and less than $9 billion in 1937, the peak year for the 1930s. Private capital expenditure could not supply the savings outlets required for an $80 billion economy short of government offsets, war, or sporadic inventory bulges. Demand deficiency could be met through tax revision designed to increase consumption relative to income, a problem created on the revenue side by Social Security collections; a steady volume of public investment as an offset to savings, in hospitals, roads, slum clearance, and other public works; and stimulus to private-sector investment in residential construction, railroad improvements, and exports. Only modest federal offsets were needed to fill gap between the current $60 to $70 billion and the desired $80 to $90 billion national income level as "we are dealing with high-powered money."[20]

In his testimony before the Temporary National Economic Committee—an antimonopoly investigation prompted by the downturn and based on Gardiner Means's theory that price rigidities delayed full recovery—Currie noted that when an individual or corporation retained a portion of income for savings (defined as the difference between the national income, or the value of goods and services produced, and the amount of that income spent on consumption), a break developed in the income flow unless that money was reinvested in plant or equipment. "Hence the problem of maintaining full employment is the problem of securing efficient outlets for the saving that will accompany full employment."

A series of tables documented private-sector income-producing expenditures in six major areas: expenditures on plant and equipment financed by depreciation allowances and issuance of stock, retained earnings, and borrowing; private housing expenditures; value of change in inventories; agriculture; net foreign balance on current account, i.e., goods sold abroad; net change in consumer credit; and net additions to disposable income attributable to government expenditure, federal and local (expenditures less tax receipts). While by 1937 capital expenditures for mining and manufactures compared favorably with the 1920s, such expenditure represented a comparatively small percentage of offsets to saving. At the same time, there existed a wide gap in expenditure on construction, especially private housing. Also troubling was the heavy dependence on inventory building and the reversal in offsets previously provided by state and local government, as the level of federal offsets in the 1930s served as a replacement for these, no more.[21]

Some years later, in Alan Sweezy's encomium to the achievements of Americanized Keynesianism, Currie recalled that he had arranged for the critical Alvin Hansen testimony before the TNEC. Currie also recruited a host of fiscal spenders, economists scattered over an assortment of government agencies. These included Richard Gilbert and others for Hopkins at Commerce; also John Kenneth Galbraith, Walter and William Salant, Alan Sweezy, Arthur Gayer, Malcolm Bryan, and Martin Krost. And he found allies elsewhere in the administration: TNEC executive secretary Leon Henderson, Harry Dexter White at Treasury, Mordecai Ezekiel and Louis Bean at Agriculture, Isador Lubin at Labor, Jerome Frank at the SEC, and Thomas Blaisdell at the National Resources Planning Board, many of whom were involved in shaping the TNEC testimony.[22]

Two variations on the new economics surfaced as the decade of the thirties ended. The more limited view relied on public works and social insurance, the latter an autonomous device for demand management. In time, based on the work of Beardsley Ruml, business-oriented economists included a policy of stable tax rates which would automatically enhance or diminish government revenues as incomes rose or fell in order to counter the economic cycle.

The predominance of the administration advocates of the new economics led by Currie and Hansen, on the other hand, envisaged a more aggressive approach to elimination of underemployment and underconsumption. Fiscal policy would take the shape of direct federal investment in the economy, or overhead demand management through a permanent system of offsets to saving, with the National Resources Planning Board responsible for stimulating demand enough to assure reemployment. In addition, tax policy and expanded provision of minimal social guarantees

would serve to equalize the benefits of production and to stimulate consumption. While Currie stressed offsets to savings based on cyclical needs,
Hansen took the argument still further, evidently carrying Currie with
him, in his portrayal of deficient private expenditure and investment as a
secular problem. The National Resources Planning Board, to which both
were attached, and the newly created fiscal advisory board would serve as
centerpieces of a government-led economy.

A good deal of economic discourse, as the decade of the thirties closed,
centered on Hansen's secular stagnation theory. Until 1937 the Minnesota-
born economist viewed the depression as an excessively lengthy trough in
the business cycle, which he regarded as fluctuating in response to technological change and misalignment of the stock of capital and labor.
Hansen's early response to the problem resembled that of the Wisconsin
school: social provision for illness, old age, and unemployment. But the
depth and persistence of the downturn led him to the belief that public
capital expenditure was required as a permanent supplement to deficient
private-sector investment.

As a protagonist of government investment for job creation, Hansen
possessed a considerable advantage over Currie. Whereas Currie's work
along these lines antedated Hansen's, service as a government economist,
particularly at the Fed, limited his audience. Hansen, on the other hand,
bridged the worlds between government-agency proponents of public-
sector investment and academe. Recruited to Harvard from the University of Minnesota, Hansen enjoyed considerable prominence as research
director of the Social Science Research Council study of international
economic relations, as chairman of a subcommittee that helped put together the Social Security Act, then as a trade adviser to Cordell Hull at
State. During this period Hansen supported the Hull trade policies and
waited patiently for a private-sector-led recovery. In 1937–38 he shifted
course, influenced by the economic downturn, John H. Williams's fiscal
policy seminar given at Harvard, and by Keynes's "Some Economic Consequences of Declining Population."

Following publication of *The General Theory,* Keynes theorized that a
decline in the rate of population growth served as a hindrance to demand.
New technologies could not absorb savings sufficient to assure full employment in the depression environment. Hansen extended on this theme
in his December 1938 presidential address before the American Economic
Association, "Economic Progress and Declining Population Growth," to

include a gloss on the Turner thesis. Stagnation theory assumed that the depression's intractability stemmed from a permanent decline in outlets for private capital investment with the frontier's disappearance.[23]

Hansen's testimony before the Temporary National Economic Committee characterized capital goods outlay on plant, equipment, and construction as essential to increased consumption, since such expenditure constituted high-powered money. "Every dollar so expended will cause consumption to rise. . . . Thus every dollar of capital outlays has a multiplier or leverage effect on income, and similarly every dollar of savings or depreciation allowances not expended on capital outlays drives the income down with a magnified effect." As for the depression, it was not simply another cyclical occurrence. Rather, it demonstrated the failure of the private sector to find adequate investment opportunities for new savings. The result was a secular decline in the rate of growth, bound to approach zero by century's end. Chronic unemployment would be the inevitable result.

Hansen viewed capital outlay of $18 billion per annum in the 1920s as an anomaly, the result of a housing boom caused by wartime backlog, an unusually high rate of exports fueled by lending, and large-scale state and local capital expenditure, all now evaporated, and by the newly developed auto industry. True, gross capital formation in 1937 matched that of the average for the New Era; but $4 billion of that figure reflected inventory buildup and a temporary boost in housing construction. Private capital outlays, he predicted, would scarcely match 1920s levels in the foreseeable future.

Full employment required long-term federal supplements to capital outlays in areas such as plant and equipment, durable goods, residential building, public works, regional resource development on the TVA model, roads, and the like. And it required as well greater community expenditure on the English model for public health and hospitals, education, low-cost housing, sewerage, and pollution abatement. Such expenditure could be financed over the business cycle and the lifetime of long-term projects or by adoption of a dual budget system.

Hansen also urged reduced social insurance taxation, a drag on consumption expenditure, and reliance instead on a pay-as-you-go system financed in part from general revenue. Federal, state, and local excise taxes, also a drag on consumption, should be replaced by increased taxes on middle incomes. The Hansen agenda embraced as well the rationalization of tax policy in order to reduce business uncertainty and lower than market interest rates on Federal Housing Authority guaranteed mortgages. Thus began "Curried Keynes," the "new official model," or the "new economics," the Americanized version of Keynesian theory.[24]

Hansen proposed study of the Danish and Swedish systems of dual budgets, since they relieved pressures on fiscal policy by treating capital expenditure as an investment by government to be amortized over a period of years. At the same time, capital provision for direct government investment in the economy and embrace of a permanent social insurance–relief–public works system would take up the slack in private investment expenditure. He believed that the NRPB and a fiscal advisory committee could readily serve as agencies for fiscal management.

While Hansen and Currie were correct in urging lower consumption (excise and sales) and social insurance taxes, there were problems with the new economics. Assumptions about the disappearance of new technologies and the permanent decline of new construction hardly proved out. The argument that larger federal offsets to savings were indicated in the 1930s as a stimulus to employment seems beyond dispute. But Hansen's claim that government debt incurred for offsets would be paid off as prosperity returned proved unlikely, as many pointed out at the time.

Other assumptions of the new economics were less than prescient. According to this school of thought, full employment required a $100 billion economy and $18 billion in investment on an annual basis. Since the private sector could supply only half of the needed investment, the balance would need to be furnished by the federal government. National income in current prices reached over $100 billion as early as 1941 and $241.9 billion by 1950. Manufacturing income alone more than quadrupled between 1939 and 1950, from $17.9 to $74.4 billion, and services grew from $8.3 to $23.1 billion. Between 1939 and 1950 gross private domestic investment in producers' durables grew from $8.5 to $21.3 billion (1954 prices), and new construction advanced from $12.2 to $27.4 billion. The American Keynesians scarcely contemplated the possibility of a second great era of enhanced demand based on global trade, private-sector investment, and new technologies. Predictions of a postwar depression, offered in the early 1940s, also proved wide of the mark, as did the underlying opinion that the private sector could no longer sustain the sort of living standard anticipated in a modern society. Equally problematic was the presumption that Congress would surrender control of taxation and expenditure—however irrational annual budgets from the point of view of economists—to executive branch experts, especially at a time when parliaments in continental Europe became ciphers in centrally managed regimes.[25]

Hansen's views came under immediate challenge, forecasting their future difficulties with economists oriented to a market economy. While Alexander Sachs was one of a cluster of economists who questioned the NRPB-Hansen bent toward an economy reliant on government investment, the Lehman Brothers economist enjoyed access to the White House considerably beyond his conveyance to Roosevelt of Albert Einstein's warning of potential development of an atomic weapon by German physicists. The president, as evidenced by his files, was an avid reader of Sachs's densely written memoranda. Stagnation theory, Sachs claimed, was fallacious as it did not account for autarky and the postwar interruption of capital expansion. Sachs put the depression in an international framework of inadequate adjustment made by the United States to its creditor position, with the collapse brought on by disrupted internal and external capital markets and world trade.[26]

Favorably disposed to elements of Keynesian theory, Sachs stressed the need to free up private-sector investment from the crippling controls and hostile atmosphere built up by the Roosevelt administration. He preferred government inducements to investment through lowered long-term interest rates in order to stimulate housing, utilities, and railroad construction, plus an end to punitive taxation, which he categorized as the anticapitalistic features of the capital gains tax and the undistributed profits tax.[27]

The argument for lowered long-term interest rates depended on an analysis of changed investment needs in the modern capital goods economy. Whereas the nineteenth century featured short-chain manufacturing, seasonal in nature, keyed to commodities, consumer goods, crops, and their distribution, the modern economy depended on meeting long-term capital needs. Interest costs were too high in the United States. Triple A bonds were priced at 3⅓ percent to 3¾ percent for new corporates, and the cost of refunding high-interest coupon bonds issued by utilities in the 1920s was well over 4 percent.[28] Sachs dismissed claims of monopoly pricing offered by New Dealers, Leon Henderson in the lead, who staffed the TNEC. Rather, he attributed the recent price advance to normal cyclical demand, additional impetus furnished by rearmament, gold bloc devaluation, and an abnormal increase in wages. Whereas wages increased by 21.5 percent (1929 to 1937), finished goods and raw materials prices languished well below 1929 levels.

Proposed deficit spending was puerile, according to Sachs, as the impact of such spending diminished over time, particularly when political decisions brought about a synthetic shortage of savings and capital. The real danger to the economy, he informed Roosevelt, stemmed from capital market and wage rigidities.[29] He wanted tax credits for replacement or modernization of plant and equipment, housing and rail rehabilitation, and slum clearance and a modus vivendi between the federal government and the private sector. Sachs, then, relied on lowered interest rates and a climate conducive to business investment. Hansen pointed to a structural flaw in the capitalist system: permanent underinvestment unable to absorb savings and provide an adequate stimulus to demand.[30]

When Sachs dispatched his conclusions to Keynes, the Cambridge economist offered a mixed review. Sachs claimed that capital markets crippled by steep surtax rates caused a liquidity preference premium, hence the diversion of capital to safe and unproductive investments: corporate gilts and tax-exempts. Keynes conceded that the recession could only have been avoided by investment in durables. Cash on balance in the previous four years suggested "an excessive craving after liquidity." But another look at Sachs's material led Keynes to observe that a reversal depended on government expenditure on housing, railroads, and utilities and the president being "reasonably kind to business."[31]

In a letter to Roosevelt, Keynes pointed to "revival of sources of demand," defining these in terms of public investment as necessary to reverse the 1937–38 recession. In the instance of the utilities, current litigation was senseless; many of the allegations against the holding companies were "wide of the mark" as the real malefactors were long since gone. While Keynes was inclined toward ownership by public boards (Sachs's 1936 proposal), if public opinion appeared unprepared for this, "what is the object of chasing the utilities round the lot every other week?" Buy the utilities out at fair prices, Keynes admonished FDR, or make peace on liberal terms, as opposed to "losses all round." As for businessmen, "you can do anything you like with them (even the big ones), if you treat them not as wolves and tigers, but as domestic animals by nature. . . . If you work them into the surly, obstinate, terrified mood of which domestic animals, wrongfully handled, are so capable, the nation's burdens will not be carried to market."

Keynes viewed a recovery in the United States as basic to world trade, a scenario that dictated state intervention for a reversal of the ongoing recession. "Durable investment must come increasingly under state direction," with emphasis on public utilities, transport, and especially housing for the working class. Reversal of the recession required either stimulus to demand by increased consumption or growth of capital goods expenditure by private investment and, when those were deficient, by government through semiautonomous or publicly owned corporations. Keynes preferred the route of capital goods expenditure to that of fiscal stimulus to consumption. Hansen, in his TNEC testimony, also emphasized the need for capital goods outlay as key to a full-employment economy.[32]

Sachs rejected the conclusions of the New Deal's "left wing," as he viewed the Hansen group, which professed internationalism yet proposed a "planned economy of the future" in the shape of government investment in plant that would compete with the private sector. A developmental economy was not as effective, he held, as the price mechanism in the allocation of resources and would induce a return to interwar autarky. Unopposed to the use of administrative agencies, Sachs insisted, nevertheless, on their accountability, an issue which "goes to the very foundation of parliamentary government and the American [legal] system." The managers of public corporations operated with other people's money yet were scarcely subject to accountability to stockholders or appraisal afforded by securities markets. Nor was business rationalization sufficient. Congress needed to be restored to its historic function, that of control over public undertakings. Big government, Sachs argued, could threaten democracy as readily as private business freed from restraint and regulation. In his view government investment should concentrate on social needs as opposed to nationalized sectors of the economy. Exorbitant profits would be heavily taxed, monopolistic profits prohibited, and profit sharing encouraged. On this score, Sachs lectured Wendell Willkie on the need as well to reorient the Republican Party, which had been "blind and unpatriotic on foreign policy and reactionary on domestic policy and devoid of contacts with [the] masses in its organizational structure," for the GOP's leadership was "profoundly wrong as the Bourbons."[33]

The NRPB-Hansen group, joined by New Deal liberals such as Leon

Henderson, envisaged chronic depression, which they attributed to private-sector underinvestment, in turn a product of a declining rate of population growth and a dearth of new technologies. Government should fill the investment void and broaden the social safety net. A system based on greater social and economic equity that embraced expanded public health services, an attack on the problem of farm tenancy, and remediation of educational deficiencies (technological unemployment) required additional federal net contribution to the economy. This would be provided by taxing the incomes of the middle classes (since the wealthy were already taxed at high rates) and corporations, by additional revenue furnished by increased business activity stimulated by new purchasing power, and by resort when needed to deficits—as opposed to regressive payroll taxes that served as a drag on purchasing power.

Developmental economists, Hansen in the lead, also broached the relationship between domestic measures and international mechanisms required for international recovery after the conclusion of the Second World War. Both Hansen and Keynes feared a postwar depression in the United States, which would cause a reversion to the protectionist trade policies of the 1930s. Only a program of public expenditures and investment for social assurance and economic growth adopted by all of the major trading nations, the United States and the United Kingdom in the lead, would ensure the emergence of a multilateral trading system as opposed to the autarkic policies of the interwar period. An international monetary mechanism would provide for exchange stability to meet another problem that had crippled trade, Hansen and Keynes agreed, when they met in London two months before Pearl Harbor.[34]

In the closing years of the Age of Roosevelt, the stage was set for a contest involving domestic policy between a congressional coalition, on the one hand, and developmental theorists given to government investment, on the other. The advocates of the "new economics" contested with an alliance of Republicans and Southern Democrats newly ascendant in the Congress. Centrist economists also challenged the concept, as Joseph A. Schumpeter put it, of erecting a capitalist facade on a socialist foundation. While they acknowledged the need for federal countercyclical spending in depression, they insisted that the private sector could spearhead economic expansion after the war.

Would Congress reassert its authority over domestic and foreign affairs as a check to presidential power that had expanded in depression and war?

Would the legislative branch cede its authority over expenditures to neutral experts independent of both branches? To what extent would authority over individual and local needs continue to reside, federal funding aside, with the community and the states? Would the nation turn to a Scandinavian model built on assurance of a minimum living standard for all? Was stagnation theory correct in its claim that long-term or permanent deficits would not impair private-sector investment? Was, in fact, the private sector incapable of sustained growth in the absence of huge public-sector investment in plant, infrastructure, and a more generous social safety net?

11 | THE NATIONAL RESOURCES
PLANNING BOARD

Rexford Tugwell offered a rationale for overhead economic management in his explanation of the "Fourth Power." Industry's mastery of technology and planning required government to rein in the economic chaos that characterized the interwar era. Artificial separation of government from industry ensured a struggle for sovereignty, as the two spheres could not be divorced. Whereas industry had mastered planning techniques for selfish ends, governmental planning had been implemented in uncoordinated bits and pieces. Planning, he argued, lacked direction when it served special interests, and "direction" was critical to the salvation of democracy.

Direction was Tugwell's goal as opposed to subsidies for agriculture and to the special interests of business or labor. He deplored group-interest politics, gains made at the expense of the whole and responsible for maladjustment of income distribution and unnecessarily high unemployment. Atomism, or Brandeisianism, had proved unrealistic in a technological world. Deficit financing, standing alone, fostered a struggle for benefits and class antagonism. Deficits, moreover, would not be permanently funded by the subsidizers who paid taxes and ultimately would revolt. Regulation in a representative system constituted negative harassment and resulted in friction.

The solution, Tugwell held, lay in abandonment of directive power by industry and the three branches of government to "a system of foresights, placements, allocation, and agreed uses," a directive movement guided by the interest of the whole in an organic society. Direction required a capital budget, managed investment, expanded services, a better and more equitable apportionment of claims, and power to assure maximum output of goods. The plan could not be built from constituent units; it must be holistic and use the experimental method that provided for adjustment to changing facts and analysis of results.

In Tugwell's view the central government as shaped by the Framers offered a study in arrested development. Wary of a strong chief executive, the drafters of the Constitution created a legislature based on disparate local interests, often representative of pressure groups and the well-to-do. Wary of a strong central government, the Framers divided sovereignty. These limitations explained the need for a Fourth Power, independent of the president, the Congress, and the judiciary, gathering information, informed by experts, not representing any particular region.

Direction, then, transcended planning. It would subordinate private to public interests. Congress would be accorded a veto by a supermajority but must refer proposals to the Fourth Power. The executive would be confined to execution of the plan, and the judiciary would be accorded no power to define or review its findings. As Tugwell viewed the scene, the National Resources Planning Board had become the nation's de facto directive agency, capable of forward planning and of absorbing this function where it existed elsewhere in government, operating eventually outside the existing political system.[1]

While Thomas C. Blaisdell Jr., chief of the NRPB's Research Division concurred with these observations, he expressed the hope that forward planning could be achieved without a major change in the structure of government.[2] Whether Tugwell took the NRPB's aspirations to its logical conclusion or, more likely, well beyond the concept of fiscal management by experts located in the executive branch based on a developmental model, the NRPB encountered the hostility of Congress. In the last analysis, the nation's lawmakers decided the issue. Southern Democrats and a revived Republican leadership objected to concentrated power in the administration, which they viewed as an intrusion on the legislative prerogative. Equally important, while liberal businessmen were persuaded by the logic of a flexible fiscal policy designed to stimulate purchasing power in an economic downturn, state direction of output and investment failed to enlist support in the business community and with most economists outside of government.

Initially, economists and administrators at the NRPB needed to decide between two versions of an economy managed by experts. Laughlin Currie carried the argument for net federal contribution, or fiscal stimulus to consumption and federal investment sufficient to take up the slack in private-sector investment, into the precincts of the NRPB. There also evolved the belief, fostered by Gardiner C. Means at Agriculture, that the depression resulted from structural deficiencies. Means offered that manufacturers restricted output and maintained prices in an oligopolistic economy, which resulted in underconsumption, depressed purchasing power, and permanent underemployment.

The National Resources Planning Board originated in Harold Ickes's Public Works Administration. Created under Title II of the National Industrial Recovery Act as the National Planning Board, it was funded by public works monies and guided by three civilian volunteers and by a staff director, Charles W. Eliot II, appointed by and accountable to Ickes. The board was charged with the selection of suitable projects for the PWA on the basis of social and economic criteria as opposed to pork-barrel politics. The NPB was chaired by FDR's uncle, Frederic A. Delano, a city and regional planner. Two academicians served with Delano on the NPB committee: the University of Chicago political scientist Charles E. Merriam and the Columbia University economist Wesley Clair Mitchell.[3]

Merriam, founder of the Chicago school, the most influential figure in the group, had built a broad constituency in government, foundations, and academe as a progressive political scientist and organizer bent on reform of government structure. Well connected, he served as president of the American Political Science Association and helped to organize the Rockefeller-funded Social Science Research Council, which underwrote many of his academic pursuits.

The careers of Merriam and Raymond Moley had significant parallels. Both were born and reared in small midwestern towns, considered the law and settled on careers in political science instead, and participated in progressive reform politics in large cities, Moley in Cleveland and Merriam in Chicago. Both demonstrated a capacity for fund-raising, with their early careers fostered by civic-minded women of substance; Moley turned to Belle Sherwin, Merriam to Helen Culver. Both championed modernized governmental practice and structures keyed to efficiency (i.e., elimination of incompetence and corruption), which appealed to New Era administrative progressives: Al Smith and Roosevelt as governors of New York, Virginia's Harry Byrd, and, at the national level, Herbert Hoover. Both Merriam and Moley emulated Woodrow Wilson's career, marrying their academic ambitions to practical politics and entering the political arena at the local level. There they effected their earliest political contacts, Merriam with Harold Ickes and Donald Richberg in Chicago, Moley with Newton Baker in Cleveland, then Louis Howe and Eleanor and Franklin

Roosevelt in New York. Both accepted corporate scale and sought to emulate business integration at the state and local levels as a means of empowerment of government. In the fashion of the era, both developed hypochondria. Moley dreaded a renewed bout with tuberculosis; Merriam dreaded stomach cancer, which felled his father. And both exited uncomfortable situations in life through reliance on illness; Moley was given to explain his departure from the Roosevelt embrace as a result of overwork and heart palpitations.

But the two political scientists differed in important respects. In his service with Roosevelt, Moley relied on experts for policy advice. Merriam built the Chicago school on a statistical, scientific approach to social and economic planning and amassed and synthesized data across social science fields in order to inform the executive branch and planning agencies. At the same time, he left to the political process the winnowing of alternatives. Whereas Merriam preferred anonymity for both himself and the several incarnations of the NRPB, Moley scarcely shunned public exposure and maintained contact with leading legislators, Key Pittman, Huey Long, James F. Byrnes, and Hiram Johnson among them. If an excess of visibility shortened Moley's public career, Merriam's insistence on avoidance of engagement with the Congress, designed to protect his cohort from politics, helped to assure its demise. Differences in style apart, Merriam filled the role vacated by Moley, as he and Roosevelt explored ideas rooted in reformist progressive thought.[4]

Merriam's summary chapter of *Recent Social Trends*, initiated by the President's (Hoover's) Committee on Social Trends and published on the eve of the Roosevelt presidency, served as a brief for the future. Merriam noted the growth in cost and compass of government, the increased use of administrative boards and authorities staffed by trained professionals, and the advance of scientific research, all bound to emulate the business model. Modernized government, in turn, required a more powerful executive, who would combine legislative and political leadership with technical administrative authority. Merriam also anticipated centralized power at the national level at the expense of the states, of the states at the expense of (especially rural) localities, and experiments with government-owned corporations, which required in turn reform of executive organization, a foreshadowing of the Brownlow Commission. The Roosevelt-Merriam collaboration lasted a decade. Its principal accomplishment was the managerial presidency.[5]

The National Planning Board evolved into the National Resources Board (July 1, 1934), funded by the allocation of emergency relief funds under the authority of the National Recovery Act. Following the *Schechter* decision, the NRB was renamed the National Resources Committee, as Roosevelt proved wary of "planning," on the grounds of possible hostility to the concept. In theory the NRC was managed by a five-member cabinet committee, chaired by Ickes and reporting to the president. In practice the advisory board, essentially Delano and Merriam, played a dominant role in determining with Roosevelt the scope of NRC studies. Ickes's role was largely that of transmission belt to the White House.

While Merriam originally conceived of a neutral, albeit progressive-reformist, approach to planning from the ground up, with reliance on local and regional agencies for water, land, forest, and electric power development related to public works needs, the NRC agenda soon embraced as well studies of population, consumption, industrial location and output, and their economic impact. In the process Merriam suggested the need for government economic planning as "business cannot protect itself effectively against the business cycle hazard." This task became the responsibility of the NRC's Industrial Committee. Thomas Blaisdell served as its chief, with Laughlin Currie, Leon Henderson, Isador Lubin, Harry Dexter White, Mordecai Ezekiel, and Gardiner C. Means its members.

A second development that emanated from the NRC gave congressional conservatives considerable pause. Progressive political scientists converged on the goal of better executive management and accountability in concert with the budgetary process and Roosevelt's need to better manage accelerated expenditures and the multiplicity of new agencies and functions. The task of bringing planning and an emergent bureaucracy under presidential control, broached by Merriam to Roosevelt in late 1935, was assigned to the President's Committee on Administrative Management (the Brownlow Committee). Chaired by Louis Brownlow, who headed the Public Administration Clearing House, the committee included Merriam and Luther Gulick, expert in fiscal and budgetary management. Technically the NRC and the new committee were separated; in reality the two committees and their goals meshed.[6]

Previous efforts at reorganization of the executive branch had rarely proved productive. Congress dominated the process since administrative agencies were accountable to its committees and legislators proved reluctant to forgo their prerogatives. Two objectives stood out: one, the managerial ideal, with presidents desirous of control over the bureaucracy; a second, congressional pressures for economy, a picture complicated by the constitutionally imposed tradition of separation of powers. In the early depression period, the Economy Acts of 1932 and 1933 empowered Hoover, then Roosevelt, to undertake reorganization with a view toward budgetary savings. Hoover failed in the face of Democratic control of the House. Roosevelt, preoccupied with economic salvage, allowed his authority to lapse.

The Merriam-Roosevelt mission emphasized managerial accountability rather than savings, since the executive branch witnessed turf warfare among the departments and the appearance of a myriad of independent agencies created to cope more expeditiously than the slow-moving bureaucracy with crisis needs. Since the emergency agencies tended to operate independently of Roosevelt's priorities, the Brownlow Report concluded that "the president needs help." Few challenged the premise.

Roosevelt's need to gain control of expanded New Deal programs and the departments through increased staffing was not in dispute. The Brownlow Report's proposed appointment of six White House staff assistants along with a Bureau of the Budget independent of the Treasury went unchallenged in subsequent congressional debate and emerged as basic components of the 1939 Reorganization Act. From the outset, nevertheless, Congress asserted its interest in the matter of executive branch reorganization by provision for committees headed in the House by James Buchanan of Texas, an intimate of Vice President John Nance Garner, and in the Senate by Harry F. Byrd of Virginia. Both looked to fiscal economy. Since Byrd, a budget hawk, distrusted Roosevelt personally and doubted the president's oft-proclaimed pledge of fiscal prudence, he engaged the Brookings Institution for an independent report.[7]

Byrd's attack on the Brownlow reorganization plan, leveled in January 1937, reflected distaste for federal spending and centralized control. Budget balance and states' rights offered a firewall against federal interference in the ways of Virginia in labor (antiunion) and race relations, as well as against federal intrusion into the political machine he had built in the Old Dominion. As Byrd saw it, government responsibility should be limited to provision of an environment in which individual initiative could flourish. And he envisaged his own success, recounted in popular publications of the times, as built on hard work. Indeed, he was a workaholic, but his rise to power in Virginia politics and his successful apple business also depended on family connections.

Much of the Byrd legend as governor, created by favorable press publicity, was overstated, with the exception of road building. Sponsorship of antilynching legislation represented the need to offer Virginia as a trouble-free zone for outside investors. The Byrd machine did not challenge the disenfranchisement of blacks and poor whites by a poll tax that had been imposed at the 1901–2 constitutional convention. Virginia under the Byrd organization remained an oligarchy, with only 11.5 percent of those eligible voting in decisive state primaries (1925–45). Virginia's progress toward a mixed economy depended on a free hand for manufacturers vis-à-vis unions. Byrd's commitment to education, like his own learning, proved minimal. He sacrificed the work of Luther Gulick's New York Bureau of Municipal Research to his patronage requirements as head of the Organization. Business progressivism, as practiced in Virginia under the Byrd machine, meant social control; benefits accrued largely to the oligarchy, and reforms were superficial. New Deal relief–public works programs served mainly to fund budget balance at the state level. Byrd proved scarcely enamored of the possibility of a nationalized economy, which he interpreted as the vision of the New Deal planners.[8]

Whereas formal studies of the southern veto based on congressional voting patterns suggest that Southern Democrats centered on maintenance of the social and racial status quo and otherwise supported the broad range of New Deal legislation, anecdotal evidence reveals otherwise. When Southern Democrats opposed components of New Deal legislation that interfered with regional interests, such as nationalizing of its low-wage labor market or disturbing customary labor patterns in agriculture, they relied on control of key committee chairmanships allocated on the basis of seniority in order to extract concessions—welfare legislation and Social Security as examples—before votes were recorded on final legislation in the House and Senate.[9]

Byrd proved too astute and experienced a politician to mount an open attack on a popular president and party leader or his program in the early phase of the New Deal. The reality that he faced election to the Senate in 1934 also tempered his hostility to the Roosevelt program. Early on he openly opposed major New Deal legislation on only a few, though important, occasions. He objected to the licensing provisions of the National

Industrial Recovery Act and the amended Agricultural Adjustment Act (1934), as well as the use of the power to tax, featured in the Bankhead Cotton Control Act, on the constitutional ground that these provisions effectively confiscated property without compensation. As for the NRA, "This is a concentration of power and the building up of a bureaucracy that I cannot approve of." The licensing of farmers would make Henry Wallace, whom he detested as an inflationist, "a supreme dictator over everyone who produces agricultural products."[10]

Informal alliance with other conservatives—Virginia colleagues Senator Carter Glass and Clifton A. Woodrum, a member of the House Appropriations Committee, and Josiah Bailey of North Carolina and Millard Tydings of Maryland—and the publication of articles on economy and limited government marked Byrd as a conservative spokesman. Byrd sought reduced WPA expenditures in 1935, from the $4.8 billion proposed by the administration to $1.9 billion. With Carter Glass, he opposed the Social Security Act on the ground that its old-age assistance feature, funded jointly by the federal government and the states, would prove too costly to Virginia, and he managed to secure an amendment that allowed the states to determine benefit levels. Average payments of $10 per month ranked the Old Dominion near the bottom in the nation.[11]

Byrd's emergence as a power identified with economy in government is indicated by his appointment as chairman of a Senate Select Committee to Investigate the Executive Agencies of Government. Initially, in this capacity, he planned to enlist John R. McCarl, a Republican appointed to the post of comptroller for a fifteen-year term in 1921, an office created to act as fiscal agent of the legislative branch. A fiscal conservative, McCarl was an open opponent of what he saw as the New Deal's wasteful spending. When Byrd's proposed advisory committee, which included Brownlow and Gulick, was preempted by the president with their appointment to the Committee on Administrative Management, he turned instead to the Brookings Institution as a fact-finding agency. Joined by Glass, Tydings, Bailey, Walter George of Georgia, and other Southern Democrats, the group, according to Bailey, determined to "salvage of the Constitution, the Congress, and the Supreme Court."[12]

The first sign of imminent difficulties for the planners came early in 1936 when FDR failed to secure permanent funding for a new national planning agency. Robert L. Doughton of North Carolina, chairman of the House Ways and Means Committee, approached by Delano, asserted he "knew nothing about the subject [planning] and had grave doubts about the advisability of doing this especially in view of recent decisions of the Supreme Court." Whereas Doughton viewed the proposal as a "money spending scheme," the liberal Texas congressman Maury Maverick, a member of a small but vocal radical bloc in the House, claimed it would rationalize public works spending, especially if dovetailed with a central budget and accounting system. Maverick and Roosevelt soon agreed on a permanent National Resources Commission as successor to the NRC. When the bill was introduced in the House and Senate, an appeal by Roosevelt to Speaker of the House Joseph W. Byrns and the Senate majority leader, Joseph Robinson, brought no result. Byrd vowed to "talk a commission to death." The contest over the agency's funding and jurisdiction lasted three years, with the NRC dependent until 1939 on the allocation of funds appropriated for relief and public works agencies.[13]

This picture was complicated by a divergence between fiscal planners lodged in the NRC and the Congress. Henry S. Dennison, a New England paper goods manufacturer committed to welfare capitalism, planning, and an organizational economy, and Beardsley Ruml, treasurer of R. H. Macy & Co., a New York department store, joined the newly created NRC as advisers in 1935. The choice of Ruml, a brilliant social scientist, appointed a director of the Federal Reserve Bank of New York in January 1937, stemmed from long association with Merriam and Ickes in their faith in economic planning.[14]

Both Dennison and Ruml advocated business-government cooperation, and both, like Eccles, proposed public spending as a stimulus to purchasing power. In 1935 manufacturers Dennison, Ralph Flanders, and Morris Leeds, together with Lincoln Filene, a department store magnate, all liberal-corporatist members of the Commerce Department's Business Advisory Council, underwrote a study of the depression. The work of John Kenneth Galbraith, it asserted that capitalism did not attain equilibrium at a high level of employment. Full employment required flexible government expenditure over the cycle, or a dual budget system, one component based on normal expenditure and the second a contingent budget authorized by Congress in advance and calibrated to kick in at precise levels of unemployment. The impact of their thinking is revealed in an NRC report to the president, December 1, 1936, also signed by Delano, a convert to purchasing-power theory; Merriam; and five cabinet members. The report stressed the need for long-term planning of public works geared to the business cycle. The goal of economic stabilization would be assigned to a national development agency or public works authority working with a fiscal advisory committee. Soon thereafter, on February 3, 1937, Roosevelt transmitted to the Congress a more restrained proposal for a permanent public works–oriented planning agency focused on water use. The agency would submit to the president a list of priorities, which would be submitted in turn to the Congress in his annual budget message. Congress would be free to add to or delete from the list, the overall plan consisting of a six-year program tailored to the business cycle. This message landed in a legislative maelstrom.[15]

The enormous gap between Democrats and Republicans in the House (331 to 89) and Senate (76 to 16) following the 1936 landslide deeply troubled Roosevelt's vice president, John Nance ("Cactus Jack") Garner. He attributed Roosevelt's failure to consult with legislative leaders as he prepared proposals for packing the Supreme Court and reorganization of the executive branch to the lack of a viable opposition. Had the GOP fielded Herbert Hoover in the presidential contest, the wily Texan believed, he could not have won but would have rallied more Republicans at the ballot box than the politically inept Alf M. Landon. Tellingly, when the liberal Texas Democrat Maury Maverick introduced the bill into the House following Roosevelt's announcement of a plan for an enlarged court on February 5, 1937, Garner, who never openly opposed the bill, offered his opinion to a group of senators by holding his nose.

For Garner and other decentralists in the Congress, the Supreme Court–packing proposal signified a turning point. While the vice president had doubts about key components of the New Deal from the outset, differences were muted or kept behind closed doors during the first term. Indeed, the old progressive was not averse to curbs on the malefactors of Wall Street or the utilities magnates. Yet the vice president was unhappy with much of the first-term legislation, especially its impact on spending levels.

Garner voiced misgivings as to the National Industrial Recovery Act, for he was wary of Washington's managerial capacity and feared the NRA's cartelizing potential. He offered behind-the-scenes encouragement to Lewis W. Douglas in his struggle for an end to deficits, and he categorized the relief–public works program as useless and destined to "bring us grief." After a visit to Uvalde, where Garner spent half the year huntin' and fishin', Raymond Moley reported to Roosevelt, "I asked him to tell me what he thought of policies, etc. and he answered in a word—the deficit. He would cut on spendin'. Notably on relief."

With the opening of Roosevelt's second term, Garner's traditional bourbon and branch water routine, or "striking a blow for liberty," took on a literal meaning. His office emerged as the nerve center for opposition to Roosevelt's attempt to increase presidential authority at the expense of the other two, presumably coordinate, branches of government, to punish anti–New Deal Democrats, and to tilt toward organized labor and continued deficit spending needed to fund relief and work programs. With Republicans ensconced cleverly on the sidelines as Democrats divided on the Supreme Court plan and as the fight raged in the Senate, its presiding officer entrained for Uvalde, "my ears ringing." An unhappy Cap'n soon pleaded for the VP's return and pledged a hardened attitude toward labor extremists and a balanced budget. "I miss you," the suitor cooed. Garner kept on huntin' and fishin'.

The sudden death of Senate Majority Leader Joseph T. Robinson in mid-July ended the bloodletting, for Roosevelt's support hinged on Robinson, who had been promised an appointment to an enlarged Supreme Court. Garner, who had joined the party's legislative powers at Little Rock, Arkansas, for the funeral, reported to the president on his return to the nation's capital. His biographer reports the scene at the White House. How was the court fight going? FDR wanted to know. Garner: "Do you want it with the bark on or the bark off, Cap'n?" FDR: "The rough way." Garner: "All right. You are beat. You haven't got the votes."

The late summer of 1937 witnessed the jelling of a coalition of conservative Southern and border-state Democrats joined by Nebraska's Edward R. Burke and New York's Royal Copeland. Self-styled Jeffersonians rallied against the "Dealers and Dreamers"—Thomas "Tommy the Cork" Corcoran, Benjamin Cohen, and James Landis[16]—and against Hopkins. Garner, at this juncture the unofficial head of the traditionalists, was convinced that the White House Janissaries, unelected and unelectable, intended to convert the Democracy to a New Deal Labor Party led by Harvard intellectuals. This was confirmed by Roosevelt's attempted purge of party conservatives in the 1938 primaries, promoted by Corcoran and the newspaper columnist Drew Pearson.

When Roosevelt insisted that disloyal Democrats might well leave the fold, Garner had his fill, and the two engaged in an acrimonious debate at their last private meeting. The purge seemingly confirmed FDR's intent to liberalize the Democracy and its program. Conservatives were also wary of the Fair Labor Standards Act's provision of minimum wages–maximum hours and a powerful labor board, on the ground that it would tilt the negotiation process toward the unions and end the southern states' low-cost labor advantage. Also in dispute were continued requests from Hopkins for the funding of WPA work relief, which Garner opposed on grounds of dependence as well as fiscal policy.[17]

The Brownlow Committee agenda thus became entangled with a contest between congressional conservatives and what they saw as an over-reaching executive branch bent on excessive spending. Presented to the president in December 1936, the report proposed the appointment of up to six White House staff assistants who would act as liaison with executive branch agencies and shelter the president from burdensome detail and meetings. It also proposed better budget control through a Bureau of the Budget lodged in the Executive Office of the president. The nearly one hundred independent agencies, including the regulatory commissions, theoretically accountable to the Congress but actually to no one, would be brought under departmental supervision. The office of comptroller general would be limited to a postaudit role in appropriations, preliminary audit having afforded it a de facto veto over New Deal expenditure. The report recommended two new departments, Public Works and Welfare, institutionalizing these functions. A permanent planning agency, renamed the National Resources Board, would be accorded legislative status and would gather economic information and manage long-range public works planning.[18]

Roosevelt's presentation of the Brownlow Committee Report in the form of a bill in a four-hour soliloquy at the White House on January 10, 1937, suggested a fait accompli to the assembled Democratic leadership of Congress. The legislators, powerful Democrats—Joe Robinson; Pat Harrison, chairman of the Senate Finance Committee; House Speaker William Bankhead of Alabama; Robert L. Doughton of North Carolina, chairman of the House Ways and Means Committee; James Buchanan and Sam Rayburn of Texas, the latter House majority leader; and Garner—were stunned. No legislator, Byrd included, had been consulted, a slight to the legislative branch soon repeated in the instance of the Supreme Court–packing proposal. Whereas the Brownlow group believed in the need for better accountability and a strengthened presidency in light of the depression at home and fascism in Europe, conservative Democrats viewed the proposal as a power grab. Byrd, in the lead, aided by a Brookings Institution report which supported his views, pressed for economy and stressed bureaucratic overreach and Congress's traditional role in fiscal management.[19]

Despite the appointment in July 1937 of James F. Byrnes of South Carolina, an astute manager of New Deal bills, as chairman of the Senate's Select Committee and the Joint Committee on Government Reorganization, the Brownlow Report stalled in a divided Congress. When debate resumed early the next year, a curtailed version sponsored by Byrnes made its way through the Senate. The Byrnes bill consisted of five titles. Title I gave the president power to reorganize various executive agencies, even though it exempted some fifteen, the Interstate Commerce Commission and Federal Reserve among them. Title II abolished the Civil Service Commission and replaced that agency with a single administrator advised by a board. Title III abolished the General Accounting Office and the office of the Comptroller General, with day-to-day budget management transferred to a director of the budget in the Executive Office of the President. Independent postaudit would be assigned to an auditor general, an agent of the Congress. Title IV created a Department of Welfare and a National Resources Planning Board to "integrate and study planning policies and the development of [national] resources." No mention was made of a Department of Public Works, a concession to economy advocates. Presented in the House by Bankhead and Rayburn as a confidence vote in the president, the bill went down to defeat on April 8, 1938. Opponents, who claimed the need to end congressional surrender of power, won recommittal by a vote of 204 to 196.[20]

At this juncture the work of the proposed NRPB was represented in an environmental–public works framework and in a planning context already undertaken in business and government. Under the Byrnes proposal the NRPB would consist of five part-time members appointed by the president and confirmed by the Senate, served by a full-time director. The agency would collect and interpret data relating to future national resource development along the lines proposed by President Hoover's Committee on Recent Social Trends. This included land resources and uses, a national water plan, public works planning, study of technological change, and coordination of planning at all levels of government. While the board would serve as a clearinghouse of planning efforts nationwide and would gather data scattered about government agencies, it would not, according to Byrnes, make final decisions on broad questions of public policy, as this responsibility was lodged in the Congress.[21]

The task of making concessions sufficient to secure passage of the reorganization bill in the House of Representatives fell on Lindsay Warren of North Carolina and John J. Cochran of Missouri, members of the House Select Committee and the Joint Committee on Government Reorganization. The Warren-Cochran bill, presented to the House on February 23, 1939, eliminated the proposed Civil Service Commission, the departments of Public Works and Welfare, and the NRPB as permanent components of the executive branch. When Roosevelt requested inclusion of the NRPB in the revamped bill, Warren demurred. He had conferred with "over 125 members of the House, including 61 of the 76 Democrats who voted against last year," Warren reported. Hostility to the NRPB was so tenacious that inclusion in the new reorganization bill would cause an adverse reaction.[22]

Senator Carl Hayden of Arizona, a New Deal stalwart committed to resource management in the Southwest, made a final effort to secure permanent status for a National Resources Board ("Planning" omitted) housed in the Executive Office of the President. Hayden introduced an amendment to the 1939 relief bill, to create a new NRB, its scope narrowed to water, forests, other natural resources, and river navigation. An amended version, satisfactory to the House, added seven department heads and the federal works administrator to the board, and three advisory members to be approved by the Senate. While Delano proved agreeable, Roosevelt concurred with Merriam, Brownlow, and Gulick who bitterly opposed the measure on the ground that it failed to incorporate "human resources," meaning social and economic planning.

Failure by Roosevelt, Merriam, Brownlow, and Gulick to support the Hayden proposal, which would have provided permanent status and congressional funding, proved a decisive tactical error. For once the board was ensconced in the Executive Office of the President under congressional authority, Hayden anticipated, its compass would have grown incrementally. Instead, under powers granted by the 1939 Reorganization Act, Roosevelt created the National Resources Planning Board, dependent for its power on the weak legal authority of the Emergency Stabilization Act of 1932. Annual funding was left to a hostile Congress.

Roosevelt appointed three citizen members to the NRPB, Delano, Merriam, and George F. Yantis, active in the NRC's Pacific Northwest regional commission. Dennison and Ruml continued as advisers whose role essentially was the same as that of the board members. With the new NRPB lodged in the Executive Office of the President and responsible directly to Roosevelt, it no longer needed to contend with Ickes's oversight. On the other hand, it also lost the shelter that the cantankerous and tenacious interior secretary could have afforded as the president became increasingly preoccupied with the worldwide conflict.[23]

As long as Congress wrestled with the issue of executive reorganization, the NRPB planners enjoyed the luxury of debate among themselves as to the best approach to recovery. Advocates of compensatory government spending confronted the structural approach of Gardiner C. Means, who would have moved the U.S. political economy toward government goals for output, employment, investment, and prices.

Means's business experience in the 1920s spurred him toward his theory of administered pricing. This theory, based on oligopoly in industry, took him to Harvard for graduate study in economics and to his work with Adolf Berle on *The Modern Corporation and Private Property*. Means's dissertation and the Berle-Means study led to the conclusion that prices reflected corporate power, not market forces. Means viewed administered prices as responsible for the depression's intractability, since production managed by large corporations emphasized maximum profit rather than maximum output. Classical economic theory, he held, had become inoperative in the contemporary environment of mass production and technology that fostered oligopoly. According to the law of supply and demand, prices would adjust to demand; actually business set prices and adjusted output to demand at that price level, hence the depression's severity and the slow pace of recovery.

Since Means's views corresponded with Tugwell's belief that the depression originated with pricing-power disparities between farmers who sold in a market environment as opposed to industry, which could indulge in managed pricing; and since both rejected antitrust as antiquated, Tugwell recruited his Columbia colleague as an adviser to Henry Wallace at Agriculture. Means's service on the NRA's Consumer Advisory Board led to the observation that restored consumer purchasing power, needed for recovery, could not be attained under the restrictive NRA business-dominated code authorities that furthered the administered pricing system that skewed price relationships against farmers, workers, and the unemployed.[24]

Means concluded that output, employment, and investment could be increased only by an industrial policy which altered certain threads of control. Coordination would be accomplished through administrative agencies on an industry-by-industry basis in the public interest. (This task could not be left to industry and labor alone as labor might well go along with restricted production as a means of dividing the spoils.) In this new arrangement of powers, government would guide the business process through a veto based on accumulated data on capacity, demand, and costs, with the details of day-to-day management of details left to management. The result would be a balance of power in the economy, an industrial policy aimed at full use of human and material resources while it equalized the interests of individuals and groups.[25]

Publication as a Senate document of *Industrial Prices and Their Relative Inflexibility* marked both the peak of Means's influence and the onset of challenges to his structural analysis of economic stagnation. Further, once the press associated Means with antitrust, his views on price-fixing were annexed to the antimonopoly noise of the late 1930s, resulting in a distortion of his message. The logic of administered price theory, he believed, hardly proved the iniquity of aggregation, which reduced transaction cost; rather, it demonstrated the relative inflexibility of prices, which should have fallen in depression. Means emphasized the lack of incentives to increased volume of sales, investment, output, and employment in the downward swing of the business cycle. With competition no longer an economic regulator, positive economic control by government representative of broad national interests should be substituted for industrial operatives acting selfishly in their own interest or in concert. When Paul T. Homans at the Brookings Institution challenged that there were more types of pricing system than he acknowledged, Means agreed that he needed more factual data on pricing, consumption, and productive capacity to mesh industrial policy with the requirements of specific industries and recovery measures, a project he undertook as research director of the National Resources Committee's Industrial Committee in 1935.[26]

Assigned the task of social and economic planning, Means examined productive capacity and consumption requirements in order to narrow the spread between the two. The argument ran that this would facilitate planning of new facilities and expanded purchasing power while reducing waste. Means's producer study led to *The Structure of the American Economy* (1939), which emphasized concentration and techniques of control.[27]

Earlier, in exchanges of viewpoint, Currie, a member of the NRC's Industrial Committee, argued the theme of deficient community expenditure, while Means supported his structural approach, or the fiction of market pricing. According to Currie, "It is in the net federal contribution to community expenditures that the greatest decrease took place in the factors tending to increase business activity." Means asserted the primacy of his price theories, for "the over-saving problem" was "a by-product of price inflexibility and not ... an independent problem." Here was the nub of the conflict between the two, and eventually between Means and Alvin Hansen. According to Means, "If I am correct, then the problem of oversaving arises as a result of insensitive prices." "If oversaving would arise as a general problem even if all prices, wage rates, etc., were sensitive, then oversaving," he conceded at most, "must be placed parallel with price inflexibility." The die was cast with the severity of the 1937–38 recession, which carried Curried Keynes into the limelight.[28]

At joint meetings of the Advisory and Industrial Committees, which contemplated the future course of NRC studies, Means found himself under added pressure. Among those present were Delano, Merriam, Eliot, Dennison, Ruml, Ezekiel, Louis Bean, Leon Henderson, Harry Dexter White, and Thomas Blaisdell. Means and Blaisdell recalled a "rambling discussion" which contemplated alternative approaches to future research: study either of balance of resources with selective use of antitrust to curb pricing or of an industrial approach combined with stimulus to consumption, as neither approach had been proven more effective. Ezekiel and Ruml demurred. Ezekiel asserted that neither Means nor Blaisdell took into account Currie's emphasis on compensatory fiscal policy, not prices, as key to an economic reversal. Ruml ventured that the issue of a compensatory budget policy had been decided, which left only the question of its thrust, toward the producer or the consumer. Defeated, Means suggested that Alvin Hansen undertake an exploratory study of fiscal and monetary policy.[29]

With publication of his *Structure of the American Economy* by the NRC as it wound up its activities in 1939, Means proposed the enlistment of distinguished economists as discussants at an informal conference designed to "obtain the maximum agreement as to the structural characteristics of the American economy." As matters developed, the newly formed NRPB, with Merriam and Delano still in command and persuaded by the views of Hansen, now a consultant and frequent contributor to its reports, scheduled part 2 of the Structure Report, *Toward Full Use of Resources*, as a critique of rather than an encomium to structural theory. Distraught, Means insisted that the two approaches, structural and operational, should be separated; later he proposed that he should research an operational study as a complement to his structural approach; then he declared that the board by associating the two approaches would create confusion and precipitate "an arid theoretical discussion." Unable to head off the publication of part 2, Means resigned from the NRPB in 1940.[30]

The Structure of the American Economy, part 2, *Toward Full Use of Resources*, a symposium on the future course of NRPB studies, signaled the board's endorsement of Hansen's new economics. In his introduction Means insisted that structural characteristics (monopoly pricing) determined operating policies.[31] Hansen dismissed Means's structural approach. Distinguishing between secular and cyclical price flexibility, Hansen held that emphasis on cyclical inflexibility of administered prices and price dispersion, or the divergence of agricultural and administered (industrial) prices, was contradicted by a growing body of opinion which stressed underinvestment as the dominant factor in cyclical movement. Hansen did not dispute price dispersion but claimed that increased income and investment would narrow the gap. Further, sharp price reductions in the capital goods sector in the early stage of depression would not necessarily induce recovery and might, to the contrary, accelerate the economy's downward movement. Deflationary movements could not be remedied by "chasing administered prices and wage rates down to the level of agricultural and other flexible prices." The result would be an accelerated income decline. "A direct attack must be made on the cycle itself and not merely upon the price dispersion"; the goal of price stability was best met by fiscal policy.[32]

Addressing the same forum, Mordecai Ezekiel proposed a functional economy nominally based on voluntarism, yet he proved willing to resort to consent decrees and the use of legislative authority where larger units dominated. Basic industries would prepare a program for expanded output and submit their plans to a proposed Industrial Expansion Administration, whose functions would include increased output facilitated by orders from a contracting agency, with excess production taken off the market by government at a discount. Ezekiel suggested government ownership of natural monopolies such as utilities, railroads, water, mines, and forests, which in his view stabilized business conditions in Sweden.

Ezekiel's approach would require businessmen in the key industries to surrender their power to establish prices and production levels to government. Industrial expansion bills along these lines, introduced into the
Congress by the "Young Turks" Thomas Amlie, Jeremiah "Jerry" Voorhis,
Maury Maverick, and Robert G. Allen, got nowhere.[33]

The NRPB adopted Hansen's formula for a full-employment economy:
public works expenditure for regional economic development financed
by deficit spending, as well as income redistribution by means of tax revision and expanded social insurance. At their meetings with Roosevelt,
Merriam and Delano projected studies of relief and reemployment, an
industrial-economic study accompanied by specific programs of action,
and a 1940 study of postdefense problems including a shelf of public works
to forestall a postwar recession or depression. Funding of such a program
(Eccles and Hansen joining in) would be accomplished by "unorthodox"
methods of financing. Merriam and Delano also proposed a report on
"The Trend of Employment and Business Activity." This included estimates of national income required to absorb the labor supply into a full-
employment economy, based partly on business expansion, partly on net
government contributions required to make up the employment deficit.

Roosevelt's posture seemed reminiscent of his fateful dispatch of Moley
to London in June 1933. "Grand," he exulted, as Merriam and Delano
broadened the compass of the NRPB; but at the same time he cautioned
against intrusion on the departments or the House Appropriations Committee. While the Merriam-Delano-Hansen prescriptions for avoidance of
another depression and better distribution of social benefits reached its
apogee with submission of the "National Resources Development Report
for 1943, Part I. Post-War Plan and Program," and the accompanying
"Security, Work, and Relief Policies," congressional displeasure also came
to a head.[34]

12 | MATURE CAPITALISM AND
DEVELOPMENTAL ECONOMICS

T
HE DEMISE OF THE NRPB and the possibilities for planning in the framework of a developmental economy are best understood within the context of the debate that emanated from the 1937–38 recession. The NRPB and fiscal-full employment planners declared that chronic private-sector underinvestment, or industry's inability to sustain full use of resources and manpower at the volume of savings, condemned the economy to equilibrium at less than full employment. Full employment necessitated a long-term program of planned federal outlay, with government's net contribution ratcheted up or downward by an administrative agency to meet the nation's annual income and consumption goals. Inability of the private sector to find adequate outlets for savings compelled the government to serve in the role of investment banker.

With the depression following the Great War a cautionary experience, John Kenneth Galbraith and Alvin H. Hansen envisaged a second postwar surge of demand followed by a severe downturn brought on by a decline in expenditure for consumption and investment. U.S. engagement in the Second World War resulted in the additional burden of absorbing millions of defense workers and draftees who would return to civilian life. As a consequence, the government should supplement private spending and investment by deployment of a shelf of public investment projects planned ahead at a minimum of six years. As advance planning would reduce lead time in a downward movement of the cycle, Congress would authorize public development expenditure within prescribed limits by a permanent fiscal agency, the Bureau of the Budget situated in the Executive Office of the President. Capable of flexible administration of federal expenditures, taxation, and borrowing, the Bureau of the Budget would also coordinate activities and functions of the government departments and regional authorities.[1]

Tax revision, a matter of social equity and required to fund federal investments, would help resolve the problem of underconsumption and an unsatisfactory pattern of income distribution. Lower payroll taxes and enhanced general revenues from middle-income tax brackets for unemployment benefits and social insurance would help meet the problem of chronic stagnation.

Stimulus to consumption as well as equity in a democratic society required adequate social provision for old age, health, disability, and mothers with dependent children. Hansen held that social provision should be funded largely from general revenues, less so from contributory taxes, as the latter were "a drag on full employment." Outpayments for unemployment insurance and old-age assistance should be increased and the waiting period for unemployment benefits shortened to diminish the lag in response to the business cycle.

Domestic economic balance should be achieved through federal investment for defense in underdeveloped regions, in postwar planning on the TVA model, and in essential industries. Such a program would remedy regional economic unbalance.[2]

One of the most formidable economic critiques of Hansen's compensatory approach was offered by Columbia University's John Maurice Clark. Like Tugwell, Clark was a socially oriented experimentalist; but Clark's views proved more moderated, especially in his prescriptions for adjustments to the modern economy. His evolutionary approach exuded awareness of the ever-changing nature of a dynamic business system which warranted state intervention yet required wariness of sure prescriptions offered by more radical institutionalists that might hamper business enterprise.[3]

Institutionalist economists of the interwar era stressed empirical research as opposed to the neoclassical emphasis on theoretical constructs. They probed the nature and development of institutions, particularly the role of collective groups, corporations, labor unions, and trade associations, and the consequent frictions that required government management for social purposes; and they noted the divergence of marketplace and social values. To this endeavor Clark contributed the concept of overhead costs, the belief that business's discard of labor in depression constituted no saving, as the community, ultimately including business, was burdened by the need for social maintenance of the unemployed. Necessarily, the government would need to mediate between labor and corporations, big and small business, agriculture and industry, in order to resolve the frictions caused by the real, as opposed to an ideal, economy. Clark came to view national planning as essential to control of the business cycle—short, however, of intruding on the operations of business enterprise. He preferred indirect mechanisms to other means of planning for which the American economy was unprepared. This was the essence of Clark's paper at the 1940 NRPB-sponsored symposium.

Clark insisted that solutions must be pragmatic, tested, suited to their times, conducive to viable competition. As for Means's price analysis, "purely structural characteristics have little or no meaning for the present problem, apart from their operational implications." Further, "The mere announcement of such an inexorable policy of public experimentation . . . might induce such a partial paralysis of private enterprise as would outweigh any stimulative effect which public policies might have." The present system offered orderly change. While he had no sympathy for businessmen who cried "wolf" at every fresh government intervention, "we [should] . . . be on guard against assuming that there will never be a wolf."

With respect to Hansen's new economics, though Clark had written on the need for countercyclical government expenditure in *The Economics of Planning Public Works* for the National Planning Board, he questioned full utilization of manpower "to do wholly useless things" or to offer inferior services financed at considerable public expense through taxes and debt. This created a fiscal burden by transferring wealth from self-liquidating private enterprise or productive use to non-self-liquidating uses. At the same time, the theory of oversaving-underinvestment remained untested and needed scrutiny.[4]

Clark distinguished between cyclical and chronic causes of underutilization. Business cycle studies demonstrated the need for price and wage flexibility in durable goods, better use of credit and fiscal policy, and restored international trade. But chronic underutilization proved more complex. Full recovery might well require several cycles and the temporary use of deficit spending, not, challenging Hansen, on the ground that "underutilization is inherent and permanent, but on the opposite ground," as it was structural in nature: involving obstacles to trade; an unsatisfactory tax system; chronic unemployables; vocational immobility, or the excess of labor supply in certain industries; cost factors due to the pressures of organized labor; and insufficiency in the flow of purchasing power. Clark held that oversaving-underinvestment might well be a symptom, not a cause, and "not all-sufficient to explain everything about a condition of underutilization." Rather, oversaving and underinvestment could be attributed to fear of the unknown, mores that warranted saving, the state of economic development, and the potential of radical government policies.

Government spending would not serve as a permanent cure. If self-liquidating, it would compete with private enterprise or absorb private power. At best, it served as a palliative, as a short-term stimulus or neutralizing force giving help to business activity; once withdrawn, such a revival would end. If permanent, it would accumulate deficits, implying heavy future taxation, burden the economy, impair business psychology, and might well be used as political bribes. Long-term recovery depended on private enterprise. Government would occasionally fill the void, but it would not serve as principal actor in full utilization of resources. "We must act daringly," Clark concluded, "but we can probably be daring without gambling away our national safety in a single roll of the dice. An experimental policy implies keeping open the possibility of withdrawal."[5]

Unpersuaded by Clark, the National Resources Planning Board plunged ahead with proposals for expanded social and economic planning. A fresh lease on life under the president's 1939 reorganization plan seemed circumscribed by the terms of the Federal Employment Stabilization Act under which it legally operated. The statute provided simply for the preparation of a long-term bank of public works recommended by the president to Congress, with annual appropriations based on employment and business activity. In practice, NRPB studies covered a long-term public works program, reemployment, taxation, power policy, regional planning, advancement of science, migration, land and water use and conservation, industrial location, youth unemployment and training, relief, and social insurance. With the coming of war in Europe, defense preparations such as plant location and expansion, steel requirements, and transport, electric, and manpower needs were added to the NRPB agenda, at least until Roosevelt, wary of Congress because it had cut the NRPB's budget request for FY 1941 by some 30 percent, insisted that the agency focus on postwar planning.[6]

A stream of publications based on the need for postwar public works planning and fiscal stimulus for a full-employment economy proselytized on behalf of the role of the central government in the nation's economic and social future. In its 1941 publication *After Defense—What?*—with over 100,000 copies distributed—the NRPB pointed to large-scale public expenditure needed to absorb some twenty-six million people currently engaged in the defense effort and the military once the war ended. As opposed to a low-level economy committed to budget balance, hence considerable unemployment, the NRPB aspired to full employment based on government investment in multipurpose regional projects modeled on TVA, a long-range public works program revised annually by Congress, rehabilitation of marginal farmland, an expanded electrical grid, planning for integrated transport and for industry, and an enhanced social welfare program that afforded security for young and old, mothers and the ill, and unemployables. These would be funded by a fiscal policy coordinated with government loans and credit and banking control and would require labor and wage regulation, price controls, and international planning.

After Defense—What? apparently followed an analysis laid out in a study directed by John Kenneth Galbraith for the NRPB, *The Economic Effects of the Federal Public Works Expenditure* (1940). Galbraith's study rejected the view that unemployment, hitherto regarded as a normal manifestation of the business cycle, could be reversed by a natural process involving the writing down of debt, wages, and interest rates. It also challenged the view of full employment as the normal or equilibrium condition, remediable by temporary reliance on deficit spending. The downward swing of the cycle could not be corrected in any substantial way by public works "shifted forward or backward to coincide with the slump." With depressions unable to correct themselves automatically, government investment in public works on a long-term basis would be required.[7]

Future funding of a bank of public works and "equal access to minimum security," planned by the NRPB group and Roosevelt in December 1940, was turned over by arrangement with Marriner Eccles to Alvin Hansen, who was appointed a special economic adviser to the Federal Reserve's Board of Governors in 1941. Authorized to explore unorthodox methods of finance, Hansen in *After the War: Full Employment* anticipated a postwar labor surplus of 12 to 16 million workers and a recurrence of the post–World War I experience, boom based on pent-up demand, then a depression. This could be avoided by maintenance of purchasing power at a high level. While private business would manage production, government would sustain demand and invigorate private enterprise through the NRPB agenda, much of it drafted by Hansen. This included urban redevelopment, low-cost housing, public health programs and hospital facilities, a nutritional program, higher educational standards, and expanded cultural and recreational facilities, in addition to more adequate provision for old age and infrastructure projects.[8]

Hansen claimed that enlarged federal functions would not test the nation's fiscal capacity since "the idleness of the decade of the thirties was responsible for the loss of $200 billions of income." A $100 billion income—a later version estimated $125 billion—would generate a full-employment economy and finance the program he had outlined by providing revenue sufficient to service any desired debt level. In the event, a public debt incurred internally bore no resemblance to private debt as it served as an instrument of public policy. It controlled national income, and when coordinated with a steeply graduated tax structure on incomes and retained profits, it facilitated lower consumption taxes.[9]

Security, Work, and Relief Policies, submitted by the NRPB to the president in December 1941, then by Roosevelt to the Congress on March 10, 1943, summarized the NRPB's agenda and sealed its fate. The security study was written by the Columbia University economist Eveline M. Burns, who had studied at the London School of Economics under William H. Beveridge, exponent of the British postwar welfare state. The report stressed access to minimum security through public work for employables unable to find work in industry; comprehensive guarantees against the hazards of accident, disease, old age, and temporary unemployment; and assurance of a minimum living standard.

A permanent federal public works agency would serve adults unemployed and willing and able to work at prevailing wages. Unemployment insurance would be extended to twenty-six weeks. Old-age pensions would be wholly administered by the federal government and social security extended to include domestics and agricultural labor. As even a full-employment policy and social insurance could not meet the needs of the aged impoverished, those unable to work, the disabled, blind, ill, and dependent children, these would benefit from a program financed jointly by state and federal funds and administered by the states under the supervision of the Social Security Board. Youths would benefit from apprenticeships or financial aid for higher education. While the report did not call for universal health insurance, it proposed expanded health services for mothers, dependent children, disease prevention, nutrition, and construction of new facilities.

An equally controversial *Post-War Plan and Program,* also released in 1943, which genuflected toward the principle of free enterprise, broached the possibility of corporations operated jointly by government and private managers after the war, based on British and dominion models. The NRPB suggested that the mixed corporation might well serve defense needs in areas such as aluminum, magnesium, basic metals, synthetic rubber, certain chemicals, shipbuilding, and aircraft production. Mixed public-private ownership also seemed suited to urban redevelopment, housing, air transport, communications, and electric power. The degree of government investment, stock ownership, and managerial authority would vary, depending on the "public interest."

Here was a charter for postwar America, a "revolutionary answer to the needs of a revolutionary age" that offered security without the loss of freedom, exulted Bruce Bliven, George Soule, and Max Lerner in the *New Republic*. The destruction of incentive and a pledge of government aid to the undeserving, public control of industry, and the wreckage of freedom, countered Robert A. Taft.[10]

According to a White House memorandum, "Mr. Corrington Gill [government economist and former aide to Harry Hopkins] called and left the following message: 'Tell Mr. Hopkins I hope he does not let the president put his neck out on the National Resources Planning Board Report on Social Benefits.'" Roosevelt, weakened by congressional opposition, was cautioned by James F. Byrnes, currently head of the Office of Economic Stabilization, against a last-ditch fight. Roosevelt would not engage the legislative branch on the issue of NRPB budgetary renewal and its charter for postwar America. "I do not want to raise any public discussion in regard to this by sending a formal communication," a conciliatory president wooed the House Appropriations Committee. Privately he proposed replacement of the current board with a new planning agency, or one made up of different personnel. To Carter Glass he promised huge savings through postwar planning and pointed to endorsement of the Committee for Economic Development and other business groups. To no avail. Whereas the Senate voted a meager $200,000 for NRPB continuance, the House Appropriations Committee voted nil and prevailed in conference. The debate over the future of planning through a developmental economy was left to Taft-led antistatists, centrist economists, and Hansen, who was bent on a "stable and large volume of public outlays."[11]

The Hansen-Taft dissonance had its origins in the 1937–38 recession and the Republican Party's Lazarus-like resurrection in the 1938 congressional contest. Although Roosevelt projected a balanced budget as a stimulus to business confidence in his January 1938 message to Congress, the recession's intractability dictated otherwise. At a Warm Springs, Georgia, meeting in March of that year, Harry Hopkins, accompanied by Leon Henderson, Aubrey Williams, deputy WPA administrator, and Beardsley Ruml, won a commitment to countercyclical spending.

While Laughlin Currie's views circulated widely among administration economists and gathered considerable support, Ruml's observations evidently sparked Roosevelt's shift to a compensatory fiscal policy. Ruml explained that a balanced budget had no impact on purchasing power. Further, proponents of budget balance assumed unrealistically that supply and demand determined price as a result of free, open, private competition, that "quantities are right" and prices fair, that a correct balance was maintained between savings and consumption, and that all who desired work could find it at the correct economic reward for the skill at offer. In reality, deficient demand would not assure a commensurate price decline sufficient to spur full production. Reasonable maintenance of demand and production required federal intervention "from time to time to provide purchasing power in the hands of the public." "The so-called pump-priming," according to Ruml, "is a crude variant of the compensatory policy. It is crude because it applies to only one phase of the compensatory problem, namely, when it is in need for expansion. Also it looks to only one side of the budget, namely, expenditures." A stable tax regime served as Ruml's preferred weapon for smoothing the cycle.

Ruml's March 1938 memorandum called for investment spending of $7 to $10 billion, public and private, to meet the goal of a full-employment economy. This required some $3 billion additional in net federal contribution as a spur to consumption. Accepting Ruml's rationale, which overcame Henry Morgenthau's objections, Roosevelt presented an emergency budget message to the Congress in April. It provided for congressional authorization of $2 billion in new expenditures and Treasury loans of $950 million, as well as desterilization of $1.4 billion of the gold hoard held by the Treasury Department. At the same time, Fed-imposed bank reserve requirements were lowered.

Roosevelt's January 5, 1939, budget message to the Congress called for continued study of the central government's role in economic stability, including the correlation between national income and government receipts and expenditures. "I believe I am expressing the thought of the most farsighted students of our economic system in saying that it would be unwise either to curtail expenditures or to impose drastic new taxes at this stage of recovery." Roosevelt also disinterred his earlier distinction between an ordinary budget and a capital budget. The latter encompassed extraordinary or long-term expenditures such as government loans and public works, which contracted or expanded with the rise or fall of national income.[12]

In a further step toward a capital budget, Roosevelt suggested a package of low-interest loans, amounting to just over $3 billion, of which $870 million would be made available commencing in 1940. This sum would be distributed to a Federal Works Agency for nonfederal public works administered by local authorities, to be used for toll roads and bridges, to create a Railroad Equipment Authority, to provide for tenant farm purchases and rural electrification, and for Export-Import Bank loans, and would be supplemented by an additional $800 million for the United States Housing Authority. The proposal resembled Scandinavian budgetary procedure, wherein capital and ordinary expenses were segregated and the legislative branch delegated to administrative officials the timing of capital investment.

While a revolving fund for capital expenditure offered the possibility of a long-range countercyclical program geared to infrastructure needs, Byrd and Taft claimed it would serve to bypass congressional authority to appropriate money on an annual basis. Cut back in the Senate, the so-called spend-lend bill did not survive debate in the House. Drawing on the views of Cleveland Trust Company economist Leonard Ayres, data furnished by the Du Pont economist Edmund E. Lincoln, and legal doctrine enunciated by his father, the Ohio senator asserted that the bill would encroach on private investors and violated the constitutional provision that designated the legislative branch as the source of appropriations. The time had come, Taft held, to let the private sector take up the employment slack and to balance the budget.[13] This initial loss on fiscal policy suffered by the Roosevelt administration; the frustrated, then diluted, reorganization plan; congressional appointment of a committee to examine the National Labor Relations Board on the ground of favoritism to the CIO, supported by a majority both of Democrats and Republicans; and repeal of the undistributed profits tax signaled Roosevelt's political weakness.[14]

With the appointment of Laughlin Currie as administrative assistant to the president, the argument on behalf of a compensatory federal budget took a decisive turn. The Currie draft of the FY 1941 budget message committed the administration to an advanced view of government expenditure. The budget served, Roosevelt now claimed, as a stimulus to national income and consumption. The resultant revenue gain would support a rising national debt. Roosevelt conceded that the recession stemmed in part from curtailed net government contributions that led to a sharp drop in consumers' purchasing power. As for the national debt, which grew by $19 billion between June 30, 1933, and December 31, 1939, it had been a prudent investment, with much of this sum spent on tangible improvements, while the credit of the national government remained unimpaired, indeed enhanced, by increased earning power.[15]

The predominance of the American Keynesians, many students of Alvin Hansen, joined by popular writers such as Stuart Chase, wanted more than the limited countercyclical budgeting offered by Currie and Roosevelt. They perceived the New Deal spending program as fitful and essentially a program of salvage. Convinced that capitalism had reached its maturity, hence the permanence of underinvestment, this group urged the need for a compensatory and "developmental" fiscal policy. Stimulus to growth and full employment required an enlarged welfare state and state investment in, or ownership of, certain "public" industries based on natural resources, communications, defense, and transport, as well as a program geared to regional and urban redevelopment. In the contest that ensued, Hansen served as this group's mover and shaker.[16]

According to Hansen, capitalism had matured in the interwar period, for the extraordinary population growth of the nineteenth century was now static and the development of new frontiers worldwide had come to an end.[17] Influenced by the British economist Ralph Hawtrey, Hansen's stagnation theory viewed capital investment as widening in the course of the industrial revolution, then deepening in the modern era. The widening of capital resulted from the development of new products, new processes of production, and new ways of utilizing natural resources, which stimulated investment and employment. Post–Civil War investment in railroads and subsequently the emergence of the automobile industry and electrification expanded investment opportunities in ancillary industries. The widening of capital gave way in the interwar years to its deepening with the introduction of labor-saving devices that required less in the way of capital investment, inducing unemployment. Hansen questioned "whether inventions and innovations are likely in the future to be capital-using to the extent experienced in the nineteenth century." How, then, to avoid secular stagnation and to absorb the flow of savings, currently held largely in institutional hands? And where could a satisfactory intermediary be found to place new investment required to meet the goal of full employment? Since equity markets had proven inadequate to the task, and in view of the large market for Treasury issues, government should serve as intermediary between savers and investment markets. Government as investment banker would enhance physical and human resources and stimulate the private sector, resulting in full employment.

Hansen's embrace of the social minima depended on his belief that recovery depended partly on a consumption-led recovery as well as on the assumption common to institutionalist economists that the individual required shelter from the vicissitudes of a dynamic but erratic capitalism. But social welfare programs alone would not suffice to meet the deficiencies in federal net contributions. Likewise, tax or monetary policy, while helpful, would hardly substitute for a developmental program in the secular transition from the old to the new economy. Low interest rates were ineffective in a framework of limited profit possibilities. With the age of extensive private capital investment past, the need existed for government capital expenditure of savings that otherwise could not find adequate outlets. The size and scope of New Deal expenditure for public works and people was too haphazard, for business depended on a steady national income. Hansen estimated that a full-employment economy, or 54 million employed by 1940 as opposed to 47.1 million, could have been attained with expenditure of $122.3 billion as opposed to $71.7 billion in the period 1929 to 1940. The resultant increase in national income and revenue could have funded the increased debt.[18]

With employment encouraged by the rise of public expenditure and national income during the Second World War, Hansen raised the bar for future public investment as a compensatory mechanism to some $18 billion annually needed to absorb savings and maintain a full-employment economy. In the next depression private enterprise would not see profit prospects adequate to warrant the risks involved. In dollar terms Hansen set an investment goal of some $6 billion targeted for public housing, $5 billion for private-sector business plant and equipment, and $5 to $7 billion for urban and valley resource development, transport, and traditional public works. Elimination of excessive regional dependence on basic commodities, unwise from both the local and national point of view, would be assigned to autonomous agencies located at the site possessing flexibility and operational responsibility. Ultimate financial and administrative control would be guided by policy directives from the Congress but lodged in the Executive Office of the President.

Planned urban redevelopment, which involved federal, state, and local governments, would serve as a major component of a developmental economy. Cities, Hansen observed, had zoned core areas for business uses no longer required. Though blighted and surrounded by decayed housing, excessive valuations for tax purposes discouraged private redevelopment of the central city. Municipalities and metropolitan areas, once they were granted legal authority by the states to buy up or condemn decayed central areas, would secure federal funding for the purpose and would be required to develop six-year plans for mixed use to be submitted to a newly created Department of Urban Affairs. Land could be leased to private or public enterprise and construction stimulated by federally subsidized housing, such underused property redeveloped according to a master plan. Expanded lending authority would enable a national financing authority to offer loans at below-market rates to insurance companies, savings institutions, and other fiduciaries for the construction of low-cost housing.

Transparently, Hansen's agenda raised the related issues of inevitable growth in public debt and its financing. Hansen argued that public debt internally held "should hardly be called a debt at all." Government debt and loan expenditure financed by idle domestic savings or bond sales to commercial banks resulted in equivalent growth in money supply, mainly in the form of demand deposits, and an increased income flow. The nub was not the size of the debt, since the federal government was not bound by the constraints facing a corporation or municipality, only by its ability to raise revenue adequate to service its indebtedness. Internal debt could be capitalized and repayment postponed. Revenue raised from increased national income would meet debt service with no net loss to the community as it would be shifted within the economic system to fiduciary institutions and individual bondholders. "In practice, an internal debt is rarely paid off; and . . . does not need to be."

Meeting postwar expenditure and debt levels required tax revision. Business enterprise would be encouraged by repeal of excess profits and capital gains taxes as well as a loss carryback (two years) and loss carryforward (five years) to induce risk-taking investments. Hansen's tax program would also eliminate sales and excise taxes other than those on tobacco, alcohol, and gasoline. This placed the tax burden on undistributed corporate earnings, with corporations allowed to deduct dividends and interest to calculate income and the balance taxed at a rate of 40 to 45 percent, and on a steeply graduated tax on individual incomes, with increased exemptions in the lower brackets as a stimulus to consumption. In both taxes and expenditures, Hansen urged flexibility in timing on the Swedish model: the legislative branch would set down parameters for a Central Fiscal Authority.[19]

A full-employment postwar program necessitated a new type of national budget based on an adequate total outlay of expenditures on goods and services, public and private, or a dual economy in which state enterprise determined its investments on a basis other than profits. Here Hansen relied on the work of the Danish economist Jørgen Pedersen, who held that "the fiscal policies of the state cannot be conceived in terms of the calculations of private enterprise but in terms of regulation and control, in terms of the impact of public policies upon the functioning of the economy as a whole." Public debt expended for the dole was deadweight debt. Swedish practice suggested to Hansen use of a capital budget geared to productive investment in state enterprises, with rate of investment determined by administrative authorities in response to the cycle. National debt incurred became an instrument of public policy and especially fruitful if financed by loan expenditure as opposed to high taxes, which impaired consumption.[20]

Ineluctably, Hansen's dual economy, based on growth induced by sustained federal investment over a generation, required administrative management by a Central Planning Agency, "a parliament of experts." Such a planning instrument would incorporate a fiscal authority charged with undertaking a flexible program of expenditure and taxation geared to cyclical needs, a department of urban affairs, and regional development authorities. While these agencies, domiciled in the Executive Office of the President, would be empowered to determine the timing of expenditures for projects authorized by the Congress, the legislative branch would not, he claimed, vest its authority in the executive. Rather, testimony by the heads of these agencies before the House and Senate and a similarly rationalized committee structure enjoying better staffing would ensure ultimate control over expenditures within authorized guidelines.

Hansen avoided the Merriam-NRPB pretense of associationalism or bottom-up planning, which required more community expertise than existed. While Hansen is not associated with structural planning or micro-management of the economy, he would have grafted government invest-ment expenditure onto a dual economy managed at the top by experts. Although the beneficiary of accolades from publications as diverse as the *New Republic* and *Fortune* and the popular economist Stuart Chase, Hansen's agenda for avoidance of a future depression entered the politi-cal arena as readily as it became part of economic discourse.[21]

In an address before a hometown Cincinnati audience, Robert A. Taft cited the work published by seven economists, members of the faculties of Harvard and Tufts Universities, which advanced countercyclical theory, as well as the TNEC testimony of Currie and Hansen, as evidence of an attack on thrift by government. Resort to borrowing, Taft predicted, would threaten national insolvency and endanger private enterprise and the American System based on limited central government. Hyperbolic or not, such views reflected a broad spectrum of opinion in rural areas and smaller communities, especially in the nation's midsection, which Taft tapped in southern Ohio during his successful 1938 campaign for the Senate.[22]

Ensconced in the Senate for the balance of his life, Taft remained true to views shaped by his father, William Howard Taft: distrust of eastern cap-ital, reliance on the commerce clause and antitrust to restrain business excess and on the law to order society, and belief in strict construction, notably emphasis on checks and balances and separation of powers. Ser-vice with Herbert Hoover at the wartime Food Administration, the Amer-ican Relief Administration, and the Paris Peace Conference reinforced these views, as did a distaste for involvement in European affairs. Active on the Chief's behalf in his presidential campaigns, the Cincinnati attor-ney characterized Hoover's 1934 manifesto, *The Challenge to Liberty*, as the expression of "the essential principles of American government." Indeed, Taft's response to the New Deal program's centralizing tendencies and his wariness of Roosevelt and his motives were encouraged by Hoover. Both stressed minimalist central government, and both provided an ideologi-cal anchor for antistatist thought and devolution of authority on social issues to the states.[23]

Herbert Hoover originated the New Deal no more than did Taft. Ac-cording to Hoover, the rights of the individual and the American System were trampled at home as readily as abroad. Democratic institutions were threatened by the delegation of legislative power to the executive for

"emergency's sake," by relinquishment of states' rights and local responsibility to central authority, by the growth of an independent bureaucracy, and by a regimented economy. He condemned just as strongly the
expenditure of "enormous sums" for public works, relief, and agriculture
not explicitly authorized by the Congress. Relief was the initial responsibility of the individual, then the local community, and ultimately the state
governments, not the reverse. Government entities, notably TVA, competed unfairly with private enterprise; the executive interfered unnecessarily with the private sector by fixing minimum wages and maximum
hours. And the Hull agenda for trade reciprocity meant that Congress had
yielded its authority over the tariff.

While Hoover accepted planning for schools, roads, hospitals, and the
like, he hammered at Rexford Tugwell's vision of a national plan as an
abandonment of individual liberty for "coercive cooperation" and centralized power. Aware of the Keynesian stress on the "ill-balance between
savings and expenditures on consumption goods," Hoover nevertheless
preferred greater attention given to budget balance. Economic security
for the individual could be achieved by unleashing the dynamism inherent in the economy and by providing insurance against unemployment,
sickness, and old age managed locally through methods that would not
"deteriorate thrift, create a group of loafers, and will not undermine the
responsibilities of state and local government." Business excess could be
reined in by regulatory powers and agencies, not by bureaucratic tyranny.
For Hoover and Taft the depression was transitory, and the principles of
limited government, associationalism, and individualism were permanent components of a free society.[24]

Like Hoover, shy, a less than engaging public speaker, not given to the
small talk and socializing characteristic of politicos, spare in friendships,
Taft relied principally on his own counsel and a narrow intellectual base
made up of Ohio associates. The hardships imposed by the depression
hardly dented his personal well-being or doctrinal consistency and pre-
conceptions rooted in antistatist premises. Like the Chief, the Ohioan attributed the depression to dislocations that emanated from the World War,
unsound lending and speculative activity, price maintenance by international cartels, excess raw materials output induced by self-containment,
and emphasis on capital goods expenditure as opposed to consumables.
Remedies depended on a modest increase in purchasing power, lower
prices, and a renewed demand.[25]

Though he declined an invitation to join the American Liberty League, Taft thoroughly sympathized with its objectives and during his early years in Washington frequently relied on the Du Pont economist Edmund E. Lincoln for the statistical basis of his ideological arguments. He regularly categorized the New Deal as revolutionary and an invitation to socialism through its attacks on wealth, price-fixing, discouragement of private enterprise, inflationary policies, reckless expenditure, and unbalanced budgets. Though he conceded the need for temporary deficits, government, he argued, was subject to the same budgetary constraints as the individual, with the exception of loan expenditure by the RFC and the urban home and farm credit institutions and for public works, subject, however, to limited federal capacity. He opposed government ownership of public utilities "whether as yardsticks or otherwise." Holding companies should be controlled by government regulation of securities issuance and rates. Overall, government's role should be limited to remediation of abuses in the system, dealt with "one by one," hence his support of the child labor amendment, "not by assuming the power . . . to regulate the details of business activity in the states." The tax system should not and could not serve effectively as an instrument of income redistribution.

Taft viewed the Social Security Act of 1935 as extravagant in its promise of benefits beyond the capacity of government, taxpayers, and employers, a "necessary evil" clothed by a humanitarian gloss. Its benefits, he claimed, should not be "more pleasant than relief is pleasant," as it induced sloth, discouraged enterprise, and placed government in the insurance business, incurring dangerous obligations.[26]

Once on the national scene, Taft moderated on social spending. He accepted social security on a pay-as-you-go basis as opposed to reliance on huge federal reserves that might well be diverted to other ends. Although he was an advocate of civil rights legislation at the national level,[27] he felt that old-age assistance, relief, and unemployment insurance should be managed by state programs administered by local authorities and funded partially by federal grants. At the same time, he opposed extension of presidential power for dollar devaluation, opposed U.S. involvement in the Second World War, sought the support of the GOP's right wing for the 1940 presidential nomination, and after the country's entry into the war, pressed for limited executive branch authority in the domestic sphere and in international affairs.[28]

Opponents of the New Deal, over time, became aware that it would not suffice to outlast Roosevelt or to hate him. Perennial tub-thumping and cries of dictatorship proved of little avail. Moderates accepted components of the New Deal, one suspects, based on personal or sectional interest; but they also feared a collectivist tide. W. W. Waymack offered the best gauge of midwestern opinion, which proved to be pivotal, in these years. Henry Wallace could not hold the nation's midsection for Roosevelt. The 1938 off-year election served as a turning point when the GOP took 764 counties as opposed to 292 for the Democrats. Farmers were no longer a majority; and the small towns, extremely conservative, anchored in tradition, offered Franklin D. Roosevelt's New Deal no gratitude for diversion of a portion of the income stream to its lawyers, merchants, and bankers. In its suffrage this group, Waymack explained in 1940, reflected "habit, tradition, a general dislike of heavy deficits, suspicion of WPA, fear of Roosevelt as an enemy of business." The New Deal sundered historic ties only to a limited extent. In Iowa, for example, Roosevelt's successes at the polls had not broken the grip of the Republican Party on county offices. Though Democratic governors were elected until 1938, the legislature never fell into the hands of Democrats. "The Iowa farm vote . . . is still largely registered in the Republican party. . . . A certain inner 'yen' to get back to the Republican fold has continued to exist." The Democratic Party could no longer rely on the fact that it had a program, Waymack noted. "Gratitude will not last forever."[29]

The balance of power between the New Dealers and the antistatists shifted in Taft's favor with the 1942 congressional election, leaving the Democrats with a narrow majority in the House and a nominal twenty-one-seat margin in the Senate, where the coalition of conservative southerners and newly elected Republicans moved to curb domestic controls and postwar plans by administration liberals and the liberal internationalists. Taft, Vandenberg, Ralph O. Brewster (Maine), and George Millikin (Colorado) found support in the new Senate GOP contingent, which included Homer Ferguson (Michigan) and Kenneth Wherry (Nebraska), and from the freshmen southern Democratic conservatives, notably James O. Eastland (Mississippi) and John L. McClellan (Arkansas). In the interim Taft cemented ties to the anti-interventionist progressive remnant, Burton K. Wheeler and Robert La Follette Jr., as well as Byrd, Walter George, and Richard Russell (Georgia).

House and Senate conservatives killed the Civilian Conservation Corps, National Youth Administration, NRPB, and WPA, as well as a bill that provided for federal aid to the states for elementary and secondary education. The Farm Security Administration and wartime agencies regarded as dominated by liberals or worse, the Office of Price Administration as an example, found their funding reduced and eventually were put out of business.[30] Congressional conservatives checked the effort by Arthur J. Altmeyer and the Social Security Board, supported by Paul McNutt, federal security administrator, to federalize unemployment compensation, part of a broader attempt incorporated in NRPB proposals to enlarge the scope and size of social security benefits in the areas of pensions, disability and health insurance, and public assistance.[31]

According to a *Chicago Journal of Commerce* reporter present at an informal Hansen talk before a group of business executives and bankers on June 27, 1942, the economist predicted:

Congress will surrender to the administration the power to tax, keeping for itself the right only to establish the broad limits within which the administration may move.

Congress will appropriate huge sums of money, surrender its power of directing when and how the money shall be spent.

Other extraordinary powers such as, for instance, to effect wholesale social reforms, will be delegated to the administration, which will retain most, if not all, of its present extraordinary wartime powers.

Noting this statement, Taft claimed that the planners contemplated the "socialization of the United States after the war." Taft also had in mind *An Economic Program for American Democracy*, which aired the Hansenite tenets of seven Harvard and Tufts economists, among them Richard V. Gilbert, George H. Hildebrand Jr., Arthur W. Stuart, Maxine Y. Sweezy, and Paul M. Sweezy. Three unnamed contributors were in government employ: Walter Salant, Emile Despres, and Alan Sweezy. Stung by Taft's version of his Chicago address, Hansen telephoned and then wrote to explain that his views had been misrepresented. A political realist in quest of rapprochement, Hansen suggested that they have lunch or dinner and discuss a postwar full-employment program, "in no sense a partisan matter," for he intended rather to avert the inevitable postwar depression. "This is not a two-by-four country and we need to plan in a large way" for developmental projects and a flexible federal budget designed to stimulate private investment. The alternative was chaos.[32]

There occurred no meeting of the minds on postwar planning and budgetary policy. With the NRPB interred by Congress, proponents of the new economics turned to the postwar reconversion process. The Kilgore-Murray bill (1944) would empower a works administrator to promote an expansionary full-employment program for housing, public works, industrial and regional development, expanded social services, foreign trade, and taxation. The usual bow to private enterprise scarcely mollified a Senate Special Committee on Post-War Economic Planning, headed by Walter George of Georgia, long an opponent of the New Deal. Taft was a member. The committee concluded that a proposed office of works administrator represented a revived NRPB. The Baruch-Hancock report on reconversion, oriented toward taking government out of business; Senate oversight by the George committee; and rapid disposal of government-financed war plant to the private sector by Will Clayton, who headed the War Surplus Property Administration, ended this aspect of the debate.[33]

Still more damaging to the developmental school, Beardsley Ruml offered a workable alternative to Hansen's program. Ruml proposed the goal of high as opposed to full employment in the postwar period, and he also predicted periodic bouts of inflation caused by demand in excess of available supply, as likely as periods of insufficiency of purchasing power. Rather than resort to public works expenditure as the principal compensatory mechanism, Ruml proposed reliance on stable tax rates calculated to maintain high employment levels and budget balance. With a progressive tax on incomes, individuals would pay less in the way of taxes in the downward trend of the cycle and a higher total tax bill in periods of expansionary pressures, with the revenue stream thus serving as an economic stabilizer. This would be supplemented by the use of monetary policy, neglected since the early 1930s.

Ruml's revenue-based system for smoothing the cycle was facilitated by an expanded tax base that included the middle and working classes in order to finance war expenditure and the use of withholding introduced to facilitate payments. The argument could now be made that long-term works projects proved wasteful, narrowly targeted, and slow to get under way as opposed to the immediate impact on purchasing power of weekly withholding and quarterly payments that rose or fell as wages and salaries shifted upward or downward. This promise of automaticity appealed to the Committee for Economic Development in the postwar years, especially as it assured the maintenance of purchasing power without resort to massive, centrally managed development projects. With business liberals won over, the Ruml proposal, amplified by Herbert Stein in 1946, served as the basis for fiscal policy in the immediate postwar era.[34]

In mid-December 1944 the War Contract Subcommittee of the Senate Military Affairs Committee, chaired by William Murray (D., Montana), proposed a national full-employment policy. The president would include in his annual budget message an employment and production budget in which he estimated the number of jobs needed to afford full employment in the next fiscal year, plus the dollar volume of output, investment, and other expenditure needed to assure the jobs goal. In the event of a potential deficiency anticipated by the planners, the president would be required to propose a program, first, to encourage private investment, then, to fill the void through federal expenditure. It was also stipulated that every American willing and able to work would be assured employment both useful and remunerative. These proved the essentials of the full-employment bill introduced by Senators Murray, Wagner, Elbert Thomas (Utah), and Joseph C. O'Mahoney (Wyoming) in January 1945.[35]

While Roosevelt adopted the NRPB's bill of economic rights in his 1944 annual message and the language of full-employment advocates in his 1945 budget message, the dual economy implied in the full-employment bill of 1945 never saw the light of day. Evidently aware of resistance in the Congress, Hansen labored on a conciliatory and awkward rewording which stressed presidential encouragement of nonfederal outlays promoting full employment. Yet he also wanted commitment—the recent British and Canadian white papers serving as models—to "a new national attitude, purpose, and responsibility of the central government," which necessarily meant maintenance of employment, production, and national income by a varied volume of total expenditure adequate to assure "sufficient employment opportunities."

Although George Terborgh's attack on stagnation theory, *The Bogey of Economic Maturity* (1945), received greater notice, the notion of economic maturity had already been undermined by other economists. Gottfried Haberler, Hansen's colleague, observed that the president already possessed the powers presumptively accorded by the full-employment bill. This was not at issue. The bill, rather, gave the impression that full employment could be maintained by a constant flow of government spending adequate to fill the gap in aggregate expenditure. Such a policy in the event of a major depression was no longer in dispute. At other times, it could well be overdone or used inappropriately, since the employment problem was complex. With depressed areas and industries often existing even when full employment obtained elsewhere, increased expenditure would simply drive up price levels in distressed areas, resulting in "the paradox of depression and unemployment in the midst of inflation," later experienced as stagflation.[36]

Another Harvard economist, Sumner H. Slichter, a specialist in management-labor relations and president of the American Economic Association (1942), questioned the concept of a national budget of employment. Democracy and capitalism, he believed, were inseparable as capitalism, despite its defects, was the sole system that dispersed power in the community. In his critique of the Murray bill, Slichter contended that government policy helped to determine volume of employment to the extent that it provided an environment conducive to private investment, a condition lacking in the 1930s. A full-employment economy depended on massive government expenditure and debt, a high-tax regime, price inflation, and regimentation. In the event, "the more mature and stagnant the economy, the greater the danger that deficits will make stagnation worse by causing government expenses to rise faster than revenues and thus limiting the increase in private employment." Massive wartime deficits, in fact, incurred in the years 1942–44, when government expenditure rose 30 percent and led to an employment increase of only 5 percent, or 2.5 million. Slichter preferred use of loans to the private sector when needed to stimulate private investment. In a series of lectures delivered at the Louisiana State University shortly before his death, Slichter questioned the efficacy of income redistribution, central planning, and the logic of stagnation-spending theory. A higher living standard and real wages depended instead on productivity-increasing technology.[37]

In his comments on plans "framed in 'capitalist' countries in order to stabilize the working of the capitalist engine," Joseph A. Schumpeter inquired, "Which kind of economy will emerge if the Murray plan becomes law and is then acted upon consistently?" The logical result, he observed, would be complete control of labor and capital markets, with the state compelled to enforce its decisions to avoid deadlock, direct private-sector expansion, and require labor to move to desired occupations and locations. For "behind the cooperation stands compulsion, at least as a last resort, and . . . the logic of things will see to it that all the major decisions about what to produce, how to provide, at what prices, wages, and profits to produce will tend to pass from the private to the public sphere." While

Schumpeter did not attribute such intent to the bill's sponsors, he thought that the proposal would necessarily lead to "Gilded Capitalism," a "midway house with a capitalist facade and a socialist basement." This, he believed, represented the temper of the times as entrepreneurship had been smothered by private and public bureaucracies.[38]

The Hansen-NRPB school was dealt a debilitating blow by powerful Democratic conservatives in the House of Representatives. In place of a policy of government spending, a national budget, and the right to employment, George Terborgh proposed an independent commission charged with steadying business activity and offering recommendations to that end to the president and the Congress. The resulting Council of Economic Advisers presented periodic reports to both the executive and a joint committee of the Congress but lacked operational powers. Hansen's developmental program, which relied on the Bureau of the Budget, was never realized to the extent he had in mind.[39]

The Employment Act of 1946 offered no commitment to any specific formula for stimulus to employment. Amendments, according to Taft, eliminated the requirement of a national budget based on compensatory spending. Government's duty to assist employment stood as only one of "many considerations which the president must take into account." Nor was the executive accorded power "to do anything which he could not have done on his own account." Finally, with Marriner Eccles determined that the budget should be balanced at war's end and Hansen wedded to a developmental program based on compensatory spending, Hansen's formal appointment as special economic adviser in the board's Division of Research and Statistics was reduced to that of occasional consultant "as needed" in 1945.[40]

There were no clear victors or losers in the controversy between the Taft-led GOP–Southern Democratic decentralist coalition and the Hansen-NRPB planners. The demise of the NRPB and the full-employment bill did not stem the growth of federal expenditure, the expansion of national programs, and the regulatory state. The GI Bill of Rights emanated from the NRPB agenda and paved the way for federal loans to college students as well as support for higher education, as it did for housing and business loans and other veterans' benefits. Expanded social insurance, modeled on the Beveridge Plan, came about through a series of amendments to the Social Security Act in the 1950s, 1960s, and 1970s which provided benefits increases above the poverty level and medical coverage for the elderly and the indigent.[41]

Yet a compensatory economy could not remediate fundamental structural problems. An exchange between Rexford Tugwell and Leon Keyserling, vice chairman of the Council of Economic Advisers in the Truman administration, underscores the frustrated aspirations of the planners. Correctly, Tugwell viewed the council as an advisory group to the chief executive, not a planning agency. Separation of powers, he held, ignored the reality of the "developmental forces of technology . . . working for interpenetration, mutual influence, [and] extended webs of relationship." While opponents associated planning with Europe's "isms," no government could exist without responsibility for "the social results of industry: unemployment, inflation, or maldistribution of income."

Keyserling, while sympathetic with Tugwell's argument—the two were longtime friends—countered that planning could hardly be divorced from politics. In Keyserling's view the 1946 Employment Act offered the potential for planning, should the council and president desire to pursue structural change. This eventuality never occurred, not at least as conceived by Alvin Hansen and the National Resources Planning Board.[42]

There were other impediments to the aspirations of the planners. The claim that the organizational structure of the New Era resumed in the postwar years as a consequence of its adoption by the NRPB urban planners and associationalists is questionable. The best hope for an organizational economy, the National Industrial Recovery Act, proved a dismal failure as readily as did welfare capitalism. Fiscal policy was never rationalized in practice. More often that not, expenditure levels were determined by wartime or defense needs or by interest group or local pressures on the Congress. This leaves us with a critical issue. What then explains the extraordinary economic expansion of the postwar era?

13 | THE ECONOMICS OF RECOVERY

IN RECENT YEARS A substantial number of historians have attributed U.S. recovery from the Great Depression to a wartime "Third New Deal" induced by Americanized Keynesianism in response to the 1937–38 recession. We are given to understand that Keynes's advocacy of a compensatory economy, or massive public spending to prevent future depressions and to sustain full employment, was validated by the level of government expenditure during the Second World War. Neither this nor other components of Third New Deal theory satisfactorily address the foundations of the postwar recovery and the basis for U.S. economic ascendancy after the war.[1]

Keynes envisaged a full-employment economy as one that tolerated a 3 to 5 percent rate of unemployment and provided for substantial government investment in self-sustaining public corporations that operated independently of government control. While he emphasized countercyclical public investment as central to economic stability, he was not an advocate of long-term deficit spending. Balance would be attained through the device of a dual budget, one for the current account and another for the government's capital account. The capital account would not be used for make-work. It would be utilized for the building of a national infrastructure that improved the quality of life, housing and electric power as examples, and would take up between 7.5 and 20 percent of the national income. The best defense against a future depression, Keynes believed, was to ensure against liquidity preference by a policy of high and stable incomes for consumers and an adequate return on investment. Budget balance would be attained through transfers of surpluses in the current budget to the capital budget in order to assure governmental countercyclical expenditure. Capital expenditure would increase when demand fell and would eliminate the current account deficit as it produced larger tax returns.

The budgetary approach taken by the United States in the postwar era did not exhibit Keynesian fundamentals. Viewed as a percentage of GDP, gross capital formation of public enterprises reached a peak of 3.5 percent in the decade 1962–72 and then ranged between 2 to 3 percent. As capital formation declined, defense expenditure, social transfers, and unemployment increased. In the process the United States fell into a situation described by the economist Hyman Minsky as "Ponzi finance," which required external funding of federal deficits, the current-account (trade) deficit, and interest on prior debt at a growing percentage of GDP.[2]

While massive wartime public expenditure led to growth in private savings that helped to fuel postwar recovery in the United States, between 1941, marked by a defense buildup, and 1945, when the Second World War ended, federal budget expenditure grew from $13 billion to $92 billion. Deficits increased from $6 billion to $47 billion, or eightfold, and outlay for wartime expenditure (fiscal years 1941–46) amounted to $320.3 billion, or 31.9 percent of GNP. Total employment in nonagricultural occupations (full- and part-time employees in mining, construction, manufacturing, wholesale and retail trade, finance, insurance and real estate, services, and government) increased from 36.2 to 40 million, a gain of some 3.8 million workers. During the depression years nonagricultural employment jumped from 23.3 million in 1932 to 32 million in 1940, an increase of 8.7 million. Bureau of Labor Statistics figures show an increase in payroll jobs of some 45 percent in Roosevelt's first term, just over 20 percent in his second term, and 8 percent in the third term, which corresponds with the Second World War. In the immediate postwar years, marked by minimal budget surpluses and deficits and by expenditure levels that never reached wartime peaks, employees in nonagricultural occupations reached over 52 million, and average weekly wages grew steadily to $82.39 by 1957.

Increased average weekly earnings in manufacturing, according to the U.S. Bureau of the Census, offer a weak argument for the presumed economic benefits afforded by entry into the Second World War. Earnings grew from $17.05 in 1932 to $25.02 in 1940, based on an average of just over 38 hours of work per week. In the years 1941 to 1945, weekly wages in manufacturing jumped from $29.58 to $44.39, or a gain of nearly $15 for a work-week of 40.6 hours in 1941 and 43.4 in 1945. But productivity is not measured by an increase in working hours or nominal wage growth, and while the consumer price index for urban consumers remained relatively stable in the 1930s, it increased some 78 percent during the war years and out-distanced wage gains.[3] According to the economists Simon Kuznets and

John Kendrick, real personal consumption per capita stagnated in wartime, and the estimates of Milton Friedman and Anna Schwartz, based on concealed price increases in the form of shifts of output to consumer items less subject to price ceilings, less desirable substitutes for rationed goods, and evasion of price controls, suggest that real personal consumption declined.

While unemployment fell to nearly nil late in the war, the decline is explained largely by absorption of some 16 million (12 million in 1945 alone) into the military and the civilian labor force that served defense needs rather than into production of consumer goods or capital needed to produce such goods at war's end. Real GDP stagnated in wartime after an advance from 100 in the base year 1939 to 119 in prewar 1941, then enjoyed a sharp postwar advance to 152 in 1948.[4]

Emphasis on the impact of wartime expenditure on regional economic balance represents a disinclination by Third New Deal proponents to reach back to earlier innovations. Income of those employed in agriculture in the interwar period was half of that enjoyed by those occupied in all industries combined. While this situation was reflected in regional income disparities, family income in urban communities in the plains and mountain regions equaled that of urban areas elsewhere.[5] That Roosevelt was aware of regional economic imbalance from the outset of the New Deal is reflected by his belief that the U.S. economy resembled that of Great Britain: exploitation of the South and the West by eastern finance and by manufacturers and processors of raw materials located in the northeastern quadrant, a situation typical of Britain's relationship with the dominions. Federal expenditure for development of the Tennessee and Columbia River valleys and innumerable programs of lesser scale, such as the Santee-Cooper in South Carolina, and for construction of rural roads, urban streets, dams, highways, tunnels, bridges, and other components of infrastructure are reflected in the Roosevelt budgets of the 1930s, which embraced urban to rural transfers for programs such as rural electrification. Further, the National Resources Production Board planned for plant location in the South and West even before U.S. engagement in the Second World War. Here, however, massive wartime expenditure expedited such undertakings.

Public expenditure in wartime transformed the trans-Mississippi West and the South into diversified economies, though the process had begun earlier in the South and Southwest and was less effective in the Old South where pockets of poverty remained. Wartime construction of new facilities in the West for manufacturing of steel, fabrication of metals such as steel and aluminum, shipbuilding and aircraft factories, the location of military bases and research facilities, and road construction resulted in a better economic mix. Similar development in the South, half financed by the federal government, half by the private sector, led to steel and aircraft production, development of facilities for petrochemicals, shipbuilding, and the emergence especially in the Southwest of a greater degree of prosperity across the board. Location of new military bases and defense industries by the government established the southern states as a major source of defense output after the war. This process encouraged a significant movement of labor and capital to urban centers. A better internal balance, however effective in creation of a more equitable national economy, was not the principal source of economic recovery after World War II or U.S. dominance in the world arena.[6] Third New Deal theory is too limited in its chronology and does not utilize the work of economists who measure economic trends over longer swings (from peak to peak) of the economic cycle and view productivity as the ratio of output per unit of work time. And it is devoid of international comparisons.

In the century following Britain's defeat of Napoleon, the United Kingdom served as the world's industrial leader. Financial primacy, established by midcentury, facilitated free trade managed by the City of London. Sterling offered a stable, convertible reserve currency, with insurance, finance, shipping, and other services earning profits from overseas trade. Profits were invested overseas albeit to the detriment of local investment in new industries. This picture changed with the impact of the First World War. The United Kingdom was weakened by manpower losses and liquidation of domestic and overseas investments in order to finance wartime expenditure. The return to gold further damaged its economy. In the interwar period, or possibly earlier, the United States' economic position surpassed that of Britain in productivity and technology. Attempts to shore up Britain's financial standing by eastern financiers and the Federal Reserve System, in the latter instance through a low interest rate policy, failed to reverse the United Kingdom's financial position. With the Great Depression, Neville Chamberlain, chancellor of the exchequer, assumed that domestic producers were unable to compete in the world economy and introduced a policy of empire protection and sterling devaluation, or abandonment of its role in the maintenance of open markets.

The Roosevelt administration was left with two options: acceptance of deflation at heavy cost in order to sustain open trade and monetary stability by staying on gold, arguments made by James P. Warburg and Lewis W. Douglas, or reliance on self-containment, reflation, and unilateral dollar devaluation until worldwide conditions changed. Roosevelt's adoption of the latter course—refusal to assume Britain's economic and financial role in the world economy, which included that of international lender of last resort—is explained by the United States' relative lack of dependence on exports beyond the needs of wheat and cotton producers. Facing massive unemployment, including "marching farmers," the president determined to protect inefficient industries as well as agriculture as these were large employers, at the expense of newer, less labor-intensive technologies.[7]

Within this compass there developed two basic viewpoints with respect to the appropriate role of the United States in the world economy. Schachtian economics, named for German economic wizard Hjalmar Schacht, found a home in Europe and Latin America and was promulgated by George Peek and Adolf Berle in the United States. Peek promoted barter, corporate controls for agricultural output and marketing, export subsidies, and a managed currency and trade regime which required protectionism. Berle extended this argument to embrace government control and management of capital investment and interest rates for public corporations, with socially desirable operations subsidized at below-market or zero interest rates. Wilsonians, on the other hand, some domiciled at the State Department under Cordell Hull's leadership, some on Wall Street, were hardly confined to the eastern elite. This cohort included Newton D. Baker, Alvin Hansen, W. W. Waymack, Henry Wallace (*America Must Choose*, 1934), Will Clayton, and others who predicated a higher living standard for the world based on the end of protectionism. This group proved correct according to recent economic analysis. Import protection in the interwar period ignored the potential of high-growth emergent industries, essentially an antigrowth policy which deepened the depression.

Contrary to revisionist history, there was no design for hegemonic power in the 1930s but rather advocacy by the internationalists of Anglo-U.S. leadership in the reinstitution of open markets facilitated by a dollar standard. Substantial diminution of London as a player in the world of finance as a consequence of the Second Great War explains creation of the International Monetary Fund, the International Trade Organization, and the International Bank for Reconstruction and Development. This development did not hinder European economic recovery. Whereas trade and gross domestic product had stagnated in the interwar years, between 1950 and 2001, on average, income per capita increased fourfold in the United States, Western Europe, and Japan, reflecting a growth rate of 2.8 percent a year. In the process the ratio of exports to world GDP increased from 5.5 percent in 1950 to 18 percent in 2001. Whereas Europeans proved to be suspicious of market forces in the immediate postwar years, the Marshall Plan and other U.S. loans and credits amounting to $25 billion led to acceptance of fair (not free) trade and to a secular investment boom, European economic integration, creation of the General Agreement on Trade and Tariffs (GATT), and the World Trade Organization (WTO).[8]

In the immediate postwar years, the United States did not dominate West European trade policy, which proved to be unilateral and restricted by currency controls and other devices left over from the 1930s; nor did it challenge European discrimination against American goods. By the 1950s U.S. insistence on liberalized trade flows resulted in a 77 percent increase in European exports and a 5 percent increase in U.S. exports. U.S. total trade was smaller than that of Europe as a whole, and even in bilateral trade the United States was not dominant. Europeans took about one-quarter of American exports, or only 1.1 percent of U.S. GNP, whereas European exports to the United States amounted to 8 percent of that region's exports, or 2 percent of Europe's GNP. While the United States enjoyed a favorable trade surplus, this was more than matched by capital outflows. In the event, Canada remained the United States' leading trading partner.

U.S. economic dominance at midcentury depended primarily on multifactor productivity (MFP), or availability and utilization of resources, capital and skilled labor, population growth, applied industrial research (R&D), willingness to adopt new technologies, managerial innovation, and educational levels that surpassed that of its competitors. "By 1950," according to Angus Maddison, the United States "had no close rivals in terms of productivity or GDP per capita" and "its productivity level was 227 percent of the average of other countries in the advanced capitalist group."[9]

Emergence of U.S. economic primacy, based on technological advance as the principal contributor to the upward trend of productivity, is centered by economists on the era 1890 to 1950. Within this period the prewar years 1929 through 1941 proved to be the most important decade for multifactor productivity growth and proved responsible for the foundations of postwar prosperity. Based on data presented by John W. Kendrick, Alexander Field calculated a compound annual average growth rate of private domestic economic MFP of 2.27 percent per year in the depression years, the most technologically progressive period in the nation's history, as opposed to 1.51 percent between 1941 and 1948. Continued moderate MFP advance in tandem with renewed capital deepening after war's end produced a "golden age of labor productivity growth and living standard improvement" in the 1950s and 1960s.

Rapid growth of productivity in the 1930s took place in both the private and government sectors as a consequence principally of acquisition and implementation of new technological knowledge. This embraced petrochemicals, nylon, Lucite, and Teflon, innovations in automobiles, communications, services, public utilities, and telecommunications, as well as utililization by government agencies of concrete in conjunction with steel in the construction of dams, bridges, and tunnels and residential construction under the auspices of the Federal Housing Authority. The bulk of street and highway construction between 1929 and 1948 took place prior to wartime and promoted postwar housing construction, which had stalled during World War II. Wartime productivity levels estimated by the War Production Board based on output of planes and in shipbuilding, which depended on government investment, were influenced by prewar advances in organizational techniques pioneered in radio, vacuum cleaners, and auto production. Output of planes and shipping also depended on wartime innovations in welding techniques and technologies for working light metals, especially aluminum. On balance, however, emphasis on military needs drained skilled workers, managers, and equipment from the private sector and proved detrimental to productivity for civilian uses.[10]

While monetary and fiscal policy, aided by social insurance, evened the economic cycle by stimulus to demand, the American Century depended on primacy in productivity as a consequence of investment in new technologies, applied research and development, the building of institutions such as the Massachusetts Institute of Technology dedicated to the advance of the sciences, and a broad emphasis on public education at the secondary and later the university levels. Although the first half of the twentieth century was marked by U.S. ascendancy in average income per capita due to its productivity lead, depression period advances provided the foundation for postwar productivity levels and GNP levels that far exceeded those of Europe, the United Kingdom, and Japan.

NOTES

COLLECTIONS

Acheson-Truman	Truman Library, Independence, Mo.
Acheson-Yale	Yale University Library, New Haven
Altmeyer Papers	Wisconsin Historical Society, Madison
Anthony Collection	Walter Lippmann Papers, Yale University Library, New Haven
Baker Papers	Manuscript Division, Library of Congress, Washington, D.C.
Baruch Papers	Seeley Mudd Library, Princeton University, Princeton, N.J.
Berry Papers	Iowa State University Library, Ames
Byrd Papers	University of Virginia Library, Charlottesville
Byrnes Papers	Cooper Library, Clemson University, Clemson, S.C.
CAB	Cabinet Papers, PRO, Kew, London
Carmody Papers	FDRL, Hyde Park, N.Y.
Chamberlain Papers	University of Birmingham, England
Clayton-Rice	Rice University, Houston, Tex.
Clayton-Truman	Truman Library, Independence, Mo.
Commons Papers	Wisconsin Historical Society, Madison
Douglas Papers	University of Arizona, Tucson
Du Pont Papers	Hagley Library, Wilmington, Del.
Eccles Papers	Marriott Library, University of Utah, Salt Lake City
Ezekiel Papers	FDRL, Hyde Park, N.Y.
FDRL	Franklin D. Roosevelt Library, Hyde Park, N.Y.
Flynn Papers	University of Oregon, Eugene
Frankfurter Papers	Manuscript Division, Library of Congress, Washington, D.C.
FRUS	*Foreign Relations of the United States*
Hansen Papers	Pusey Library, Harvard University, Cambridge, Mass.
Harrison Papers	Butler Library, Columbia University, N.Y.
HHPL	Herbert Hoover Presidential Library, West Branch, Iowa
Hope Papers	Kansas Historical Society, Topeka
Hopkins Papers	FDRL, Hyde Park, N.Y.
House Papers	Yale University Library, New Haven
Hurja Papers	FDRL, Hyde Park, N.Y.
Lamont Papers	Baker Library, Graduate School of Business, Harvard University, Cambridge, Mass.
Lauck Papers	University of Virginia Library, Charlottesville
Leffingwell Papers	Yale University Library, New Haven

Leiserson Papers   Wisconsin Historical Society, Madison
Leith-Ross Papers   PRO, Kew, London
Lippmann Papers   Yale University Library, New Haven
Means Papers   FDRL, Hyde Park, N.Y.
Mills Papers   Manuscript Division, Library of Congress, Washington, D.C.
Moley Diary and   Hoover Institution on War, Revolution and Peace
  Papers   Archives, Stanford, Calif.
Morgenthau Diary,
  Farm Credit
  Diary, and Papers   FDRL, Hyde Park, N.Y.
OF   President's Official File, FDRL, Hyde Park, N.Y.
PPF   President's Personal File, FDRL, Hyde Park, N.Y.
PPI   Post-Presidential: Individual, HHPL, West Branch, Iowa
PRO   Public Records Office, Kew, London
PSF   President's Secretaries File, FDRL, Hyde Park, N.Y.
Reno Papers   Special Collections, University of Iowa, Iowa City
Rockefeller Archive
  Center   Tarrytown, N.Y.
Rogers Papers   Yale University Library, New Haven
Rosenman, *PPA*   Samuel I. Rosenman, comp., *The Public Papers and Addresses of
                          Franklin D. Roosevelt* (New York, 1938)
Sachs Papers   FDRL, Hyde Park, N.Y.
Stimson Diary   Yale University Library, New Haven
T   Treasury Papers, PRO, Kew, London
Taft Papers   Manuscript Division, Library of Congress, Washington, D.C.
Thomas Papers   Carl Albert Center, University of Oklahoma, Norman
Tugwell Diary and
  Papers   FDRL, Hyde Park, N.Y.
Wallace Papers   Special Collections, University of Iowa, Iowa City
Warburg Diary   Columbia University Oral History Collection
Warburg Papers   John F. Kennedy Library, Boston
Warren Papers   Cornell University Library, Ithaca, N.Y.
Waymack Papers   Iowa Historical Society, Iowa City
M. L. Wilson Papers   University of Montana, Bozeman
Willkie Papers   Lilly Library, University of Indiana, Bloomington
Witte Papers   Wisconsin Historical Society, Madison
Wood Papers   HHPL, West Branch, Iowa
Young Papers   St. Lawrence University, Canton, N.Y.

INTRODUCTION

1. Ellis W. Hawley, "Herbert Hoover, the Commerce Secretariat, and the Vision of an Associative State," *Journal of American History* 61 (June 1974): 116–40; Hoover address, "Some Phases of the Government in Business," Cleveland Chamber of Commerce, May 7, 1924, Public Statements File, Hoover to Gerard Swope, draft of letter, Oct. 1926, box 190, Commerce Papers, Hoover address, "Republican Policies," Republican County Committee, New York City, Oct. 16, 1928, The Bible, vol. 26, no. 648, HHPL.

2. Susan P. Lee and Peter Passell, *A New Economic View of American History* (New

York and London, 1979), 368–69; Peter Temin, *Did Monetary Forces Cause the Great Depression?* (New York, 1976), 4.

3. Michael M. Weinstein, *Recovery and Redistribution under the NIRA* (Amsterdam, 1980), 28; Kristen Forbes, "A Reassessment of the Relationship between Inequality and Growth," *American Economic Review* 90 (Sept. 2000): 869–87; Claudia Goldin, "Labor Markets in the Twentieth Century," in *Cambridge Economic History of the United States*, vol. 3, *The Twentieth Century,* ed. Stanley L. Engerman and Robert E. Gallman (Cambridge, 2000), 555, 584; Robert M. Solow, "Mysteries of Growth," *New York Review of Books,* July 3, 2003, 50; Alan H. Meltzer, *A History of the Federal Reserve* (Chicago, 2003), 1:416, 565–68.

4. W. W. Waymack to Paul H. Appleby, Nov. 22, 1943, box 44, Waymack Papers.

1 | FINANCIAL CRISIS

1. *Memoirs of Herbert Hoover,* vol. 2, *The Great Depression, 1929–1941* (New York, 1952), 4.

2. Telegram no. 175, American Embassy, London, to Secretary of State, June 8, 1931, 2 A.M., telegram no. 177, June 8, 1931, midnight, in Foreign Affairs File: Financial, box 1-G/880, Hoover Diary, June 5–18, 1931, Foreign Affairs File: Financial, box 1-G/891, HHPL; Stephen A. Schuker, *American "Reparations" to Germany,* Princeton Studies in International Finance, no. 61 (July 1988), 47–68.

3. Schuker, *American "Reparations" to Germany,* 9–70; Russell C. Leffingwell, "Debt Suspension Matter," and Thomas W. Lamont to Hoover, June 5, 1931, box 98, Lamont Papers; Thomas Ferguson, "From Normalcy to New Deal: Industrial Structure, Party Competition, and American Public Policy in the Great Depression," *International Organization* 38 (Winter 1984): 79; John W. Owens to Owen D. Young, June 13, 1931, box 30, f. 135, Young Papers.

4. "Subjects for Laval Conversation," Sept. 1931, box 1-G/883, "Memorandum of Conversation between Secretary Stimson and the British Ambassador, Sir Ronald Lindsay," Oct. 29, 1931, box 1-G/881, Foreign Affairs File: Financial HHPL; Robert H. Ferrell, *American Diplomacy in the Great Depression: Hoover-Stimson Foreign Policy, 1929–1933* (New York, 1957), 198–204; James R. Moore, "A History of the World Economic Conference, London, 1933" (Ph.D. diss., State University of New York at Stony Brook, Dec. 1971), chap. 1.

5. Herbert Feis, "Memorandum of Exchange of Views at Meeting in Federal Reserve Bank of New York, Oct. 19, 1931, to Discuss Various Financial and Economic Matters That May Arise during the Visit of Premier Laval," Oct. 20, 1931, Foreign Affairs File: Financial, box 1-G/884, HHPL.

6. Lawrence Richey to William R. Castle, Oct. 28, 1931, for transmission to Ambassador Dawes [Great Britain], and Dawes to Secretary of State, Oct. 29, 1931, ibid..

7. Stimson Diary, Oct. 23, 24, 1931, copy in box 1-G/890, ibid.; T/188/74, Leith-Ross Papers.

8. Herbert Feis to Felix Frankfurter, Nov. 5, 1931, and "Note on the Present Status of the International Debt and Reparations Negotiations," Nov. 2, 1931, box 54, Frankfurter Papers; William Starr Myers, ed., *The State Papers and Other Public Writings of Herbert Hoover* (Garden City, N.Y., 1934), 2:20.

9. Myers, *Hoover State Papers* 2:72–75; *Congressional Record,* 72d Cong., 1st sess., vol. 75, Dec. 7, 1931–Jan. 19, 1932, 297, 794, 1081–82; Arnold J. Toynbee, *Survey of International*

Affairs: 1931 (London, 1932), 140. Section 5 of the House-Senate Joint Resolution reads: "It is hereby declared to be against the policy of Congress that any of the indebtedness of foreign countries to the United States should be in any manner cancelled or reduced; and nothing in this joint resolution shall be construed as indicating a contrary policy, or as implying that favorable consideration will be given at any time to a change in the policy hereby declared." H.J. Res. 147, Dec. 17, 1931, Foreign Affairs File: Financial, box 1-G/884, HHPL.

10. American Embassy, London [Charles Dawes], to Secretary of State, Dec. 16, 1931, and American Embassy, Paris [Walter Edge], to Secretary of State, Dec. 17, 1931, Foreign Affairs File: Financial, box 1-G/884, HHPL.

11. Moore, "World Economic Conference," 11 ff., 34; cable 260 from Gibson in Geneva to secretary of state for the president and the secretary, June 20, 1932, and memorandum of transatlantic conversation between "Mr. Castle and Mr. Hugh Gibson and Norman Davis," from Geneva, July 1, 1932, Foreign Affairs File: Financial, box 1-G/886, HHPL.

12. Stimson Diary, July 11–14, 1932; Myers, *Hoover State Papers* 2:235; *New York Times,* July 24, 1932.

13. Herbert Feis, *Europe the World's Banker, 1870–1914* (reprint, New York, 1964), 3–17; Sir Charles Morgan-Webb, *The Rise and Fall of the Gold Standard* (New York, 1934), 1–6; Morgan-Webb, *The Money Revolution* (New York, 1935); Barry Eichengreen, *Golden Fetters: The Gold Standard and the Great Depression, 1919–1939* (New York, 1992), 4–7; D. E. Moggridge, *British Monetary Policy, 1924–1931: The Norman Conquest of $4.86* (London, 1972), 3–7.

14. Moggridge, *British Monetary Policy,* 1–96; Charles P. Kindleberger, *The World in Depression, 1929–1939* (Berkeley, Calif., 1973), 43–54, 157–60; David Williams, "London and the 1931 Financial Crisis," *Economic History Review,* 2d ser., 15:3 (1963): 514–27; Diane B. Kunz, *The Battle for Britain's Gold Standard in 1931* (London, 1987), 89; Eichengreen, *Golden Fetters,* 216–20.

15. Kindleberger, *World in Depression,* 162–63; American Embassy, London [Dawes], to Secretary of State [Stimson], Nov. 4, 1931, Foreign Affairs File: Financial, box 1/884, HHPL.

16. W. Randolph Burgess to Ogden Mills, "Summary of the Principal Measures Adopted since Sept., 1931, Which Affect World Trade and Balance of Payments, Jan. 30, 1933," and preliminary tables for "Analysis of Proposal for Devaluation of the Dollar," box 11, Mills Papers.

17. Susan Howson, *Sterling's Managed Float: The Operations of the Exchange Equalisation Account, 1932–1939,* Princeton Studies in International Finance, no. 46 (Nov. 1980), 1–19; Keith Hutchison, *The Decline and Fall of British Capitalism* (Hamden, Conn., 1966), 253–54; Introduction, 10–11, Donald Winch, "Britain in the Thirties: A Managed Economy?" 47–67, and Forrest Capie, "The British Tariff and Industrial Protection in the 1930's," 93–96, 98–99 (table), in *The Managed Economy: Essays in British Economic Policy and Performance since 1929,* ed. Charles Feinstein (Oxford, 1983); "Policy of H.M. Government in Regard to Public Works," extracts from speeches by the chancellor of the exchequer on March 8, 22, 1933, in T188/71, Leith-Ross Papers; Neville Chamberlain, "Notes on Proceedings in Cabinet & Elsewhere on Formulation of Government Policy on Balance of Trade," January 1932, NC 8/18/1, Neville to Ida Chamberlain, Jan. 23, 1932, NC 18/1/768, to Arthur Chamberlain, Feb. 11, 1932, NC 7/16/19, clipping, *Observer,* Feb. 7, 1932, copy in NC 8/17/1, N.C., "Notes for Speech," n.d., NC 4/3/9, N.C.

Notebook, "Trade Notes," 1931, NC 2/27, Chamberlain Papers; Sidney Pollard, *The Development of the British Economy, 1914–1967* (London, 1969), 114–17.

18. Pollard, *British Economy,* 136–44; John A. Garraty, *The Great Depression* (San Diego, Calif., 1986), 57–59, 61–69, 72–74; U.S. Department of Commerce, Bureau of the Census, *Historical Statistics of the United States: Colonial Times to 1957* (Washington, D.C., 1960), Series U 163, 164, "Trade With the United States as Reported by the United Kingdom," 555; N.C. Notebook, "Trade Notes," 1931, NC 2/27, Chamberlain Papers.

19. Gerald M. Craig, *The United States and Canada* (Cambridge, Mass., 1968), 192–95; Ian M. Drummond, *Imperial Economic Policy, 1917–1939: Studies in Expansion and Protection* (Toronto, 1974), 30–31, 173, 180–81, 235, 254, 282–83; Pollard, *British Economy,* 197; Neville to Hilda Chamberlain, June 11, 1932, NC 18/1/786, to Ida Chamberlain, July 17, 1932, NC 18/1/791, to Arthur Chamberlain, Oct. 24, 1932, Chamberlain Papers.

20. Notes of conversation with M. Flandin, Nov. 1932, included in Neville Chamberlain to Lord Tyrell, Nov. 17, 1932, NC 7/11/25/47, Neville to Hilda Chamberlain, Dec. 6, 1931, Jan. 17, May 15, Nov. 26, Dec. 4, 10, 1932, NC 18/1/764, 767, 781, 807–9, Chamberlain Papers.

21. Mr. Gardner to Eugene Meyer, "Effect of the Depreciation of Sterling Exchange on British Prices," Aug. 23, 1932, W. Randolph Burgess to Ogden Mills, Jan. 28, 1933, enclosing address of George Roberts, National City Bank of New York, Jan. 25, 1933, Burgess to Mills, Jan. 30, 1933, "Preliminary Analysis of the Proposal for Devaluation of the Dollar," box 11, Mills Papers.

22. Federal Reserve Bank of New York, "Preliminary Draft, Second Section of Analysis of the Proposal for Devaluation of the Dollar, Jan. 30, 1933," Third Section, Feb. 8, 1933, Fifth Section, Feb. 6, 1933, and Sixth Section, Feb. 1, 1933, box 11, ibid.; Meltzer, *Federal Reserve* 1:265, 271, 277–79.

23. Ogden L. Mills to Owen D. Young and George Harrison, Dec. 16, 1932, box 9, Mills Papers (copy in box 12, Harrison Papers).

24. Telegram, Hoover to Roosevelt, Nov. 12, 1932, in Myers, *Hoover State Papers* 2:483–86.

25. Kenneth McKellar to Dabney Crump, Dec. 13, 1932, to Will L. Clayton, Dec. 26, 1932, Clayton to McKellar, Dec. 17, 1932, box 6, Clayton-Rice.

26. Rexford G. Tugwell, *The Democratic Roosevelt* (Garden City, N.Y., 1957), 256; Adolf A. Berle Jr. to Raymond Moley, Nov. 15, 1932, item 40/6, Moley Papers; Moley, *The First New Deal* (New York, 1966), 24; Felix Frankfurter note on Moley's stationery, in f. Felix Frankfurter, box 150, PSF; Tugwell Diary, Dec. 20, 1932.

27. Tugwell Diary, Dec. 20, 1932; Myers, *Hoover State Papers* 2:554–59; Moley, *First New Deal,* 39–41; Herbert Feis, *1933: Characters in Crisis* (Boston, 1966), 47; Stimson Diary, Dec. 21, 1932.

28. Stimson Diary, Jan. 9, 15, 20, 1933, and "Memorandum of Conversation between President Hoover and Governor Roosevelt," following entry of Jan. 20; Moley, *After Seven Years* (New York, 1939), 86; Tugwell Diary, Jan. 22, 1933.

29. William Starr Myers and Walter H. Newton, *The Hoover Administration* (New York, 1936), 336–44; Hoover to Frank B. Knox, April 3, 1933, PPI; "Ex-President in New York," reminiscences of John M. Carmody, Aug. 1, 1958, box 57, Carmody Papers; Russell C. Leffingwell to B. H. Inness-Brown, April 14, 1934, box 1, Leffingwell Papers.

30. Henry A. Wallace to Henry Morgenthau Jr., Aug. 19, 1932, to William Hirth, Aug. 20, 1932, to George F. Warren, Aug. 26, 1932, to George N. Peek, Aug. 29, 1932, Peek to Wallace, Aug. 30, 1932, reel 15, Peek to Roosevelt, Oct. 25, 1932, reel 17, Wallace Papers.

2 | NATIONALIZING THE ECONOMY

1. Franklin D. Roosevelt to Irving Fisher, June 8, 1934, PPF 431.

2. Cordell Hull, *Memoirs* (New York, 1948), 1:150–53; "true" copy of the Democratic Party platform, appended to A. Mitchell Palmer to Newton D. Baker, July 16, 1932, box 183, Baker Papers.

3. J. Ramsay MacDonald to Neville Chamberlain, Jan. 5, 1933, NC 7/11/26/25, Chamberlain Papers. For assignment of culpability in the shattering of international cooperation in the 1930s to Roosevelt's policies, see Schuker, American *"Reparations"* to Germany, 102; David Marquand, *Ramsay MacDonald* (London, 1977), 733–34.

4. Paul Mazur to Robert F. Wagner, Dec. 3, 1932, attached to Mazur to Raymond Moley, Jan. 24, 1933, item 113/6, Ralph Robey to Moley, "National Policy," Jan. 31, 1933, item 53/1, box 116, Alexander Sachs, "Intranationalism as a Synthesis of Economic Nationalism and Internationalism," Jan. 27–31, 1933, item 53/4, Sachs, "Intra-Nationalism as a Program," item 120/129, Moley Papers.

5. René Léon to Raymond Moley, Oct. 13, 1932, Léon, "A Solution to the Debt Installment Problem," n.d., Léon to Moley, Saturday, and proposed statement, item 11/25, box 31, FDR to Moley, Jan. 18, 1933 (with notation, "This is Rene Léon's solution. See me about it."), box 107, Moley Papers. That Roosevelt was aware of the potential of the Gold Embargo or Trading with the Enemy Act as early as Jan. 7 is indicated by a note in Moley's hand, "look up," in RM Notebook, Jan. 7, 1933, box 1, Moley Papers.

6. Frank Freidel, *Franklin D. Roosevelt: Launching the New Deal* (Boston, 1973), 329–30; Charles O. Hardy, *Is There Enough Gold?* (Washington, D.C., 1936), 165; Rosenman, *PPA* 2:141–44.

7. Russell C. Leffingwell to Thomas W. Lamont, Feb. 8, 14, 1933, box 4, Leffingwell Papers; draft, Thomas W. Lamont to FDR, March 25, 1933, f. 29, box 127, Lamont Papers; Secretary to Mr. Thomas Lamont to Marvin H. McIntyre, March 21, 1933, PPF 70; Meltzer, *Federal Reserve* 1:360–61, 428, 442; Elmer Thomas to Lloyd H. Smith, Jan. 20, 1933, Carl Snyder to Thomas, Feb. 9, 1933, Thomas Papers.

8. B. S. Carter to Russell C. Leffingwell, April 28, 1933, Leffingwell to Carter, May 9, 1933, to E. C. Grenfell, April 19, 1933, boxes 1 and 3, Leffingwell Papers.

9. James P. Warburg Diary, 67ff., 284–85; Warburg to Arthur Schlesinger Jr., Jan. 15, 1957, box 20, Warburg Papers; Moley, *First New Deal*, 395; Warburg, *The Long Road Home* (Garden City, N.Y., 1964), 107; Moley Diary, Jan. 23, 1933; "Monetary and Economic Conference, Cabinet Committee," M.E.C. (33) Series, 6th Meeting, May 23, 1933, CAB 29/140.

10. "Notes of a Conversation in the Treasury Board Room," July 2, 1933, CAB 21/375.

11. Moley, *First New Deal*, 127–99; Milton Friedman and Anna Jacobson Schwartz, *The Great Contraction, 1929–1933* (Princeton, N.J., 1963, 1965), 55–63.

12. Warburg Diary, 245–308, 312–13; Kindleberger, *World in Depression*, 202–4.

13. Kindleberger, *World in Depression*, 207–8; Warburg Diary, 583–84, 612–19; telegram, Sir John Simon to Sir Ronald Lindsay, April 21, 1933, indicating Chamberlain's concurrence, in T188/78, Leith-Ross Papers; Monetary and Economic Conference Series, M.E.C. Memorandum no. 4, "Policy of the United Kingdom on Main Questions Raised in Agenda," memorandum by F. W. Leith-Ross and Sir F. Phillips, especially, "(b) Relative Value of Principal Currencies," CAB 29/140.

14. Warburg Diary, 701–7; Moley, *First New Deal*, 396–98; Kindleberger, *World in*

Depression, 208; Herbert Feis to Felix Frankfurter, box 54, Frankfurter Papers; Lewis W. Douglas to James Stuart Douglas, May 27, 1933, box 31, Douglas Papers.

15. Hull, *Memoirs* 1:171–75, 248–50; Moley, *First New Deal,* 402; Kindleberger, *World in Depression,* 214; *FRUS, 1933* 1:587ff.; Warburg Diary, 648; Ernest K. Lindley, *The Roosevelt Revolution: First Phase* (New York, 1933), 186; memorandum, State Department, on British-Argentinean exchange controls, 1933, PSF.

16. Moley, *First New Deal,* 403–6; syndicated article and radio address, Appendix D and Appendix E in Moley, *After Seven Years,* 406–14.

17. Hull, *Memoirs* 1:248–49, 255; Moley, *First New Deal,* 422–24; Freidel, *FDR: Launching the New Deal,* 466–67; Hull to Acting Secretary of State, June 13, 1933, Phillips (Roosevelt) for Hull, June 20, 1933, Phillips to Hull, June 26, 1933, *FRUS, 1933* 1:636–40, 650, 657.

18. Moody's Daily Index of Staple Commodity Prices, the dollar-pound exchange rate, and the Dow Jones Industrial Average, April 1–Aug. 1, 1933, in Kindleberger, *World in Depression,* 222–24; James P. Warburg to Raymond Moley, memorandum, May [?], 1933, item 37xx/55, box 102, Moley Papers; press release, "OK'd by Secretary Woodin and Ray Moley, 7:15 PM, 6/16/33, STE [Stephen Early]," box 1, OF 17; Neville Chamberlain Diaries and Journals, 1926–33, June 29, 1933, NC 2/22, Chamberlain Papers.

19. The Agricultural Adjustment Act of May 12, 1933, authorized the president, upon determining that the foreign trade of the United States had been adversely affected by currency depreciation of other governments, to direct the secretary of the treasury to issue unbacked currency to redeem maturing federal obligations up to $3 billion per annum; to reduce the dollar's gold content up to 50 percent; to engage in silver purchases at a fixed ratio to gold and to monetize such purchases; to accept silver in payment of war debts and to issue silver certificates based on such payments; and to permit the Federal Reserve to raise or lower reserve requirements for member banks. Roosevelt never made use of his authority to issue unbacked currency. Subj. 16, f. 10, Thomas Papers.

20. Kindleberger, *World in Depression,* 217; Moley, *First New Deal,* 425–27; Freidel, *FDR: Launching the New Deal,* 468–69; Sprague to Woodin, June 16, 1933, Warburg to the president, June 16, 1933, Phillips to Hull, June 17, 1933, *FRUS, 1933* 1:642–46; Ernest Lindley to Moley, June 8, 1939, box 31, Roosevelt's June 17 cable, original draft, item 37xx/62a, box 102, Moley Papers.

21. Moley, *First New Deal,* 427–40; *FRUS, 1933* 1:650.

22. Moley, *First New Deal,* 396–98; Paul Mazur to Moley, June 19, 1933, box 77, Frank Altschul to Moley, June 20, 1933, box 63, Moley Papers, copy in OF 229; Frank Altschul to Stephen Early, June 23, 1933, H. M. Kannee to Altschul, June 26, 1933, box 1, OF 17.

23. Edward M. House to B. H. Inness-Brown, June 19, 1933, box 63b, House Papers; Roosevelt to House, June 12, 1933, and telegram, June 20, 1933, PPF 222; Freidel, *FDR: Launching the New Deal,* 470–78. William K. Finley, Coordinator of Special Collections, College of Charleston Library, and Judith W. Mellins, Manuscripts Associate, Harvard Law School Library, assisted in identification of Inness-Brown. Raymond Teichman of the Roosevelt Library helped to search out his correspondence. See also *College of Charleston Magazine,* June 1900; *Harvard Law Review,* Nov. 1902; Harvard Law School Class of 1904, "List of Members, First Report," 1909, p. 5, Harvard Law School Library; Edgar B. Nixon, *Franklin D. Roosevelt and Foreign Affairs* (Cambridge, Mass., 1969), 1:247–48.

24. B. H. Inness-Brown, memorandum, April 25, 1933, and "Memorandum on the Fallacy That Cutting the Gold Content of the Dollar Automatically Increases Commodity Prices," April 26, 1933, Inness-Brown to House, May 25, 1933, House to Inness-Brown, June 25, 1933, box 63b, House Papers; Inness-Brown to James H. Rand Jr., June 15, 1933, OF 229; Inness-Brown to House, June 19, 1933, PPF 222; Inness-Brown to Walter Lippmann, May 24, 25, 1933, box 79, Lippmann Papers.

25. B. H. Inness-Brown to William C. Bullitt, June 23, 29, 1933, box 63b, House Papers.

26. John M. Keynes, "Can We Cooperate with America," *Daily Mail* and New York *Herald Tribune*, June 27, 1933, reprinted in D. E. Moggridge, ed., *The Collected Writings of John Maynard Keynes* (London, 1971–89), 21:264–68.

27. Georges Bonnet to Neville Chamberlain, June 28, 1933, NC 7/11/26/5, and Chamberlain Diaries and Journals, June 29 and July 27, 1933, NC 2/22, Chamberlain Papers.

28. Moley, *First New Deal,* 453–57; "Paraphrase of the 'Declaration' Proposed by the French and the British on June 29, 1933," in Moley, *After Seven Years,* 417–18; Chamberlain Diaries and Journals, June 29, 1933, NC 2/22, Chamberlain Papers; Ernest K. Lindley to Moley, June 8, 1939, box 31, Moley Papers; Acheson to the president, June 27, 1933, box 1, OF 17, FDRL; "Conclusions of the 18th Meeting of the U.K. Delegates," July 2, 1933, and "The Draft Currency Declaration," M.E.C. Memorandum no. 16, pt. 1, CAB 29/142.

29. Moore, "World Economic Conference," 218–19, 329; Moley, *First New Deal,* 481–86; Kindleberger, *World in Depression,* 219–20; Freidel, *FDR: Launching the New Deal,* 480–84; *FRUS, 1933* 1:669–70; Sir Basil Blackett, "Sanctity of Contract and the Gold Standard," *Economic Forum* 1 (Jan.–Dec. 1933): 253.

30. Russell C. Leffingwell, "The Dollar and the Conference," June 29, 1933, box 8, Leffingwell Papers.

31. John M. Keynes, New York *Herald Tribune,* July 13, 1933, in Moggridge, *Collected Writings of Keynes* 21:277–80.

32. "Imperial Preference, Joint Memorandum by the Dominions Office and the Board of Trade," June 14, 1933, and "Draft Conclusions of the 19th Meeting of the U.K. Delegates," July 3, 1933, CAB 29/142; "Conclusions of the 6th Meeting, British Commonwealth Delegations, Monetary and Economic Conference," July 4, 1933, and 10th meeting, July 18, 1933, CAB 29/143.

33. Neville Chamberlain Diaries and Journals, London, July 4, 17, 24, 27, 1933, NC 2/22, 23A, and Neville to Hilda Chamberlain, July 10, 23, 1933, NC 18/1/835, 837, Chamberlain Papers; Keith Feiling, *The Life of Neville Chamberlain* (Hamden, Conn., 1970), 224; "Declaration by Delegations of the British Commonwealth," July 27, 1933, CAB 29/143.

34. Neville to Hilda Chamberlain, July 10, 1933, NC18/1/835, to Ida Chamberlain, July 15, 1933, NC 18/1/836, Chamberlain Papers.

35. B. H. Inness-Brown to Edward M. House, July 5, 21, 1933, box 63b, House Papers.

3 | DOLLAR DEVALUATION AND THE MONETARY GROUP

1. Walter Lippmann, "The Permanent New Deal," *Yale Review* 24 (June 1935): 649–67.

2. Eichengreen, *Golden Fetters,* 342–47; Lester V. Chandler, *America's Greatest Depression, 1929–1941* (New York, 1970), 171–74; Harrison conversation with Black re: open market operations, Sept. 16, 1933, binder 46, Harrison Papers.

3. Warburg Diary, 1126–30.

4. Warburg memorandum for the president, July 16, 1933, draft of letter for Roosevelt to MacDonald, Warburg Diary, July 16, 1933, box 6, Warburg Papers.

5. Warburg Diary, July 20, 1933, 1166.

6. Moley handwritten notes, boxes 108, 116, Moley Diary, March 24, 1933, Moley Papers; Owen D. Young to Franklin D. Roosevelt, Jan. 11, 1933, Copybook 59, box 834, Young Papers.

7. James M. Cox to James P. Warburg, Sept. 7, 1933, box 7, Warburg Papers; Warburg Diary, 1560; Jordan Schwarz, *The Speculator: Bernard M. Baruch in Washington, 1917–1965* (Chapel Hill, N.C., 1981), 276–77; Henry Morgenthau Jr., Farm Credit Diary, July 30, 1933, 54, FDRL.

8. Warburg Diary, July 21, 1933, 1168–69.

9. Tugwell Diary, May 3, 1933.

10. [Warburg] memorandum for the president, July 24, 1933, "Domestic Currency Problem," with notation "read to the president and left with him July 24th," distributed to Douglas, Moley, Acheson, Woodin, Black, Sprague, Harrison, and shown to Stewart, Warren, and Rogers, box 7, Warburg Papers, and box 248, Douglas Papers; Warburg Diary, July 24, 1933, 1187–89.

11. Warburg Diary, July 24, 1933, 1190.

12. Henry A. Wallace, "Further Facts on Raising the Price of Gold," *Journal of Farm Economics* 40:3 (Aug. 1958): 713.

13. James Harvey Rogers, *America Weighs Her Gold* (New Haven, 1931), 1–127, 167–80, 206–8.

14. Rogers, "The Abrogation of Bank Credit," 63–70, paper delivered before the American Statistical Association, Washington, D.C., Dec. 1931, box 27, published in *Econometrics* 1 (Jan. 1933), Rogers, "The Bugaboo of Inflation," [July 1932], box 27, Rogers to Adolf Berle, Feb. 2, 1933, box 11, "President Butler's Committee on Economic Questions," Jan. 30, 1933, list of subcommittees and topics assigned, meeting of April 14, 15, 1933, and "Program Recommended to Butler Commission," n.d., box 50, Rogers, "International Currency Devaluation, Presented to Prof. Moley, Memo on Discussion of Previous Evening," April 23, 1933, box 53, Rogers, summary of address before Connecticut Chapter of the American Statistical Association, April 26, 1933, box 28, Rogers to Warburg, draft of letter [April 1933], and Rogers to Warburg, May 2, 1933, box 12, Rogers Papers; W. W. Rostow, *DAB*, s.v. "Rogers, James Harvey"; *New York Times*, April 17, 1933.

15. "Domestic Currency Problem," Aug. 2, 1933, box 6, Warburg Papers; Warburg Diary, Aug. 8, 1933, 1251–54, 1260–61; Warren Diary, Aug. 8, 1933, Warren Papers.

16. George F. Warren, untitled memorandum, Aug. 7, 1933, and memorandum beginning "Reflation necessary," n.d., box 59, Acheson-Yale, also in box 53, Rogers Papers.

17. Warburg Diary, Aug. 8, 1933.

18. O. M. W. Sprague, "Memorandum for Mr. Acheson on Monetary Policy, and Memorandum on Changing the Price of Gold," n.d., Acheson to the president, n.d., Acheson-Yale; Meltzer, *Federal Reserve* 1:258.

19. Acheson to the president, n.d., and [Acheson], "Monetary Policy," box 59, Acheson-Yale; Arthur M. Schlesinger Jr., *The Coming of the New Deal* (Boston, 1958), 240; A. A. Berle Jr., "Managed Currency," July 10, 1933, box 28, Warren Papers, and box 54, Rogers Papers; Berle [?], "Recommendations for Stabilizing Prices," July 12, 1933, box 54, Rogers Papers.

20. Warburg, "Suggested Agenda for the Monetary Group," Aug. 14, 1933, box 6, Warburg Papers, copy in box 248, Douglas Papers, and box 59, Acheson-Yale; Warburg Diary, Aug. 14–15, 23, 1933, 1269–81, 1348.

21. "Interim Monetary Report, Final Draft," Aug. 29, 1933, box 7, Warburg Papers; Albert U. Romasco, *The Politics of Recovery: Roosevelt's New Deal* (New York, 1983), 95–98.

22. O. M. W. Sprague to James P. Warburg, Aug. 30, Sept. 5, 7, 1933, Warburg to Sprague, Aug. 31, Sept. 1, 1933, box 7, Warburg Papers.

23. John D. Williams, "International Effect of Greenback Issue," and Williams to Governor Harrison, "Subject: Mr. Warburg's Currency Proposal," Aug. 3, 1933, box 3, Harrison conversation with Governor Black re: open market operations, Sept. 16, 1933, binder 46, Harrison Papers.

24. Warburg Diary, Sept. 19, 1933, 1446; Walter Isaacson and Evan Thomas, *The Wise Men: Six Friends and the World They Made, Acheson, Bohlen, Harriman, Kennan, Lovett, and McCloy* (New York, 1986), 108–16.

25. Warburg memorandum to Roosevelt, Sept. 20, 1933, box 7, Warburg Papers, and box 248, Douglas Papers.

26. Warburg Diary, Sept. 21, 1933, 1458–61; handwritten notations by Roosevelt, Special folder, PPF 540; Douglas Diary, Sept. 21, 1933, box 236, Douglas Papers.

27. Douglas Diary, Sept. 25–26, 1933, box 236, Douglas Papers; Warburg Diary, Sept. 21–23, 1933, 1461–77.

28. Warburg Diary, Sept. 21–23, 1933, 1494–97, Sept. 27, 1933, 1512–14; Warburg, "Motion to Be Put before Monetary Group, Monday, Sept. 25 [1933]," and William Woodin to the president, Sept. 28, 1933, with report for the president, box 248, Douglas Papers.

29. Warburg to Woodin, Sept. 29, 1933, box 6, Warburg Papers.

30. FDR to William Woodin, Sept. 30, 1933, PPF 258; Romasco, *Politics of Recovery*, 100; FDR to Woodin, Oct. 9, 1933, PSF 97: Treasury; Warburg to Acheson, Oct. 12, 13, 1933, box 7, Warburg Papers.

31. Rogers to Dean Acheson, memorandum marked "Prices," Oct. 20, 1933, box 248, Douglas Papers; Acheson to the president, Oct. 21, 1933, with memorandum attached, "How to Raise Prices," box 59, Acheson-Yale; Romasco, *Politics of Recovery*, 102.

32. Warburg Diary, Oct. 18, 1933, 1611; Feis, *Characters in Crisis*, 264–65; Sir Frederick Leith-Ross, "Note of a Conversation with Mr. Warburg on Oct. 18, 1933," "Note of Conversation with Mr. Walter Stewart on Oct. 13, 1933," "Note of a Conversation with Mr. Douglas, Nov. 7, 1933," T188/74, Leith-Ross Papers.

33. Sir Frederick Phillips, "Recovery from the Trade Depression, Also Comparison of Recovery Programs in the United Kingdom and United States," Sept. 21, 1933, T188/72, H. D. Henderson to Sir Frederick Leith-Ross, Sept. 28, 1933, and "Group on International Monetary Problems, Note for Autumn Discussion," Sept. 12, 1933, T188/72, Sir Frederick Leith-Ross, "Note of a Conversation with Mr. Acheson on Nov. 6, and with Mr. Douglas on Nov. 7, 1933," T188/74, Leith-Ross Papers; "Monetary and Economic Conference, United Kingdom Delegation, Imperial Preference, Joint Memorandum by the Dominion Office and the Board of Trade," June 14, 1933, "Note Prepared in the Board of Trade: The Depreciation of the Dollar and Its Effect on United Kingdom Industry," [Summer 1933], CAB 29/142; Rogers, "Diary Notes," Sept. 1933, f. 743, box 52, Rogers Papers; Richard N. Kottman, *Reciprocity and the North Atlantic Triangle* (Ithaca, N.Y., 1968), 7, 38, 42, 75.

34. Henry Morgenthau Jr., Farm Credit Administration Diary, Oct. 1, 18, 19, 22–23, 26, 27, 28–29, 31, Nov. 4, 13, 1933, 65–67, 69, 71 73–75, 75–81, 81, 83, 83A,; 86–90, 91, 96, 100,

Roosevelt's handwritten instructions for the gold purchases, which indicate a goal of 10-cent cotton and 90-cent wheat, FDRL; Kindleberger, *World in Depression*, 225–27.

4 | MONETARY POLICY AND THE HOOVER-STRAWN GROUP

1. Eichengreen, *Golden Fetters*, 35–36.

2. Rexford Guy Tugwell to author, May 5, 1964, author's papers, HHPL.

3. Warburg Diary, Oct. 20–21, 1933, 1618–24; memo, "Ogden Mills telephoned," March 9, 1933, box 439, PPI.

4. "The Fourth Fireside Chat," Oct. 22, 1933, Rosenman, *PPA* 2:425–27.

5. Warburg Diary, Oct. 24, 1933, 1633–42. At the same time Warburg's Chicago contacts expanded to include Melvin Traylor of the First National Bank, at one time regarded by conservatives as a contender for the Democratic Party's 1932 nomination; Albert Lasker, chairman of the board of Lord & Thomas, a Chicago advertising agency, head of the U.S. Shipping Board in the Harding administration; also Charles F. Glore and Russell Forgan, partners in the investment bank of Glore, Forgan & Co. Forgan, vice chairman of the Crusaders, offered the services of that group.

6. Hoover to John C. O'Laughlin, Oct. 12, 1933, box 457A, PPI.

7. Hoover to Walter F. Brown, April 16, 25, Dec. 27, 1933, box 289, to Harry Chandler, April 27, 1933, Inflation File, box 298, to Simeon D. Fess, April 27, May 4, 1933, box 328, to Samuel Crowther, June 8, 19, 1933, box 308, to Richard Lloyd Jones, Dec. 15, 1933, box 381, ibid.

8. Chester A. Moores to C. Gordon Moores, July 17, 1933, Hoover to C. Gordon Moores, July 21, 1933, box 443, Mark Requa to Hoover, Oct. 12, 1933, box 475, Hoover to John Richardson, Oct. 13, 1933, box 477, to Earle S. Kinsley, Oct. 22, 1933, box 392, to Frank Knox, Nov. 28, 1933, box 396, to Ogden Mills, Nov. 18, 24, 1933, box 439, ibid.

9. Hoover to Adolph Miller, copy to Lewis Strauss, Aug. 25, 1933, box 437, Edwin W. Kemmerer to Hoover, Oct. 13, 1933, Hoover to Kemmerer, Oct. 12, 1933, box 388, PPI.

10. Warburg Diary, Oct. 31, Nov. 2, 1933, 1685–1707.

11. Ibid., Oct. 24, 30, 1933, 1636ff., 1674; *New York Times*, Nov. 13, 1933.

12. *New York Times*, Nov. 4, 1933; Sir Frederick Leith-Ross, "Note of a Conversation with Mr. James Warburg on Nov. 9th, 1933," T188/74, Leith-Ross Papers.

13. Warburg Diary, Oct. 31, Nov. 19, 1933, 1686–99, 1768; *New York Times*, Nov. 19, 1933; Silas Strawn to Herbert Hoover, Dec. 22, 1933, box 522, PPI; Romasco, *Politics of Recovery*, 133.

14. Federal Advisory Council, statement, Sept. 26, 1934, copy in folder: Walter Lichtenstein, box 405, PPI.

15. *New York Times*, Nov. 28, 1933.

16. George L. Harrison to Roosevelt, Dec. 12, 1933, Roosevelt, memorandum, Dec. 19, 1933, "Memorandum of Conversation between George L. Harrison . . . and Montagu Norman," PSF 97; memoranda of conversations between Harrison and Norman, Harrison and Roosevelt, and Harrison and Henry Morgenthau Jr., binders 22 and 46, Harrison Papers; Confidential [Leith-Ross] to Bewley, Dec. 13, 1933, Dollar File, T188/78, Leith-Ross Papers.

17. Warburg to René Léon, Nov. 29, 1933, box 10, to Sir Frederick Leith-Ross, Dec. 15, 1933, box 6, Warburg Papers; F. W. Leith-Ross to Warburg, Dec. 22, 1933, to Robert Boothby, Jan. 8, 1935, H. Leak, Board of Trade, to Sir Frederick Leith-Ross, Dec. 7, 1933, Sir Warren Fisher to Chancellor of the Exchequer, Feb. 16, 1934, T188/78, T118/300, Leith-

Ross Papers; Herbert Feis, *Characters in Crisis*, 294; Atherton to Treasury, American Embassy, London, Feb. 2, 1935, PSF 87.

18. Feiling, *Chamberlain*, 252–54.

19. Romasco, *Politics of Recovery*, 136.

20. Leffingwell to Roosevelt, Oct. 2, Nov. 23, 1933, Leffingwell, "Gold, Money and Prices," Dec. 26, 1933, box 7, Leffingwell Papers, copy in PPF 866.

21. B. H. Inness-Brown to Walter Lippmann, Nov. 15, 1933, Jan. 15, 18, 1934, box 79, Lippmann Papers, copies in box 63b, House Papers, forwarded to Roosevelt.

22. Kindleberger, *World in Depression*, 225–28.

23. Frederic A. Delano to FDR, Oct. 4, 1933, accompanied by Frank W. Taussig, "Sterling, Gold, and Dollars," Sept. 25, 1933, OF 229, Irving Fisher to Roosevelt, Dec. 1, 1933, PPF 431; Walter Lippmann, "Today and Tomorrow," Jan. 3, 17, 19, 25, 1934, reel 9, Anthony Collection.

24. J. H. Rand to Henry Morgenthau Jr., telegram, Feb. 3, 1934, box 16, Warren Papers; Hoover to William Allen White, May 11, 1934, box 553, PPI.

25. John Morton Blum, *Roosevelt and Morgenthau* (Boston, 1972), 56–60; Roosevelt to Governor Eugene Black, Federal Reserve Board, Dec. 29, 1933, PSF 97; statement for the press, Jan. 31, 1934, Henry Morgenthau Jr., approved by the president, Jan. 31, 1934, OF 229.

26. Eichengreen, *Golden Fetters*, 342–47, 352; Margaret G. Myers, *A Financial History of the United States* (New York, 1970), 337–38; Friedman and Schwartz, *Monetary History of the United States*, 512–14, 532; Mark Toma, *Competition and Monopoly in the Federal Reserve System, 1914–1951* (Cambridge, 1997), 88–95.

27. FDR to Duncan U. Fletcher, Nov. 8, 1933, OF 229.

5 | FISCAL POLICY AND REGIONAL DIVERSITY

1. William J. Barber, *From New Era to New Deal: Herbert Hoover, the Economists, and American Economic Policy, 1921–1933* (Cambridge, 1985), 22, 189–90, 194.

2. Myers, *Hoover State Papers* 2:48, 57–72, 104–6, 206; B. Hollister to Robert A. Taft, April 21, 1932, box 34, Taft Papers; Jordan Schwarz, *The Interregnum of Despair: Hoover, Congress, and the Depression* (Urbana, Ill., 1970), 139.

3. Owen D. Young to Franklin D. Roosevelt, Jan. 11, 1932, 87.2.27, no. 109B, Young Papers.

4. Friedman and Schwartz, *Monetary History of the United States*, 330–31 n. 43; James Stuart Olson, *Herbert Hoover and the Reconstruction Finance Corporation, 1931–1933* (Ames, Iowa, 1977), 48, 50–51, 117–19; Barber, *New Era to New Deal*, 170–74; Thomas Corcoran to Felix Frankfurter, undated [ca. Oct.–Nov. 1932], box 49, Frankfurter Papers.

5. James S. Olson, *Saving Capitalism: The Reconstruction Finance Corporation and the New Deal, 1933–1940* (Princeton, N.J., 1988), 127, 224.

6. Herbert Stein, *The Fiscal Revolution in America* (Washington, D.C., 1990), 34–38, 43–44; Ross McKibbin, "The Economic Policy of the Second Labor Government," *Past and Present* 68 (Aug. 1975): 96 and passim.

7. F. P. [Frederick Phillips] to Sir Frederick Leith-Ross, "Recovery from Trade Depression," Sept. 21, 1933, T188/72, Leith-Ross Papers.

8. Chandler, *America's Greatest Depression*, 122; Richard P. Adelstein, "'The Nation as an Economic Unit': Keynes, Roosevelt, and the Managerial Ideal," *Journal of American History* 78:1 (June 1991): 162, 172–73. Adelstein uses a multiplier of three, whereas I rely

on the estimate formulated by Keynes and Kahn. On my statistics, see Department of Commerce, Bureau of the Census, *Long Term Economic Growth, 1860–1965* (Washington, D.C., Oct. 1966), ser. A 27, 170–71.

9. Five memoranda, probably Baruch, n.d., box 63, Moley Papers.

10. Archibald B. Roosevelt to Lewis W. Douglas, May 4, 1932, Douglas to Roosevelt, May 5, 1932, John W. Davis to Douglas, May 9, 1932, Grenville Clark to Douglas, telegram, June 13, 1932, and proposed plank on veterans' relief intended for the Democratic Party platform, Clark to Douglas, Clark to Royal Johnson, House of Representatives, South Dakota, June 24, 1932, Jack [John J. McCloy] to Douglas and Grenville Clark, July 29, 1932, Douglas to McCloy, Aug. 6, 1932, box 214, Douglas Papers.

11. Robert Paul Browder and Thomas G. Smith, *Independent: A Biography of Lewis W. Douglas* (New York, 1986), 2–24, 70, 145ff.; David M. Kennedy, *Over Here: The First World War and American Society* (New York, 1980), 146; Lewis W. Douglas to James Stuart Douglas, May 3, 29, 1932, box 31, Douglas Papers.

12. "Balancing the Budget," speech of Hon. L. W. Douglas, *Cong. Record*, 72d Cong., 1st sess., Feb. 16, 1932, Baruch to Douglas, March 4, 1932, Douglas to Baruch, March 5, 1932, LWD speech notes, n.d., box 214, excerpt from the *Cong. Record*, May 3, 1932, and Douglas notes for address, box 217, Douglas to Timothy A. Riordan, June 9, 1932, to Bernard Baruch, Feb. 27, 1932, to S. P. Applewhite, box 232, to Raymond Moley, May 4, 1964, box 119, Frank R. Kent, "The Great Game of Politics: The Budget Director," *Baltimore Sun*, Feb. 26, 1933, box 234, Douglas Papers; Schwarz, *Interregnum of Despair*, 156–72.

13. Browder and Smith, *Independent*, 64–65, 70, 73–78; James E. Sargent interview with Lewis W. Douglas, f. 4, box 119, Douglas to Ben. J. McKinney, Feb. 13, 1932, box 232, to Frank C. Brophy, Dec. 29, 1932, box 77, Lewis to James Stuart Douglas, Dec. 8, 1932, Douglas to Franklin D. Roosevelt, Dec. 7, 1932, box 31, and Jan. 19, 1933, box 118, Douglas Papers.

14. Lewis to James S. Douglas, Jan. 16, March 1, 1932, box 31, Raymond Moley to Lewis Douglas, March 27, 1964, Douglas to Moley, May 4, 1964, box 118, Douglas Papers; Schuyler C. Wallace to Raymond Moley, Dec. 29, 1932, Jan. 4, 1933, box 102, Wallace, "Balancing the Budget," n.d., box 86, Moley Papers; Elliott Roosevelt, ed., *F.D.R.: His Personal Letters, 1928–1945* (New York, 1950), 1:321–22.

15. Moley, *First New Deal*, 200–205; Freidel, *FDR: Launching the New Deal*, 245–46; Browder and Smith, *Independent*, 87.

16. *Historical Statistics of the United States*, ser. Y 254–57, "Summary of Government Finance," 711.

17. E. Cary Brown, "Fiscal Policy in the Thirties: A Reappraisal," *American Economic Review* 46 (Dec. 1956): 857–79; Chandler, *America's Greatest Depression*, 136–40, summarizes Brown's conclusions; on RFC lending, see Olson, *Saving Capitalism*, 127 and passim.

18. Barber, *New Era to New Deal*, 15–20, 107; Schwarz, *Interregnum of Despair*, 160–73.

19. Schwarz, *Interregnum of Despair*, 54–55; Joseph Dorfman, *The Economic Mind in American Civilization* (New York, 1959), 4:339–51; William T. Foster and Waddill Catchings, *The Road to Plenty* (Boston, 1928), 127–28; Arthur Schlesinger Jr., *The Politics of Upheaval* (Boston, 1960), 237; Alan Brinkley, *The End of Reform: New Deal Liberalism in Recession and War* (New York, 1995), 74–76; W. Randolph Burgess to Everett Case, Nov. 30, 1929, 87.2.204, no. 344B, Young Papers.

20. Schlesinger, *Crisis of the Old Order*, 134–36; William Trufant Foster, "We Want

Work," *Bowdoin Quarterly,* March 1931, and "A Discussion of Bills, Banks, Bonuses, and Budgets," *Economic Forum* 1:1 (1932), typescript copies in PSF 149. On the Liberal Party–Lloyd George public works proposals, see Derek H. Aldcroft, *The Inter-War Economy: Britain, 1919–1939* (New York, 1970), 318.

21. Lord Astor to Roosevelt, March 9, 1933, PPF 5235; Astor to Keynes, March 9, 1933, in Moggridge, *Collected Writings of Keynes* 21:167.

22. For a contrary interpretation, see James E. Sargent, "FDR and Lewis W. Douglas: Budget Balancing and the Early New Deal," *Prologue* 6:1 (Spring 1974): 33–36.

23. Swagar Sherley, "A Study of the Problem of Federal Economy," n.d., box 237, Lewis Douglas to Raymond Moley, May 4, 1964, box 118, to James S. Douglas, March 12, 1933, box 31, Douglas Papers; New York *Herald Tribune,* March 20, 1933.

24. Moley, *First New Deal,* 270–71.

25. Joint resolution, April 21, 1933, f. 5, box 249, Lewis W. Douglas to James S. Douglas, April 23, 1933, box 31, "Memorandum Relating to Sources of Revenue," April 28, 1933, box 249, "Memorandum to Mr. Douglas," May 8, 1933, box 248, "Tentative Tax Program," box 248, Lewis W. Douglas to Francis C. Newton, May 24, 1933, Douglas Papers; New York *Herald Tribune,* May 14, 16, 1933; *New York Times,* May 17, 23, 1933.

26. David Lawrence, "The Twin Budgets," *Saturday Evening Post,* Sept. 2, 1933, 23, 51–53.

27. Douglas, "Budget Years, Misc. Background Material," f. 5, box 118, Douglas Papers.

28. Douglas memoranda for the president, July 20, Oct. 12, Nov. 2, 1933, box 236, Lewis W. Douglas to James S. Douglas, Nov. 4, 1933, box 31, ibid.

29. Moley, *First New Deal,* 271–78; Chandler, *America's Greatest Depression,* 193–201. Hopkins also headed the FERA, created by law on May 12, 1933, with an initial appropriation of $500 million.

30. Lewis W. Douglas to James S. Douglas, Nov. 20, 1933, box 31, "Conference with the President: Ray Moley and Myself Present. Subject: Budget Message," Dec. 29, 1933, "Conference, Round Room, White House, Subject: Budget Message," Dec. 30, 1933, box 236, Douglas Papers.

31. Lewis W. Douglas to the President, memorandum, Dec. 30, 1933, box 237, Lewis W. Douglas to James S. Douglas, Jan. 6, 1934, box 31, ibid.; "Government's Cash Requirements for Emergency Program for Period Ending June 30, 1934," PSF 118 (Bureau of the Budget).

32. Stein, *Fiscal Revolution,* 63, 68; Rosenman, *PPA* 3:16–23; Lewis W. Douglas, "Estimate of Receipts and Expenditures for the Fiscal Year Ending June 30, 1935," n.d. [Dec. 1933], box 237, Douglas Papers; Dean Acheson to James P. Warburg, Jan. 7, 1934, box 13, Warburg Papers.

33. Douglas notes of cabinet meeting, White House, March 16, 1934, box 236, Douglas Papers.

34. Sargent interview with Douglas, f. 5, p. 40, box 119, Douglas, "Memorandum on Possible Veto of Independent Offices Bill Because of Increased Veterans Benefits," March 22, 1934, and FDR veto message, March 27, 1934, box 243, Lewis W. to James S. Douglas, March 28, April 5, 1934, box 31, ibid.

35. "Dictated at Meeting of Mr. Douglas Stuart, Mr. Kendall, and Mr. D., Afternoon of April 5, 1934, Mr. D's Office," box 237, and memorandum for the president, April 13, 1934, box 236, ibid. Douglas Stuart was one of the principals in the Chicago-based Warburg-Hoover sound money–government economy group.

36. Lewis W. Douglas to William R. Mathews, April 7, 1934, to James S. Douglas, May 25, 1934, box 31, "White House Conference, Subject: Additional Appropriations for Relief, Public Works, etc.," April 23, 1934, box 236, Douglas Papers.

37. Sargent interview with Douglas, f. 5, pp. 40–41, box 119, "Memorandum to the President, June 6, 1934, Copies to John Nance Garner, Hon. James Buchanan, . . . and Senator Carter Glass," and note attached to Douglas to Byrnes, June 11, 1934, "Original White House Draft of Letter . . . and Letter of 6/11 Prepared by President—Signed by Mr. Douglas—Actually Sent Sen. Byrnes, and Memorandum," June 11, 1934, "Notes of White House Meeting, Monday, June 11, 1934," box 236, ibid.; Douglas to James F. Byrnes, June 11, 1934, OF 79.

38. LWD notes, June 14, 15, 1934, Douglas to Marvin H. McIntyre, June 19, 1934, box 236, Douglas Papers.

39. Douglas notes, June 28, 1934, box 236, Lewis W. to James S. Douglas, June 30, 1934, box 31, ibid.; The Secret Diary of Harold L. Ickes: The First Thousand Days (New York, 1953), 174.

40. Lewis W. Douglas to James S. Douglas, July 20, 1934, box 31, to Franklin D. Roosevelt, Aug. 30, 1934, box 236, Douglas Papers and PPF 1914.

41. Copy of longhand notes on visit with the president, Aug. 30, 1934, and addenda, box 236, and on Douglas's flirtation with the American Liberty League, unsigned telegram to Robert Stroud (Douglas's assistant), Aug. 25, 1934, box 237, Lewis W. Douglas to James S. Douglas, Sept. 3, 1934, box 31, Douglas Papers.

42. Addresses by Lewis W. Douglas and Stuart Chase, "A Federal Fiscal Policy Conducive to Recovery," Economic Club of New York, Dec. 12, 1934, Consensus 19:3 (Jan. 1935), box 6, Warburg Papers.

43. James P. Warburg, Hell Bent for Election (Garden City, N.Y., 1935); Warburg to Virgil Jordan, Sept. 18, 1935, box 25, Pierre S. du Pont to Warburg, Oct. 25, Nov. 20, 1935, Warburg to Du Pont, Oct. 31, 1935, Du Pont to S. Clay Williams, Jan. 2, 1936, box 9, Warburg Papers; file 765, box 2, Pierre S. du Pont Papers.

44. Virgil Jordan to James P. Warburg, Sept. 17, 1935, Warburg to Jordan, Sept. 18, 1935, box 25, Warburg, "What of 1936?" Chicago Association of Commerce, Jan. 15, 1936, box 23, Warburg to Charlton McVeigh, April 2, 1936, to Ogden L. Mills, April 24, 1936, box 10, Warburg Papers.

45. Stein, Fiscal Revolution, 57, 61; McKibbin, "Labor Government Economic Policy," 99–100; Arthur Smithies, "The American Economy in the Thirties," American Economic Review, Supplement, 36:2 (May 1946): 13.

46. "Depression and Recovery in the United Kingdom and the United States," Conference Board Bulletin 12:14 (Dec. 19, 1938); McKibbin, "Labor Government Economic Policy," 95–97, 100–8, 121–23.

47. Roosevelt to Irving Fisher, June 8, 1934, PPF 431; Historical Statistics of the United States, ser. Y 254–57, "Summary of Government Finance," 711; memorandum, E. E. Lincoln, "Federal Non-recoverable Relief Expenditures by States, Compared with Internal Revenue Collections, July 1, 1933, to June 30, 1937 . . . and accompanying table," file 771, box 1, Pierre S. du Pont Papers; "Summary Operations Report of Federal Funds Loaned and Expended from New and Emergency Appropriations, March 4, 1933, through December 31, 1937," Cong. Record, Senate, April 14, 1938, 7064–65.

6 | THE MYTH OF A CORPORATE STATE

1. Otis L. Graham Jr., *Toward a Planned Society: From Roosevelt to Nixon* (New York, 1976), 1–14; Schwarz, *Speculator*, 4–6, 51–52, 73–77, 82–84; Colin Gordon, *New Deals: Business, Labor, and Politics in America, 1920–1935* (New York, 1994), 31–86, 128–59; Robert D. Cuff, *The War Industries Board: Business-Government Relations during World War I* (Baltimore, 1973), 1–7; Donald R. Brand, *Corporatism and the Rule of Law: A Study of the National Recovery Administration* (Ithaca, N.Y., 1988), 312.

2. Summary of Edward Batson, "A Note on the Nature and Significance of Economic Planning," *South African Journal of Economics* 4:1 (March 1936), copy in box 101, Sachs Papers; *New York Investment News*, Sept. 17, 1931, and Gerard Swope, "Discussion of Stabilization of Industry," Academy of Political Science, Nov. 13, 1931, box 87.2.8, f. 25V, Young Papers.

3. Stuart Chase, *A New Deal* (New York, 1932), 182–83, 213.

4. "Proposal for an Economic Council," reprinted in R. G. Tugwell, *The Brains Trust* (New York, 1968), 525–28; Tugwell, "The Principle of Planning and the Institution of Laissez Faire," *American Economic Review* 22:1, Supplement (March 1932): 75–92; Tugwell radio address, NBC, box 1, and "Discourse in Depression," box 2, Tugwell Papers; Ellis W. Hawley, *The New Deal and the Problem of Monopoly* (Princeton, N.J., 1966), 44–45.

5. Owen D. Young to Henry Goddard Leach, June 12, 1931, box 87.2.204, f. 364F, press release, May 11, 1932, box 87.2.206, f. 3640, Young Papers.

6. Robert F. Himmelberg, *The Origins of the National Recovery Administration* (New York, 1976), 166, 182.

7. Ibid., 167; M. L. Wilson to Rexford Tugwell, July 12, 1932, Henry I. Harriman, "An Economic Program," Feb. 10, 1933, item 118/21, United States Chamber of Commerce Referendum no. 58, "On the Report of the Special Committee on Continuity of Business and Employment," box 113, Moley Papers; Harriman address on "Stabilization of Business and Employment," Dec. 4, 1931, and radio address, "Economic Planning," March 22, 1932, in Agricultural Policy, National Chamber of Commerce, Harriman, H. I., CD F 77, and M. L. Wilson to Tugwell, July 25, 1932, CD F 90, Correspondence, Tugwell, M. L. Wilson Papers; and Moley, *First New Deal*, 285–86.

8. Moley, *First New Deal*, 286; H. G. Moulton to Moley, March 6, 1933, and "A Plan for Business Recovery," Frederick Delano to FDR, March 9, 1933, box 67, Herbert Feis to Moley, March 8, 1933, Marvin McIntyre to Moley, March 28, 1933, item 109/19, box 73, Moley Papers.

9. Warburg Diary, 201–2, 221, 243, 249, 258, 261, 364, 371–73, 376; "Industrial Stabilization," box 7, folder 2, Warburg Papers.

10. Warburg Diary, 221, 382, 493–94; Warburg to Fred I. Kent and W. Jett Lauck, April 18, 1933, to David L. Podell, April 19, 1933, box 7, Warburg Papers.

11. James P. Johnson, *The Politics of Soft Coal* (Urbana, Ill., 1979), 118–21, 195–96; Melvyn Dubofsky and Warren Van Tyne, *John L. Lewis* (New York, 1977), 41; Valerie Jean Conner, *The National War Labor Board: Stability, Social Justice, and the Voluntary State in World War I* (Chapel Hill N. C., 1983), vii–viii, 4–158, 169–70, 173–81; John A. Ryan to W. Jett Lauck, June 20, 1918, William Ogburn to Lauck, July 18, 1918, [Ogburn], "Memorandum on Cost of Living Information Needed in Settling Labor Disputes by the War Labor Board," n.d., box 66, Lauck to Woodrow Wilson, Aug. 5, 1919, box 37, Lauck Papers.

12. Lauck to Philip Murray, Jan. 11, 1928, box 41, "Brief Analysis of the Copeland-Jacobstein Coal Bills," Jan. 4, 1928, box 232, [Lauck], "Memorandum of Constructive Proposal for Coal Industry, Prepared for Mr. Lewis," April 9, 1928, box 233, Watson bill, S. 4490, box 230, Lauck to John T. Flynn, Jan. 28, 1937, box 35, Lauck Papers.

13. "United Mine Workers of America, John L. Lewis, President, Investigation by Senate Committee on Interstate Commerce," Feb. 25–May 17, 1928, in f. Docket 1928, box 173, Lauck to Benjamin A. Javits, March 19, 1929, box 37, to Lewis, Aug. 26, 1931, Lewis to Lauck, Aug. 31, 1931, box 39, Lauck, Emergency Stabilization Procedure," f. Docket 1931, box 174, Lauck to Lewis, Sept. 4, 30, Oct. 20, 1931, Lewis to Lauck, Oct. 28, 1931, box 39, f. Stabilization of Industry, 1931, Lewis statement, box 231, "What the Davis-Kelly Bill . . . Actually Provides Is," and H.R. 7536 (Kelly bill) in f. Stabilization of Coal Industry Bill, on the Origin of Section 7(a), box 230, "Statement of John L. Lewis . . . to Finance Committee of the United States Senate," Feb. 17, 1933, box 231, Lauck Papers.

14. Note to W. J. L., Aug. 4, 1932, and memorandum to W. J. L., Aug. 8, 1932, box 232, "Fundamental Principles Advocated," Aug. 29, 1932, box 283, Docket: Coal & Stabilization, Oct. 18, 1932, box 165, Philip Murray to Lauck, Oct. 24, 1932, box 41, Lauck to Roosevelt, Nov. 21, 1932, box 44, Lauck Papers.

15. Docket, April 19, 20, 1933, box 165, ibid.

16. John T. Flynn, "Whose Child Is the NRA?" 9, "Working Periods in Industry, Report of the Special Committee, Chamber of Commerce of the United States," April 1933, J. F. Bennett, Secretary, to Mr. Litchfield, April 13, 1934, with Litchfield "Memorandum for Mr. Flynn," April 12, 1934, attached, and "Statement of Henry I. Harriman . . . before the Committee on Labor, United States House of Representatives, the Black Bill," April 27, 1933, f. MSS Unpublished New Deal Book, box 11, Flynn Papers; Moley, *First New Deal*, 287; George Martin, *Madam Secretary: Frances Perkins* (Boston, 1976), 260–63; Stanley Hoffman, "Look Back in Anger," *New York Review of Books*, July 17, 1997, 48; Kindleberger, *World in Depression*, 254.

17. Himmelberg, *Origins of the NRA*, 201–5.

18. Moley Notebook, May 2, 1933, Moley Papers.

19. John Dickinson to Raymond Moley, April 26, 1933, accompanied by "Memorandum of Criticisms of the Black Bill as Amended, Memorandum of Proposals for Accomplishing Objects of Black Bill by Measure Drawn along Different Lines," item 104/34, box 67, ibid.

20. Memorandum, April 29, 1933, Meyer Jacobstein and Harold G. Moulton, "A Plan for Economic Recovery Tentative Rough Draft, Title, Industrial Coordination Federal Emergency Administration of Public Works, and Tentative Rough Draft, Supplemental to the Foregoing (Submitted by Economists Associated with the Department of Agriculture by Way of a Combination of the Kent and Rorty Plans)," box 249, Douglas Papers; Docket: Coal & Stabilization, April 21, 1933, box 165, Docket, April 25, 26, 1933, box 172, Lauck to Franklin D. Roosevelt, Nov. 13, 1934, box 44, Lauck Papers.

21. Lauck, Moulton, Kelly, Industrial Control–Wagner bill, May 1, 1933, box 286, William Hard, "Industrial Control Act Is Believed to Contain Germs of Economic Revolution," *Washington Star*, "Sunday, 14, 1933," and interview with Clyde Kelly, in f. NRA clippings, box 170, Lauck Papers; Warburg Diary, 637.

22. Donald T. Critchlow, *The Brookings Institution, 1916-1952* (DeKalb, Ill., 1985), 14–15, 54, 114–21; John Kennedy Ohl, *Hugh Johnson and the New Deal* (DeKalb, Ill., 1985), 96–101.

23. The analysis is based on a comparison of the "Industry Control–Wagner Bill, Presented by Lauck, Supported by Moulton, to the Second Wagner Conference, and Turned Over to Enlarged Drafting Committee Headed by John Dickinson," May 1, 1933,, box 286, Lauck Papers, with an annotated copy of the National Industrial Recovery Act, Office of the Messrs. Rockefeller, RGII 2F, Economic Interests Series, Rockefeller Archive Center. The Harriman plan is discussed above. The Swope proposal for business stabilization and welfare capitalism is found in Gerard Swope to Herbert Hoover, discussion of "Stabilization of Industry," container 1-F/754, and Thomas D. Thacher to Hoover, Oct. 1, 1931, container 1-E/87, HHPL. The Lauck-Podell split on licensing is described in Docket: Coal & Stabilization, April 28, May 1, 1933, Lauck Papers.

24. Lauck to John T. Flynn, April 27, 1936, box 287, Lauck Papers; "Resolution Adopted at Meeting, National Association of Manufacturers, Mayflower Hotel, Washington, D.C.," June 3, 1933, box 278, PPI; John T. Flynn, "Whose Child Is the NRA?," 19, Flynn Papers.

25. Michael M. Weinstein, *Recovery and Redistribution under the NIRA* (Amsterdam, 1980), vii, 19, 25–28, 47–48, 57–61, 63, 112, 146–49.

26. Hawley, *New Deal and Problem of Monopoly,* 19–20, 33–35, and passim; Michael A. Bernstein, *The Great Depression: Delayed Recovery and Economic Change in America, 1929–1939* (Princeton, N.J., 1987), 194; Leverett S. Lyon et al., *The National Recovery Administration* (Washington, D.C., 1935), 292, 578, 756–60, 766–69, 817.

27. Sachs to Charles F. Roos, July 25, 1935, box 63, Sachs Papers; Sachs, "Extracts from Memo. Dated Jan. 22, 1934," OF 1983; Sachs letters to Hugh Johnson, box 37, Sachs Papers, also in Alexander Sachs, *Selected Memoranda on Problems of National Recovery,* reprinted from Charles F. Roos, *NRA Economic Planning* (Bloomington, Ind., 1937), box 44, Lauck Papers; Roos, *NRA Economic Planning,* Appendix III, 520–36.

28. Mordecai Ezekiel to [Federal Farm] Board Members, Aug. 25, 1932, including further estimates on unemployment and payrolls by industrial groups, and Ezekiel to Stone et al., Aug. 22, 1932, "Unemployment Heaviest in Groups Producing Capital Goods," box 1, Ezekiel Papers.

29. Sachs, "Extracts from Memo: Dated Jan. 22, 1934," OF 1983; Sachs, "National Recovery Administration Policies and the Problem of Economic Planning," in *America's Recovery Program,* ed. A. A. Berle Jr. et al. (London, 1934), 109–90.

7 | THE LIMITS OF PLANNING

1. Section 7(a) of the National Industrial Recovery Act reads: "Every code of fair competition . . . shall contain the following conditions: (1) That employees shall have the right to organize and bargain collectively through representatives of their own choosing, and shall be free from the interference, restraint, or coercion of employers of labor, or their agents, in the designation of such representatives or in self-organization or in other concerted activities for the purpose of collective bargaining; . . . (2) that no employee and no one seeking employment shall be required as a condition of employment to join any company union or to refrain from joining, organizing, or assisting a labor organization of his own choosing; (3) that employers shall comply with the maximum hours of labor, minimum rates of pay, and other conditions of employment, approved or prescribed by the president."

2. William H. Wilson, "How the Chamber of Commerce Viewed the NRA: A Reevaluation," *Mid-America* 44:2 (April 1962): 95–108; Henry I. Harriman, "Current

National Problems: A Statement to the Board of Directors, Chamber of Commerce of the United States," Sept. 21, 1934, box 216, Witte Papers; Tom L. Girdler, address, "Tomorrow's Markets for Steel," American Society for Metals, New York City, Oct. 4, 1934, box 39, Hurja Papers; text of "Report of the Joint Conference for Business Recovery," *New York Times*, Dec. 20, 1934.

3. Herbert Hoover to William S. Bennet, July 2, 1933, box 278, PPI; Willard M. Kiplinger to Raymond Moley, May 16, Aug. 3, 1934, Kiplinger Special Letter, July 7, 1934, box 28, Moley Papers.

4. Bernstein, *Depression and Economic Change*, 198–200; Robert M. Collins, *The Business Response to Keynes, 1929–1964* (New York, 1981), 32.

5. Morgan Farrell, "What the Swope Plan Is," *Electrical Manufacturing*, Jan. 1934.

6. Owen D. Young to Gerard Swope, Oct. 4, 1933, f. 25C, box 87.2.8, Young to James P. Warburg, July 31, 1934, box 836, bk. 64, 280, Young Papers.

7. John W. Owens to Young, June 24, 1935, and "Forgotten Men of the New Deal . . . ," *Baltimore Sun*, June 23, 1935, f. 135, box 30, ibid.

8. Robert E. Wood to Henry J. Allen, Aug. 17, 1928, box 47, to Arthur Vandenberg, April 21, 1944, box 18, Wood Papers.

9. Justus D. Doenecke, "General Robert E. Wood: The Evolution of a Conservative," *Journal of the Illinois State Historical Society* 71 (Aug. 1978): 162–66; Wood to Chester H. McCall, May 18, 1936, box 10, and [Wood], memorandum for the president, Oct. 19, 1936, box 15, Wood Papers.

10. [Wood], memorandum for the president, Oct. 19, 1936, box 15, Wood Papers; Tugwell Diary, Jan. 29, 1935, box 17, Tugwell Papers; "Address by R. G. Tugwell," Olympic Auditorium, Los Angeles, Oct. 28, 1935, copy in box 217, Baker Papers; Rexford G. Tugwell, *The Industrial Discipline and the Governmental Arts* (New York, 1933).

11. *Railroad Retirement Board v. Alton Railroad Co.*, 295 U.S. 330 (1935).

12. Hawley, *New Deal and Problem of Monopoly*, 170–81; N. I. Stone, review of Mordecai Ezekiel, *$2,500 a Year: From Scarcity to Abundance* (New York, 1936), in *Society for Advancement of Management Journal* 2:1 (Jan. 1937): 30–32, and John Shute, "Streamlining the Dismal Science," *Mechanical Engineering* 58:10 (Oct. 1936): 641–42, box 19, Ezekiel Papers.

13. Tugwell Diary, May 9, 19, 30, 31, June 5, 1935, Tugwell to Paul T. Homan, Feb. 6, 1952, and Milo Perkins memorandum for Tugwell, June 5, 1935, Tugwell Papers; Haas to Secretary Morgenthau, transmitted to FDR, "The Business Situation," Dec. 23, 1935, box 118, PSF; Lyon et al., *National Recovery Administration*, 873.

14. David S. Painter, *Oil and the American Century: The Political Economy of U.S. Foreign Oil Policy, 1941–1954* (Baltimore, 1986), 5–7; Northcut Ely, "The Conservation of Oil," *Harvard Law Review* 51:7 (1938): 1209–44.

15. Brand, *Corporatism and the Rule of Law*, 175–87; Painter, *Oil and the American Century*, 3, 6–7; August Giebelhaus, *Business and Government in the Oil Industry: A Case Study of Sun Oil, 1876-1945* (Greenwich, Conn., 1980), 125–47, 200–201, 302–3; Bernstein, *Depression and Economic Change*, 63–70; G. John Ikenberry, *Reasons of State: Oil Policies and the Capacities of American Government* (Ithaca, N.Y., 1988), 66–67; Gerald D. Nash, *United States Oil Policy, 1890–1964* (Pittsburgh, 1968), 128–56; Gary D. Libecap, "The Political Economy of Crude Oil Cartelization in the United States, 1933–1972," *Journal of Economic History* 49:4 (Dec. 1989): 833–40; Norman E. Nordhauser, *The Quest for Stability: Domestic Oil Regulation* (New York, 1979), 74–165; Joseph E. Pogue to Alexander

Sachs, Jan. 2, 19, 1932, "Collective Planning in the Petroleum Industry," boxes 57, 58, Sachs Papers.

16. Pamela Pennock, "The National Recovery Administration and the Rubber Tire Industry, 1933–1935," *Business History Review* 71:4 (Winter 1997): 543–68.

17. Federal Trade Commission, *Report on Motor Vehicle Industry* (Washington, D.C., 1959), 7 (table 6), 22, 1074; John B. Rae, *American Automobile Manufactures* (Philadelphia, 1959), 191–92; A. T. Court (Automobile Manufacturers Association) to Alexander Sachs, Nov. 5, 1935, box 28, Sachs Papers; Sidney Fine, *The Automobile under the Blue Eagle: Labor, Management, and the Automobile Manufacturing Code* (Ann Arbor, Mich., 1963), 1–12, 48–53, 58–60, 128–30; Alexander Sachs, "Extracts from Memo, Jan. 22, 1934, on Economic Statesmanship of Original Recovery Program," OF 1983.

18. Alfred P. Sloan Jr. to R. C. Fulbright, Oct. 24, 1935, box 14, Clayton-Truman.

19. Bernstein, *Depression and Economic Change,* 202.

20. James P. Johnson, *The Politics of Soft Coal: The Bituminous Industry from World War I through the New Deal* (Urbana, Ill., 1979), 2–8, 14, 135–36, 156, 163–69, 182–83, 190–91, 195, 198–245; Hawley, *New Deal and Problem of Monopoly,* 72–80; "Statement of John L. Lewis . . . at the Hearing on a Code for the Bituminous Coal Industry, before the National Recovery Administration," Washington, D.C., Aug. 10, 1933, and National Recovery Administration, "Code of Fair Competition for the Bituminous Coal Industry," box 286, A. D. L. to Jett Lauck, n.d. [1935], enclosure, "The Bituminous Coal Industry: A Discussion of the Necessity for and Methods of Production Control," box 279, Lauck Papers.

21. Bernstein, *Depression and Economic Change,* 200–201.

22. Louis Galambos, *Competition and Cooperation: The Emergence of a National Trade Association* (Baltimore, 1966), 89–288.

23. Corporate Profits, box 13, Ezekiel Papers; *Historical Statistics of the United States,* ser. P 3–4, "Manufactures Summary," 409. Louis Galambos and Joseph Pratt, *The Rise of the Corporate Commonwealth: United States Business and Public Policy in the 20th Century* (New York, 1988), 124–25; Giebelhaus, *Oil Industry,* 146; Robert Sobel, *The Age of Giant Corporations: A Microeconomic History of American Business, 1914–1970* (Westport, Conn., 1972), 122–26; Bernstein, *Depression and Economic Change,* 66.

24. Bernstein, *Depression and Economic Change,* 32–40, and passim; Solomon Fabricant, *Employment in Manufacturing, 1899–1939: An Analysis of Its Relation to the Volume of Production* (New York, 1942), 16–27; Weinstein, *NIRA,* 28–31.

25. Alexander Sachs, "Notes on Purchasing Power as a Fulcrum of Recovery and a New Economic Equilibrium," July 28, 1933, "transmitted by F. R. Robinson to Miss Le Hand . . . for the president," OF 1989, Sachs, extracts from memo, Jan. 22, 1934, "Economic Statesmanship of Original Recovery Plan," OF 1983; Sachs to Raymond Moley, April 29, 1933, box 47, "Conversation with Mr. J. E. Pogue," Aug. 6, 19[33], box 57, Sachs to Charles F. Roos, July 23, 1935, box 63, Sachs Papers.

26. Sachs to Joseph Pogue, Dec. 17, 1937, box 57, Sachs Papers; Thomas K. McCraw, *Prophets of Regulation* (Cambridge, Mass., 1984), 186–87.

27. On housing, see Sachs to Raymond Moley, April 29, 1933, box 47, to Charles F. Roos, July 23, 1935, and Sachs, "Establishment of Mortgage Rediscounting System and Stimulation of Building," Nov. 28, 1933, box 95, Sachs Papers; Olson, *Saving Capitalism,* 172–77, 195, 225; Friedman and Schwartz, *Monetary History of the United States,* 244–45.

28. Sachs to Roosevelt, Nov. 5, 1934, Roosevelt to Sachs, July 15, 1935, and [Joseph East-

man], "Memorandum on Alexander Sachs' Integrated Railroad Plan for the Administration," [July 1935], box 63, Sachs Papers; Olson, *Saving Capitalism*, 117–22, 196–98.

29. Alexander Sachs to O. T. Falk, Sept. 21, 1934, box 23, to Winfield Riefler, Oct. 13, 1934, box 61, Sachs to FDR, Nov. 5, 1934, box 63, Pierson M. Tuttle, Bonbright & Co., to Sachs, Nov. 6, 1933, box 81, Sachs Papers; Jordan A. Schwarz, *The New Dealers: Power Politics in the Age of Roosevelt* (New York, 1993), 228–29.

30. Frank R. McNinch, radio address, National Broadcasting Company, Dec. 10, 1934, in McNinch—and Federal Power Commission, box: Willkie, pre-1940, f. June 1937, National Power Proposal, Willkie Papers; Joseph P. Lash, *Dealers and Dreamers* (New York, 1988), 193.

31. Paul K. Conkin, "Intellectual and Political Roots," 3–32, and Richard Lowitt, "The TVA, 1933–1945," 35–36, in *TVA: Fifty Years of Grass-Roots Bureaucracy*, ed. Erwin C. Hargrove and Paul K. Conkin (Urbana, Ill., 1983).

32. *Investigation of Executive Agencies of the Government, Report to the Select Committee, No. 4, Report on the Governmental Activities in the Field of Mineral Resources and Power Prepared by the Brookings Institution* (Washington, D.C, 1937), 108.

33. Schlesinger, *Politics of Upheaval*, 310, 320, 363; William H. Droze, "The TVA, 1945–80: The Power Company," in Hargrove and Conkin, *TVA*, 66–67; Henry Steele Commager, ed., *Documents of American History*, 7th ed. (New York, 1963), 2:255–57.

34. Ellsworth Barnard, *Wendell Willkie: Fighter for Freedom* (Marquette, Mich., 1966), 78–109, 105, 111, 115, 117, 118–19; Thomas P. Hughes, *Networks of Power: Electrification in Western Society, 1880–1930* (Baltimore, 1983), 393–401; Willkie to James P. Warburg, Sept. 7, 1934, box 22, Warburg Papers; Alexander Sachs, "High Lights from . . . Basic Elements of Preliminary Arrangement and Eventual Plan for Southeastern Cooperative Pool for Publicly and Privately Owned Utilities," Sept. 29, 1936, box 63, Sachs Papers. Sachs compared Central Illinois Light's ability to convert preferred stock to a 4.2 percent yield, as opposed to Tennessee Electric Power Company's inability to refund its 8.5 percent preferred.

35. Sachs to O. T. Falk, Sept. 21, 1934, box 23, to Roosevelt, Nov. 5, 1934, box 63, Sachs, "A Concrete Illustration of the Necessity for Positive Planning in Federal Utility Regulation," April 2, 1935, box 47, to G. O. Muhlfeld, copy to John Hancock, June 4, 1935, box 48, Sachs Papers.

36. Unsigned to Alexander Sachs, left by Sachs for the president to read, Feb. 28, 1936, Ben Gray to Roosevelt, March 20, 1936, OF 1983; Hughes, *Networks of Power*, 388–401.

37. Lash, *Dealers and Dreamers*, 191–214.

38. David Lilienthal to Wendell Willkie, April 25, 1936, Willkie to Lilienthal, May 5, 1936, box 89, to Roosevelt, May 21, 1936, box 63, Sachs Papers; Sachs telegram to Marguerite Le Hand, May 17, 1936, OF 1983.

39. "Conference with Mr. Basil Manly, Vice Chairman, Federal Power Commission," June 8, 1936, box 44, Sachs Papers; Basil Manly memorandum for the president, June 8, 1936, note in FDR's hand, Aug. 8, 1936, "Luncheon Conference . . . July 24, 1936," OF 1983.

40. Alexander Sachs, "Integral Plan and Preliminary Arrangement for Southeastern Power Pool for Public and Private Utilities," May 20, June 8, Aug. 11, Sept. 16, 1936, for conferences with President Roosevelt and Federal Power Commission, box 63, Sachs Papers; Hughes, *Networks of Power*, 352, 354, 356.

41. Sachs, "High Lights from . . . Basic Elements of Preliminary Arrangement and Eventual Plan for Southeastern Cooperative Pool for Publicly and Privately Owned Util-

ities," Sept. 29, 1936, and "Conference at Federal Power Commission between Vice Chairman Basil Manly, Louis B. Wehle, and Alexander Sachs," Sept. 25, 1936, box 63, Sachs Papers.

42. FDR to Sachs, Sept. 17, 1936, and White House press release, ibid.

43. [Sachs], "Perspective on Tasks Arising from President's Power Pool Conference with Special Reference to the TVA and Commonwealth & Southern," White House conference, Sept. 30, 1936, OF 1983.

44. Morris L. Cooke to the president, Nov. 6, 1936, box 141, George W. Norris to Roosevelt, Nov. 13, 1936, Roosevelt to Norris, Nov. 19, 1936, box 158, PSF.

45. Wendell L. Willkie to Franklin D. Roosevelt, Sept. 30, 1936, copy, box 89, Sachs Papers.

46. Sachs to FDR, Jan. 25, 1937, Administrative Assistant to the President to Sachs, Jan. 27, 1937, OF 1983.

47. David E. Lilienthal to Wendell L. Willkie, Jan. 29, 1937, Willkie to Lilienthal, Feb. 1, 1937, box 89, Sachs Papers.

8 | TRADE RECIPROCITY OR THE LAND USED AS CONCEALED DOLE

This chapter is informed in part by a reading of the Milo Reno Papers (Farm Holiday Movement), Clifford Hope Papers, Elmer Thomas Papers, and Don Berry Papers.

1. Temin, *Monetary Forces and Depression,* 150–51.

2. Alan Brinkley, *Voices of Protest: Huey Long, Father Coughlin, and the Great Depression* (New York, 1983), 167; Simon Kuznets, *National Income: A Summary of Findings* (New York, 1946), 6 (table 2), 24 (table 8), 27 (table 9), and 6–7, 23, 27–29, 32–33, 41.

3. *Historical Statistics of the United States,* ser. D, 48–56, 73; "Employees in Nonagricultural Establishments by Major Industry Division: 1919–1957"; ser. F, 34–43, "Percent Distribution of National Income or Aggregate Payments, by Industry, in Current Prices: 1869–1948 (based on NBER estimates of national income)," 73, ibid.; ser. K 122–38, "Farm Cash Receipts and Income and Indexes of Prices Received and Paid by Farmers, and Parity Ratio: 1910–1957," 283, ibid.

4. Rexford G. Tugwell to Carey McWilliams, May 6, 1940, box 6, Tugwell to Bruce Bliven, Dec. 5, 1940, box 2, Tugwell Papers; "Standards of Living and of Life," *New Republic,* Dec. 9, 1940, 777–78; Gavin Wright, *Old South; New South: Revolutions in the Southern Economy since the Civil War* (New York, 1986), chap. 7; Sally H. Clarke, *Regulation and the Revolution in United States Farm Productivity* (Cambridge and New York, 1994).

5. George E. Roberts to Gardner Cowles Jr., Sept. 2, 1936, box 4, Waymack Papers; Leroy Quance and Luther G. Tweetsen, "Policies, 1930–1970," in *Size, Structure, and Future of Farms,* ed. A. Gordon Ball and Earl O. Heady (Ames, Iowa, 1972), 22; Richard S. Kirkendall, *Social Scientists and Farm Politics in the Age of Roosevelt* (Columbia, Mo., 1966), 74–76, 81–87; *Historical Statistics of the United States,* ser. E 101–12, "Wholesale Prices of Selected Commodities," 125, and ser. U 73–93, "Exports of Selected United States Merchandise," 547.

6. Gilbert C. Fite, *George N. Peek and the Fight for Farm Parity* (Norman, Okla., 1954), 4–202; Owen D. Young to Benjamin F. Porter, Dec. 29, 1930, box 87.2.204, no. 364, Young to Frank O. Lowden, May 16, 1932, and Lowden to Young, May 19, 1932, box 87.2.10, f. 30, Young Papers; Murray R. Benedict, *Farm Policies of the United States, 1790–1950: A Study of Their Origins and Development* (New York, 1953), 211–14; Wayne Cole, *Roosevelt and the Isolationists, 1932–45* (Lincoln, Nebr., 1983), 95.

7. Fite, *Peek*, 249–66; Schwarz, *The Speculator*, 208–10, 280–85; Benedict, *U.S. Farm Policies*, 283–84; Henry A. Wallace to Dante Pierce, March and April 1933, reel 18, Wallace Papers.

8. Fite, *Peek*, 270–72, 278; Hull, *Memoirs*, 352; Alonzo Taylor, *The New Deal and Foreign Trade* (New York, 1935), 14–37, 45, 180–200, 225, 231, 278–80; George N. Peek to the president, and draft of Foreign Trade Board Bill, July 16, 1935, PSF 73, Cordell Hull to the president, Nov. 28, 1934, accompanied by [Francis B. Sayre], memorandum, "The United States Trade Agreements Program and Most-Favored-Nation Treatment," [1934], and "Memorandum on Generalization of Concessions," [1934], Hull memorandum for the president, Feb. 15, 1934, PSF 87.

9. Schlesinger, *Coming of the New Deal*, 253–57; Hull, *Memoirs*, 359–60.

10. Schlesinger, *Coming of the New Deal*, 255–58; Aldcroft, *Inter-War Economy* (New York, 1970), 348; George N. Peek to Bernard M. Baruch, Aug. 26, 1935, and "Explanation of Foreign Trade Board Bill," General Correspondence, box 190, Baruch Papers.

11. George N. Peek, Special Adviser to the President on Foreign Trade, May 23, Aug. 30, 1934, Baruch Papers; Fite, *Peek*, 274–85.

12. Moley to Father Charles E. Coughlin, Nov. 6, 1935, box 10, Moley Papers; Walter Millis, *The Road to War* (reprint, New York, 1970).

13. Roosevelt to Moley, Nov. 23, 1935, Moley to Roosevelt, Nov. 30, 1935, box 1, Safe File, Moley Papers, also in PPF 743. For background, see Robert Dallek, *Franklin D. Roosevelt and American Foreign Policy, 1932–1945*, paperback ed. (Oxford, 1981), 102–21.

14. Peek address, "The Foreign Trade Problem of the United States," National Industrial Conference Board, New York City, Oct. 24, 1935, General Correspondence, box 190, Baruch Papers; "America's Choice," address before Members of the War Industries Board Association, New York City, Nov. 11, 1935, and editorial, *Washington Herald*, Nov. 26, 1935, PSF 73.

15. George N. Peek, with Samuel Crowther, *Why Quit Our Own?* (New York, 1936), 324. An isolationist and economic nationalist, Crowther had written *America Self-Contained* (1933), serialized in the anti–New Deal *Saturday Evening Post*. The Chemical Foundation of New York, a high-tariff group, distributed 100,000 copies of the Crowther book. Fite, *Peek*, 288–90; William S. Culbertson, *Reciprocity: A National Policy for Foreign Trade* (New York, 1937), 122.

16. Culbertson, *Reciprocity*, 130–31; Christiana McFadyen Campbell, *The Farm Bureau and the New Deal* (Urbana, Ill., 1962), 35–37, 140–148; Fite, *Peek*, 288; William W. Waymack to Walter T. Fisher, July 25, 1936, box 3, Waymack Papers.

17. W. W. Waymack to Lewis H. Brown, May 21, 1936, to Walter Fisher, June 24, 1936, to Richard F. Cleveland, June 29, 1936, box 3, to Francis P. Miller, June 15, 1936, box 47, Waymack Papers. On the problem of regional shifts in output under federal crop control programs, see Will W. Clayton to George Fort Milton, Jan. 15, 1940, box 8, Clayton-Rice.

18. *New York Times*, Jan. 5, 6, 1934; Alvin Hansen to W. W. Waymack, Feb. 6, 1934, box 1, Hansen to Waymack, March 17, 21, 1934, Waymack to Hansen, March 26, April 18, 1934, box 82, Waymack Papers; *International Economic Relations: Report of the Commission of Inquiry into National Policy in International Economic Relations* (Minneapolis, 1934), 5–11.

19. Minutes of the Organization Committee of the Committee on Economic Policy, Dec. 4, 1937, box 78, Waymack to George Fort Milton, Dec. 23, 1937, box 47, G. S. Nollen to Raymond Leslie Buell, Dec. 15, 1937, to Buell, Dec. 30, 1937, to Joseph P. Chamberlain,

Dec. 30, 1937, Buell to Waymack and to M. L. Wilson, Dec. 13, 1937, to Nollen, Dec. 21, 1937, to Waymack, Dec. 21, 1937, Waymack to Buell, Dec. 23, 1937, and "Committee on Economic Policy: Statement of Purposes," revised, box 75, Waymack Papers; Mark Lincoln Chadwick, *The Warhawks: American Interventionists before Pearl Harbor* (New York,, 1970), 43; Gabriel Kolko, *The Politics of War: The World and United States Foreign Policy, 1943–1945* (New York, 1968), 484–86.

20. Membership, Committee on Economic Policy, box 75, Waymack Papers; Raymond L. Buell to Thomas W. Lamont, Feb. 2, 1938, box 26, f. 11, Economic Policy Committee, Lamont Papers; Alexander Sachs to Richard F. Cleveland, Oct. 6, 1938, box 57, Sachs Papers.

21. Douglas to Arthur W. Kiddy, March 18, 1935, box 251, to Walter Parker, Jan. 4, 1935, box 255, Douglas Papers.

22. On the inevitability of war, see Baker to Charles B. Welsh, April 9, 1934, to Raymond Rich, March 8, 1934, box 241, correspondence with R. E. Desvernine, box 83, to John W. Davis, Jan. 18, 1935, box 84, to Bainbridge Colby, June 1, 1935, box 74, to John H. Clarke, May 15, June 18, Nov. 26, 1936, to Carl B. Dick, April 15, 1937, box 60, to Frederic R. Coudert, Oct. 20, Nov. 11, 1936, box 78, Baker Papers.

23. Robert A. Divine, *The Illusion of Neutrality: Franklin D. Roosevelt and the Struggle over the Arms Embargo* (Chicago, 1968), 48–80; Michael Dunne, *The United States and the World Court, 1920–1935* (New York, 1988), 1, 231–52; Hamilton Fish to Baker, July 17, 1933, box 97, Norman Davis to Baker, July 21, 1933, Allen Dulles to Baker, July 25, 1933, box 88, League of Nations Association and S. Van B. Nichols to Baker, Dec. 19, 1933, box 145, John W. Davis to Baker, Nov. 13, 1935, Baker to Ralph W. Smith, [Nov. 1935], box 176, Carnegie Endowment for International Peace, Conference held at Chatham House, London, March 5–7, 1935, box 145, Baker Papers; Nicholas Murray Butler to Thomas W. Lamont, April 1, 1935, Lamont to Butler, April 15, 1935, Lamont notes for talks at Saturday Butler dinner, box 85, Lamont Papers.

24. Lamont notes on Anglo-American cooperation, box 81, Lamont to S. Parker Gilbert, July 1, 1935, "Abroad Memorandum for T. W. L. in re B.I.S.," [1935], and "Stabilization [Lamont notes for London talks]," f. 15, box 131, Lamont to Russell Leffingwell, July 9, 1935, box 83, Lamont Papers.

25. Lippmann to Norman H. Davis, March 22, 29, 1935, box 66, to Newton D. Baker, Jan. 22, 1936, Baker to Lippmann, Jan. 27, 1936, box 54, Lippmann to Lewis W. Douglas, March 16, 27, 1936, Douglas to Lippmann, March 23, 28, April 2, 1936, "Tentative Draft of Declaration of Principles," box 67, Lippmann Papers. The Lippmann draft is also found in box 149, Baker Papers; Ronald Steel, *Walter Lippmann and the American Century* (New York, 1980), 315–18.

26. Lippmann to Frank Knox, July 10, 1936, Knox to Lippmann, box 82, Lippmann to Lewis W. Douglas, July 30, 1936, box 67, Lippmann Papers.

27. Lewis W. Douglas to W. R. Mathews, June 25, 1936, box 78, Douglas statement, Oct. 22, 1936, box 251, Douglas to Grenville Clark, Oct. 30, 1936, box 252, Douglas Papers.

28. Grenville Clark, "Notes on the Election, Second and Final Chapter," and Clark to Douglas, Oct. 30, 1936, box 252, ibid.

29. Dean G. Acheson, address, Churchman's Club of Maryland, May 8, 1934, box 13, Acheson to James P. Warburg, Oct. 8, 1935, to editor, *Baltimore Sun*, Oct. 17, 1936, box 13, Warburg Papers; Acheson to Alexander Sachs, Jan. 10, 1935, box 28, and generally, f. 3, box 2, Acheson-Yale.

30. Donald R. McCoy, *Landon of Kansas* (Lincoln, Nebr., 1966), 302–5; Theodore Saloutos, *The American Farmer and the New Deal* (Ames, Iowa, 1982), 229–30; W. W. Waymack to Gilbert Stinger, Sept. 24, 1936, box 88, Waymack Papers; Fite, *Peek,* 290–92.

31. Fite, *Peek,* 279–91; Peek, "Memorandum on the Canadian Trade Agreement," Dec. 8, 1935, "Agriculture and the Election," Aug. 15, 1936, and "Facts for American Farmers," radio address, Oct. 31, 1936, General Correspondence, box 190, Baruch Papers; *Historical Statistics of the United States,* ser. U 116–33, "Values of Exports," 550; ser. 134–52, "Value of General Imports," 552; Saloutos, *American Farmer,* 147; Henry J. Haskell, "The Reciprocity Agreements," *Kansas City Times-Star,* Sept. 25, 1936, reprinted in Culbertson, *Reciprocity,* 280–82.

32. Clayton testimony, Senate Committee on Finance, 66th Cong., 3d sess., 347–51, March 1, 1940; Clayton to Ben J. Williams, Oct. 24, 1940, box 8, Clayton-Rice.

33. Frederick J. Dobney, *Selected Papers of Will Clayton* (Baltimore, 1971), 1–4; Ross J. Pritchard, "Will Clayton: A Study of Business-Statesmanship in the Formulation of United States Economic Foreign Policy" (Ph.D. diss., 1955, Faculty of the Fletcher School of Law and Diplomacy, Tufts University), 5–32.

34. Clayton, "What Congress Can Do for the Cotton Farmer," April 15, 1930, ACCO speech file, "The Struggle for the World's Cotton Market," Feb. 1931, and "The World's Economic Tangle," April 1931, Clayton address, *Texas Weekly,* Jan. 9, 1932, box 3, Clayton-Rice; A. R. Erskine to Will Clayton, Dec. 12, 16, 17, 24, 1932, Clayton to Erskine, Dec. 16, 17, 1932, W. T. Ferris to Clayton, Dec. 13, 1932, box 6, Clayton-Truman. On the southern cotton mills as high-cost operators, vulnerable to imports, see Wright, *Old South, New South,* 151–55.

35. Form Cotton 4, Dec. 18, 1933, U.S. Department of Agriculture, Agricultural Adjustment Administration, Washington, D.C., box 9, W. L. Clayton, "Our National Cotton Policy," statement before the Commission of Inquiry on National Policy in International Economic Relations, Houston, May 7, 1934, box 16, Clayton-Truman; Clayton to James E. Bennett, June 13, 1934, to Marvin Jones, Sept. 19, 1934, to Henry A. Wallace, Oct. 11, 1934, box 4, Clayton-Rice; Benedict, *U.S. Farm Policies,* 307; Clifton Luttrell, *The High Cost of Farm Welfare* (Washington, D.C., 1989), 15.

36. Clayton to Sir Arthur Steel-Maitland, Jan. 2, 1934, box 9, Clayton-Truman; Clayton to Chester Davis, Sept. 14, 1935, box 5, Clayton-Rice.

37. Henry A. Wallace to Senator Ellison D. Smith, March 2, 1939, "Available Supply of American Cotton . . .," table 26, reel 21, Wallace Papers.

38. Clayton, "The Southwest's Stake in Cotton," address, Chamber of Commerce of the United States, Kansas City, Mo., Nov. 8, 1935, in *ACCO Press,* Dec., 1935, box 17, Clayton-Truman; Clayton to Wallace, Oct. 24, 1934, box 4, to Richard C. Patterson, Jan. 21, 1939, box 7, Clayton-Rice; George B. Tindall, *The Emergence of the New South, 1913–1945* (Baton Rouge, La., 1967), 400–402; Luttrell, *Farm Welfare,* 35–36; Lamar Fleming to W. W. Waymack, Oct. 13, 1937, box 18, Waymack Papers; Alexander Sachs to Economics Group, "Note on Effect of Defeatist AAA Policy on Cotton and Other Crops," April 3, 1935, box 92, Sachs Papers; Dobney, *Clayton,* 5.

39. Dobney, *Clayton,* 6–7; Clayton, "A Speech on World Trade," Washington, D.C., May 5, 1938, box 6, Clayton to Leon O. Wolcott, Oct. 26, 1939, box 7, Clayton-Rice; Clayton to Walter Parker, Oct. 17, 1934, box 6, Clayton address to the Cotton Research Congress, June 27, 1940, reprinted in *ACCO Press,* July 1940, box 10, Clayton-Truman.

40. Jim F. Couch and William Shugart II, *The Political Economy of the New Deal*

(Northampton, Mass., 1998), 37–38, and chap. 2; Paul K. Conkin, *The New Deal*, 2d ed. (Arlington Heights, Ill., 1975), 37–38; Gilbert Fite, *American Farmers: The New Minority* (Bloomington, Ind., 1984), 61–62.

41. Benedict, *U.S. Farm Policies*, 314–15; Clarke, *Farm Productivity*, 162–200; John Leonard Fulmer, *Agricultural Progress in the Cotton Belt since 1920* (Chapel Hill, N.C., 1950), table 15, "Trend in Labor Requirements of Three Major Staple Crops in the United States," 61, and table 18, "Trend in Number and in Ratio to All Farms of Sharecroppers . . . ," 74, also 75–81; Wright, *Old South, New South*, 248–49.

42. Jack Temple Kirby, *Rural Worlds Lost: The American South, 1920–1960* (Baton Rouge, La., 1987), 60; Richard Lewontin, "Genes in the Land!" *New York Review of Books*, June 21, 2001, 84; Robert D. Plotnick, Eugene Smolenski, Eirick Evenhouse, and Siobhan Reilly, "The Twentieth Century Record of Inequality and Poverty in the United States," in Engerman and Gallman, *Cambridge Economic History of the United States* 3:261–53.

9 | RELIEF, PUBLIC WORKS, AND SOCIAL INSURANCE

1. John Joseph Wallis and Walter E. Oates, "The Impact of the New Deal on American Federalism," in *The Defining Moment*, ed. Michael E. Bordo, Claudia Goldin, and Eugene N. White (Chicago, 1998), 155–79.

2. William R. Brock, *Welfare, Democracy, and the New Deal* (Cambridge, 1988), 162–69, 177, 199–200; J. Joseph Huthmacher, *Senator Robert F. Wagner and the Rise of Urban Liberalism* (New York, 1968), 110, 127–28, 143–44; George McJimsey, *Harry Hopkins* (Cambridge, Mass., 1987), 51–53; Moley, *First New Deal*, 264–70; Chandler, *America's Greatest Depression*, 192.

3. Chandler, *America's Greatest Depression*, 199–201; Harry Hopkins to the president, Nov. 8, 1934, and executive order, box 95, Hopkins Papers; Brock, *Welfare and the New Deal*, 204; Bonnie Fox Schwartz, *The Civil Works Administration, 1933–1934: The Business of Emergency Employment in the New Deal* (Princeton, N.J., 1984), viii–ix, 3, 26–28, 30–33, 36–38, 43–63, 69, 71, 181–212; McJimsey, *Hopkins*, 55–59.

4. McJimsey, *Hopkins*, 62; Harry Hopkins, "Draft of Message to Congress," n.d., box 95, Hopkins Papers; Lester G. Seligman and Elmer E. Cornwell Jr., eds., *New Deal Mosaic: Roosevelt Confers with His National Emergency Council, 1933–1936* (Eugene, Oreg., 1965), meeting no. 3, Jan. 23, 1934, 76.

5. Seligman and Cornwell, *New Deal Mosaic*, 27–29, 38–39, 111; McJimsey, *Hopkins*, 59–60; annual budget message, Jan. 3, 1934, Rosenman, *PPA* 4:21; Chandler, *America's Greatest Depression*, 199 (table), 200; "Reports of the Committee on Economic Security, Corrington Gill, Unemployment Relief," box 69, Witte Papers; Schwartz, *Civil Works Administration*, ix, 195–96, 214–17.

6. Schwartz, *Civil Works Administration*, 252; annual message to Congress, Jan. 4, 1935, Rosenman *PPA* 4:19–20; Chandler, *America's Greatest Depression*, 207; FERA report, Nov. 1934; Brock, *Welfare and the New Deal*, 280; President's Economic Security Program, box 65, Witte Papers.

7. Brock, *Welfare and the New Deal*, 271; Rosenman, *PPA* 4:19–23, 163–68; Schlesinger, *Politics of Upheaval*, 268; Robert H. Bremner, *From the Depths: The Discovery of Poverty in the United States* (New York, 1956), 263.

8. David A. Rochefort, *American Social Welfare Policy: Dynamics of Formulation and Change* (Boulder, Colo., 1986), 1–10; Harold Wilensky and Charles Lebeaux, *Industrial Society and Social Welfare* (New York, 1965), 14–15, 47, 62–63, 77–79; Raymond Richards,

Closing the Door to Destitution: The Shaping of the Social Security Acts of the United States and New Zealand (University Park, Pa., 1994), viii, 64–65.

9. Richards, Closing the Door to Destitution, vii–xxiii; Jill Quadagno, The Transformation of Old Age Security: Class and Politics in the American Welfare State (Chicago, 1988), 3–19, 180, 185; Introduction and Ann Shola Orloff, "The Political Origins of America's Belated Welfare State," 37–80, in The Politics of Social Policy in the United States, ed. Margaret Weir, Orloff, and Theda Skocpol (Princeton, N.J., 1988); Skocpol, Protecting Soldiers and Mothers: The Political Origins of Social Policy in the United States (Cambridge, Mass., 1992), 24–29.

10. Gordon, New Deals, 4, 13–14, 240–79; Murray W. Latimer, Industrial Pension Plans (New York, 1932–33); Paul H. Douglas, Social Security in the United States (New York, 1936), 88, 247–78; Richards, Closing the Door to Destitution, 43–44; U.S. Dept. of Labor, Unemployment Series, "Unemployment Benefit Plans in the United States and Unemployment Insurance in Foreign Countries," July 1931, 1–13, 276–95; F. R. Lyon to R. C. Hill, Feb. 25, 1933, box 35, f. 304, Office of the Messrs. Rockefeller: Business Interests, RG 2, Rockefeller Archive Center.

11. Martin, Frances Perkins, 3–4, 7–8, 37–38, 91–121, 171–241, 495–96; Frances Perkins, The Roosevelt I Knew (New York, 1946), 10, 13–14, 17–18, 24–25, 54–57, 100–103, 107; Bernard Bellush, Franklin D. Roosevelt as Governor of New York (New York, 1955), 126–32, 182–90. On AFL opposition to the Perkins appointment, Matthew Woll to Owen D. Young, Nov. 9, 1932, Jan. 18, 1933, 87.2.27, no. 109B, Young Papers.

12. Frances Perkins, "Unemployment Insurance: An American Plan to Protect Workers and Avoid the Dole," Survey, Nov. 1931, 117–19, 173; U.S. Dept. of Labor, Unemployment Series, "Unemployment Benefit Plans," 1–13, 276–95.

13. Irving Bernstein, A Caring Society: The New Deal, the Worker, and the Great Depression (Boston, 1985), 44–51; Perkins, Roosevelt I Knew, 5; Edward D. Berkowitz, America's Welfare State from Roosevelt to Reagan (Baltimore, 1991), 15–16, 29; Rosenman, PPA 3:287–92, 321–22; Edwin E. Witte, The Development of the Social Security Act (Madison, Wis., 1963), 8–9, 29–30, 38, 201–2.

14. Charles McKinley and Robert W. Frase, Launching Social Security: A Capture-and-Record Account (Madison, Wis., 1970), 9–10; Bernstein, A Caring Society, 52; John Ikenberry and Theda Skocpol, "Expanding Social Benefits: The Role of Social Security," Political Science Quarterly 102 (Fall 1987): 406; House Committee on Ways and Means, Economic Security Act: Hearings on H.R. 4120, 74th Cong., 1st sess., Appendix, List of Committees Advisory to the Committee on Economic Security, 60–61; J. Douglas Brown, An American Philosophy of Social Security: Evolution and Issues (Princeton, N.J., 1972), 21–22; "Labor Chiefs Swing to Work Insurance," New York Times, July 23, 1932, and William Green to William M. Leiserson, Oct. 17, 1932, box 2, Leiserson Papers. Others in the advisory group included the AFL's William Green, professionals, and representatives of the public, among them Paul U. Kellogg, editor of the survey, and Grace Abbott, University of Chicago, former chief of the federal Children's Bureau.

15. Rockefeller address, "Representation in Industry," Dec. 5, 1918, War Emergency and Reconstruction Congress, Chamber of Commerce, box 20, f. 169, Office of the Messrs. Rockefeller: Economic Interests, C. J. Hicks to Walter C. Teagle, and Teagle to John D. Rockefeller Jr., Oct. 15, 1928, box 133, f. 991, Office of the Messrs. Rockefeller: Business Interests, RG 2, Rockefeller Archive Center; Howard M. Gitelman, Legacy of the Ludlow Massacre: A Chapter in American Industrial Relations (Philadelphia, 1988).

16. Mr. Jones to Mr. Fosdick, memorandum, July 6, 1921, Subject: Industrial Relations Research, box 6, f. 45, Mark M. Jones Papers, Rockefeller Archive Center. For the inception, activities, and funding of Industrial Relations Counselors, Inc., see Raymond B. Fosdick to John D. Rockefeller Jr., April 27, 1933, box 12, f. 87, and on its reputation for expertise, see Isador Lubin, Commissioner of Labor Statistics, to E. K. Wickman, The Commonwealth Fund, May 5, 1934, in folder: Retainer Clients, 1934–35, box 16, Office of the Messrs. Rockefeller: Economic Interests, RG 2, ibid.

17. For the spirited academic debate on the issue of welfare capitalist domination of the process and the sources that shaped my conclusions, see Quadagno, *Welfare, Class, and Politics,* 90, 97, 116; Gitelman, *Ludlow Massacre,* xi–xii, 28–29, 50, 145, 156, 177, 331–33; Edwin Amenta and Sunita Parikh, "Capitalists Did Not Want the Social Security Act: A Critique of the 'Capitalist Dominance' Thesis," *American Sociological Review* 56 (Feb. 1991): 124–29; *New York Times,* Nov. 11, 1934; Stuart D. Brandes, *American Welfare Capitalism, 1880–1940* (Chicago, 1984), 81, 123–26, 130, 141–47; Bryce M. Stewart, *Planning and Administration of Unemployment Compensation in the United States* (New York, 1938), 604; Theda Skocpol and Edwin Amenta, "Did Capitalists Shape Social Security," and Jill Quadagno, "Two Models of Welfare State Development: Reply to Skocpol and Amenta," *American Sociological Review* 50 (Aug. 1985): 572–78; Magnus W. Alexander, president, National Industrial Conference Board, *Unemployment Benefits and Insurance* (New York, 1931), vi–vii, 123–24; Anthony J. Badger, *The New Deal: The Depression Years, 1933–1940* (New York, 1989), 230; J. Craig Jenkins and Barbara G. Brents, "Social Protest, Hegemonic Competition, and Social Reform: A Political Struggle Interpretation of the Origins of the Welfare State," *American Sociological Review* 54 (Dec. 1989): 898; Arthur J. Altmeyer, *The Formative Years of Social Security* (Madison, Wis., 1968), 8, 11–13; Brown, *Philosophy of Social Security,* 3–21; Abraham Epstein, *Insecurity: A Challenge to America* (New York, 1936), 676, 698; G. J. Anderson to Mr. Fosdick, May 9, 1923, box 13, f. 104, Office of the Messrs. Rockefeller: Economic Interests, RG 2, Industrial Relations Counselors, Inc., n.d., and John D. Rockefeller Jr. to John A. Brown, Nov. 13, 1934, box 16, f. 127, Rockefeller Archives Center; for opposition to unemployment insurance by Wisconsin manufacturers, see Merrill G. Murray, Wisconsin Committee for Unemployment Reserve Legislation, to John R. Commons, and letter attached, Nov. 20, 1931, box 11, Commons Papers; Edwin E. Witte to John R. Commons, Oct. 27, 1933, box 1, to Walter Slack, Young Radiator Company, Racine, April 5, 1935, box 33, to Wilbur J. Cohen, Nov. 15, 1935, box 2, Witte Papers; for the NAM position on unemployment insurance, see *New York Times,* Dec. 7, 1934; on the incapacity of business to pass on payroll taxes to consumers in depression, see U.S. Senate Committee on Finance, *Economic Security Act: Hearings on S. 1130,* 74th Cong., 1st sess., testimony of William M. Leiserson, 278–79, and Alvin Hansen's testimony that such ability varied from industry to industry, depending on conditions of supply and demand, 447ff.; on the United States Chamber of Commerce reversal, see *New York Times,* May 3, 1935.

18. Thomas H. Eliot, *Reflections of the New Deal* (Boston, 1992), 75–89; Patrick D. Reagan, *Designing a New America: The Origins of New Deal Planning, 1890–1943* (Amherst, Mass., 1999).

19. Charles R. Hook to Raymond Moley, Sept. 8, 1934, box 23, Moley Papers; Roy Lubove, *The Struggle for Social Security, 1900–1935* (Cambridge, Mass., 1968), 171–74; Schlesinger, *Coming of the New Deal,* 302; Douglas, *Social Security,* 16–17; Horace S. Keifer to William M. Leiserson, Feb. 11, 1931, box 20, Abraham Epstein to Leiserson, Sept.

4, 16, 1933, Leiserson to Epstein, Sept. 6, 25, 1933, box 2, Isaac M. Rubinow to Leiserson, Dec. 2, 1932, Leiserson to Wilbur M. Morse, Jan. 24, 1934, box 35, Leiserson Papers.

20. Felix Frankfurter to Raymond Moley, July 25, 1934, box 17, Moley Papers; Joseph P. Harris, "The Social Security Program in the United States," *American Political Science Review* 30 (June 1936): 463; Edwin E. Witte to William Green, Oct. 19, 1932, to Joseph P. Chamberlain, Oct. 24, 1932, box 1, "Views of Justice Brandeis on an Economic Security Program," interview, Aug. 19, 1934, and Witte to James S. Thomson, March 30, 1936, box 2, to Harry A. Millis, Oct. 26, 1938, box 4, to Wilbur J. Cohen, Aug. 29, 1940, to John D. Black, Sept. 7, 1940, box 6, Witte, address, twenty-eighth annual meeting, American Association for Labor Legislation, in joint session with the American Statistical Association, Chicago, Dec. 27, 1934, published in *American Labor Legislation Review* 25 (March 1935): 1, box 257, Witte Papers.

21. Douglas, *Social Security*, 113, 176–78.

22. Minutes, Conference on Economic Security, minutes of meetings, Technical Board on Economic Security, Sept. 24, 1934, Bryce Stewart, "Proposal for a Federal Subsidy Plan of Unemployment Insurance," minutes of meetings of the Technical Board, Oct. 30, 1934, minutes of the meetings of the Committee on Economic Security, Nov. 9, 1934, "Report of the Advisory Council to the Committee on Economic Security," Dec. 18, 1934, Thomas Kennedy, testimony, Nov. 14, 1935, box 65, first tentative draft, "Report of the Committee on Economic Security," Dec. 1934, box 201, Joseph Harris, "Statement concerning the Report of the Committee on Social Legislation of the Business and Advisory Council for the Department of Commerce," April 10, 1935, box 216, Witte to Wilbur J. Cohen, Sept. 7, 1940, to A. V. Miller, Dec. 9, 1940, box 6, Witte on "Experience Rating" and pooled funds in address, May 13, 1941, box 258, on the AFL position, "Economic Security for Workers," *American Federationist*, March 1935, 254–60, and Witte's notes, box 216, on the business position, "Report of Committee on Social Legislation (Robert G. Elbert, Morris E. Leeds, Walter C. Teagle, and Gerard Swope, chairman), Business Advisory Council for the Department of Commerce," April 10, 1935, box 212, Witte Papers; Witte, *Social Security Act*, 29, 56–59, 62–73, 112–18, 121–24; Harris, *Social Security*, 464; Berkowitz, *America's Welfare State*, 28–37; Bernstein, *A Caring Society*, 53–56; Lubove, *Social Security*, 173–74; Douglas, *Social Security*, 32, 44–54, 92, 95–96; Eliot, *New Deal Recollections*, 98, 100, 111; Committee on Economic Security, *Social Security in America* (Washington, D.C., 1937), 96 and table 22; Epstein, *Insecurity*, 701–2, 711–14; Tugwell Diary, Dec. 31, 1934, 171–72, box 16. For Roosevelt's insistence on a cooperative federal-state undertaking, see Arthur J. Altmeyer to Arthur Schlesinger Jr., March 31, 1958, box 1, Altmeyer Papers, and in "Altmeyer Reminiscences: Social Security Project," 26, CUOH.

23. Mr. Haas to Secretary Morgenthau, "Report of the Committee on Economic Security," Jan. 5, 1935, bk. 3, 37–47, Morgenthau Diary; Aubrey Williams, "Suggestions for Message to Congress," Dec. 14, 1934, box 13, and [Hopkins notes at Georgia Warm Springs Foundation], n.d., box 50, Hopkins Papers; Witte to M. Albert Linton, Nov. 15, 1935, box 2, to Arthur J. Altmeyer, Dec. 17, 1936, box 33, Witte Papers; [A. A. Berle Jr.], "Memorandum on Certain Phases of National Policy, 1934–1935," box 99, PSF.

24. Carl Shoup, Roy Blough, and Mabel Newcomer, *Facing the Tax Problem: A Survey of Taxation in the United States and a Program for the Future* (New York, 1937), 451–60, 495–500; Witte, *Social Security Act*, 18, 74, 146–54, 173–89; Douglas, *Social Security*, 11, 56–62, 88, 97–99; Berkowitz, *America's Welfare State*, 16–27, 40–49; Schlesinger,

Coming of the New Deal, 306–10; Perkins, *Roosevelt I Knew,* 293–94; Richards, *Closing the Door to Destitution,* 9, 26–27; Committee on Economic Security, *Social Insurance in America,* 224; U.S. House, *Report of the Committee on Economic Security: Message of the President Recommending Legislation on Economic Security,* 74th Cong., 1st sess., Jan. 17, 1935, H. Doc. 81, 25; Henry J. Aaron, *Economic Effects of Social Security* (Washington, D.C., 1982), 3–8; Eliot, *New Deal Reflections,* 101–4; Mark Leff, "Taxing the 'Forgotten Man': The Politics of Social Security in the New Deal," *Journal of American History* 70:3 (Sept. 1983): 359, 366–80; Witte, "Suggestions for a Long-Time and Immediate Program for Economic Security," n.d. [1934], box 48, Hopkins Papers; "Security for Children," Dec. 1, 1934, minutes of the meetings of the Technical Board on Economic Security, the Executive and Old Age Committees, Nov. 12, 22, 1934, Witte, "The Economic Security Act," box 65, Witte to J. Douglas Brown, March 18, 28, 1936, box 2, to Edith Abbott, Oct. 18, 1939, box 5, to Wilbur J. Cohen, Sept. 7, 1940, to Leon O. Wolcott, Jan. 8, 1941, box 6, to George B. Robinson, Dec. 6, 1948, to Carl T. Curtis, Dec. 16, 1953, to Carl T. Schletterbeck, Jan. 8, 1954, box 35, *Report to the President of the Committee on Economic Security* (Washington, D.C., 1935), 30, box 165, table, "Progress of Reserve under Proposed Old Age Insurance Plan, Old Age Security Volume, Reports of the Committee on Economic Security, and Old Age Security Staff Report to Mr. Witte," and table, "Comparison of Income and Outgo under Combined Old Age Pension Plan and Contributory Old Age Annuity, in Comments of the Actuarial Committee on the Recommendations for Old Age Security," box 68, Edwin E. Witte, "The Social Security Act and Sales Taxes, and Statement of the Secretary of the Treasury on the Economic Security Bill, Presented to the House Ways and Means Committee, February, 1935," box 216, Witte Papers; U.S. House Committee on Ways and Means, *Hearings,* 74th Cong., 1st sess., statement of Hon. Frances Perkins, 11; Altmeyer, *Social Security,* 16; U.S. Department of Commerce, Office of Business Economics, "National Income and Product Accounts of the United States, 1929–1965" (1966), 52; McJimsey, *Hopkins,* 77–78; Henry Morgenthau Jr. to FDR, Sept. 4, 1935, PSF 99.

25. Witte, *Social Security Act,* 143–45; Martha H. Swain, *Pat Harrison: The New Deal Years* (Jackson, Miss., 1978), 88–89; Altmeyer, *Social Security,* 34; Douglas, *Social Security,* 100; Richards, *Closing the Door to Destitution,* 23–25; Beth Stevens, "Blurring the Boundaries: How the Federal Government Has Influenced Welfare Benefits in the Private Sector," in Weir, Orloff, and Skocpol, *Politics of Social Policy,* 129; Eliot, *New Deal Recollections,* 111–12; Badger, *New Deal,* 234.

26. Lubove, *Social Security,* 137–43, 175–79; Epstein, *Insecurity,* 723–25, 761–71; Epstein testimony, U.S. Senate Committee on Finance, *Economic Security Act: Hearings on S. 1130,* 74th Cong., 1st sess., Jan. 22–Feb. 20, 1935, 458–70, 512–14, "Statement of Abraham Epstein, Expressed at a Meeting of the Social Security Advisory Council," Dec. 10, 1937, "Views of Abe Epstein on the Amendments to the Old Age Insurance Law, Presented to the Interim Committee of Social Security Advisory Council, at New York, Nov. 4, 1938," box 4, "Views of Miss Edith Abbott . . . on a Feasible Program for Economic Security," Aug. 25, 1934, box 216, Witte, "Notes on the Concept of Social Insurance," Dec. 11, 1937, box 4, Witte Papers; Witte, "What to Expect of Social Security," *American Economic Review, Supplement* (March 1944): 212–15; Epstein, "Social Security—Fiction or Fact?" *American Mercury,* Oct. 1934; "Our Social Insecurity Act," *Harper's Monthly,* Dec. 1935; "Away from Social Insecurity," *New Republic,* Jan. 4, 1939. On Senator Vandenberg's opposition to a full reserve system, see "Affirmative Republican Position Taken in the

75th Congress, Social Security, Republican National Committee, Political Parties," 66, box 786, Taft Papers.

27. Bernstein, *A Caring Society,* 183–85; Berkowitz, *America's Welfare State,* 44–48; J. S. Parker, *Social Security Reserves* (Washington, D.C., 1942), 54–57, 261–84; "Amendments Discussed at Meeting at Chicago, Dec. 29, 1936, Prepared for Dr. Altmeyer by His Staff, . . . To Provide for the Beginning of Benefit Payments in 1938, and to Make Other Changes," draft, Dec. 11, 1936, and Witte to Arthur J. Altmeyer, Nov. 21, Dec. 7, 1936, box 33, Witte to Wilbur J. Cohen, March 27, 1938, box 2, to Richard [Reinhard] A. Hohaus, June 30, 1938, box 4, to Theresa S. McMahon, Oct. 7, 1937, to William R. Williamson, Jan. 20, 1938, to Arthur J. Altmeyer, March 16, 1938, box 34, to James S. Parker, Sept. 4, 1940, box 6, Witte, "Suggestion for a Tentative Summation of the Present Thinking of the Members of the Social Security Advisory Council on the Financing of Old Age Insurance; Position of the Members . . . in Favor of Reduction of the Title VIII Tax Rates; Position of the Members Who Oppose . . . Any Declaration in Favor of Reducing the Title VIII Tax Rates, Prepared August 1938," box 216, Reinhard A. Hohaus, "Democracy and Security," presidential address, American Institute of Actuaries, Nov. 2–3, 1939 and Albert M. Linton, "Security through Individual Enterprise; The Proper Role of Social Insurance," *Annalist* 54:1406, (Dec. 28, 1939): 825–26, 855, box 202, George B. Robinson to Witte, Feb. 8, 1948, box 35, Witte Papers; *New York Times,* May 5, Aug. 8, 1937; Shoup, Blough, and Newcomer, *Facing the Tax Problem,* 407, 451–60, 496–500; J. Douglas Brown, "Current Social Insurance Problems," *American Labor Legislation Review* 27:1 (March 1938): 7; Brown, in Sumner Slichter, chairman, "The Economic Aspects of an Integrated Social Security Program," *American Economic Association, Proceedings* (1935), 123; Brown to Witte, March 24, 1936, box 2, Witte Papers.

28. Edwin E. Witte, "In Defense of the Federal Old Age Benefit Plan," *American Labor Legislation Review,* Jan. 1937, 27–32; Witte to J. Douglas Brown, Jan. 10, 1938, to William R. Williamson, Jan. 7, Feb. 4, 1938, box 34, to John J. Corson, June 4, 1938, box 4, Witte, "Thoughts Relating to the Old-Age Insurance Titles of the Social Security Act and Proposed Changes Therein, Presented to the Social Security Advisory Council," Feb. 18, 19, 1938, box 57, Witte Papers; Witte, "Social Security—1940 Model," *American Labor Legislation Review,* Sept. 1939, 101–9.

29. Marriner S. Eccles, "How Are We to Put Idle Men, Money, and Machines to Work?" address before the ninth special meeting of the Harvard Business School Alumni, Boston, June 16, 1939, in *Economic Balance and A Balanced Budget: Public Papers of Marriner S. Eccles,* ed. Rudolph L. Weissman (New York, 1973), 268–69.

30. Witte to Wilbur J. Cohen, March 30, 1939, to Theresa McMahon, March 31, 1939, box 5, to George Robinson, March 23, 1949, box 35, Witte Papers; Berkowitz, *America's Welfare State,* 191.

10 | THE NEW ECONOMICS

1. Alvin H. Hansen, *Fiscal Policy and Business Cycles* (New York, 1941), 47; Laughlin Currie memorandum, April 19, 1939, box 73, Eccles Papers.

2. When asked by John M. Carmody, acquainted with Herbert Hoover through membership in the Society of Industrial Engineers, what he might have done otherwise in dealing with the depression crisis, the ex-president replied, unhesitatingly, "Repudiate all debts." Reminiscence by John M. Carmody, Aug. 1, 1958, box 57, Carmody Papers.

3. Marriner S. Eccles, "Depression: Its Causes, Effects, and Suggested Remedies,"

Utah State Bankers Convention, June 17, 1932, and clipping, Ogden *Standard-Examiner,* June 19, 1932, box 76, "Paper Prepared by Mr. M. S. Eccles," Ogden, Utah, Feb. 24, 1933, box 63, Eccles Papers; Schlesinger, *Politics of Upheaval,* 237–39.

4. Eccles, "Reconstructing Economic Thinking," address before the Utah Education Association, Salt Lake, Oct. 27, 1933, box 76, Eccles Papers; Marriner S. Eccles, *Beckoning Frontiers* (New York, 1951), 118–30.

5. Eccles, *Beckoning Frontiers,* 132–33, 142–61, 183–84.

6. Ibid., 165–74; memo given to the president, Nov. 3, 1934, "Desirable Changes in the Administration of the Federal Reserve System," box 4, Eccles Papers; Sydney Hyman, *Marriner S. Eccles: Private Entrepreneur and Public Servant* (Stanford, Calif., 1976), 154–60; Roger J. Sandilands, *The Life and Political Economy of Laughlin Currie* (Durham, N.C., 1990), 62–64.

7. Friedman and Schwartz, *Monetary History of the United States,* 445–59; Sandilands, *Currie,* 66–67; Hyman, *Eccles,* 186–87.

8. Laughlin Currie, "The Failure of Monetary Policy to Prevent the Depression of 1929–32," *Journal of Political Economy* 43:2 (April 1934), copy in box 6, Means Papers.

9. J. Raymond Walsh, Laughlin Curry, John B. Crane, John M. Cassels, Robert K. Lamb, and Alan R. Sweezy to the president, Jan. 25, 1934, OF 229; Alan Sweezy, "The Keynesians and Government Policy, 1933–1939," papers and proceedings of the 84th annual meeting of the American Economic Association, *American Economic Review* 62:2 (May 1972): 117–18; J. Bradford De Long, "Fiscal Policy in the Shadow of the Great Depression," in *The Defining Moment: The Great Depression and the American Economy in the Twentieth Century,* ed. Michael D. Bordo, Claudia Goldin, and Eugene N. White (Chicago, 1998), 67–69, 80.

10. Laughlin Currie, "Comments on Pump Priming," Nov. 30, 1934, and "A Suggested Works Program," March 6, 1935, box 72, Eccles Papers.

11. J. Ronnie Davis, *The New Economics and the Old Economists* (Ames, Iowa, 1971), and Davis, "Chicago Economists, Deficit Budgets, and the Early 1930s," *American Economic Review* 58 (June 1968): 476–82; Laughlin Currie and Martin Krost, "Federal Income-Increasing Expenditures, 1932–1935," May 1935, box 72, Eccles Papers. Dates assigned this memorandum and the other Currie memoranda cited are based on handwritten notes entered in the Eccles Papers, box 72, likely by Currie.

12. Byrd L. Jones, "Laughlin Currie, Pump Priming, and New Deal Fiscal Policy, 1934–1936," *History of Political Economy* 10 (Winter 1978): 521; Sandilands, *Currie,* 77; Collins, *Business Response to Keynes,* 39–43.

13. Currie, "Comments and Observations," *History of Political Economy* 10 (Winter 1978): 542–44.

14. Friedman and Schwartz, *Monetary History of the United States,* 520–26; Meltzer, *Federal Reserve,* 518; Currie, "The Present Status and Problems of the Recovery Movement," Dec. 22, 1936, box 72, Eccles Papers.

15. Currie to Eccles, "Fiscal Program," Feb. 17, 1936, and "The Proposed Tax on Undistributed Earnings," May 15, 1936, box 72, Eccles Papers; W. Elliot Brownlee, *Federal Taxation in America: A Short History* (Cambridge, 1996), 78; Swain, *Pat Harrison,* 117–21.

16. Currie to Eccles, "A Tentative Program to Halt the Business Recession," Oct. 13, 1937, and Currie, "The Current Situation," Oct. 26, 1937, box 73, Eccles Papers.

17. Leon Henderson to Harry Hopkins, Oct. 12, 1937, box 54, Hopkins Papers; Leon

Henderson, "Summary Statement, Boom and Bust," March 29, 1937, PSF 155; Sandilands, *Currie*, 91–92.

18. Currie, "Causes of the Recession," April 1, 1938, box 73, Eccles Papers.

19. Sandilands, *Currie*, 88; Friedman and Schwartz, *Monetary History of the United States*, 526–27, 543–45; Meltzer, *Federal Reserve* 1:271–74, 415–18, Currie to Morrill, "Would a Further Expansion of Money Be Injurious?" Jan. 26, 1937, Currie, "An Appraisal of Current Prospects and a Tentative Program," May 18, 1937, and statement for the president, not used, May 24, 1937, box 72, Eccles Papers.

20. Currie, "The Transition Problems in Compensatory Fiscal Policy," Oct. 29, 1938, "Memorandum on the Question: 'The Claim Is Made That Private Industry by Itself Cannot Profitably Absorb Current Savings,'" April 19, 1939, "Notes on Fiscal Policy," April 26, 1939, "Some Potentialities in the Field of Public Investment," April 26, 1939, "Some Possibilities for the Expansion of Private Investment," April 27, 1939, box 72, Eccles Papers; Currie, "Industrial, Railroad, and Electric Utility Plant, Equipment, and Maintenance Expenditure," Jan. 24, 1938, box 274, Sachs Papers.

21. Laughlin Currie, "Statement Submitted to the Temporary National Economic Committee," May 16, 1939, and table, "Shift since 1929 toward Taxes with Regressive Effects on Cconsumption," April 26, 1939, box 73, Eccles Papers; and Currie's testimony, U.S. Cong., Senate, Temporary National Economic Committee, Investigation of Concentration of Economic Power, Hearings, 76th Cong., 1st sess., pts. 7–9, March–May 1939, 3520–38.

22. Sandilands, *Currie*, 92–103; Currie, "Discussion: The Keynesian Revolution and Its Pioneers, the Keynesians, and Government Policy, 1933–1939," papers and proceedings, American Economic Association, *American Economic Review* 62 (May 1972): 141. Albert Lepawsky, "The Planning Apparatus: A Vignette of the New Deal," *Journal of the American Institute of Planners* 42:1 (Jan. 1976): 17, numbered the group at some five hundred in 1939.

23. Perry G. Mehrling, *The Money Interest and the Public Interest* (Cambridge, Mass., 1997), 81–134; Robert Skidelsky, *John Maynard Keynes: The Economist as Savior, 1920–1937* (New York, 1995), 632; Currie, "Paper for Symposium on Keynes's Doctrines," April 29, 1937, box 25, Warburg Papers; William J. Barber, *Designs within Disorder: Franklin D. Roosevelt and the Shaping of American Economic Policy, 1933–1945* (Cambridge, 1996), 124.

24. Barber, *Designs within Disorder*, 128–29; Mehrling, *Money Interest*, 120–25; U.S. Cong., Senate, TNEC, Hearings, 76th Cong., 1st sess., March–May 1939, pts. 7–9, 3493–3518, 3538–59, 3837–59; "Statement of Testimony of Dr. Alvin H. Hansen . . . before the Temporary National Economic Committee at the Hearings on Savings and Investment, May 16, 1939," box 809, Taft Papers. The terms originate with Barber and Sandilands.

25. *Historical Statistics of the United States*, ser. F 67–86, "Gross National Product by Type of Product in Current Prices," 142, ser. F 22–33, "National Income by Industrial Origin," 140, and ser. F 87–103, "Gross National Product by Major Type of Product, in 1954 Prices," 143; Paul Krugman, "Once and Again," *New York Times*, Jan. 2, 2000; Mark Mazower, *Dark Continent: Europe's Twentieth Century* (New York, 1999).

26. Sachs, "Point-Counterpoint Summary of the Stagnation Hypothesis," New School, March 24, 1939, box 52, Sachs, "Comments from a Liberal Standpoint on the Eccles-Byrd Controversy and Historic Refutation of Eccles's Theory about Budget Defi-

cits and Public Debt," Jan. 27, 1938, box 80, Sachs to Frances Perkins, May 18, 1939, box 56, Sachs to Elliott Thurston, June 5, 1939, box 81, Sachs to Benjamin Graham, March 26, 1940, box 29, Sachs Papers; Mehrling, *Money Interest*, 118–19.

27. Sachs to Moley, March 28, 1935, and "Summary of Main Conclusions as to the Economic Misplanning of the Proposed Utility Legislation," March 1935, box 110, Moley Papers.

28. Sachs to Lawrence Seltzer, March 13, 23, 1937, Seltzer to Sachs, March 25, 1937, box 70, Sachs to Elliott Thurston, March 23, 1937, box 81, to Raymond Leslie Buell, Dec. 27, 1937, box 11, Sachs Papers.

29. Sachs to Maurice Hutton and Thomas Balogh, July 8, 1937, box 48, to O. T. Falk, Aug. 17, 1937, to Thomas Balogh, Jan. 7, 1938, box 23, to Raymond L. Buell, Dec. 27, 1937, box 11, to Dorothy Thompson, Jan. 3, 1938, box 80, to Shelby Cullom Davis, Jan. 27, 1938, box 19, ibid.; FDR to Morgenthau, April 29, 1937, OF 1983; Sachs memorandum, "Variable Behavior Patterns of Commodity Prices and Production during and by Stages of Major Recoveries in Business Cycles from Depression to Emergence to Next Ensuing Depression," April 19, 1937, box 313, Morgenthau Papers. Roosevelt's note to Morgenthau suggests, likely in jest, that he "read the enclosed from Alexander Sachs, an outstanding professor from whom you—and even I can learn much." FDR to Missy Le Hand, Feb. 2, 1939, OF 1983: "Having had much experience with Alex Sachs's language, the president is perfectly able to understand it."

30. Sachs, with F. M. Judd, "How Enterprise-Stifling Our Present Taxation Compared with Past and British," unpublished paper, March 1939, box 25, Sachs to Frances Perkins, May 18, 1939, box 56, to Sumner Slichter, Dec. 30, 1941, box 72, Sachs Papers; Sachs, Appendix 1, "Taxation and Capital Formation," The Second Fortune Round Table, *Fortune*, May 1939, 118–23.

31. Sachs to J. M. Keynes, Dec. 24, 1937, Jan. 14, 1938, Keynes to Sachs, Jan. 3, April 30, 1938, box 39, Sachs Papers.

32. J. M. Keynes to Roosevelt, Feb. 1, 1938, PPF 5235; Jan A. Kregel, "Keynesian Stabilisation Policy and Post War Economic Performance," in *Explaining Economic Growth: Essays in Honor of Angus Maddison*, ed. A. Szirmai, B. Van Ark, and Dirk Pilat (Amsterdam, 1993), 434–37.

33. Sachs to Dorothy Thompson, Oct. 27, 31, 1938, box 80, Sachs, "Danger Issues Confronting Willkie," Aug. 21, 1940, box 89, Sachs to Benjamin Graham, March 16, 1940, box 29, "Notes on Fundamental Schisms in Internal-External Government, R. L. Buell with A. S.'s Comments," July 1941, box 11, Sachs Papers. Sachs, as did much of the internationalist cohort, joined numerous groups that urged aid to France and Britain, including the Committee to Defend America by Aiding the Allies. Membership in such groups shows continuity from the Economic Policy Committee and the National Policy Committee. On this, see telegram, Lewis W. Douglas to Sachs, Nov. 28, 1940, box 20, and Sachs to Clark Eichelberger, May 22, 1940, box 15, f. Citizens for Victory, ibid.

34. Hansen, "The Importance of Anti-Depression Policy in the Establishment and Preservation of Sound International Relations," HUG (B)-H145.72, Hansen to Geofrey Crowther, Aug. 1, 1941, Crowther to Hansen, Nov. 14, 1941, HUG (FP)-3.10, box 1, Hansen to Henry A. Wallace, May 6, 1941, HUG (FP)-3.10, box 2, Alvin Hansen and C. P. Kindleberger, "Anglo-American Pitfalls: Foreign Trade," Nov. 18, 1941, HUG (FP)-3.16, box 2, Hansen Papers.

11 | THE NATIONAL RESOURCES PLANNING BOARD

1. Rexford G. Tugwell, "The Fourth Power," *Planning and Civic Comment,* April–June, 1939, pt. 2, 1–31; Michael V. Namorato, *Rexford Tugwell: A Biography* (New York, 1988), 134–38; Tugwell to Joseph Dorfman, Jan. 24, 1946, box 3, to Alfred E. Emerson, Dec. 4, 1946, box 4, to William F. Ogburn, Oct. 22, 1941, box 9, Tugwell, "A Third Economy," address before the Rochester, N.Y., Teachers' Association, April 9, 1935, box 38, Tugwell Papers.

2. Thomas C. Blaisdell to Tugwell, Oct. 12, 1939, box 16, Tugwell Papers.

3. Schlesinger, *Coming of the New Deal,* 350–51; Philip W. Warken, "National Resources Planning Board," in *Franklin D. Roosevelt: His Life and Times, an Encyclopedic View,* ed. Otis L. Graham Jr. and Meghan R. Wander (Boston, 1985), 277–78; Warken, *A History of the National Resources Planning Board, 1933–1943* (New York, 1979), Introduction; Marion Clawson, *New Deal Planning: The National Resources Planning Board* (Baltimore, 1981), 40–43; Brinkley, *End of Reform,* 246. Mitchell resigned at the close of 1935.

4. Barry D. Karl, *Charles E. Merriam and the Study of Politics* (Chicago, 1974), ix, 1–210; Raymond Moley, "The State Movement for Efficiency and Economy" (Ph.D. diss., Faculty of Political Science, Columbia University, 1918); author's interviews with Moley, HHPL; Moley, *Reality and Illusions: Autobiography* (New York, 1980); Clawson, *New Deal Planning,* 214, 221–22; Warken, *History of the NRPB,* 45–46.

5. C. E. Merriam, "Government and Society," in *Recent Social Trends in the United States: Report of the President's Research Committee on Social Trends* (Westport, Conn., 1970), 2:1521, 1534–35.

6. Karl, *Merriam,* 132–36, 149, 201–29, 265; Clawson, *New Deal Planning,* 40–46, 72, 149–50, and passim; Merriam, "Planning Agencies in America," *American Political Science Review* 29 (April 1935): 202–7, quoted in Brinkley, *End of Reform,* 247; Henry Wallace, Harold Ickes, Frances Perkins, and Harry Hopkins to the president, June 26, 1934, and Delano to the president, June 26, 1934, M. H. McIntyre to Ickes, June 7, 1935, and press release, "Executive Order Creating the National Resource Committee," June 8, 1935, Frederic Delano to FDR, transmitted by Ickes, Nov. 23, 1935, box 1, OF 1092; Peri E. Arnold, *Making the Managerial Presidency: Comprehensive Reorganization Planning, 1905–1986* (Princeton, N.J., 1986), 100; Richard Polenberg, *Reorganizing Roosevelt's Government, 1936-1939* (Cambridge, Mass., 1966), 11–15.

7. Polenberg, *Reorganizing Roosevelt's Government,* 3–9, 31–35; Arnold, *Managerial Presidency,* 3–80; Matthew Dickinson, *Bitter Harvest: FDR, Presidential Power, and the Growth of the Presidential Branch* (Cambridge, 1997), 71–74, 86, 99–100; W. Elliot Brownlee, "The Public Sector," in Engerman and Gallman, *Cambridge Economic History of the United States* 3:1045.

8. Ronald L. Heinemann, *Harry Byrd of Virginia* (Charlottesville, Va., 1996), 15–170; Heinemann, *Depression and New Deal in Virginia: The Enduring Dominion* (Charlottesville, Va., 1983), chap. 7.

9. Ira Katznelson, Kim Geiger, and Daniel Kryder, "Limiting Liberalism: The Southern Veto in Congress, 1933–1950," *Political Science Quarterly* 108:2 (Summer 1993): 283–306; Lee J. Alston and Joseph P. Ferrie, *Southern Paternalism and the American Welfare State* (Cambridge, 1999), 40–46. Gavin Wright, *Old South, New South,* 8 and passim, emphasizes the historic isolation of the southern labor market as basic to the section's

political economy, with elements of the New Deal program undercutting its low-wage structure.

10. Heinemann, *Byrd,* 160–61, 165; Harry F. Byrd to William O. Bailey, July 5, 1933, to Walter E. Harris, July 18, 1934, box 152, to R. T. Barton, July 14, 1934, box 129, Byrd, "Bureaucracy and the Farmer," *Scientific American,* Aug. 1934, box 293, Byrd Papers.

11. Heinemann, *Byrd,* 167–71; Heinemann, *Depression and New Deal in Virginia,* 157–62; Virginia Manufacturers Association press release, n.d., box 293, C. H. Morrissett, State Tax Commissioner, to Byrd, Oct. 10, and Byrd to Morrissett, Oct. 22, 1935, box 144, Byrd to Governor George C. Perry, Oct. 22, 1935, box 146, Byrd Papers; Rexford G. Tugwell to Harry [Hopkins], n.d., and Paul H. Appleby to Tugwell, June 26, 1935, box 40, Tugwell Papers.

12. "Senator Byrd," n.d. [1936], and list of names, box 165, Henry Breckinridge to Byrd, July 21, 1936, Josiah Bailey to Byrd, July 7, 1936, box 129, Byrd Papers; Polenberg, *Reorganizing Roosevelt's Government,* 23.

13. Frederic A. Delano to Maury Maverick, Jan. 8, 1936, Maverick to Roosevelt, Feb. 11, 1936, Roosevelt to Maverick, Feb. 12, 1936, Delano to the Chairman [Ickes], Jan. 31, 1936, FDR memorandum for the Speaker [Byrns] and Senator Robinson, April 20, 1936, Morris L. Cooke to Marvin H. McIntyre, two letters, June 2, 1936, box 1, OF 1092.

14. Collins, *Business Response to Keynes,* 56–69; Clawson, *New Deal Planning,* 73–74; Harry Dexter White to Secretary Morgenthau, April 3, 1939, box 312, Morgenthau Papers; Henry S. Dennison, Lincoln Filene, Ralph E. Flanders, and Morris E. Leeds, *Toward Full Employment* (New York, 1939), 9, 18–26, 215–38, 288–97; Patrick D. Reagan, *Designing a New America: The Origins of New Deal Planning, 1890–1943* (Amherst, Mass., 1999), 166–67, 184–95.

15. Harry H. Woodring, M. L. Wilson, Daniel C. Roper, Frances Perkins, Frederic A. Delano, Charles E. Merriam, Henry S. Dennison, and Beardsley Ruml, transmitted by Harold L. Ickes to the president, Dec. 1, 1936, box 1, OF 1092.

16. Lash, *Dealers and Dreamers.*

17. Rosen, "'Not Worth a Bucket of Warm Piss': John Nance Garner as Vice President," in *At the President's Side: The Vice Presidency in the Twentieth Century,* ed. Timothy Walch (Columbia, Mo., 1997), 45–53; Bascom N. Timmons, *Garner of Texas* (New York, 1948), chaps. 13, 14; Moley to the president, Sept. 19, 1934, PPF 743, Garner to Roosevelt, July 19, 1936, June 20, 1937, accompanying Hopkins to Roosevelt, June 2, 1937, with attachments, PPF 1416; Garner to Roosevelt, June 19, 1937, Roosevelt to Garner, July 7, 1937, PSF 188; "Said Tom Corcoran," [8/21/35], PPF 1560; James Rowe, memorandum for the president, July 19, 1942, PSF, 148; William E. Leuchtenburg, *Franklin D. Roosevelt and the New Deal, 1932–1940* (New York, 1963), 252–54; James T. Patterson, *Congressional Conservatism and the New Deal: The Growth of the Conservative Coalition in Congress, 1933–1939* (Lexington, Ky., 1967). On the 1938 purge, see Thomas G. Corcoran to the president, Aug. 1, 1938, and R. R. Lawrence, Regional Director, Textile Workers Organizing Committee, to Sidney Hillman, July 25 and July 26, 1938, and attachment, "South Carolina," Clark Foreman to the president, Aug. 5, 1938, R. R. Lawrence, "Notes of Senatorial Campaign in Georgia," n.d. [1938], PSF 151, Theodore Huntley to Mr. Early, Aug. 23, 1938, PSF 188, James Rowe, Jr., memorandum for the president, July 19, 1942, PSF 148; Sean J. Savage, *Roosevelt: The Party Leader 1932–1945* (Lexington, Ky., 1991), 120–23, 129–35.

18. Dickinson, *Bitter Harvest,* 104–13; Arnold, *Managerial Presidency,* 104–7.

19. Arnold, *Managerial Presidency*, 109–14; Polenberg, *Reorganizing Roosevelt's Government*, 41–42; Byrd, "Government Reorganization," radio address, National Broadcasting Company, Jan. 11, 1936, and address, "Need for Moderation in Affairs of Government and Economy of Operation," May 28, 1937, University of Richmond, reprinted in the *Cong. Record*, 75th Cong., 1st sess., box 165, Byrd Papers.

20. Timmons, *Garner*, 232; Heinemann, *Byrd*, 179–81; Polenberg, *Reorganizing Roosevelt's Government*, 163–80; James F. Byrnes to Joseph P. Kennedy, April 12, 1936, folder 23, summary of S. 3331, n.d., folder 30, and "History of Reorganization," box: Legislation, 1933–41, f. Ra-Reorganization, Byrnes Papers.

21. "6. National Resources Planning Board," box: Legislation, 1933–41, folder: Ra-Reorganization, Byrnes Papers.

22. FDR to James F. Byrnes, Feb. 11, 1939, folder 35(1), Roosevelt 1939–41, Byrnes Papers; David L. Porter, *Congress and the Waning of the New Deal* (Port Washington, N.Y., 1980), 89–108; FDR to Lindsay Warren, Feb. 7, 1939, Warren to Roosevelt, Feb. 10, 1939, John J. Cochran to Roosevelt, Feb. 8, 1939, box 3, OF 1092.

23. Carl Hayden to Marvin H. McIntyre, and copy of S. 19, Jan. 5, 1939, box 2, FDR to Byrnes, June 22, 1939, enclosing Delano to the president, June 17, 1939, and H.J. Res. 326, June 1939, incorporating Hayden's amendments, E. M. W. memorandum for the president, June 29, 1939, FDR to General Watson, June 30, 1939, box 3, OF 1092; Roosevelt to Senator Byrnes, June 20, 1939, and telegrams, Luther Gulick to the president, June 19, and Charles E. Merriam to the president, June 18, 1939, folder 35(1), and Reorganization Plan No. I, folder 35(2), Roosevelt 1939–41, Byrnes Papers; Clawson, *New Deal Planning*, 40, 49–51, 217–18.

24. Theodore Rosenof, *Economics in the Long Run: New Deal Theorists and Their Legacies, 1933–1993* (Chapel Hill, N.C., 1997), 31–35; Bernard Sternsher, *Rexford Tugwell and the New Deal* (New Brunswick, N.J., 1964), 51; Gardiner C. Means to Miss Falke, Oct. 1, 1934, Rexford Tugwell to Means, May 31, 1938, box 8, Tugwell, "Design for Government," Nov. 26, 1933, box 36, Tugwell, "The Farmer's Control of Industry," June 1934, box 50, Means to Tugwell, March 17, 1953, box 22, Tugwell Papers.

25. Gardiner C. Means, "NRA and AAA and the Reorganization of Industrial Policy Making," Aug. 29, 1934, box 116, Moley Papers; Means to H. I. Harriman, Oct. 27, 1934, and Means, "The Distribution of Control and Responsibility in a Modern Economy," proof copy of article published in *Political Science Quarterly*, box 2, Means, "The Major Causes of the Depression," Oct. 15, 1935, box 3, Means Papers.

26. Means, "Proposed Changes in NRA, Model Code Outline," Nov. 18, 1933, and "Memorandum Re: The Commodity Dollar and the Reorganization of the American Economy," n.d., box 1, Paul T. Homans to Means, Oct. 24, 1934, Means to Homans, Oct. 27, 1934, box 2, Means Papers; Means, "The Administered-Price Thesis Reconfirmed," *American Economic Review* 62:3 (June 1972): 292–93, U.S. Senate, *Industrial Prices and Their Relative Inflexibility*, 74th Cong., 1st sess., 1935, Sen. Doc. 13; Rosenof, *Economics in the Long Run*, 36.

27. "Progress Report of the Industrial Section of the National Resources Committee," [1935], box 7, Means Papers; Hawley, *New Deal and Problem of Monopoly*, 172–73; National Resources Committee, *The Structure of the American Economy*, pt. 1, *Basic Characteristics* (Washington, D.C., 1939); Rosenof, *Economics in the Long Run*, 66–67.

28. Laughlin Currie to Means, March 4, 1935, and Currie, "Comment on the Recovery Spending Program," box 2, John M. Keynes to Means, March 18, 1935, Means to

Keynes, July 6, 1935, box 4, Means to Henry A. Wallace, "The Relations between Government and Economic Activity," July 25, 1934, box 5, "Materials on Government Expenditures," Nov. 23, 1935, box 7, Currie, "Causes of the Recession," April 1, 1938, box 6, fragment in folder, Industrial Commission, 1938, box 7, Means Papers.

29. "Summaries of Discussion between the Advisory Committee and the Industrial Committee," June 5, 1938, Ezekiel to Tom Blaisdell, June 14, 1938, memo to Messrs. Eliot, Merrill, Means, Currie, Ezekiel, White, Lubin, Henderson, Bean, Corwin Edwards, Ben Cohen, and Jerome Frank from Thomas C. Blaisdell Jr., July 9, 1938, box 7, ibid.; Rosenof, *Economics in the Long Run*, 66–67.

30. Means, "Proposed Informal Economic Conference," n.d. [1939], Means to National Resources Planning Board, Nov. 20, 1939, minutes of the 45th meeting of the Industrial Committee, Jan. 13, 1939, Means to Thomas G. Blaisdell, March 12, 1940, to Delano, July 1, 1940, box 7, Means Papers.

31. Means, "Basic Structural Characteristics and the Problem of Full Employment," and "The Controversy over the Problem of Full Employment," 3–17, in *The Structure of the American Economy*, pt. 2, National Resources Planning Board, *Toward Full Use of Resources* (Washington, D.C., June 1940).

32. Alvin H. Hansen, "Price Flexibility and the Full Employment of Resources," ibid., 27–34.

33. Ezekiel, "Economic Policy and the Structure of the American Economy," ibid., 35–45; Harry Dexter White to Henry Morgenthau Jr., Feb. 25, 1939, box 312, Morgenthau Papers; Ezekiel, "The Future of the New Deal," *Common Sense*, n.d., box 3, Means Papers; R. L. Duffus, "Another Plan for a New Era," *New York Times* book review, Feb. 12, 1939, box 12, memorandum for the secretary, Feb. 15, 1937, "How to Prevent Another 1929 in 1940," n.d., "What to Do If March, 1938, Resembles March, 1933," box 2, H.R. 7325, June 1, 1937, and remarks by Allen, Voorhis, and Amlie, "Planning for Abundance," and industrial expansion bill, June 23, Aug. 10, 21, 1937, a bill to create an Industrial Expansion Board, Industrial Expansion Administration, H.R. 10924, June 14, 1938, box 10, Ezekiel, "Pump Priming and Corporate Price Policy," Cosmos Club, Nov. 19, 1938, box 33, Ezekiel Papers; Allan G. Gruchy, *Modern Economic Thought: The American Contribution* (New York, 1967), 386–87; Hawley, *New Deal and Problem of Monopoly*, 179–84.

34. "Report of the Conference of National Resources Planning Board with the President at the White House," Oct. 17, 1939, box 3, Delano memorandum to the president, Dec. 31, 1940, with appendixes, Delano to the president, July 23, 1941, box 4, Delano to the president, April 4, 1941, box 6, OF 1092.

12 | MATURE CAPITALISM AND DEVELOPMENTAL ECONOMICS

1. Alvin H. Hansen, "A Full Employment Program," n.d., HUG (FP)- 3.42, box 2, Hansen, "Preparedness for Peace: Program of Public Works and Services," n.d., HUG (FP)-3.42, box 3, Hansen to John K. Jessup, Aug. 6, 1943, HUG (FP)-3.10, box 1, Hansen Papers; Hansen to Robert A. Taft, Jan. 22, 1943, box 529, Taft Papers.

2. Delano to the president, Sept. 15, 1939, NRPB memorandum for the president, "Reorientation of Work of the National Resources Planning Board," April 16, 1940, box 3, OF 1092, Laughlin Currie, memorandum for the president, "Basic Conditions of Recovery," March 18, 1940, OF 264, Delano, Merriam, and Yantis to the president, Dec. 31, 1940, OF 264 and OF 1092; Alvin H. Hansen, "Memorandum on the Present Social Security Program and the Problem Whether It Constitutes a Drag on Recovery," n.d.,

[1939], box 12, Ezekiel Papers; Marriner S. Eccles to the president, March 30, 1939, box 5, Eccles Papers; Hansen, "Frontiers of Public Welfare Programs," n.d. [1940], HUG (FP)-3.42, box 2, "Summary of the Discussions and Recommendations of the Group of Economists Called to Advise the Secretary of the Treasury on Proposed Social Security Legislation," Jan. 20–21, 1939, HUG (FP)-3.42, box 4, Hansen Papers; Mehrling, *Money Interest*, 123–25.

3. Allan G. Gruchy, *Modern Economic Thought* (New York, 1967), 337–40; Dorfman, *Economic Mind* 3:201–5; Yuval P. Yonay, *The Struggle over the Soul of Economics: Institutional and Neoclassical Economists in America between the Wars* (Princeton, N.J., 1998), 27, 35–43, 131.

4. Yonay, *Struggle over the Soul of Economics*, 50–112, 121–23; Gruchy, *Modern Economic Thought*, 342–401; Tugwell to Paul H. Homan, Jan. 21, 1931, to Allan G. Gruchy, July 16, 1946, box 5, Tugwell Papers; Brinkley, *End of Reform*, 77, and n. 36, 305; Dorfman, *Economic Mind* 5:459–63.

5. John Maurice Clark, "The Attack on the Problem of Full Use," in *Structure of the American Economy*, pt. 2, 20–26; Clark, "An Appraisal of Compensatory Devices," *Conference Board Bulletin* 13:8 (April 14, 1939): 80–86; Clark, "Effects of Public Spending on Capital Formation," HUG (B)-145.72, box 1, Clark to Hansen, Feb. 13, 1939, HUG (FP)-3.10, box 1, Hansen Papers.

6. Frederick A. Delano to the president, Aug. 25, Dec. 9, 1939, memorandum for the president, "Reorientation of the NRPB, FY 1941," box 3, Delano to the president, April 24, 1941, box 6, OF 1092, Delano, Merriam, and Yantis to the president, raw file drawer, May 1941, PSF 159. On Roosevelt's difficulties with Congress on the NRPB's continuance, E. M. Watson to Director of the Budget, Jan. 5, 1940, presidential memorandum to William H. Whittington, Feb. 14, 1940, Charles W. Eliot memorandum of conference with the president, Feb. 12, 1940, and generally box 3, OF 1092. On the claim that the NRPB exceeded its statutory authority, see address by Robert A. Taft, "How Long Shall We Submit to the Usurpation of Power by the President," Indianapolis, March 11, 1944, box 159, Taft Papers; Senate debate between Kenneth McKellar (Tennessee) and Taft, May 27, 1943, *Cong. Record*, 78th Cong., 1st sess., vol. 89, pt. 4, 4924.

7. National Resources Planning Board, *After Defense—What? Post Defense Planning* (Washington, D.C., Aug. 1941); Delano to the president, July 23, 1941, box 4, OF 1092; "Items for Conference with the President" and accompanying memorandum, Dec. 4, 1941, PSF 175; Charles W. Eliot [to Hansen], and "Agenda, War-Time Planning for Continuing Full Employment, NRPB," Feb. 20, 1942, HUG (FP)-3.16, box 2, Hansen Papers.

8. CWE [Eliot] to Mr. Forster, Dec. 4, 1940, Delano memorandum for the president, Dec. 3, 1940, box 3, Delano memorandum for the president, Dec. 31, 1940, read by Laughlin Currie, Jan. 14, 1941, box 4, OF 1092.

9. Alvin H. Hansen, *After the War: Full Employment* (Washington, D.C., 1942). There are three editions of the NRPB pamphlet, each showing a revised assumption for national income after the war reflecting income growth during the conflict. Hansen's analysis of the distinction between the economic impact of personal or business indebtedness versus that of internal governmental debt was drawn from a paper by the Danish economist Jørgen Pedersen, "Some Problems of Public Finance," n.d. [ca. 1938 or 1939], in HUG (FP)-3.10, box 2, Hansen Papers.

10. "Toward Security," PSF 175; *Washington Review*, sec. 3, March 13, 1943, 9–12, copy in box 5, OF 1092; *National Resources Development Report for 1943*, pt. 1, *Post-War Plan*

and Program (Washington, D.C., Jan. 1943), 29–30; Bruce Bliven, George Soule, and Max Lerner, "Charter for America," pt. 2, *New Republic,* April 19, 1943; Taft speech notes, f. Economic Study—Spending Theory, 1943–45, box 529, Taft Papers.

11. White House memorandum, "Mr. Corrington Gill Called," Jan. 13, 1933, FDR to Clarence Cannon, Chairman, House Appropriations Committee, Feb. 16, 1943, to Carter Glass, March 24, 1943, James F. Byrnes to the president, March 12, 1943, box 5, OF 1092; Warken, *History of the NRPB,* 244–45.

12. Rosenman, *PPA,* 1939 volume, 27–28, 36–53, 221–33; Beardsley Ruml, "The Retailer's Interest in National Fiscal Policy," May 22, 1939, attached to Paul H. Appleby to W. W. Waymack, June 10, 1939, box 44, Waymack Papers; FDR to Secretary of the Treasury, Jan. 21, 1939, box 96, Hopkins Papers; Stein, *Fiscal Revolution,* 105–11, 116.

13. Stein, *Fiscal Revolution,* 120–23; Roosevelt to James F. Byrnes, June 21, 1939, folder 35 (1), Roosevelt, 1939–41, Byrnes Papers; Henry Morgenthau Jr. to the president, July 26, 1936, PSF 100, Samuel I. Rosenman to Mr. president, n.d. [1938?], PSF 155, E. M. Watson for the president, July 19, 1939, PSF 115; Patterson, *Congressional Conservatism,* 311, 316–23; Taft address, "Citizens of the United States of America," n.d., n.p., "Statement of Secretary Morgenthau before the Senate Committee on Banking and Currency," S. 2759, July 18, 1939, Taft notes on constitutional doctrine, and amendment to S. 2759, Taft notes on speech, spend-lend bill, 1939, copy of S. 2759, July 10, 1939, copy of S. 2864, July 22, 1939, memorandum on S. 2864, Barkley Act, f. Spending-Lending—For the Floor (1939), "Lending Program Embraces A. A. Berle's Low Interest Rates for Socially Desirable Projects," *Goldsmith Washington Service,* July 22, 1939, confidential annotated bill for the Self-Liquidating Projects Act of 1939, July 12, 1939, Leonard Ayres, address, "Lending Our Way to Prosperity," Graduate School of Banking, Rutgers University, June 23, 1939, E. E. Lincoln to Members of the Du Pont Executive Committee, "Federal Spending, Industrial Production, and Wholesale Prices," June 19, 1939, Taft address, Institute of Public Affairs, University of Virginia, July 14, 1939, and miscellaneous speech notes, boxes 808 and 809, Taft Papers; on the Revenue Acts of 1938 and 1939, which repealed the undistributed profits tax and reduced the tax on capital gains, see Swain, *Pat Harrison,* 175–79, 187–89; Mark Leff, *The Limits of Symbolic Reform: The New Deal and Taxation, 1933–1939* (Cambridge, 1984), 231–75.

14. Mary T. Norton to the president, May 16, 1939, PSF 140, E. M. Watson for the president, July 19, 1939, PSF 115; Clyde P. Weed, *The Nemesis of Reform: The Republican Party during the New Deal* (New York, 1994), 169–83.

15. Currie, "Background of Budget Policy for Fiscal Year 1941," and "The Public Debt," Dec. 14, 1939, PSF 118; annual budget message, Jan. 3, 1940, Rosenman, *PPA,* 1940 volume, 10–24.

16. Alvin Hansen to Ralph E. Flanders, April 20, 1938, HUG (FP)-3.10, box 1, Hansen to D. H. Robertson, Sept. 29, 1939, HUG (FP)-3.10, box 2, fragment of letter, HUG (FP)-3.11, Hansen comments on George Terborgh's address at the National Industrial Conference Board, Nov. 23, 1943, "Public and Private Investment after the War," HUG (FP)-3.42, box 4, Hansen Papers.

17. Hansen to David McCord Wright, July 10, 1945, HUG (FP)-3.10, box 2, ibid.

18. Hansen, "Mr. Keynes on Unemployment Equilibrium," review of Keynes, *The General Theory of Employment Interest, and Money,* in *Journal of Political Economy* 64:5 (Oct. 1936): 667–86; "Economic Progress and Declining Population Growth," *American Economic Review* 29:1 (March 1939): pt. 1, 1–15; address, "Toward Full Employment,"

March 15, 1940, University of Cincinnati, from notes taken before the Business and Professional Men's Group, box 1, "Postwar Financial Problems," n.d. [ca. 1943], box 3, "Public Expenditures and Debt," *Financial and Investment Review*, copy in folder S.E.C. Testimony, HUG (FP)-3.42, box 4, "Some Introductory Observations, First Draft of Paper, Seminar on Capital Formation and Its Elements," National Industrial Conference Board, Nov. 9, 1937, Nicholas Kaldor, review of Hansen, *Full Recovery or Stagnation?* (1938), in *Economic Journal*, March 1939, Hansen, "Underlying Problems Confronting American Business," *Conference Board Bulletin* 13:8 (April 14, 1939): 77–79, HUG (B)-145.72, box 1, Hansen, "Model I, Full Employment in Thirties," HUG (FP)-3.16, box 2, Hansen Papers; Mehrling, *Money Interest*, 88–122.

19. Hansen, "Postwar Financial Problems," n.d. [ca. 1943], HUG (FP)-3.42, box 3, Hansen comments, "A Symposium: A Postwar National Fiscal Program," reprinted from *New Republic*, Feb. 28, 1944, 27–28, Hansen, "Should Corporation Taxes Be Abolished?" Town Meeting, Blue Network, Dec. 14, 1944, Hansen, "The Role of Urban Redevelopment and Housing in a Full Employment Program," typescript, n.d., HUG (B)-145.72, box 1, Hansen, "Urban Redevelopment and Comprehensive Urban Planning," n.d., HUG (FP)-3.42, box 8, Hansen and Harvey S. Perloff, *Regional Resource Development*, National Planning Association Pamphlet no. 16 (Washington, D.C., Oct. 1942), Hansen, "Postwar Economic Controls," *Chicago Journal of Commerce*, Aug. 31, 1942, HUG (B)-145.72, box 2, Hansen, "Postwar Financial Problems," HUG (B)-145.72, box 3, Richard M. Bissell Jr. to Hansen, Dec. 14, 1938, Hansen to John K. Jessup, Aug. 3, 1943, HUG (FP)-3.10, box 1, Hansen Papers; Hansen, *Fiscal Policy*, 447–48; Hansen and Guy Greer, "The Federal Debt and the Future," *Harper's Magazine*, April 1942, 489–500; Alvin Hansen and Guy Greer, "Toward Full Use of Our Resources," *Fortune*, Nov. 1942; Hansen, "The Postwar Economy," in *Postwar Economic Problems*, ed. Seymour E. Harris (New York, 1943), 9–26.

20. Hansen, *Fiscal Policy*, 144–45; Hansen, notes on Jørgen Pedersen's views, Hansen to Herbert U. Nelson, April 11, 1944, HUG (FP)-3.10, box 2, "How Shall We Deal with the Public Debt?" Nov. 17, 1943, and "Fiscal Policy for Full Employment," 1946, Institute on Postwar Reconstruction, New York University, HUG (B)-145.72, boxes 2 and 3, "Stagnation and Under-employment Equilibrium," Keynes issue, *Rostra Economica Amstelodamensia*, Nov. 15, 1966, 7–9, HUG (FP)-3.42, box 7, Hansen Papers.

21. Hansen's notes, "Suggested Title: Partial Quotation and Use of Sources," in reference to Harold G. Moulton, *The New Philosophy of Public Debt* (Washington, D.C., 1943), Hansen's untitled notes on Moulton's critique, n.d., HUG (FP)-3.16, box 2, Hansen to John K. Jessup, Aug. 6, 1943, HUG (FP)-3.10, box 1, Hansen Papers; *Fortune*, Supplement, Dec. 1942; Stuart Chase, "From War to Work: How to Get Full Employment and Keep It Going," special edition, *Survey Graphic*, May 1943.

22. Robert Taft, *An Economic Program for American Democracy* (New York, 1938); address of Senator Taft before the Cuvier Press Club, Cincinnati, Ohio, March 27, 1941, box 664, Taft Papers; Collins, *Business Response to Keynes*, 11–12, and nn. 33–34, 216.

23. James T. Patterson, *Mr. Republican: A Biography of Robert A. Taft* (Boston, 1972), 49–51; Taft to Herbert Hoover, Dec. 24, 1934, box 34, Taft Papers.

24. Herbert Hoover, *The Challenge to Liberty* (New York, 1934), 1–179 and n. 175.

25. Taft, "What Do I Want to Work Out?" Aug. 25, 1933, box 1291, Taft Papers.

26. Taft to W. H. Stayton, Nov. 9, 1934, box 101, address, Warren, Ohio, Chamber of Commerce, "The New Deal: Reform, Recovery, and Revolution," April 1935, and before Women's National Republican Club, f. Speeches, 1936, address, possibly at Columbia

University, 1936, box 1291, Taft to Charles C. Burlingham, Jan. 30, 1936, box 103, Taft notes, Taft to Judson King, May 8, 1936, to Arthur A. Craven, June 20, 1936, box 104, "[Taft Replies to] Questions Put by the *Cincinnati Post*," June 1936, address, Women's Republican Club of New Hampshire, April 30, 1936, box 105, Edmund E. Lincoln to Taft, Aug. 3, 1939, with enclosure, "Industry Trends," and Aug. 7, 1939, with enclosure, "Some Popular Misconceptions and Current Fallacies Regarding Our Foreign Trade and Tariff Policies," box 493, copy of E. E. Lincoln to Members of the [Du Pont] Executive Committee, "Federal Spending, Industrial Production, and Wholesale Prices," June 19, 1939, box 809, Lincoln to Taft, July 29, 1940, box 483, June 28, 1944, box 837, Aug. 16, 1944, box 533, Taft to Lincoln, Aug. 5, 1939, box 493 ("The information you give me is just what I want, and will be useful in preparing speeches for the fall"), Taft Papers. Taft actively sought the support of the Du Ponts, the Chicago-based Silas Strawn group, and the Pews of Sun Oil Company in his quest for the 1940 Republican nomination. Taft to Silas Strawn, Lester Armour, and Charles G. Dawes, Oct. 24, 1939, Strawn to Taft, Oct. 25, 1939, Aug. 6, 1940, box 124, Taft to C. Douglas Buck, Governor of Delaware, March 18, April 15, 1940, with lists of names, box 122, ibid.

27. Undated speeches in folders marked "speech material," 1937 and 1938, press release, Taft for Senate Headquarters, six debates with Democratic incumbent Robert J. Bulkley, 1938, Taft address, Republican Convention, Sept. 14, 1938, box 1292, extract from address of Robert A. Taft, Madisonville School, May 11, 1938, box 118, advertisement in the *Ohio Farmer*, Oct. 22, 1938, box 119, S. 2721, introduced by Taft, Arthur Vandenberg, and New Jersey's W. Warren Barbour, on June 29, 1939, box 777, Taft address, Institute of Public Affairs, University of Virginia, July 14, 1939, box 142, folder, Political, 1940, Taft policies, box 148, Taft to Vincent Starzinger, March 29, 1940, box 125, ibid.; Patterson, *Mr. Republican,* 170–78.

28. Speech of Hon. Robert A. Taft, Bureau of Advertising Dinner, New York City, April 27, 1939, box 494, Taft Papers. On the discontinuation of presidential authority to devalue the dollar, Taft was aided by a number of orthodox economists, including Thomas Jefferson Coolidge, a onetime assistant to Henry Morgenthau Jr. who resigned in 1936, George L. Harrison, Jay Crane, and W. Randolph Burgess at the New York Fed, the Cleveland Trust's Leonard Ayres, Princeton's Edwin Kemmerer, and Walter Spahr's Economists' National Committee on Monetary Policy. Coolidge to Taft, March 8, 1939, box 494, "Economists' National Committee: 55 Members Recommend Termination of President's Power to Devalue the Dollar," box 519, George E. Harrison to Taft, March 21, 1939, and enclosure, April 4, 1933, "Analysis of the Proposal for Devaluation of the Dollar," box 519, Taft speech notes in boxes 494, 495, 529, Taft Papers.

29. Edgar Eugene Robinson, *They Voted for Roosevelt: The Presidential Vote, 1932–1944* (Stanford, Calif., 1947), 53; Waymack to J. H. Frandsen, Nov. 13, 1940, box 14, to Henry Hazlitt, Nov. 22, 1938, box 8, Waymack Papers; Weed, *Nemesis of Reform,* 197–98.

30. Patterson, *Mr. Republican,* 252–53, 259–61; Brinkley, *End of Reform,* 141; Alston and Ferrie, *Southern Paternalism,* 95–97.

31. Thomas M. Quinn to Herschel C. Atkinson, Administrator, Ohio Bureau of Unemployment Compensation, Oct. 15, 1941, Atkinson to Taft, Oct. 17, 1941, Taft to Atkinson, Oct. 20, 1941, National Association of Manufacturers, *Economic Security Bulletin,* Feb. 1942, Taft to George B. Chandler, March 2, 1942, and "Steps in the Federalization of Unemployment Compensation," n.d. [1942], box 802, Taft Papers; Bernstein, *A Caring Society,* 180–81; Berkowitz, *America's Welfare State,* 52–55.

32. Hansen, "Postwar Controls: Fate of Private Enterprise Hinges on Successful Postwar Reconversion and Full Employment," *Chicago Journal of Commerce,* Aug. 31, 1942, HUG (B)-H 145.72, box 2, Hansen Papers; Taft address, "We Need a Courageous and Independent Congress," *Cong. Record,* Appendix, 78th Cong., 1st sess., vol. 89, pt. 9, A32–A35; Richard V. Gilbert, ed., *An Economic Program for American Democracy, by Seven Harvard and Tufts Economists* (New York, 1938); Hansen to Taft, Jan. 22, 1943, box 529, Taft Papers.

33. Brinkley, *End of Reform,* 236–45, 260–61; Schwarz, *Speculator,* 458–66; *Cong. Record,* Senate, 78th Cong., 1st sess., vol. 89, pt. 2, 1929, March 12, 1943; Taft address, U.S. Senate, "The George Bill for Reconversion a Constructive Plan: The Murray-Kilgore Bill a New Deal Grab for Money and Power," box 159, Taft Papers.

34. Stein, *Fiscal Revolution,* 181–87, 193–94; Collins, *Business Response to Keynes,* 81–87, 129–52; Beardsley Ruml and H. Chr. Sonne, *Fiscal and Monetary Policy,* National Planning Association Pamphlet no. 35 (Washington, D.C., July 1944); Beardsley Ruml, *Tomorrow's Business* (New York, 1945).

35. E. E. Lincoln to Taft, Jan. 12, 1945, enclosing National City Bank of New York *Bulletin,* Jan. 1945, 5–7, box 159, Taft Papers.

36 Hansen, "Suggested Revision of Full Employment Bill (1945)," July 28, 1945, HUG (FP)-3.42, box 2, Hansen Papers; Stein, *Fiscal Revolution,* 175–76; Gottfried Haberler, *Prosperity and Depression* (Geneva, 1941), 503–7; "Five Views on the Murray Full Employment Bill: Alvin H. Hansen, Seymour Harris, Gottfried Haberler, Sumner H. Slichter, Malcolm P. McNair," *Review of Economic Statistics* 27:3 (Aug. 1945): 102–3, 106–9.

37. "Five Views on the Murray Full Employment Bill: Alvin H. Hansen, Seymour Harris, Gottfried Haberler, Sumner H. Slichter, Malcolm P. McNair," *Review of Economic Statistics* 27:3 (Aug. 1945): 109–12; "The Conditions of Expansion," *American Economic Review* 32 (March 1942): 1–21; excerpt from "Public Policies and Postwar Employment," box 39, Means Papers; Slichter, *Economic Growth in the United States* (Baton Rouge, La., 1961), 1–12, 17–18, 25.

38. Schumpeter, "Preface to the Hebrew Edition," translation, May 1945, HUG (B)-145.72, box 3, Hansen Papers; Robert Lekachman, Joseph A. Schumpeter, *Can Capitalism Survive?* (New York, 1950), xi.

39. Barber, *Designs within Disorder,* 165–67; Stein, *Fiscal Revolution,* 202.

40. Taft to Evans F. Stearns, Jan. 16, 1946, box 881, Taft Papers; R. F. Leonard to Hansen, July 13, 1945, HUG (FP)-3.ll, and press clippings, including item, "Hansen Is Dropped by Reserve Board," *New York Times,* Aug. 15, 1945, HUG (FP)-3.16, box 2, Hansen Papers.

41. Reagan, *Designing a New America,* 239–40; Berkowitz, *America's Welfare State,* 56–82, 171–76.

42. Leon Keyserling to Rexford Tugwell, March 25, 1948, Tugwell to Keyserling, March 30, 1948, box 7, Tugwell Papers; Tugwell, "The Utility of the Future in the Present," *Public Administration Review* 8:8 (1948): 49–59.

13 | THE ECONOMICS OF RECOVERY

1. John W. Jeffries, *Wartime America: The World War II Homefront* (Chicago, 1996), 35–42.

2. Kregel, "Keynesian Stabilization Policy," 429–46.

3. *Historical Statistics of the United States,* ser. D 627–28, "Hours and Earnings . . . in Manufacturing," 92, ser. D 48, "Employees in Nonagricultural Establishments," 73; James D. Savage, *Balanced Budgets and American Politics* (Ithaca, N.Y., 1988), 290; *New York Times,* Sept. 28, 2003; Bureau of Labor Statistics, "Consumer Price Index, All Urban Consumers, All Items, 1982–84 = 100," available on the internet.

4. Robert Higgs, "Wartime Prosperity? A Reassessment of the U.S. Economy in the 1940s," *Journal of Economic History* 52 (March 1992): 41–53; Michael Edelstein, "War and the American Economy in the Twentieth Century," in Engerman and Gallman, *Cambridge Economic History of the United States,* 3:338, 342 (table), 394, 398; Friedman and Schwartz, *Monetary History of the United States,* 557–58.

5. Simon Kuznets, *National Income: A Summary of Findings* (New York, 1946), 6–7, 23–29, 32–33.

6. Gerald D. Nash, *The American West Transformed* (Bloomington, Ind., 1985), 3–5, 17–19; Nash, *The Crucial Era: The Great Depression and World War II, 1929–1945* (New York, 1992), 162–65; Bruce J. Schulman, *From Cotton Belt to Sunbelt: Federal Policy, Economic Development, and the Transformation of the South, 1938–1980* (New York, 1991), 10, 72–109.

7. Patrick Karl O'Brien, "The Pax Britannica and American Hegemony: Precedent, Antecedent, or Just Another History?" 3–27, and Andrew Gamble, "Hegemony and Decline: Britain and the United States," 120–32, in *Two Hegemonies: Britain, 1846-1914, and the United States, 1941–2001,* ed. O'Brien and Armand Clesse (Burlington, Vt., 2001); Kindleberger, *World in Depression,* 291–98.

8. Angus Maddison, "The West and the Rest in the International Economic Order," in *Development Is Back,* ed. Jorge Braga de Macedo, Colm Foy, and Charles P. Oman (Paris, 2002), 31–45; Peter H. Lindert, "United States Foreign Trade Policy in the Twentieth Century," in Engerman and Gallman, *Cambridge Economic History of the United States* 3:407–8, 456, 458.

9. Angus Maddison, *Economic Growth in the West* (New York, 1964), 160–67, 170, 182; Maddison, "The Nature of U.S. Economic Leadership: A Historical Overview," in O'Brien and Clesse, *Two Hegemonies,* 187–93; Robert M. Solow, "Mysteries of Growth," *New York Review of Books,* July 3, 2003, 50.

10. The preceding analysis of multifactor productivity, sometimes referred to as Total Factor Productivity (TFP), is based on Alexander Field, "The Most Technologically Progressive Decade of the Century," *American Economic Review* 93 (Sept. 2003): 1399–1414; see also John Kendrick, *Productivity Trends in the United States* (Princeton, N.J., 1961), tables A-XXII, A-XXIII, 334–35, 339–40; Moses Abramovitz and Paul A. David, "American Macroeconomic Growth in the Era of Knowledge-Based Progress: The Long-Run Perspective," in Engerman and Gallman, *Cambridge Economic History of the United States* 3:1–92.

INDEX

Italicized page numbers refer to tables

old-age insurance, 167–68, 169, 171; recession of 1937–38 and, 169, 179; Ruml on, 229; Sachs on punitive, 187; undistributed profits tax, 179–80, 187, 219; for unemployment insurance, 163–64, 165–66
Teagle, Walter C., 158, 161
technology, 4, 6, 184, 206, 239, 240
Temporary National Economic Committee (TNEC): antimonopolists and, 181; Currie's testimony before, 182–83, 224; Hansen's testimony before, 5, 183, 185, 189, 224
Tennessee Valley Authority (TVA): Chamber of Commerce criticizes, 63; Commonwealth & Southern–TVA controversy, 122–31; Hansen on, 5; Hoover on, 225; National Resources Planning Board using as model, 4, 212, 215; as regional economic development, 70
Terborgh, George, 230, 232
Texas Railroad Commission, 117
Third New Deal, 6, 234, 236, 237
Thomas, Elbert, 230
Thomas, Elmer, 26
Thomas, Norman, 88
Thomas Amendment (Agricultural Adjustment Act of 1933): and FDR's fix of price of gold, 50, 52, 69; Hoover on, 58, 60; Keynes on, 36; on reducing dollar's gold content, 32, 48, 57, 69; Warburg's opposition to, 54
tire manufacturing, 117–18
Townsend movement, 171
trade. See international trade
Trade Agreements Act (1934), 136–38, 140, 143
trade associations, 94–95, 104, 105, 109, 111, 115
trade reciprocity. See reciprocal trade agreements
Trading with the Enemy Act (1917), 25
Traylor, Melvin, 251n5
Treasury Department: becoming coproducer of money and credit, 69; dollar's nationalization opposed by internationalists at, 58; FDR on transferring gold from Federal Reserve to, 69; FDR's economic advisers at Commerce, not, 45; gold purchases by, 48, 56; Morgenthau becomes secretary, 83; Warburg wanting all monetary projects concentrated in, 47; Woodin as secretary, 26, 32, 47, 50

Tripartite Agreement (1936), 140
Tugwell, Rexford: on currency stabilization negotiations, 44; on direction, 192–93; Eccles and, 174; on Fourth Power, 192, 193; Harriman and, 97; Hoover criticizing, 225; *Industrial Discipline and the Governmental Arts*, 114; on industrial planning, 96, 192–93, 233; on interference in economic policy, 57; intranationalist economic theory of, 24; land-purchase program under, 133–34; Means and, 206; on overhead economic management, 115–16; "The Principle of Planning and the Institution of Laissez Fair," 96; radical policies advocated by, 70, 113–16; and Stimson on British wartime debt, 21
TVA. See Tennessee Valley Authority (TVA)
Twentieth Century Fund, 168, 169
Tydings, Millard, 199

underconsumption, 79, 183, 194
underinvestment, 188, 190, 211, 213–14, 221
undistributed profits tax, 179–80, 187, 219
unemployment: in capital goods industries, 108; Chamberlain attempts to reduce British, 16; FDR's provisions for relieving, 81; Hansen on possibility of chronic, 185; in midst of inflation, 231; persistence of, 4; public works programs as remedy for, 73–74; "rules of the game" causing, 62; structural, 120–21; surplus labor due to mechanization of agriculture, 121, 132–33, 149–50; in Swope Plan, 95; Third New Deal as cure for, 6; wartime, 236. See also unemployment insurance
unemployment insurance, 163–66; attempt to federalize, 228; FDR sees as permanent, 157; Perkins's plan for, 160; private sector plans, 158; *Security, Work, and Relief Politics* on, 216; social justice reflected in, 3; Taft on, 226; Warburg on, 88; workmen's compensation as model for, 151, 163
unionization: cost-price pressures resulting from, 181; economic growth affected by, 6–7; Fair Labor Standards Act and, 6, 203; National Industrial Recovery Act promoting, 6, 63, 106
United Kingdom. See Great Britain
United Mine Workers, 99–101, 118